Nicholas Schmidt 5th grade

HABITAT Jaguars live in North, Central, and South America. Their habitats are swamplands, rainforests, dry grasslands, scrub, and deserts.

BODY COVERING Most jaguars have brownish-yellow fur with dark rosettes, or spots, that look like paws.

D1605049

SELF-PROTECTION Jaguars are one of only four wild cats that roar. A jaguar roars to scare other animals away from its territory.

TEETH The strong jaws and sharp teeth of a jaguar allows it to bite into prey.

Science

Jaguar

Harcourt
SCHOOL PUBLISHERS

Orlando   Austin   New York   San Diego   Toronto   London

Visit *The Learning Site!*
www.harcourtschool.com

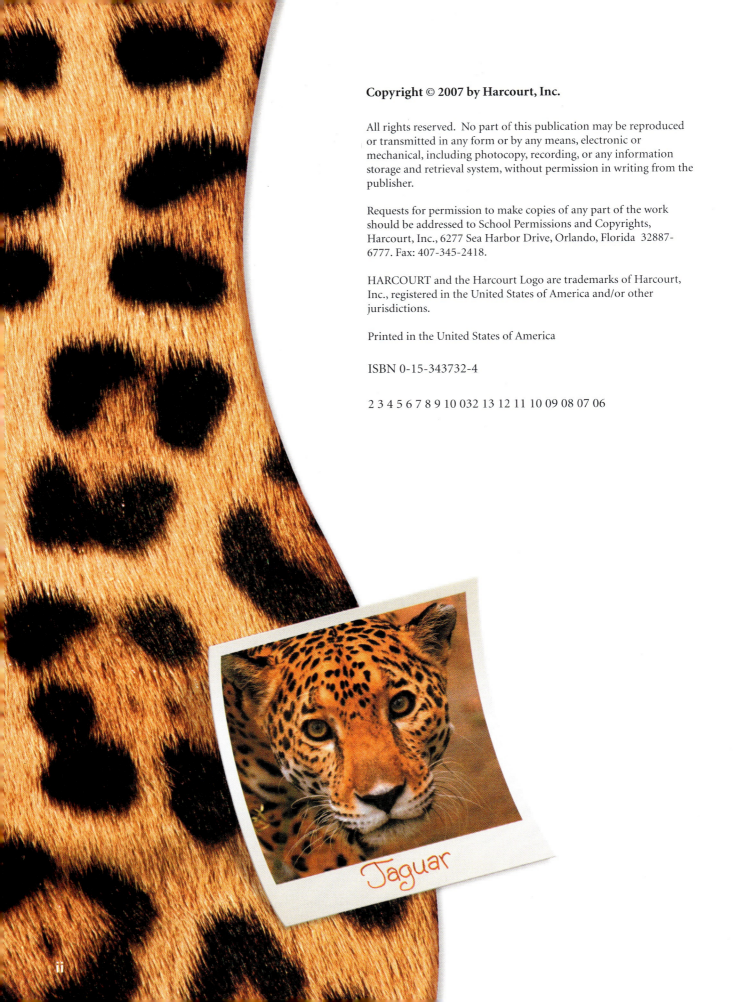

ISBN 0-15-343732-4

2 3 4 5 6 7 8 9 10 032 13 12 11 10 09 08 07 06

Jaguar

Consulting Authors

Michael J. Bell
*Assistant Professor of Early
    Childhood Education*
College of Education
West Chester University of
    Pennsylvania

Michael A. DiSpezio
Curriculum Architect
JASON Academy
Cape Cod, Massachusetts

Marjorie Frank
Former Adjunct, Science Education
Hunter College
New York, New York

Gerald H. Krockover
*Professor of Earth and Atmospheric
    Science Education*
Purdue University
West Lafayette, Indiana

Joyce C. McLeod
Adjunct Professor
Rollins College
Winter Park, Florida

Barbara ten Brink
Science Specialist
Austin Independent School
    District
Austin, Texas

Carol J. Valenta
Senior Vice President
St. Louis Science Center
St. Louis, Missouri

Barry A. Van Deman
President and CEO
Museum of Life and Science
Durham, North Carolina

Senior Editorial Advisors

Napoleon Adebola Bryant, Jr.
Professor Emeritus of Education
Xavier University
Cincinnati, Ohio

Robert M. Jones
Professor of Educational Foundations
University of Houston-Clear Lake
Houston, Texas

Mozell P. Lang
Former Science Consultant
Michigan Department of Education
Science Consultant, Highland Park
    Schools
Highland Park, Michigan

PHYSICAL SCIENCE

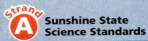
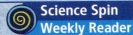

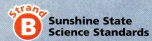
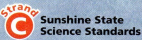
v

EARTH SCIENCE

Processes That Shape the Earth 210

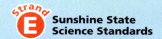

LIFE SCIENCE

How Living Things Interact with Their Environments   424

Getting Ready for Science

Lesson 1 What Tools Do Scientists Use?

Lesson 2 What Inquiry Skills Do Scientists Use?

Lesson 3 What Is the Scientific Method?

Vocabulary

FCAT-Tested
investigation
experiment
scientific method

Other Terms
microscope
balance
inquiry

What do YOU wonder?

This rocket won't travel into space, but it works in the same way as the rockets that carried people to the moon. How do rocket scientists try out their designs? What variables can they test to make a rocket fly farther and faster?

What Tools Do Scientists Use?

Fast Fact

That's a BIG Kite! One of the largest kites ever flown is the Megabite. It is 64 m (210 ft) long (including tails) and 22 m (72 ft) wide. That's only about 6 m (20 ft) shorter than a 747 jet airliner! Kite fliers around the world are always trying to set new records. How high can a kite go? How big or small can a kite be? Setting a record depends on accurate measurements. In the Investigate, you'll practice several different ways of measuring objects.

Measuring Up!

Materials
- balloon
- ruler
- tape measure
- hand lens
- string
- spring scale

Procedure

1. Observe the empty balloon with the hand lens. Copy the chart, and record your observations.

2. Measure the length and circumference of the balloon. Record your measurements.

3. Use the spring scale to measure the weight of the balloon. Record its weight.

4. Now blow up the balloon.

5. Match a length of string to the length of the balloon. Measure that string length with the ruler or tape measure. Record the length.

6. Measure the circumference of the balloon as in Step 5. Record your measurement.

7. Measure the weight of the balloon with the spring scale. Record your measurement.

Draw Conclusions

1. How did the measurements change when you blew up the balloon? Why?

2. Do you think that your measurement of the length of the empty balloon or the blown-up balloon was more accurate? Why?

3. **Inquiry Skill** Work with another group to identify variables in your measurements. What variables caused different groups to get different measurements?

Step 2

	Balloon	Balloon with Air
Hand lens		
Length		
Circumference		
Weight		

Investigate Further

How can you find the volume of a blown-up balloon? Plan and conduct a simple investigation to find out.

Reading in Science

SCIENCE CONCEPTS
► how tools are used to make better observations
► why a balance and a scale measure different things

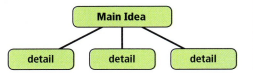 **READING FOCUS SKILL**

MAIN IDEA AND DETAILS Look for details about how and when each tool is used.

```
          Main Idea
      /       |       \
  detail   detail   detail
```

Using Science Inquiry Tools

People in many jobs must use tools. Cooks use pots and pans. Mechanics use screwdrivers and wrenches. Scientists use tools to measure and observe objects in nature.

Your Science Tool Kit includes a dropper to move liquids, as well as forceps to pick up solids. A hand lens and a magnifying box help you see details. You can measure temperature with the thermometer, length with the ruler or tape measure, and volume with the measuring cup. The spring scale measures weight.

 MAIN IDEA AND DETAILS What are four tools you can use to measure objects?

◄ **A thermometer measures the temperature of liquids and the air. It measures in degrees Celsius (°C).**

▲ **Use a dropper to move small amounts of liquid or to measure volume by counting drops.**

A tape measure helps you measure the length of curved or irregular surfaces. ▶

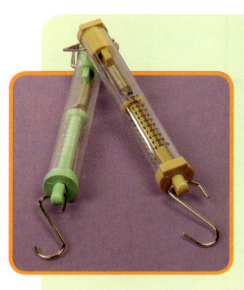

◀ A spring scale measures forces, such as weight or friction. It measures in units called newtons (N).

A ruler measures the length and width of objects in centimeters (cm) and millimeters (mm).

▲ You can place an insect, pebble, or other small object in the magnifying box. Looking through the lid helps you see the object clearly.

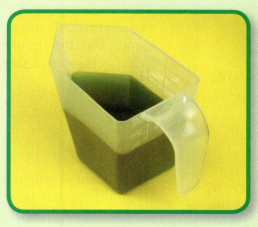

▲ A measuring cup is used to measure the volume of liquids. It measures in liters (L) and milliliters (mL).

◀ Forceps help you pick up or hold small objects. They are handy for holding small objects under the hand lens.

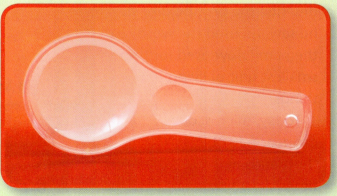

▲ A hand lens makes objects look larger and helps you see more detail.

Microscopes

Without a telescope, you can't identify what look like tiny objects in the sky. In the same way, you can't see tiny parts of an insect, colored particles in a rock, or cells in a leaf without a microscope. A <mark>microscope</mark> is a tool that makes small objects appear larger. It lets you see details you couldn't see with your eyes alone.

People have known for a long time that curved glass can *magnify,* or make things look larger. An early Roman scholar read books through a glass ball filled with water. People started making eyeglasses a thousand years ago. They called the curved glass a *lens* because it looked like a lentil—a bean!

An early scientist named Anton van Leeuwenhoek (LAY•vuhn•hook) used a lens to see creatures in a drop of pond water. He called them animalcules.

In the late 1500s, a Dutch eyeglass maker put a lens in each end of a hollow tube. Changing the length of the tube made tiny objects look three to nine times their actual size. This was probably the first "modern" microscope.

In the 1600s, Robert Hooke used a microscope to study thin slices of cork. To describe the tiny, boxlike structures he saw, he used the word *cell,* the name now used for the smallest unit of living things.

Today, microscopes can magnify objects thousands of times. So a tiny "animalcule" might look as large as a whale!

▲ Van Leeuwenhoek was the first person to see microscopic organisms. He placed tiny samples on the tip of a needle and looked at them through a single lens.

Using a simple microscope, you can make things look up to 400 times their actual size! ▼

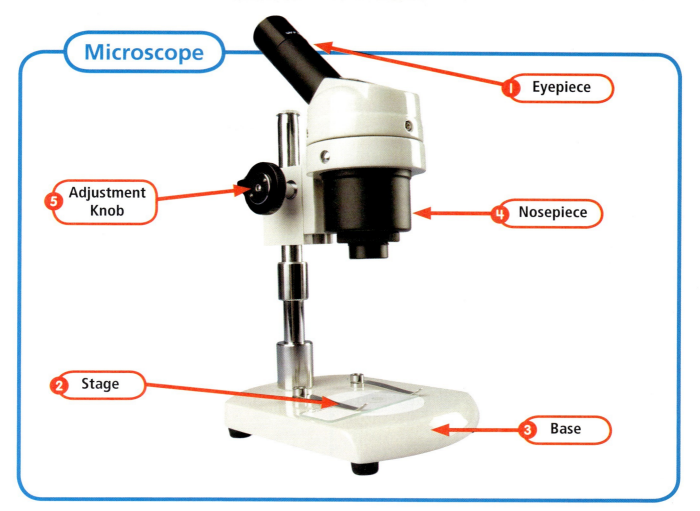

Microscope

1 Eyepiece

5 Adjustment Knob

4 Nosepiece

2 Stage

3 Base

Most classroom microscopes have several main parts:

1. The eyepiece contains one lens and is mounted at the end of a tube.

2. The stage holds the slide or object you are looking at.

3. The base supports the microscope. It usually holds a lamp or mirror that shines light through the object.

4. A nosepiece holds one or more lenses that can magnify an object up to 400 times.

5. Adjustment knobs help you focus the lenses.

MAIN IDEA AND DETAILS What are the main parts of a microscope?

Research microscopes can magnify objects 5000 times. These microscopes are used for everything from studying diseases to solving crimes. ▼

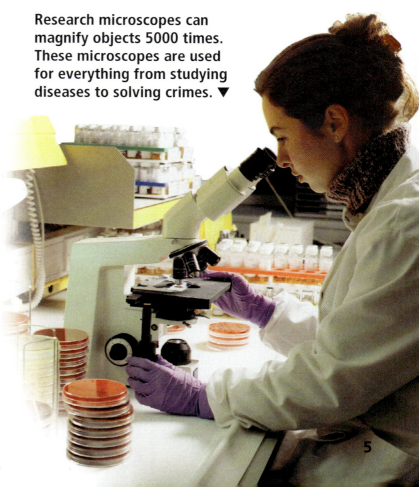

5

Measuring Temperature

"Boy, it's hot today! It feels much hotter than yesterday." Without a thermometer, temperature isn't much more than how a person feels.

In 1592, an Italian scientist named Galileo found that a change in temperature made water rise and fall in a sealed tube. This device, a simple thermometer, helped Galileo study nature in a more precise way.

In the early 1700s, a German scientist named Fahrenheit sealed mercury in a thin glass tube. As it got warmer, the liquid metal took up more space. The mercury rose in the tube. As it cooled, the mercury took up less space. So the level of liquid in the tube fell. But how was this thermometer to be marked? What units were to be used?

Fahrenheit put the tube into freezing water and into boiling water and marked the mercury levels. Then he divided the difference between the levels into 180 equal units—called degrees.

In 1742, a Swedish scientist named Celsius made a thermometer with 100 degrees between the freezing and boiling points of water. The Celsius scale is used in most countries of the world. It is also the scale used by all scientists.

Thermometers can't measure extreme temperatures. For example, many metals get to several thousand degrees before they melt. Scientists have other temperature-sensing tools to measure very hot and very cold objects.

 **MAIN IDEA AND DETAILS** How does a thermometer work?

Temperature Scales

Measured on a Celsius thermometer, water boils at 100 degrees and freezes at 0 degrees. On a Fahrenheit thermometer, water boils at 212 degrees and freezes at 32 degrees.

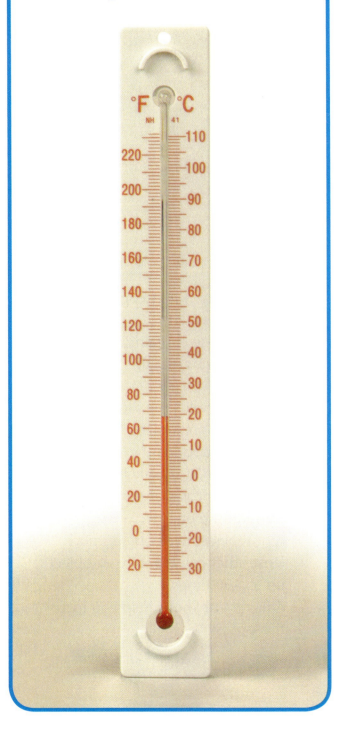

Balance or Spring Scale?

Suppose you're a merchant in Alaska in the early 1900s. A man wants food in exchange for some gold he got from the bottom of a river. But how much is the gold worth?

To find out, you use a tool that looks like a small seesaw. You place the gold at one end of a beam. Then you add objects of known mass at the other end until the beam is level. The objects balance! A **balance** is a tool that measures the amount of matter in an object—the object's *mass*.

The balance in your classroom measures mass by balancing an unknown object with one or more objects of known mass. Mass is measured in grams (g) or kilograms (kg).

When you want to measure an object's weight, you use a spring scale. You hang an object from a hook on the scale and let gravity pull it down. Gravity is a force that pulls on all objects on or near Earth. Weight is a measure of the force of gravity's pull. The unit for this measurement is the newton (N).

People often confuse mass and weight. But think what happens to the mass of an astronaut as he or she goes from Earth to the International Space Station. Nothing! The astronaut's mass stays the same, even though his or her weight goes down. The pull of gravity from Earth is countered by the space station's great speed in orbit.

 MAIN IDEA AND DETAILS What does a balance measure? What does a spring scale measure?

▲ Find an object's mass, or amount of matter, by first placing the object on one pan. Then add a known mass to the other pan until the pointer stays in the middle.

▲ When you hang an object on the hook of the spring scale, you measure the force of gravity pulling on the object. This is the object's weight.

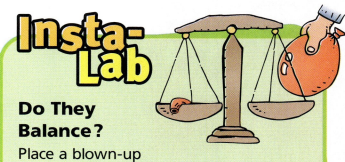

Insta-Lab

Do They Balance?

Place a blown-up balloon on one pan of a balance and an empty balloon on the other pan. Do they have the same mass? Why or why not?

Safety in the Lab

Working in the lab is fun. But you need to be careful to stay safe. Here are some general rules to follow:

- Study all the steps of an investigation so you know what to expect. If you have any questions, ask your teacher.
- Be sure you watch for safety icons and obey all caution statements.

Scientists in the lab wear safety goggles to protect their eyes. Smart students do the same thing! When you work with chemicals or water, a lab apron protects your clothes.

Be careful with sharp objects!

- Scissors, forceps, and even a sharp pencil should be handled with care.
- If you break something made of glass, tell your teacher.
- If you cut yourself, tell your teacher right away.

Be careful with electricity!

- Be especially careful with electrical appliances.
- Keep cords out of the way.
- Never pull a plug out of an outlet by the cord.
- Dry your hands before unplugging a cord.
- If you have long hair, pull it back out of the way. Roll or push up long sleeves to keep them away from your work.
- Never eat or drink anything during a science activity.
- Don't use lab equipment to drink from.
- Never work in the lab by yourself.
- Wash your hands with soap and water after cleaning up your work area.

 MAIN IDEA AND DETAILS What are four ways to keep safe in the lab?

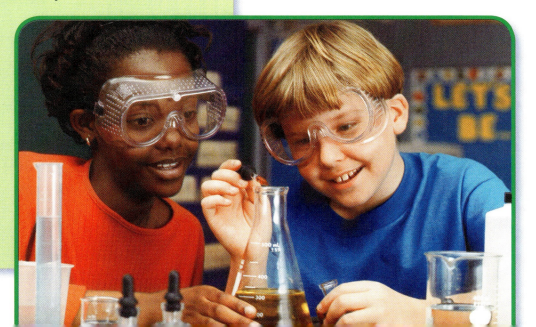

1. MAIN IDEA AND DETAILS Draw and complete this graphic organizer.

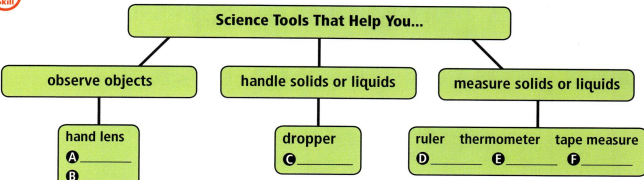

Science Tools That Help You...

observe objects

handle solids or liquids

measure solids or liquids

hand lens
Ⓐ_____
Ⓑ_____

dropper
Ⓒ_____

ruler   thermometer   tape measure
Ⓓ_____ Ⓔ_____   Ⓕ_____

2. SUMMARIZE Write two sentences that tell the most important information in this lesson.

3. DRAW CONCLUSIONS Why are different tools used to measure mass and weight?

4. VOCABULARY Write one sentence describing each vocabulary term.

FCAT Prep

5. Read/Inquire/Explain You are doing an investigation and accidentally spill water on the floor. How could this be a safety problem?

6. Why is using a thermometer or measuring cup more scientific than estimating temperature or volume?

A. It is easier.

B. It is more accurate.

C. It looks more scientific.

D. It uses up more class time.

Links

Writing

Narrative Writing

Use reference materials to learn about the life of Anton van Leeuwenhoek. Write a **story** that includes what he is famous for and what kinds of things he observed using his microscope.

Math

Choose Measuring Devices

A bottle is half full of water. Describe three things you could measure about the water, and name the tools to use for the measurements.

Health

Measuring for Health

Which science tools are also used by doctors, nurses, lab workers in hospitals, or others involved in health care? Describe how they are used.

 For more links and activities, go to **www.hspscience.com**

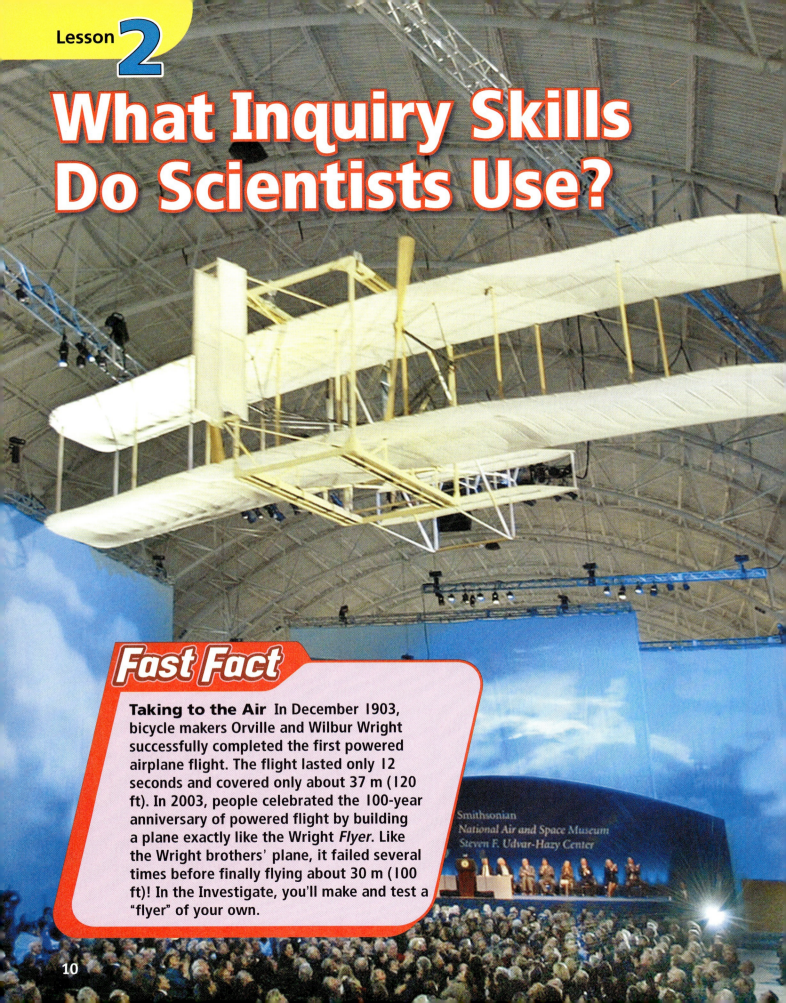

What Inquiry Skills Do Scientists Use?

Fast Fact

Taking to the Air In December 1903, bicycle makers Orville and Wilbur Wright successfully completed the first powered airplane flight. The flight lasted only 12 seconds and covered only about 37 m (120 ft). In 2003, people celebrated the 100-year anniversary of powered flight by building a plane exactly like the Wright *Flyer*. Like the Wright brothers' plane, it failed several times before finally flying about 30 m (100 ft)! In the Investigate, you'll make and test a "flyer" of your own.

Design an Airplane

Materials
- **thick paper**
- **tape**
- **stopwatch**
- **tape measure**

Procedure

1 Design a paper airplane. Then fold a sheet of thick paper to make the plane.

2 Measure a distance of 10 m in an open area. Mark one end of the distance as a starting line, and place a stick or stone every half meter from the starting line.

3 Test-fly your plane. Have a partner start the stopwatch as you're releasing the plane and stop it when the plane lands. Record the flight time in a table like the one shown.

4 Measure the distance the plane flew. Record the distance in the table.

5 Repeat Steps 3 and 4 for a second and a third trial.

6 Make a second airplane, with wings half as wide as your first plane.

7 Test-fly your second plane three times. Record all your measurements in the table.

Draw Conclusions

1. How did changing the width of the wings affect the way your plane flew?

2. **Inquiry Skill** Why did some students' planes fly farther or longer than those of others? Write a hypothesis to explain your thinking.

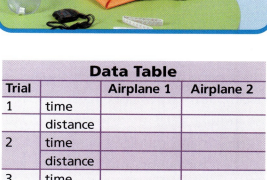

Step 1

Data Table			
Trial		Airplane 1	Airplane 2
1	time		
	distance		
2	time		
	distance		
3	time		
	distance		

Investigate Further

On one of your planes, add a paper-clip weight. Then fly the plane. What happens to the distance and time it flies? Infer the weight's effect on the plane.

Reading in Science

 SC.H.1.2.2.5.1 scientists use different kinds of investigations; **SC.H.1.2.5.5.2** compare using models; **LA.A.2.2.1** main idea and details

VOCABULARY

investigation p. 12
inquiry p. 12
experiment p. 15

SCIENCE CONCEPTS

▶ how inquiry skills help you gather information

▶ how an investigation differs from an experiment

READING FOCUS SKILL

MAIN IDEA AND DETAILS Look for information on when to use different inquiry skills.

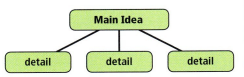

What Is Inquiry?

Suppose you wanted to learn about the way parachutes work. How would you begin? You might read a book about parachutes. Or you might investigate the subject on your own. An **investigation** is a procedure that is carried out to gather data about an object or event. An investigation can be as simple as measuring an object or observing a response to a stimulus. In this lesson, you investigated the way in which wing size affected flight.

So how can you begin your investigation about parachutes? Scientists usually begin an investigation by asking questions. Then they use inquiry skills to answer their questions. **Inquiry** is an organized way to gather information and answer questions. What questions do you have about parachutes?

Inquiry Skills

Observe—Use your senses to gather information about objects and events.

Measure—Compare the length, mass, volume, or some other property of an object to a standard unit, such as a meter, gram, or liter.

Gather, Record, and Display Data—Gather data by making observations and measurements. Record your observations and measurements in an organized way. Display your data so that others can understand and interpret it.

Use Numbers—Collect, display, and interpret data as numbers.

How does a parachute enable a person to jump from an airplane without getting hurt? ▶

How can you get answers to your questions? First, you might observe how parachutes are made. Look for diagrams in books or on the Internet. Go to a local airport, and ask to see some parachutes. Then gather, record, and display the data you collected. Measure and use numbers to express the data if possible.

You might wonder how a round parachute compares to a parachute like the one pictured on the previous page. What do they have in common? How are they different? What other shapes can a parachute have?

Once you compare different shapes, you can classify them. Some parachutes are used for doing tricks. Others are used to gently land heavy objects, such as space capsules. Some help sky divers land on a small target.

Now you've gathered a lot of data. The next step is to interpret the data. For example, how does the size or shape of the parachute relate to its use? Is there any pattern in the data? What shape of parachute appears easiest to control?

Data and observations can be used in many ways. It all depends on what questions you want to answer. You can use the data and logical reasoning to draw conclusions about things you haven't directly observed. For example, you might notice that narrow parachutes are used for tricks. From that, you can infer that this shape is easier to control. Or you might predict which parachute might win a sky-diving contest.

 MAIN IDEA AND DETAILS What are inquiry skills used for?

Inquiry Skills

Compare—Identify ways in which things or events are alike or different.

Classify—Group or organize objects or events into categories based on specific characteristics.

Interpret Data—Use data to look for patterns, to predict what will happen, or to suggest an answer to a question.

Infer—Use logical reasoning to come to a conclusion based on data and observations.

Predict—Use observations and data to form an idea of what will happen under certain conditions.

How does the size or shape of a parachute affect the way it works? ▶

Using Inquiry Skills

Suppose you were in a contest to find a way to drop a raw egg from a balcony without breaking the egg. What kind of parachute would you use?

First, you might plan and conduct a simple investigation. You might make parachutes of different shapes and sizes. You could tie weights on them, drop them, and see how they behave. How long do they stay in the air? How gently do they land? You could make observations and take measurements.

Plan and Conduct a Simple Investigation—Use inquiry skills to gather data and answer questions.

Hypothesize—Suggest an outcome or explanation that can be tested in an experiment.

Experiment—Design a procedure to test a hypothesis under controlled conditions.

This experiment tested hypotheses about the type of parachute that would prevent a dropped egg from breaking! What variables were involved? ▼

14

Control Variables—Identify and control the factors that can affect the outcome of an experiment.

Draw Conclusions—Use data and experimental results to decide if your hypothesis is supported.

Communicate—Share results and information visually, orally, or electronically.

With that information, you could hypothesize. What design has the best chance to protect the egg? You may think that a large, round parachute is the best design. You could experiment to test your hypothesis. An **experiment** is a procedure you carry out under controlled conditions to test a hypothesis.

An experiment has more steps than a simple investigation. You have to decide what you will test. Then you have to be sure you control variables.

What are variables, and how can they be controlled? A variable is a factor, such as size, that can have more than one condition, such as large and small. You wouldn't test both the size and shape of parachutes at the same time. Why not? You wouldn't know whether the size or the shape caused the results. Suppose you compared a small, square parachute and a large, round one. How would you know if the size or the shape made a difference?

To test your hypothesis that large, round parachutes are best, you could first test round parachutes of different sizes. Everything except parachute size would be the same. You'd use the same egg size for each drop. You'd drop the eggs from the same height. And you'd drop each one several times to check the results. Then you'd do the whole thing again, using parachutes with different shapes instead of sizes! As before, you'd control all other variables.

During the experiment, you'd be careful to write down exactly what you did and how you did it. You'd record all observations and measurements.

The final step in an experiment is to draw conclusions. Did your experiment support your hypothesis? Was a large, round parachute the best way to protect the egg? What did the experiment show?

Finally, you'd write up your experiment to communicate your results to others. You might include tables for your data or draw diagrams of your parachute design.

 MAIN IDEA AND DETAILS Why do you have to control variables in an experiment?

Insta-Lab

What Causes Lift?

Cut a strip of newspaper or notebook paper about 2–3 cm wide and 10 cm long. Hold the end of the strip in your hand, and blow gently over the top of it. What happens? How might the result relate to airplane wings?

Models, Time, and Space

Have you ever watched a leaf fall from a tree? You might think of a falling leaf as a model for a parachute. It could give you ideas for a parachute design. Or you might make a model and test it before making an actual parachute. That can be very practical. Companies that build rockets, for example, save a lot of time and money by making and testing models before building the real things.

How will your parachute interact with what is attached to it? Thinking about time and space relationships is an important inquiry skill. For example, how do you make sure the parachute in a model rocket pops out at the right time? There's a lot to think about! Inquiry skills are ways to make sure your thinking and tests really work.

MAIN IDEA AND DETAILS How do models help an investigation?

Inquiry Skills

Make a Model—Make a mental or physical representation of a process or object. Use a model that someone else has built or something from nature that is similar to what you are investigating.

Use Time/Space Relationships—Think about ways in which moving and nonmoving objects relate to one another. Figure out the order in which things happen.

Inexpensive models are a good way to test an idea before building the real thing. ▼

1. MAIN IDEA AND DETAILS Draw and complete this graphic organizer.

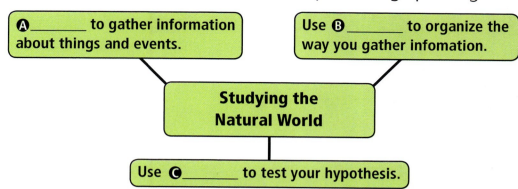

A _____ to gather information about things and events.

Use **B** _____ to organize the way you gather infomation.

Studying the Natural World

Use **C** _____ to test your hypothesis.

2. SUMMARIZE Use your completed graphic organizer to write a lesson summary.

3. DRAW CONCLUSIONS If you wanted to learn more about birds, would you be more likely just to make observations first or to experiment first?

4. VOCABULARY Use the vocabulary terms in a paragraph describing how scientists study the natural world.

FCAT Prep

5. Read/Inquire/Explain Alberto shines red light on one group of plants and blue light on another. He measures the height of the plants each day. What hypothesis is he testing?

6. A factor that can affect the outcome of an experiment is called a

A. hypothesis.　　**C.** variable.

B. prediction.　　**D.** model.

Links

Writing

Narrative Writing
What inquiry skills do you use in everyday life? Write a screenplay about a day in your life. **Describe** how you use inquiry skills.

Math

Displaying Data
Make three different charts, tables, or graphs that show how many of your classmates were born in each month of the year.

Social Studies

Making Inferences
Use reference materials to find out how archaeologists make inferences. What information do they use to infer what life was like hundreds of years ago?

 For more links and activities, go to **www.hspscience.com**

What Is the Scientific Method?

Fast Fact

Reaching for the Stars In October 2004, *SpaceShipOne* traveled nearly 112 km (70 mi) above the surface of Earth. The ship reached a speed of Mach 3—three times the speed of sound. However, *SpaceShipOne* wasn't built or launched by a government or a major aerospace company. It was the first successful launch of a private spaceship! In the Investigate, you too will build your own rocket.

Build a Rocket!

Materials
- string, 5 m
- safety goggles
- drinking straw
- 2 chairs
- balloon
- tape
- timer/stopwatch
- tape measure

Procedure

1. **CAUTION: Wear safety goggles.** Thread one end of the string through the straw.

2. Place the chairs about 4 m apart, and tie one end of the string to each chair.

3. Blow up the balloon, and pinch it closed.

4. Have a partner tape the balloon to the straw, with the balloon's opening near one chair.

5. Release the balloon. Use the stopwatch to time how long the balloon keeps going.

6. Measure and record the distance the balloon traveled. Also record its travel time.

7. Repeat Steps 3–6 with more air in the balloon. Then repeat Steps 3–6 with less air in the balloon than on the first trial.

Draw Conclusions

1. Why did the balloon move when you released it?

2. How did the amount of air in the balloon affect the travel time and distance?

3. **Inquiry Skill** Would changing the shape of the balloon affect the distance it travels? Predict what would happen if you used a large, round balloon and a long, skinny balloon with the same amount of air.

Step 2

Step 4

Investigate Further

Plan an investigation to find out how the angle of the string affects the travel time and distance. How do you think the results will change when the angle is varied?

Reading in Science

SC.H.1.2.1.5.1 scientific evidence should be replicable;
SC.H.2.2.1.5.1 make predictions; **SC.H.1.2.3.5.2** scientists
communicate; **LA.A.2.2.1** main idea and details

VOCABULARY
scientific method p. 20

SCIENCE CONCEPTS
▶ what steps are in the scientific method
▶ how scientists use the scientific method

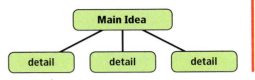 **READING FOCUS SKILL**

MAIN IDEA AND DETAILS Look for information on the steps of the scientific method.

```
          Main Idea
         /    |    \
    detail  detail  detail
```

The Scientific Method

In the Investigate, you predicted what would happen if you changed the shape of the balloon. How can you tell if your prediction is right? You could just play around with some balloons and see what happens. But a true experiment involves a series of steps that scientists use. The steps are called the **scientific method**.

Scientists use the scientific method to plan and carry out experiments. Some of the steps are the same as inquiry skills. And some inquiry skills are used in planning experiments.

There are five steps in the scientific method:

1. Observe, and ask questions.
2. Form a hypothesis.
3. Plan an experiment.
4. Conduct an experiment.
5. Draw conclusions, and communicate the results.

1 Observe, and Ask Questions

- Use your senses to make observations.
- Record *one* question that you would like to answer.
- Write down what you already know about the topic of your question.
- Do research to find more information on your topic.

2 Form a Hypothesis

- Write a possible answer to your question. A possible answer to a question is a *hypothesis*. A hypothesis must be a statement that can be tested.
- Write your hypothesis in a complete sentence.

Suppose you follow the steps of the scientific method. You form a hypothesis, and your experiment supports it. But when you tell other people your results, they don't believe you!

This is when the scientific method works especially well. You recorded your procedures. You have all your observations and data. All that another person has to do is repeat exactly what you did. That's one way scientists can check each other's experiments. If another person doesn't get the same results, you can try to figure out why. You can ask, "Did I do something differently? Were there variables I didn't control?"

Scientists can use the scientific method to repeat the experiments of other scientists. This helps them make sure that their conclusions are correct.

 MAIN IDEA AND DETAILS What are the steps of the scientific method?

③ Plan an Experiment

- Decide how to conduct a fair test of your hypothesis by controlling variables. Variables are factors that can affect the outcome of the experiment.
- Write down the procedure you will follow to do your test.
- List the equipment you will need.
- Decide how you will gather and record data.

④ Conduct an Experiment

- Follow the procedure you wrote down.
- Observe and measure carefully.
- Record everything that happens, including what you observe and what you measure.
- Organize your data so it is easy to understand and interpret.

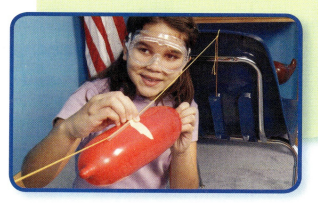

⑤ Draw Conclusions/ Communicate Results

- Make charts, tables, or graphs to display your data.
- Analyze your observations and the data you collected.
- Write a conclusion. Describe the evidence you used to determine whether the experiment supported your hypothesis.
- Decide whether your hypothesis was supported or not.

Before and After

People don't always start with the scientific method. Suppose you have questions about something scientists have already studied. All you need to do is read about it. But when studying the natural world, you often find new problems that puzzle you. You think, "I wonder what would happen if. . . " That's when inquiry skills, investigations, and experiments come in handy.

What happens after you've done an experiment? Even if an experiment supports your hypothesis, you might have other questions—about the same topic—that can be tested. And if your hypothesis wasn't supported, you might want to form another hypothesis and test that.

Scientists never run out of questions. The natural world is filled with things that make people wonder. By asking questions and using the scientific method, scientists have learned a lot. They've learned how to send people to the moon. They've learned to cure many diseases. But there are still many things to be learned. Who knows? Maybe you're the one to make the next big discovery!

 MAIN IDEA AND DETAILS What do scientists do when experiments show their hypotheses to be incorrect?

▲ Computers can be used to research a problem, display data, and share the results of experiments with scientists all over the world.

Tables and charts make it easy for other people to understand and interpret your data. ▼

Insta-Lab

Make a Helicopter

Cut a piece of paper 3 cm wide and 13 cm long. Draw lines on the paper like those on the diagram above. Cut along all the solid lines. Fold one flap forward and one flap to the back. Fold the base up to add weight at the bottom. Drop your helicopter, and watch it fly. How does adding a paper clip to the bottom change the way the helicopter flies?

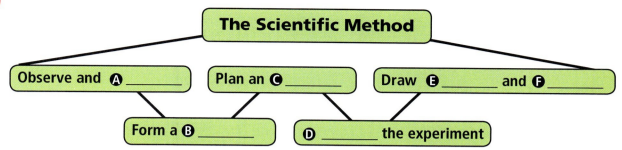

1. MAIN IDEA AND DETAILS Draw and complete this graphic organizer.

The Scientific Method

Observe and **A** _____

Plan an **C** _____

Draw **E** _____ and **F** _____

Form a **B** _____

D _____ the experiment

2. SUMMARIZE Use your graphic organizer to write a paragraph telling the steps of the scientific method.

3. DRAW CONCLUSIONS During which step of the scientific method would you identify variables and figure out how to control them?

4. VOCABULARY For each letter in *scientific method,* write a science-related word starting with the same letter. Skip repetitions of a letter.

FCAT Prep

5. Read/Inquire/Explain Karla heard that for making ice cubes, hot water is better than cold water because it freezes faster. How could she test that idea as a hypothesis?

6. What does an experiment test?

A. a fact   **C.** a theory
B. a hypothesis   **D.** a variable

Links

Writing

Expository Writing
Write a letter to a friend, **explaining** how he or she could use the scientific method to test a balloon rocket.

Math

Display Data
Make a table to display how long the balloon rockets flew in the Investigate. Then make a graph of the results.

Social Studies

Scientific Method
Use reference materials to compare how the Greeks studied science and what Francesco Redi added to their method. Write a story about what he showed.

 For more links and activities, go to **www.hspscience.com**

Review and FCAT Preparation

Vocabulary Review

Use the terms below to complete the sentences. The page numbers tell you where to look in the chapter if you need help.

microscope p. 4   **inquiry** p. 12
balance p. 7   **experiment** p. 15
investigate p. 12   **scientific method** p. 20

1. An organized way to gather information is called _____.

2. A tool used to measure the mass of an object is a _____.

3. To test a hypothesis, you plan and conduct a(n) _____.

4. A tool that makes objects appear larger is a _____.

5. A series of steps used by scientists to study the physical world is the _____.

6. When you gather information about an object or event, you _____.

Check Understanding

Write the letter of the best choice.

7. Which tool is used to measure volume in the metric system?
   A. balance   **C.** spring scale
   B. measuring cup   **D.** thermometer

8. **MAIN IDEA AND DETAILS** Which of the following steps to solve a problem is done first?
   F. test a hypothesis
   G. interpret data
   H. form a hypothesis
   I. observe, and ask questions

9. Which inquiry skill can be used to save time and money before doing an experiment?
   A. form a hypothesis
   B. make and use models
   C. classify objects
   D. draw conclusions

The diagram shows four tools. Use the diagram to answer questions 10 and 11.

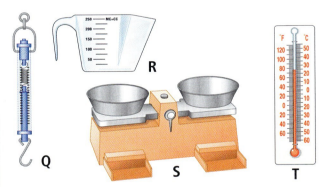

10. Which tool is used to measure the weight of an object?
    F. Tool Q   **H.** Tool S
    G. Tool R   **I.** Tool T

11. Which tool measures in grams?
    A. Tool Q   **C.** Tool S
    B. Tool R   **D.** Tool T

12. MAIN IDEA AND DETAILS Comparing, measuring, and predicting are examples of what process?

    F. communicating **H.** inquiry
    G. hypothesizing   **I.** investigating

13. When conducting an experiment, which is the best way to record data?

    A. Make a bar graph while taking the measurements.
    B. Write everything down after you are finished.
    C. Make a table to record your data as you collect it.
    D. Write things down on a sheet of paper and organize it later.

14. Juan is making and flying airplanes with different shaped wings. What is he doing?

    F. experimenting **H.** investigating
    G. hypothesizing   **I.** communicating

15. Why do scientists do each part of their investigation several times?

    A. to be sure their data is accurate
    B. to make their experiment look more impressive
    C. to use up all of their materials
    D. because it's fun

16. If you wanted to see more detail on the surface of a rock, what tool would you use?

    F. dropper   **H.** microscope
    G. forceps   **I.** thermometer

Inquiry Skills

17. Andrea is testing balloon rockets by using balloons with different amounts of air. **Identify three variables** Andrea will need to control.

18. Which boat would you **predict** will finish second in the race?

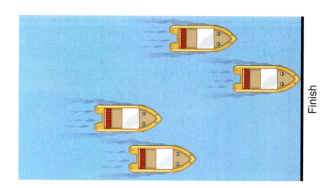

Finish

Read/Inquire/Explain

19. Why are safety goggles important when students are doing an investigation with scissors or glass?

20. The diagram shows an experiment. Different amounts of water were placed in 4 beakers. The beakers were heated at the same rate. The data shows how long it took each beaker to boil.

2.0 min   4.0 min   6.0 min   7.9 min

Part A What conclusion is supported by the experiment? Explain.

Part B What variables were controlled in the experiment?

The Nature of Matter

PHYSICAL SCIENCE

 The chapters in this unit address these Grade Level Expectations from the Florida Sunshine State Standards.

The investigations and experiences in this unit also address many of the Grade Level Expectations in Strand H, The Nature of Science.

Science in Florida

Port St. Joe

The Sunshine State

USA

Dear Marta,

Today our class took a field trip to Port St. Joe to learn how paper is made. First, trees are cut down, the bark is removed, and the wood is cut into small chips. The wood chips are heated and chemicals are added to soften the wood, forming a slurry. Then the slurry is drained and pressed into thin sheets. It's amazing to think that this postcard started out as a tree and went through so many changes to become paper!

Talk to you soon, Doug

FCAT Writing

Writing Situation

Write a story about being at the beach and finding a message in a bottle.

Experiment!

Make Your Own Paper Many people throw away old paper instead of recycling it. When paper is recycled, it goes through several changes before it can be used again. Find out how to recycle paper. Does the strength of a sheet of recycled paper depend on the type of paper that was recycled? Plan and conduct an experiment to find out.

Matter and Its Properties

Vocabulary

FCAT-Tested

matter	liquid
mass	gas
volume	mixture
density	solution
solid	

Other Terms

state of matter

solubility

suspension

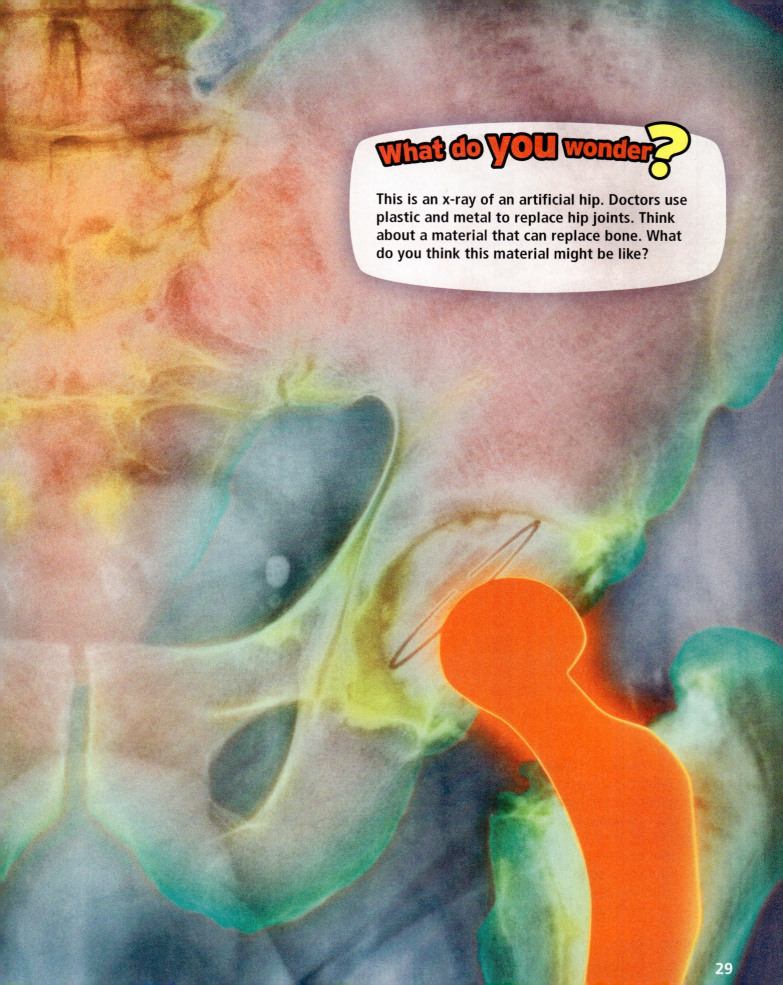

How Can Physical Properties Be Used to Identify Matter?

Fast Fact

Amazing Water Density affects the floating of liquids and solids. Water is unusual. It's less dense when it is solid ice than when it is liquid water. That's why ice floats on water. No other common material has this property of being denser as a liquid than as a solid. In the Investigate, you will find the densities of three liquids. Amazing water is one of them.

Measuring the Densities of Liquids

Materials
- graduate
- vegetable oil
- balance
- corn syrup
- water

Procedure

1. Make sure the graduate is empty, clean, and dry. Then use the balance to find its mass. Record the mass.

2. Add 10 mL of water to the graduate. Measure and record the mass. Empty the graduate, wash, and dry it.

3. Repeat Step 2, using 10 mL of vegetable oil.

4. Repeat Step 2, using 10 mL of corn syrup.

5. Subtract the mass of the empty graduate from each of the masses you measured in Steps 2, 3, and 4. Record each result.

6. To find the densities, divide the mass of each liquid by its volume, 10 mL. Record and compare the densities.

Draw Conclusions

1. Which liquid has the greatest density? Which has the least? Compare the amount of matter in each liquid.

2. **Inquiry Skill** Scientists often use graphs to display data thay have collected. Display data by making a bar graph that shows the density of each liquid you measured.

Step 2

Step 4

Investigate Further

Tint 10 mL of water red. Pour it into the graduate. Then add 10 mL of corn syrup. Observe what happens. How do you explain your observation?

VOCABULARY
matter p. 32
mass p. 33
volume p. 34
density p. 34

SCIENCE CONCEPTS
▶ how physical properties can be used to identify substances
▶ how density can be determined

READING FOCUS SKILL

MAIN IDEA AND DETAILS Find out how physical properties help identify matter.

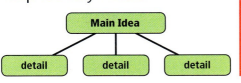

Matter

What is matter? Just about everything! Everything that takes up space is **matter**. This includes you, your skateboard, the clothes you're wearing, and the sidewalk under you. Breakfast cereal is matter. Your bowl, your spoon, and the milk you pour on the cereal are all matter, too.

If you can taste, smell, or touch something, it's matter. Even a breeze is matter, because air takes up space. You prove that when you blow up a balloon. The air you blow into the balloon pushes out its sides. The air inside the balloon takes up space.

Some things exist without taking up space, so they are not matter. What is not matter? Heat, light, and ideas are examples of things that are *not* matter. Even though they exist, they don't take up any space.

 MAIN IDEA AND DETAILS Define *matter*, and name three examples.

◀ What do you have in common with a skateboard?

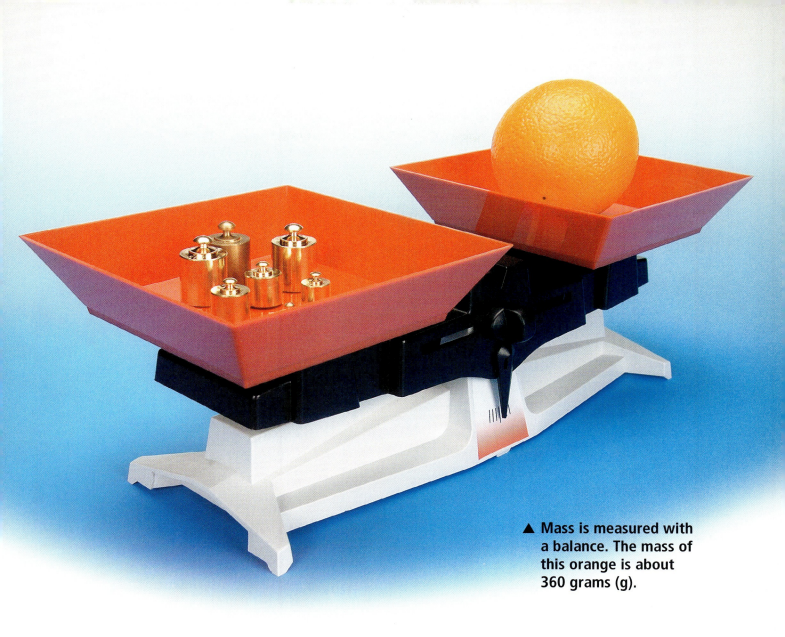

▲ Mass is measured with a balance. The mass of this orange is about 360 grams (g).

Mass

Matter not only takes up space but also has mass. **Mass** is the amount of matter something contains. A heavy object has more mass than a light object. Finding mass is a way of measuring matter.

All matter is made of tiny particles. You can see them only under the strongest microscopes. In general, the more particles an object has, the more mass it has. The more mass it has, the heavier it is. An object's mass doesn't change if you cut up the object or change its shape.

A golf ball and a table tennis ball both are made of matter. The balls are about the same size. However, the golf ball is heavier because it has more mass.

The mass of an object is one of its physical properties. A physical property is something you can observe or measure. You can measure mass. Other physical properties include an object's look and texture.

 MAIN IDEA AND DETAILS Define *mass.* Name one object with a lot of mass and one with little mass.

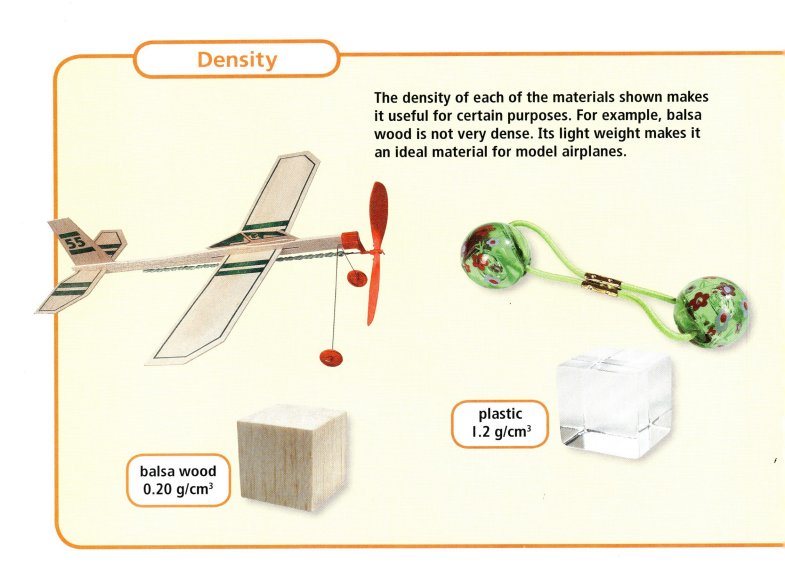

The density of each of the materials shown makes it useful for certain purposes. For example, balsa wood is not very dense. Its light weight makes it an ideal material for model airplanes.

plastic
1.2 g/cm³

balsa wood
0.20 g/cm³

Volume and Density

Volume is the amount of space that matter takes up. Scientists say that volume is conserved. The amount of space a measured volume takes up doesn't change if we move it, divide it, or change its shape. Some objects, such as a blown-up balloon, have little mass (few particles). Yet a balloon takes up a lot of space. A marble has more mass but takes up little space. How can we show this relationship between mass and space?

The answer is density. Density is the amount of matter in an object compared to the space it takes up. In the Investigate, you measured density. You divided the masses

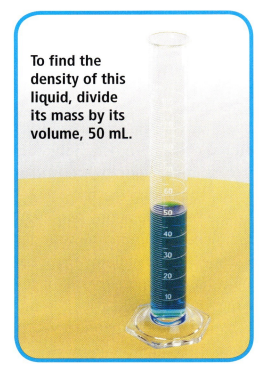

To find the density of this liquid, divide its mass by its volume, 50 mL.

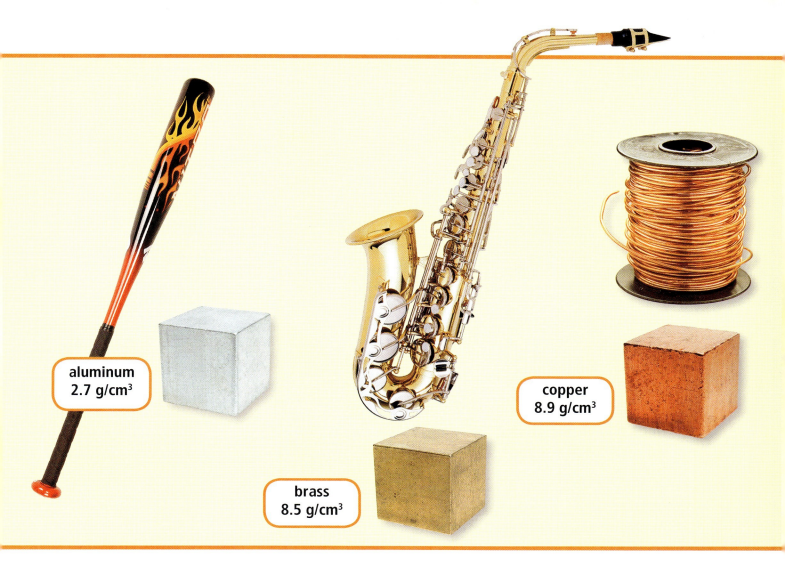

aluminum
2.7 g/cm³

copper
8.9 g/cm³

brass
8.5 g/cm³

of three liquids by their volumes. Each liquid had the same volume but a slightly different mass. This explains why each liquid had a different density.

You can find the density of a solid object by dividing its mass by its volume. For example, a certain wooden block has a mass of 20 grams. Its volume is 10 cubic centimeters. When you divide its mass by its volume, the answer is 2 grams per cubic centimeter. So, the block has a density of 2 grams per cubic centimeter (2 g/cm³).

MAIN IDEA AND DETAILS How are mass and density different?

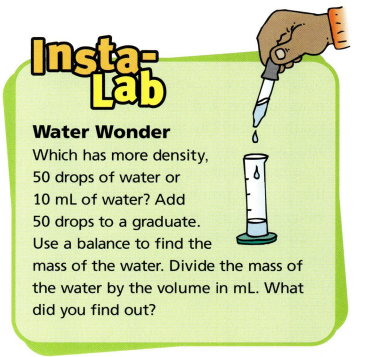

Insta-Lab

Water Wonder
Which has more density, 50 drops of water or 10 mL of water? Add 50 drops to a graduate. Use a balance to find the mass of the water. Divide the mass of the water by the volume in mL. What did you find out?

The foam tube is soft and green. It bends easily. ▶

▲ The foil is shiny and thin. It crushes easily.

You can tell these objects apart by observing their physical properties.

The glass is clear. It breaks easily. ▶

Other Properties of Matter

Suppose two marbles have the same mass, volume, and density. How can you tell them apart? By their colors, of course! You can tell one object from another by their physical properties. You have learned that physical properties include mass, volume, and density.

Color is another physical property. Shape and texture are two more physical properties. You use your senses to detect physical properties.

In the next lesson, you will learn that another physical property of matter is state. Matter might be a liquid, a solid, or a gas. How matter dissolves in a liquid is also a physical property.

The ability to transfer heat and electricity is another physical property. Some substances, such as copper, transfer heat and electricity easily. Others, such as plastic, do not.

You use physical properties to identify substances every day.

 MAIN IDEA AND DETAILS What physical properties could you use to describe a rock?

Focus Skill

1. MAIN IDEA AND DETAILS Draw and complete this graphic organizer.

Ⓐ_____ is the relationship between mass and volume.

Two objects with high density:

Ⓑ_____ **Ⓒ**_____

Two objects with low density:

Ⓓ_____ **Ⓔ**_____

2. SUMMARIZE Write a summary of the lesson by using the lesson vocabulary words in a paragraph.

3. DRAW CONCLUSIONS Two clear bags each contain a different unknown object. What physical properties can you use to tell the objects apart?

4. VOCABULARY In a sentence or two, explain why you must measure mass before you can determine density.

FCAT Prep

5. Read/Inquire/Explain Which senses help you determine an object's physical properties?

6. Which physical property can be the same for both a large marble and a small one?

A. color
B. mass
C. volume
D. weight

Links

Writing

Informative Writing

Suppose you are a scientist who has discovered a new substance. Write a **report** to describe its physical properties.

Math 9÷3

Find the Density

A green ball has a mass of 100 grams and a volume of 200 cubic centimeters. A yellow ball has a mass of 50 grams and a volume of 10 cubic centimeters. Which ball has the greater density?

Physical Education

Catch This!

You can use an air pump to change the density of air inside a soccer ball or basketball. What happens when you pump more air into the ball?

For more links and activities, go to
www.hspscience.com

How Does Matter Change States?

Fast Fact

Ice Cold Every March, ice artists like this one gather at the World Ice Art Championships in Fairbanks, Alaska. The artists depend on changing states of matter to shape and polish the giant sculptures. In the Investigate, you will have a chance to observe changes of state.

Melt, Boil, Evaporate

Materials
- 4 ice cubes
- hot plate
- safety goggles
- pot holders
- pan
- graduate

Procedure

1. Draw the ice cubes and describe their physical properties. Be sure to tell how they look and feel.

2. **CAUTION: Put on safety goggles.** Put the ice in the pan. Your teacher will help you carefully heat the pan. If you must touch the handle, use a pot holder. Predict the changes you expect to see in the ice cubes.

3. When the ice cubes melt, your teacher will pour the hot water into the graduate. Record its volume.

4. Use a pot holder as you pour the water back into the pan. Your teacher will put it on the hot plate again. Let the water boil. Predict what will happen this time.

   CAUTION: Remember to turn off your hot plate. Remove the pan from the heat before it is dry. Place the pan on a burn-proof surface.

Step 2

Step 4

Draw Conclusions

1. What caused the water to change?

2. **Inquiry Skill** Scientists often infer after making observations. Infer where the water is now. When it evaporated, what did the liquid water become?

Investigate Further

Using pot holders, pick up an ice cube in each hand. Push the cubes together without touching them with your hands. Explain what you observe.

Reading in Science

VOCABULARY
state of matter p. 40
solid p. 40
liquid p. 41
gas p. 41

SCIENCE CONCEPTS
▶ what three states of matter are
▶ how temperature can change the state of a substance without matter being lost or gained

READING FOCUS SKILL

CAUSE AND EFFECT Look for things that cause changes in a state of matter.

cause → effect

States of Matter

Every day, you see and touch three **states of matter**: solid, liquid, and gas. But why is an apple solid, while milk is liquid? What makes the air you breathe a gas? The answer lies in the particles that you read about earlier.

All matter is made of particles. The way those particles are arranged determines whether the matter is a solid, a liquid, or a gas.

In a **solid**, the particles are packed together in a tight pattern. A solid is rigid. This pattern gives solids an exact shape, so the solid takes up a certain amount of space. When you roll a bowling ball, the particles stay tightly packed. As a result, the ball does not change its shape.

The particles in matter are always moving. Particles in solids are packed too tightly to move around much. They vibrate in place instead.

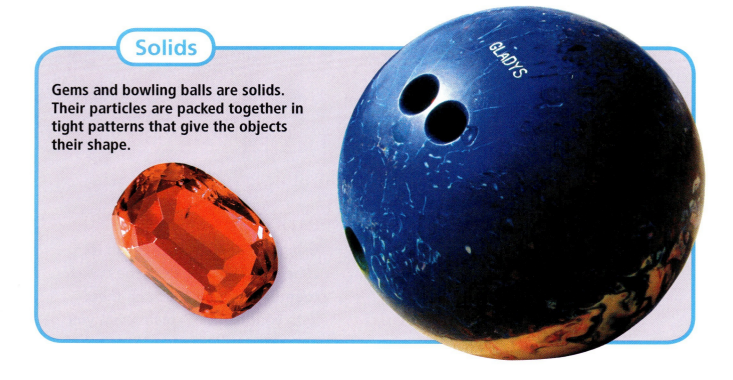

Solids

Gems and bowling balls are solids. Their particles are packed together in tight patterns that give the objects their shape.

GLADYS

Liquids

Liquids take the shape of their containers and have definite volume.

Gases

Gases take the shape of their containers but have no definite volume.

Particles in a **liquid** have more movement. They slide around, taking the shape of their container. A liquid can be poured from one container into another. They are able to move a little, so liquids change shape and flow. A liquid also takes up a certain amount of space. However, if you spill a liquid, its shape changes as its particles slide around.

A **gas** has no definite shape or volume. In a gas, the particles are far apart. Particles move fastest in a gas. When you open a container and release a gas into the air, its particles move away quickly. That's why you smell perfume after it is sprayed. Then the scent gets weaker because its gas particles move away and spread out.

CAUSE AND EFFECT What causes solids to keep their shape?

Insta-Lab

Spaces and Places

Fill a glass with water until the water bulges above the top. Next, slowly sprinkle 2 teaspoons of salt into the glass. The glass is full of water, so where does the salt go?

Changes of State

Water clearly shows how heating and cooling change the state of matter. Heat makes particles in matter move faster. If a solid gains energy, its particles move faster. They begin to slide around each other. The solid loses its shape and becomes a liquid. At 0°C (32°F), ice *melts*. It changes from a solid to a liquid.

Particles in a liquid move around and take the shape of the container. If you pour the liquid into another container, the liquid particles take that shape. However, the volume of the water stays the same.

If you keep adding heat to a liquid, its particles move even faster. Some of them escape, and become a gas. This a process is called *evaporation*. The gas particles bounce into each other and spread out in all directions. At 100°C (212°F), liquid water *boils*. It changes rapidly from a liquid to a gas.

Cooling gas particles slows their movement. The particles come together to form a liquid. This process is called *condensation*. Water vapor condenses as it cools, forming liquid water.

If a liquid gets cold enough, the particles form a solid once again. At 0°C (32°F), water *freezes* to form ice.

Although heat can change the state of matter, it can not change the amount of matter. For example, as the ice in a glass of ice water melts, the water level in the glass stays the same.

 CAUSE AND EFFECT How does heat change the state of water?

Heat Makes the Difference

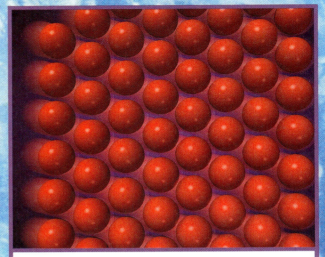

Ice is water in its solid state. The particles in ice are arranged in a tight, evenly spaced pattern. The particles still vibrate.

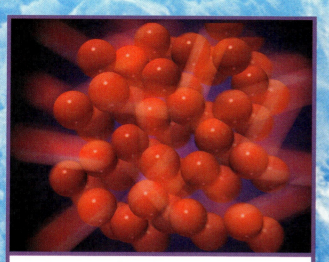

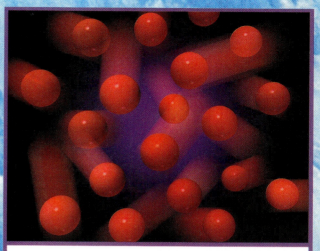

As ice warms, it melts into a liquid—water. As the particles warm up, they move and slide around one another. The even spaces between the particles become different-size spaces.

As the water is heated in the teapot, the particles move faster and faster. The liquid boils and becomes a gas. They bounce off one another and fly out of the spout, but they are invisible. As this water vapor cools, it condenses back into tiny drops of water, called steam.

 For more links and activities, go to www.hspscience.com

43

All Materials Change States

Water isn't the only material that changes state. All metals melt with heat, and even boil. And some materials change state in different ways. For example, dry ice is solid carbon dioxide. Carbon dioxide changes directly from a solid into a gas by a process called *sublimation*.

Some gases change directly into solids. Frost forms this way. Solid crystals of frost form from water vapor in the air. This process is called *deposition*.

 CAUSE AND EFFECT What causes dry ice to change state?

Math in Science
Interpret Data

Freezing and Boiling Points

Almost anything will melt or boil if its temperature gets high enough or low enough. Which of these substances would be useful in an industry in which resistance to heat is important?

Substance	Melting Point	Boiling Point
Iron	1538°C (2800°F)	2862°C (5184°F)
Mercury	−39°C (−38°F)	357°C (675°F)
Nitrogen	−209°C (−344°F)	−196°C (−321°F)
Oxygen	−218°C (−360°F)	−183°C (−297°F)

Dry ice changes from a solid directly into a gas.

Metals become liquid at very high temperatures. After a metal is cooled in a mold, it becomes a solid again. Now it has a new shape.

1. CAUSE AND EFFECT Draw and complete each graphic organizer.

CAUSE ⟶ EFFECT

| Heat warms ice particles. | | **Ⓐ** _____ |

CAUSE ⟶ EFFECT

| **Ⓑ** _____ | | Water particles turn into gas. |

2. SUMMARIZE Write a summary of this lesson. Begin with this sentence: There are three common states of matter on Earth.

3. DRAW CONCLUSIONS What do you think happens when gas particles cool off?

4. VOCABULARY Make a crossword puzzle that has the vocabulary terms as answers. Write clear clues for the words.

FCAT Prep

5. Read/Inquire/Explain How can you change the state of water?

6. In which state of water are the particles the most organized?

A. ice   **C.** liquid

B. gas   **D.** water vapor

Links

Writing

Narrative Writing
Suppose you are a drop of water. Write a **story** about how you experience all three states of matter in one day.

Math

Using Numbers
The metal mercury melts at about –40°C. In which state is mercury at room temperature? How do you know?

Language Arts

Name Origins
We use two temperature scales: Celsius and Fahrenheit. Find out when and how these scales were created and named.

 For more links and activities, go to **www.hspscience.com**

What Are Mixtures and Solutions?

Fast Fact

Salty Shore Most lakes have fresh water, but some lakes are saltier than the ocean. Mono Lake, in California, has salts and minerals dissolved in it. In warm weather, its water evaporates, leaving behind some of the salts and other minerals. In the Investigate, you will find out how salt and other solids dissolve in water.

Which Solids Will Dissolve?

Materials
- water
- teaspoon
- sand
- 4 clear containers
- stirrer
- salt
- sugar
- baking soda

Procedure

1. Half-fill each container with water.

2. Put 1 spoonful of sand into one container. Observe and record what happens.

3. Stir for 1 minute, and then record what you see.

4. Put 1 spoonful of salt into another container. Observe and record what happens. Repeat Step 3.

5. Put 1 spoonful of sugar into another container. Observe and record what happens. Repeat Step 3.

6. Put 1 spoonful of baking soda into the last container. Observe and record what happens. Repeat Step 3.

Draw Conclusions

1. Which solid dissolved the most? Which did not dissolve at all?

2. **Inquiry Skill** Scientists often plan a simple investigation to test an idea quickly. What idea did this activity test? What is another simple investigation you could do with these materials?

Step 2

Step 4

Investigate Further

Dissolve table sugar and powdered sugar in separate containers of water. Compare how quickly the two kinds of sugar dissolve. Explain your results.

Reading in Science

SC.A.1.2.4.5.1 physical combinations; **SC.A.1.2.4.5.2** mixtures and solutions; **LA.A.2.2.1** main idea and details

VOCABULARY

mixture p. 48
solution p. 50
solubility p. 51
suspension p. 52

SCIENCE CONCEPTS

▶ how a mixture, a solution, and a suspension differ

▶ differences in how substances dissolve

READING FOCUS SKILL

MAIN IDEA AND DETAILS Look for details about mixtures.

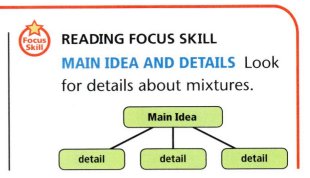

Main Idea

detail — detail — detail

Mixtures

Do you like salad? Salad is a mixture. A **mixture** is two or more substances that are combined without being changed. The substances in a mixture aren't permanently combined, and their properties don't change. They can be separated from each other again. For example, if you don't like onions, you can take them out of your salad.

Mixtures can contain different amounts of the substances. Your salad might have a lot of lettuce and just a little bit of onion.

oatmeal flakes

nuts

raisins

dried cranberries

This spoonful of granola is a mixture of good things to eat. ▶

48

Not all mixtures are made of solids. Salt water is a mixture of a solid and a liquid. Fog is a mixture of water drops and air. Air itself is a mixture of nitrogen, oxygen, carbon dioxide, and other gases.

Most materials found in nature are mixtures. Sand at the beach is a mixture of rocks, broken shells, and other materials. You can separate the materials on the beach by sifting or by other methods. The individual pieces keep their original properties.

The pictures show how one mixture can be separated. The mixture begins as a pile of rocks, dirt, salt, and bits of iron. First, larger rocks and particles are screened from the mixture. Only the smaller particles can pass through the holes in the screen.

Next, a magnet draws out the iron bits. Then, water is added to the remaining mixture. The wet dust, dirt, and salt are poured through a filter. Water and dissolved salt pass through. The dust and dirt are left behind.

Finally, the salty water is heated. The water boils away, leaving the salt behind.

All the substances in the original mixture are separated. Being in the mixture did not change them.

MAIN IDEA AND DETAILS
Define the term *mixture*, and name three examples.

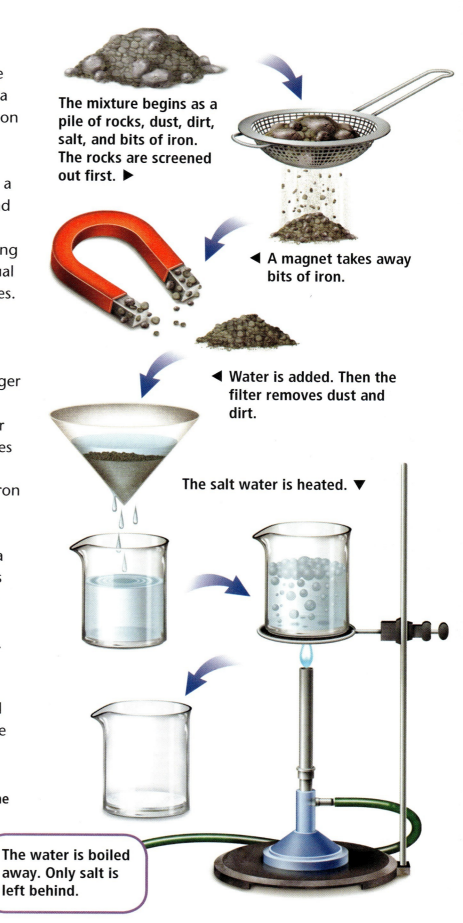

The mixture begins as a pile of rocks, dust, dirt, salt, and bits of iron. The rocks are screened out first. ▶

◀ **A magnet takes away bits of iron.**

◀ **Water is added. Then the filter removes dust and dirt.**

The salt water is heated. ▼

The water is boiled away. Only salt is left behind.

Solutions and Solubility

A solution is a kind of mixture. In a **solution**, different kinds of matter are mixed completely with each other. Salt water is a solution. The salt and the water are so evenly mixed that you cannot see the salt. You can tell it is there by tasting the water. Solutions can be combinations of solids, liquids, and gases. For example, the air you breathe is a solution. It is a combination of several gases that are mixed completely.

On the other hand, a bowl of salad is not a solution. You can always tell the ingredients apart. The tomatoes might all be on top. Most of the lettuce might be on the bottom.

When a solid forms a solution with a liquid, the solid dissolves in the liquid. In the Investigate, you found that sugar dissolves easily in water. The water particles pull the sugar particles away from one another. All the particles are moving, so the sugar particles spread evenly through the water.

However, sand does not dissolve in water. Water cannot pull sand particles apart. Instead, they fall to the bottom of the container without changing form. So, sand in water is not a solution.

Sugar crystals are added to water.

Water particles start pulling the sugar crystals apart.

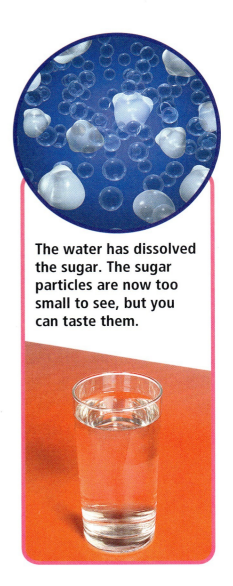

The water has dissolved the sugar. The sugar particles are now too small to see, but you can taste them.

What would happen if sand dissolved in water as easily as salt does?

This salt was once dissolved in ocean water. After the water evaporated, particles of solid salt were left.

You found in the Investigate that substances dissolve differently. **Solubility** (sahl•yoo•BIL•uh•tee) is a measure of how much of one material will dissolve in another. For example, 204 g (7.2 oz) of sugar will dissolve in 100 mL (3.4 oz) of water at room temperature. So, sugar has a solubility of 204 g/100 mL. However, no sand will dissolve in water. Sand has a solubility of zero. So does oil. That's why a bottle of salad dressing needs to be shaken before it is used.

 MAIN IDEA AND DETAILS Name two things besides sand and oil that are not soluble in water.

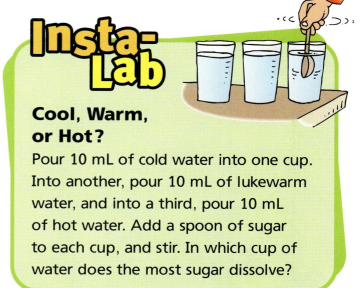

Insta-Lab

Cool, Warm, or Hot?

Pour 10 mL of cold water into one cup. Into another, pour 10 mL of lukewarm water, and into a third, pour 10 mL of hot water. Add a spoon of sugar to each cup, and stir. In which cup of water does the most sugar dissolve?

Other Mixtures

In some mixtures, the ingredients are not spread out evenly. When these mixtures sit, some of the ingredients settle to the bottom. Other ingredients rise to the top. This kind of mixture is called a <mark>suspension</mark>. Particles of one ingredient are suspended, or floating, in another ingredient.

If you have taken a walk on a foggy day, you have walked through a suspension. Droplets of water are suspended in the air. If you dip water out of a muddy creek, you will see a suspension. Bits of soil are suspended in the water.

 MAIN IDEA AND DETAILS How can you tell whether a mixture is a suspension?

You must shake the orange juice container because the pulp settles out of the juice. ▶

You must also shake most salad dressings. Otherwise, you might have just oil on your salad! ▶

Fog is a suspension of water droplets in air.

1. MAIN IDEA AND DETAILS Draw and complete this graphic organizer. List two details about each main idea.

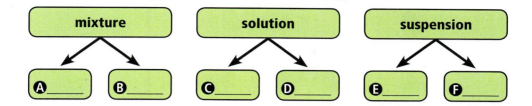

2. SUMMARIZE Use your completed graphic organizer to write a lesson summary.

3. DRAW CONCLUSIONS Why is lemonade made from a powdered mix a solution and not a suspension?

4. VOCABULARY Write two sentences. Use all four vocabulary words.

FCAT Prep

5. Read/Inquire/Explain Name two mixtures you have eaten in the past week. Explain whether each is a simple mixture, a solution, or a suspension.

6. Which of these is a mixture?

A. apple   **C.** carrot stick

B. broccoli   **D.** ham sandwich

Links

Writing

Narrative Writing
Suppose you are out walking on a rainy day. Write a **description** of what you see, and mention at least four mixtures. Include one solution and one suspension in your description.

Math

Make a Bar Graph
Use a graph to show the solubility of each of these substances in 100 mL of water at room temperature: sugar, 204 g; salt, 36 g; baking soda, 7 g; and sand, 0 g.

Social Studies

The Bronze Age
Bronze is a mixture of the metals tin and copper. Find out why people mix these two metals. Then research the Bronze Age. Find out what years it covered, and name an important event from that time.

 For more links and activities, go to **www.hspscience.com**

FIGHTING FIRES WITH DIAPERS

Firefighters usually use water and chemicals to fight wildfires. But firefighters battling a wildfire near Jackson, Wyoming, fought a fire with a new weapon: disposable diapers.

Well, actually it is the chemical found in disposable diapers that is used. The chemical is now being used across the country as an effective weapon against fire.

Fire-Fighting Gel

Inside a disposable diaper is a chemical called *polyacrylate.* This chemical draws moisture away from babies' bottoms. Scientists have been able to use the chemical, in a gel form, as a fire retardant.

What happens is that when a fire breaks out near a house, firefighters can spray the gel, nicknamed "green slime", wherever they need it. The gel stays put for hours and can be rinsed off with a hose once danger has passed.

During the Jackson, Wyoming, fires, the gel was sprayed on nearly 200 houses. Because the green slime doesn't burn, it protects the houses from the fire. And as one fire department official said, "It is well worth being slimed to save your house."

THINK ABOUT IT

1. Why is it important that homeowners be able to wash the green slime away with water?
2. Why would putting the chemicals into a gel form help fight fires?

Spin-In **Find out more! Log on to www.hspscience.com**

SC.H.3.2.1.5.1 technology has improved human lives; SC.H.3.2.1.5.2 some inventions lead to others

55

MARIE CURIE
Scientific Pioneer

Marie Curie (1867–1934) was a French scientist. She changed science forever and was the first woman to win the Nobel Prize.

A Nobel Prize medal

Marie worked with her husband, Pierre. Together, they discovered the element radium. They also explored the idea of radiation. Now, doctors use radiation to find and treat diseases.

Marie Curie was born in Warsaw, Poland, on November 7, 1867. Her father inspired her to study science. He taught high school physics. Later, Curie moved to France. That's where she met and married Pierre Curie.

Career   Nuclear Medicine Technologist

A nuclear medicine technologist uses radiation to help take pictures of a medical patient. First, a patient swallows a liquid that has a safe dose of radioactive material in it. The technologists then use special cameras to take 3-D pictures. By looking at how the liquid moves through a patient, a doctor can learn if there are any problems.

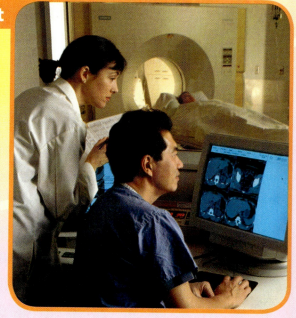

SCIENCE Projects
for Home or School

You Can Do It!

Quick and Easy Project

Don't Be Dense!

Materials
- deep container of water
- 2 identical marbles
- 2 balloons

Procedure

1. Find the mass of each marble to make sure they are identical.

2. Put a marble inside each balloon.

3. Knot one balloon close to the marble.

4. Blow some air into the other balloon, and knot the balloon close to its mouth.

5. Drop both balloons in the water, and observe what happens.

Draw Conclusions

Which balloon has more mass? Which has more volume? Which has more density? Which balloon floats? Explain.

Design Your Own Investigation

Cooling Off

You have learned that particles move more slowly as their temperature drops. How could you use a round balloon, a tape measure, and a freezer to prove that air particles move closer together as they get colder? Write the steps for a procedure and the results you expect—your prediction. Then carry out the experiment to test your prediction.

57

Chapter 1

Review and FCAT Preparation

Vocabulary Review

Use the terms below to complete the sentences. The page numbers tell you where to look in the chapter if you need help.

mass p. 33
volume p. 34
density p. 34
state of matter p. 40
solid p. 40
liquid p. 41
solubility p. 51
suspension p. 52

1. When some solids get warm enough, they become a _____.

2. When liquid particles get cool enough, they become a _____.

3. Mass divided by volume is _____.

4. The amount of a substance that can be dissolved in another substance is a measure of _____.

5. Gas is one, a _____.

6. If particles settle out of a mixture, the mixture is a _____.

7. The amount of space an object takes up is its _____.

8. _____ is the measure of the amount of matter an object has.

Check Understanding

Write the letter of the best choice.

9. Which of these is a mixture?
   A. pail of sand and soil
   B. copper wire
   C. ring of pure gold
   D. pinch of salt

10. Which of these is made of matter?
    F. a dream   H. happiness
    G. a book   I. an idea

11. **MAIN IDEA AND DETAILS** Which of these is an example of a solution?
    A. granola   C. pizza
    B. iced tea   D. salad

12. Which of these has no definite volume?
    F. gas   H. matter
    G. liquid   I. solid

13. **CAUSE AND EFFECT** Which of these probably has the **most** mass?
    A. apple   C. brick
    B. balloon   D. golf ball

14. Which term best describes the contents of this glass?

    F. density   H. suspension
    G. mass   I. volume

15. Which is a measure of how closely particles are packed together?
    A. density   C. solubility
    B. matter   D. volume

16. Which has mass and takes up space?

   F. height   **H.** volume

   G. matter   **I.** weight

Inquiry Skills

17. Contrast the arrangement of particles in a solid with the arrangement of particles in a gas.

18. Two boxes are the same size and density. What can you **infer** about their masses?

Read, Inquire, Explain

19. You have a red box and a black box that are exactly the same size. The red box is heavier than the black one. What does this tell you about the physical properties of the boxes?

20. The air around us is a mixture of nitrogen, oxygen, carbon dioxide, and other gases. This morning, the air outside looked like Picture A. Right now, the air outside looks like Picture B.

Part A Use the terms *solution* and *suspension* to describe the air this morning and the air right now.

Part B Explain how air can be a mixture, a solution, and a suspension.

Picture B

Picture A

Chapter 2

Changes in Matter

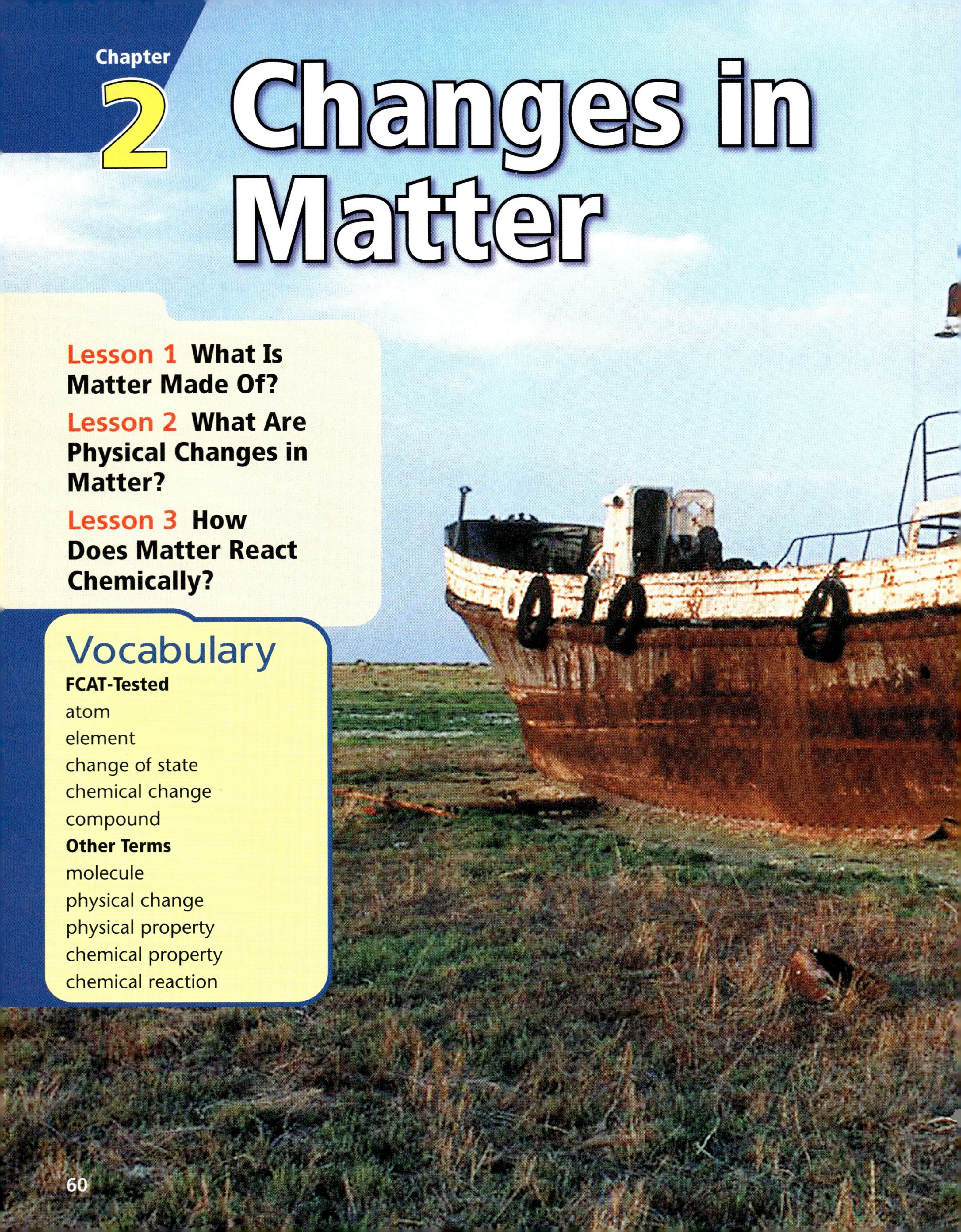

Lesson 1 What Is Matter Made Of?

Lesson 2 What Are Physical Changes in Matter?

Lesson 3 How Does Matter React Chemically?

Vocabulary

FCAT-Tested

atom

element

change of state

chemical change

compound

Other Terms

molecule

physical change

physical property

chemical property

chemical reaction

The shrinking of a sea left this ship behind. What happened to the sea floor? What is happening to the outside of the ship?

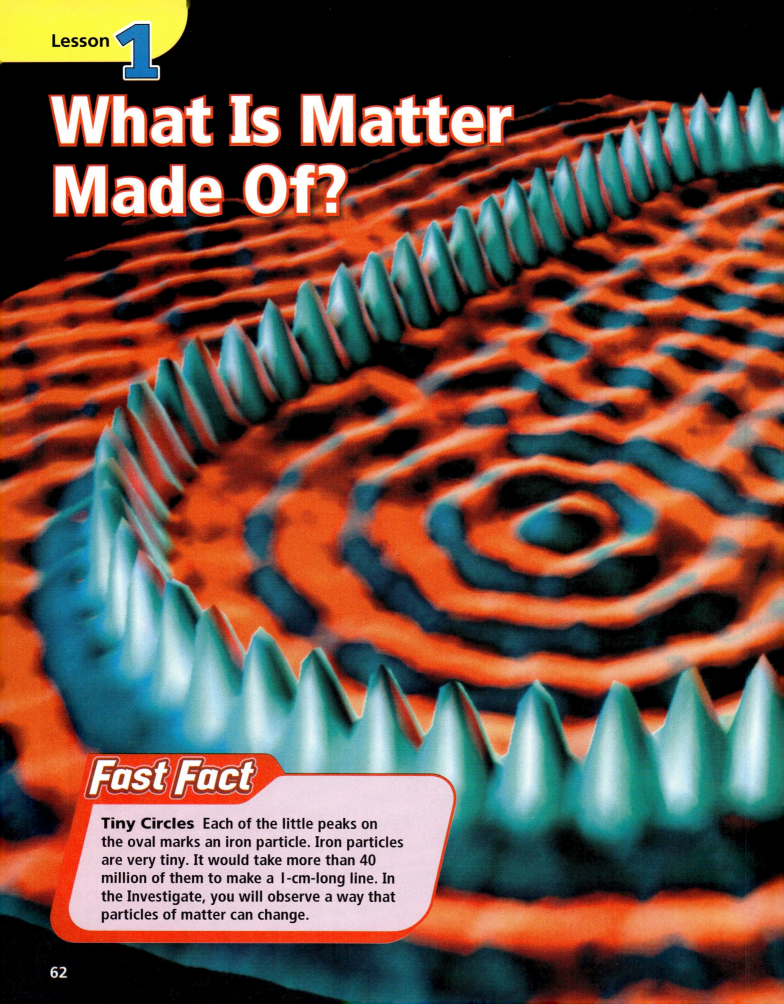

What Is Matter Made Of?

Fast Fact

Tiny Circles Each of the little peaks on the oval marks an iron particle. Iron particles are very tiny. It would take more than 40 million of them to make a 1-cm-long line. In the Investigate, you will observe a way that particles of matter can change.

A Solution to the Problem

Materials
- iodized salt
- kosher salt
- sea salt
- granulated sugar
- powdered sugar
- brown sugar
- 6 spoons
- 6 plates
- 6 plastic cups
- water

Procedure

1. Place a small amount of each kind of salt and each kind of sugar on its own plate.

2. Compare and contrast each sample for color and texture. Record your observations.

3. Compare and contrast the grain size of each sample. Record your observations.

4. Place the same amount of water in each of six cups. Use a clean spoon to place the same amount of each sample in its own cup. Stir. Record your observations.

Step 1

Draw Conclusions

1. Which samples—the light-colored ones or the darker-colored ones—mixed into the water more quickly?

2. Which samples—the ones with larger grains or the ones with smaller grains—mixed into water more quickly?

3. **Inquiry Skill** Scientists interpret data to draw conclusions. What can you conclude about how color and grain size affect the speed with which a sample mixed into water?

Step 4

Investigate Further

Sequence the samples by how quickly they mixed into water. **Predict** where sugar cubes fit in your list. Test your prediction.

Reading in Science

SC.A.2.2.1.5.1 materials have microscopic parts;
LA.A.2.2.1 main idea and details

VOCABULARY
atom p. 66
molecule p. 66
element p. 68

SCIENCE CONCEPTS
▶ that matter is made up of atoms
▶ that an element is a substance made up of just one kind of atom

Focus Skill **READING FOCUS SKILL**
MAIN IDEA AND DETAILS Look for details about atoms.

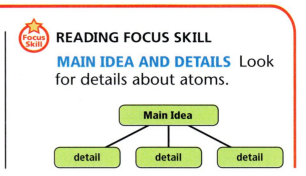

Basic Properties of Matter

What do your bed, the water in the ocean, and the air in your classroom all have in common? Not much, really. In fact, they have only one thing in common—they are all examples of matter. As you learned earlier, matter is anything that has mass and takes up space.

Sunlight is not matter. A light room does not have more mass than a dark room. An idea also is not made of matter. Your brain doesn't take up more space when you think hard.

What is matter made of? You know that it has different properties. How does it come together to make the things you see and touch?

Like matter, these toy pieces can be put together to form objects of many shapes and sizes. Each object has mass and takes up space. ▶

The soccer ball at the right has more mass than the one at the left. Where does the extra mass come from? ▶

Air is something around you everywhere. You need it to breathe. You know it is matter. The two soccer balls on this page show that you can squeeze different amounts of it into a container.

The fact that you can squeeze more and more air into a container gives a hint as to what matter is made of. It hints at the size of the particles of matter. You can't see the particles. With an air pump you can pack more and more of them into the same space. So they must be very small.

Other properties of matter also provide hints. Substances have properties such as solubility, mass, and hardness. As you learned in the Investigate, some materials act differently when mixed with water. You also know that metal knives are heavier and harder than plastic ones. So, some particles must be heavier or hold together more tightly. These differences are due to the fact that the tiny particles that make up each substance are different. In the rest of this lesson, you'll learn more about these particles.

 MAIN IDEA AND DETAILS How do you define *matter*?

Diving Bell

Hold a cup upside down in a bowl of water, and then remove it. Is it wet inside? (If you can't tell, tape a wadded-up tissue inside the bottom of the cup and try again.) What do you think happened?

Particles of Matter

More than 2000 years ago, a Greek thinker named Democritus (dih•MAHK•ruh•tuhs) had an idea about matter. Democritus said that all matter is made up of tiny particles, or bits. He said that different kinds of matter are made up of different kinds of particles. And he thought that these particles could not be broken down into smaller parts.

Democritus didn't experiment or test his ideas in any way. Still, it turns out that he was right. We now know that matter can be broken down only so far. If you divide something smaller and smaller, you end up with an atom. An **atom** is the smallest possible particle of a substance. A **molecule**

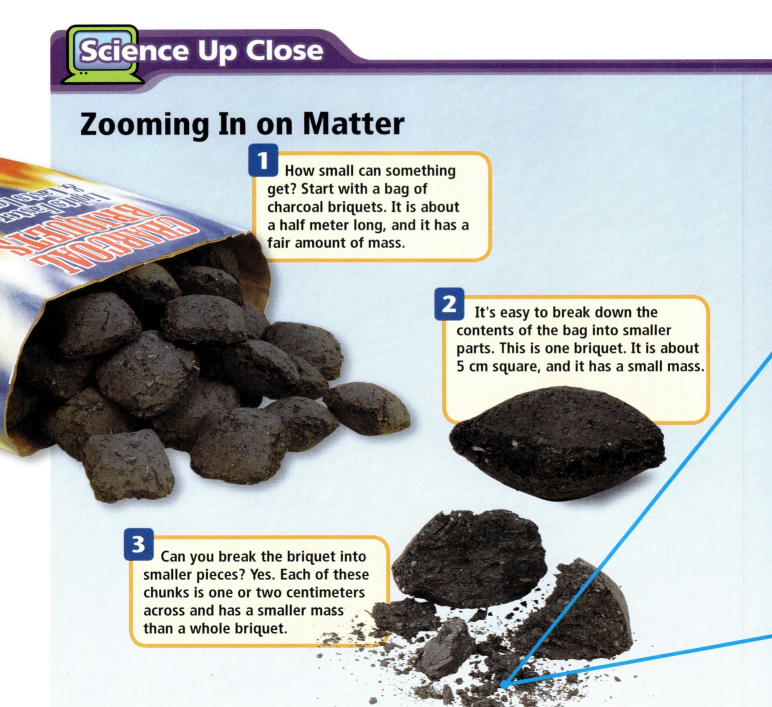

Science Up Close

Zooming In on Matter

1 How small can something get? Start with a bag of charcoal briquets. It is about a half meter long, and it has a fair amount of mass.

2 It's easy to break down the contents of the bag into smaller parts. This is one briquet. It is about 5 cm square, and it has a small mass.

3 Can you break the briquet into smaller pieces? Yes. Each of these chunks is one or two centimeters across and has a smaller mass than a whole briquet.

(MAHL•ih•kyool) is made up of two or more atoms joined together.

As you might guess, atoms and molecules are very small. They are really, really small. In fact, they are so small that you can't see them. Even with a regular microscope you couldn't see an atom or a molecule. Why not? Because single atoms and molecules are too small to reflect light! So there's no way you can see an atom or molecule at all unless you use a special microscope.

Democritus made up the word *atom*. It comes from a word that means "cannot be divided." Think about a tank of oxygen. You can divide all the oxygen inside into smaller and smaller parts. But when you get to an oxygen atom, you have to stop. If you break it up further, it won't be oxygen anymore.

MAIN IDEA AND DETAILS What is an atom?

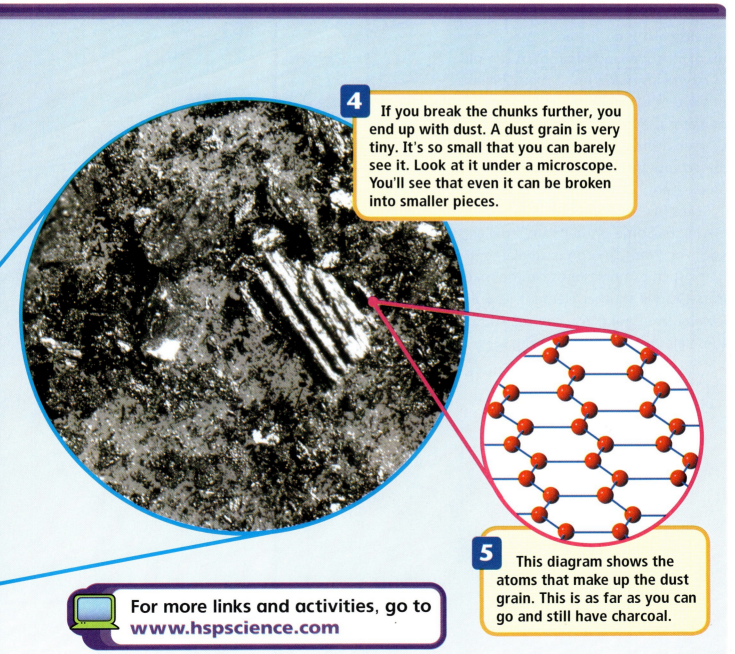

4 If you break the chunks further, you end up with dust. A dust grain is very tiny. It's so small that you can barely see it. Look at it under a microscope. You'll see that even it can be broken into smaller pieces.

5 This diagram shows the atoms that make up the dust grain. This is as far as you can go and still have charcoal.

For more links and activities, go to **www.hspscience.com**

Elements

You just read that if you were to break all the oxygen inside a tank into smaller and smaller parts, you would end up with an oxygen atom. What if you did the same thing with a drop of water? Would you end up with a single water atom? No, because there is no such thing as an atom of water. The smallest possible particle of water is a molecule made up of two different kinds of atoms—two hydrogen atoms and one oxygen atom.

Hydrogen and oxygen are elements. An **element** is a substance that is made up of just one kind of atom. A sample of oxygen is made up of many billions of oxygen atoms only. But a sample of water is made up of billions of oxygen atoms and hydrogen atoms joined together. So, water is not an element.

Scientists have identified 116 elements. Some of them are familiar to you. For example, iron is an element. Useful items such as horseshoes can be made from iron. Gold is another element. People make jewelry from gold. You can see some of these elements on these two pages.

MAIN IDEA AND DETAILS What is an element?

Remember the atoms in charcoal? They were carbon atoms. Carbon is also the element that makes up the point of a pencil.

You've already read that oxygen is an element. It is one of several elements that people must have in order to live.

Elements

Have you ever seen a mercury switch in a thermostat? As you can see, mercury is a shiny, silver-colored element.

Iron is another common element. You probably see things made of iron every day. You may also see things made of steel. Steel is made up of iron and a small amount of carbon.

Another shiny, silver-colored element is silver. Silver is somewhat rare. Many people call forks and spoons "silverware." However, only fancy, expensive silverware is really made of silver.

Sulfur is another element. It is a nonmetal. If you try to stretch it out, it breaks. ▼

▲ Gold is an element. It is a metal. It can be drawn out into thin wire and used in jewelry and in electronics.

Some Groups of Elements

You've probably noticed that scientists classify things into groups. Forming groups helps people see how things are like each other and how they are different from each other. Scientists have grouped elements several different ways. One of these ways divides elements into metals and nonmetals.

Many metals, like iron, gold, and silver, are elements. However, not all metals are elements. Steel, for example, is made up of at least two elements, iron and carbon.

What are some ways in which all metals are alike? For one thing, most metals are shiny. They can also be pounded into thin sheets or stretched out into long, thin wires.

How are nonmetals different from metals? First of all, nonmetals aren't shiny. They're dull. And they can't be pounded or stretched out. Most nonmetals are brittle. If you try to pound them or stretch them, they just break.

 MAIN IDEA AND DETAILS Name two groups of elements.

1. **MAIN IDEA AND DETAILS** Draw and give examples to complete this graphic organizer.

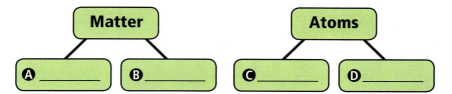

2. **SUMMARIZE** Write a summary of this lesson by using each of the lesson vocabulary words in a sentence.

3. **DRAW CONCLUSIONS** The scientific name for table salt is sodium chloride. Why do you think it has this name?

4. **VOCABULARY** Make a word puzzle by using the lesson vocabulary words. Be sure to write a clue for each word.

FCAT Prep

5. **Read/Inquire/Explain** Why is "anything you can touch and pick up" not a good definition of *matter*?

6. Which is the smallest particle of an element?

   A. atom   **C.** chunk
   B. bit   **D.** grain

Links

Writing

Narrative Writing
Imagine that you have been shrunk down to the size of an atom. Write a short **story** about what you see and do.

Math

Identify Place Value
You have read that you would have to line up more than 40 million iron particles (atoms) to get a line of them 1 cm long. How do you write the numeral for 40 million?

Social Studies

Explore the History of Science
Did everyone accept Democritus's ideas about atoms 2000 years ago? Do some research. Then write a paragraph about people's reactions to Democritus's ideas.

 For more links and activities, go to **www.hspscience.com**

What Are Physical Changes in Matter?

Fast Fact

Bubble Life Span A scientist once kept a bubble in a jar for three months! It never popped, but it eventually shrank down until the air in the bubble was gone. The shape of the bubble changed, but the substance didn't. In the Investigate, you will observe changes in three liquids over time.

Drop by Drop

Materials
- 3 droppers
- water
- vegetable oil
- rubbing alcohol
- 3 plates
- safety goggles

Procedure

1. **CAUTION: Wear safety goggles.** Place 3 drops of water on one plate, 3 drops of vegetable oil on the second plate, and 3 drops of rubbing alcohol on the third plate. Be sure to use a different dropper for each liquid.

2. Record your observations of each liquid.

3. Repeat Step 2 every half hour for the rest of the school day. Make and record your observations each time.

Draw Conclusions

1. What did you observe at the end of the day?

2. **Inquiry Skill** When scientists give a possible explanation for what they observe, we say they are making a hypothesis. Then the scientists test the hypothesis. What hypothesis can you make from your observations?

Step 1

Step 2

Investigate Further

What could you do to test your hypothesis? Plan and carry out an investigation to find out.

VOCABULARY
change of state p. 74
physical change p. 76

SCIENCE CONCEPTS
▶ that solid, liquid, gas are three states of matter
▶ that physical changes do not make new substances

READING FOCUS SKILL

COMPARE AND CONTRAST
Look for similarities and differences in states of matter.

alike	different

States of Matter

Have you ever seen ice cubes melt in a glass? The ice becomes water. Or maybe you've seen water boil away on a stove. It seems to disappear. Whatever you've experienced, you probably figured out long ago that water, ice, and water vapor are all the same thing.

But this fact isn't as easily known as you might think. After all, ice is cold and hard, and water is wet and soft. Water vapor is water, too, but you can't see it.

So, how is it that water can have three forms that are so different? Actually, every substance on Earth can exist as a solid, as a liquid, or as a gas. These are called the *three states of matter.*

A **change of state** occurs when a substance changes from one state to another. Each change of state has its own name. If a solid is heated enough, it will eventually turn into a liquid.

Liquid
The particles of water in this glass are close to each other. They move quickly and slide past each other easily.

These monkeys get warm by sitting in a hot spring. They are surrounded by water in all three of its states. ▶

This is called *melting*. If a liquid is cooled enough, it will turn into a solid. This is called *freezing*.

If a liquid is heated enough, it will turn into a gas. This is called *boiling*. If a gas cools, it will turn into a liquid. This is called *condensing*.

You know that all matter is made up of tiny particles. These particles are always moving. Since ice, water, and water vapor are all the same substance, they are made up of the same kind of particles—water molecules.

The difference between them is in the way the particles move. Ice particles don't move around at all; they just vibrate in place. Water particles move easily. Water vapor particles quickly fly all over the place.

 COMPARE AND CONTRAST How are particles of ice, water, and steam different? How are they the same?

Solid
The particles of ice are locked in place, although they're still vibrating.

Gas
The particles of gas in this balloon include water vapor. Water vapor particles are far apart and are moving quickly.

Physical Changes

Look at the pictures of the icicles melting and the water boiling. What do they have in common? They both show changes of state.

Now look at the pictures on the next page. One sheet of paper is being shredded, another sheet of paper is being cut, and wood is being carved with a chain saw. Those pictures have something in common with the pictures on this page. Do you know what it is?

The paper and wood are being changed, but none of these changes is a change of state. So that's not it. But, all the pictures on these two pages show physical changes. A **physical change** is a change that does not result in a new substance. Changes of state are examples of physical changes. So are shredding, cutting, and carving.

How do you know that a change of state is a physical change? Well, you know that ice, water, and water vapor are all different

◄ The icicles are melting into liquid water. Ice and water are two forms of the same thing.

The water is boiling into water vapor, a gas you cannot see. Water and water vapor are two forms of the same thing. ▼

Both of these photos show changes of state. A change of state is a physical change.

The shredder is changing paper into many, many thin strips of paper. ▼

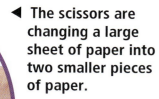
◄ The scissors are changing a large sheet of paper into two smaller pieces of paper.

This artist is using a chain saw to change a log into a deer statue and wood chips. ▼

forms of the same thing. If ice changes to water or water changes to water vapor, no new substance is made. So, that change is a physical change.

After you shred a sheet of paper, what do you get? You get shreds of paper. And when you cut a sheet of paper in two, you get two smaller pieces of paper. The size and shape are different, but they are all still paper.

The chain saw makes lots and lots of wood chips. They're small, but they're still wood. Since wood is not being changed into another substance, the change is a physical change.

Focus Skill
COMPARE AND CONTRAST What do all physical changes have in common?

Insta-Lab

Change It

Take an everyday object, such as a piece of chalk or a sheet of paper. Describe its physical properties—is it smooth or rough, hard or soft, shiny or dull? Now break it or tear it. What are the physical properties of the pieces?

Dissolving

You know that a change of state is a kind of physical change. This picture shows another kind of physical change—*dissolving*. The sugar dissolves, or becomes evenly mixed into, the hot water in the beaker. The result is a solution of sugar water.

How can you tell that dissolving is a physical change? You can let the water in the beaker *evaporate*, which is another physical change. After the water evaporates, the sugar is left behind in the beaker. The sugar doesn't change into another substance. It's still there.

Focus Skill **COMPARE AND CONTRAST** How is dissolving like evaporating?

The sugar dissolves in the hot water.

After the water evaporates, the sugar is left behind.

1. COMPARE AND CONTRAST Copy and complete the graphic organizer.

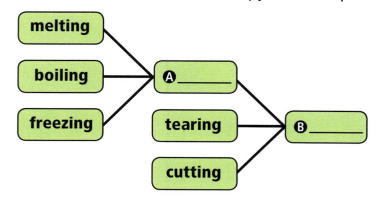

melting

boiling → Ⓐ _____

freezing

tearing → Ⓑ _____

cutting

2. SUMMARIZE Write a summary of this lesson. Begin with this sentence: *Matter can be in one of three states.*

3. DRAW CONCLUSIONS A glass falls to the floor and smashes into hundreds of tiny pieces. Is this a physical change? Why or why not?

4. VOCABULARY Write a fill-in-the-blank sentence for each vocabulary term. Show the right answers.

FCAT Prep

5. Read/Inquire/Explain A cook adds oil to vinegar and then mixes it to make salad dressing. Is this a physical change? Why or why not?

6. Which might occur if you heat a substance?

A. boiling **C.** shredding

B. freezing **D.** none of these

Links

Writing

Expository Writing

Imagine that you are helping a younger student learn about science. Write a short **explanation** of what changes occur when a substance goes through a change of state.

Math

Estimate Measurements

Nancy combines 950 mL of vinegar with 800 mL of oil. About how many liters is that in all?

Health

Food Changes

When you eat, your body changes food so that you can digest it. Make a diagram that shows two places in the body in which food undergoes a physical change. (Hint: Read about digestion.)

 For more links and activities, go to **www.hspscience.com**

How Does Matter React Chemically?

Fast Fact

Bang! Zoom! The energy made by two chemical reactions is enough to lift the space shuttle into orbit. Believe it or not, the substance that is made by one reaction is water. In the Investigate, you will find out about another reaction that involves water.

Wet Wool

Materials
- 3 small pieces of steel wool
- water
- 2 plates
- bowl

Procedure

1. Put one piece of steel wool on a plate.

2. Soak another piece of steel wool in water. Then put it on the other plate.

3. Fill the bowl with water, and put the third piece of steel wool in the water. Make sure none of it sticks out above the water.

4. Place all three samples in the same area, away from direct sunlight. Examine them every day for a week. Record your observations.

Step 2

Draw Conclusions

1. How do the three samples compare?

2. **Inquiry Skill** Scientists can draw conclusions from the results of their experiments. What two things can you conclude caused the changes?

Step 3

Investigate Further

What do you predict will happen if you place the three samples in direct sunlight? Experiment to find out.

Reading in Science

SC.A.1.2.5.5.1 chemical combinations; **SC.A.1.2.5.5.2** physical and chemical changes; **LA.A.2.2.7** compare and contrast

VOCABULARY
physical property p. 83
chemical property p. 83
chemical change p. 84
chemical reaction p. 84
compound p. 84

SCIENCE CONCEPT
▶ that one or more new substances are produced during a chemical change

READING FOCUS SKILL
COMPARE AND CONTRAST
Compare chemical changes to physical changes.

| alike | — | different |

Chemical and Physical Properties

How would you describe a pencil? You might say that it's yellow, that it's long and thin, and that it has six sides. You might say that you use it to write, and that the tip breaks easily. You could even say that it is a thin column of carbon wrapped with wood.

All of these descriptions have something in common—they all describe the pencil itself.

Can you also describe something in relation to another substance? Yes, you can. You can describe something by the way it interacts with other substances.

Think about the wood in the pencil. If there is oxygen near the wood and the temperature is hot enough, the wood will

Properties of Matter

	Physical Properties	
Water	• colorless • odorless • liquid at room temperature	• boils at 100°C • melts at 0°C
Silver	• shiny • soft • silver in color	• boils at 2163°C • melts at 962°C
Iron	• shiny • hard • grayish silver in color	• boils at 2861°C • melts at 1538°C
Sulfur	• dull • brittle • yellow	• boils at 445°C • melts at 115°C

burn. So, another description of the pencil might be "It burns if there is oxygen near it and the temperature is very high."

So, now you know two different ways to describe a substance. One way is to describe its physical properties. **Physical properties** are traits that involve a substance by itself.

Another way to describe a substance is to describe its chemical properties. **Chemical properties** are properties that involve how a substance interacts with other substances.

Look at the table. You're probably familiar with most of these substances. You're probably also familiar with some of these changes. Have you ever seen rusted iron or tarnished silver?

 COMPARE AND CONTRAST How are physical properties different from chemical properties?

Math in Science
Interpret Data

Boiling Mad
Boiling point is a physical property of a substance. Which substance has the highest boiling point? Which has the lowest boiling point?

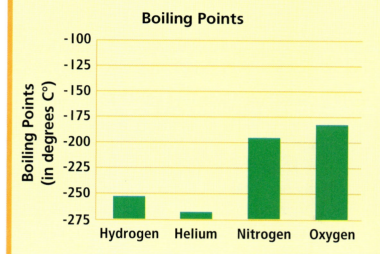

Boiling Points

Boiling Points (in degrees C°)

- -100
- -125
- -150
- -175
- -200
- -225
- -250
- -275

Hydrogen   Helium   Nitrogen   Oxygen

This glass contains liquid nitrogen, which would still boil on the coldest winter day.

Chemical Properties
• made up of hydrogen and oxygen
• does not react with many other substances • does not react with air • reacts with ozone or sulfur to form tarnish ✓
• reacts easily with many other substances • reacts with oxygen to form the minerals hematite and magnetite • reacts with oxygen in presence of water to form rust ✓
• reacts with any liquid element • reacts with any solid element except gold and platinum • reacts with oxygen to form sulfur dioxide, a form of air pollution ✓

◄ Notice in the table that one particular word is used in nearly every line. That word is *react* or *reacts*. What does that word mean in science? Well, it's an important topic, and you'll start reading about it on the next page.

Chemical Changes

You know that hydrogen and oxygen are usually gases. Do you know what happens when hydrogen burns? It combines with oxygen to form water.

This change results in a new substance—water. Clearly the formation of water is not a physical change. A physical change does not result in a new substance. This change is a chemical change. A <mark>chemical change</mark> is a change that results in one or more new substances. Another term for a chemical change is <mark>chemical reaction</mark>. Now you know the word *reacts* means "goes through a chemical change."

You know that an element is something made up of only one kind of atom. Since water is made up of hydrogen and oxygen atoms, it is not an element. It's a compound. A <mark>compound</mark> is a substance made up of two or more different elements that have chemically combined.

COMPARE AND CONTRAST How is a chemical change different from a physical change?

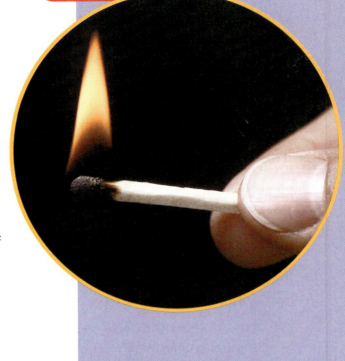

Sulfur in the match head is what helps the match light quickly.

Iron reacts with oxygen in the presence of water to form rust.

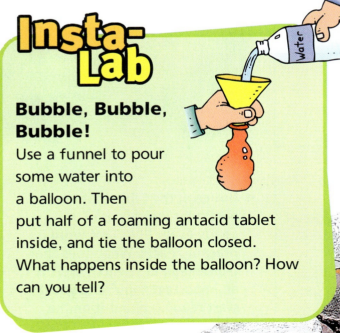

Insta-Lab

Bubble, Bubble, Bubble!

Use a funnel to pour some water into a balloon. Then put half of a foaming antacid tablet inside, and tie the balloon closed. What happens inside the balloon? How can you tell?

Silver reacts with sulfur to form tarnish. This helps you know that either sulfur or compounds that contain sulfur were in the air.

Sulfur reacts with oxygen to form sulfur dioxide. *Reacts with oxygen* often means that a substance burns.

Recognizing Chemical Changes

Water is made up of two gases— oxygen and hydrogen. They react to form a liquid. It's easy to understand that a chemical reaction took place. Water is a liquid, not a gas!

There are clues that help you know that chemical changes have taken place. Sometimes gas bubbles form, such as when you pour hydrogen peroxide on a cut. A change in color may also tell you that a chemical change has occurred. Fireworks are a good example of this. Some additional chemical-change clues are listed in the table. Just remember that none of these clues is absolute. When water freezes, it becomes solid—a new physical property. But freezing is a physical change, not a chemical change.

COMPARE AND CONTRAST Suppose you bake bread. Suppose you draw with a marker on paper. How are the changes in color that occur different from one another?

Before bread dough is baked, it's white or very pale tan.

After the bread is baked, its crust is dark brown. That's because baking causes a chemical change.

The smell of eggs frying tells you that a chemical change is taking place. So does seeing the egg yolk change from a runny liquid to a solid. ▶

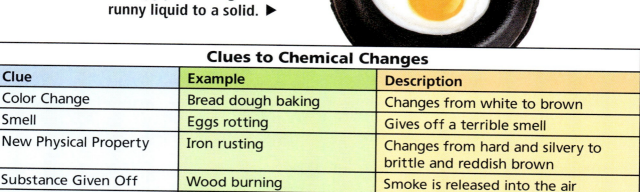

Clues to Chemical Changes

Clue	Example	Description
Color Change	Bread dough baking	Changes from white to brown
Smell	Eggs rotting	Gives off a terrible smell
New Physical Property	Iron rusting	Changes from hard and silvery to brittle and reddish brown
Substance Given Off	Wood burning	Smoke is released into the air
Heat Given Off	Sulfur burning	Fire is hot

1. COMPARE AND CONTRAST Copy and complete the graphic organizer.

	PHYSICAL	BOTH	CHEMICAL
Properties	deal with a substance by itself	**Ⓐ** _____	**Ⓑ** _____
Changes	**Ⓒ** _____	involve a change in appearance	**Ⓓ** _____

2. SUMMARIZE Write a summary of this lesson by using the lesson vocabulary terms in a paragraph.

3. DRAW CONCLUSIONS A car engine uses gasoline and oxygen. The exhaust given off has water and the gas carbon dioxide. Was this a chemical reaction? Explain.

4. VOCABULARY Use each of the lesson vocabulary terms in a sentence.

FCAT Prep

5. Read/Inquire/Explain Explain why the burning of wood is a chemical change. List as many clues as you can.

6. Which is a chemical property of a substance?
  A. what color it is
  B. whether it floats
  C. whether it burns when oxygen is present
  D. what its melting temperature is

Links

Writing

Expository Writing
It is often easier to remember something you've learned if you describe it to someone else. Write a **friendly letter** telling a relative what you learned in this lesson.

Math

Estimate Sums
A lab has 22 grams of iron, 14 g of sulfur, 31 g of sodium, and 29 g of potassium. Estimate the total mass of these four chemicals.

Art

Illustrate a Reaction
Choose one of the chemical reactions described in this lesson. Draw or paint a picture illustrating this reaction.

 For more links and activities, go to **www.hspscience.com**

WHAT A Taste Test

What do you get when you cross blueberries with meat? Sometimes you get a blueberry hamburger! Some scientists hope that blueberry burgers will soon be on your school cafeteria's menu.

Food scientist Al Bushway told *Weekly Reader* (*WR*) that his lab has experimented with adding blueberry powder and blueberry puree (pyoo•RAY) to beef, chicken, and turkey. Puree is a thick paste. It's made when fruit is mashed in a blender.

Why the odd food combination? Bushway says it's a way to increase the nutrition in meat and to make school lunches more healthful. Blueberries are rich in special chemicals that help fight diseases, such as cancer. A serving of blueberries can give kids plenty of calcium, magnesium, vitamin C, and vitamin A. The combination of the vitamins and minerals in the meat and the fruit makes for a more healthful meal than just meat alone.

A Colorful Combo?

Do blueberries turn the meat blue? "In beef, you can't see the difference," Bushway told *WR*. "However, ground turkey turns a grayish blue color."

So far, many adult taste tasters have been giving the food the thumbs up. But will it be a hit with kids? One 8-year-old from Illinois said she would love to try a blueberry burger. Her 11-year-old sister didn't feel the same. "I like my hamburger with ketchup," she said.

At Home Taste Test

With an adult's help, kids can try this fruit-and-meat combo at home. Allow about one half to one ounce of frozen blueberries to come to room temperature. Then, again with an adult's help, use a blender to puree them. Finally, add the puree to ground hamburger meat.

THINK ABOUT IT

1. What other foods can help you stay healthy?
2. What are some food combinations that you like to eat?

Spin-In

Find out more! Log on to
www.hspscience.com

HIGH-FLYING SCIENTIST

In 1991, the United States government sent chemist Peter Daum to the Middle East. Daum was not there to fight in the first Persian Gulf War, however. He was sent there to study the environmental effects of the oil fires set by the retreating Iraqi army during the war.

Daum works for the U.S. Department of Energy's Brookhaven Laboratory. He studies pollution that is in Earth's atmosphere.

When Daum is at home in the U.S., he and other scientists spend a lot of time flying in a plane that is an airborne laboratory. The plane's equipment can measure the levels of pollutants in the air.

Career   Food Manufacturer

This is a job to sink your teeth into. People who make, or manufacture, food work with raw fruits, vegetables, grains, meats, and dairy products. They change the raw materials into finished, packaged goods to sell to grocery stores or restaurants.

SCIENCE Projects
for Home or School

You Can Do It!

Materials
- 3 ordinary objects

Quick and Easy Project

Practicing Changes

Procedure

1. Gather three ordinary objects — for example, a piece of paper, an old button, and a tissue.
2. List at least four physical properties of each object.
3. For each object, try to change each of the properties you listed without changing the substance itself. In other words, put the object through physical changes but not chemical changes.

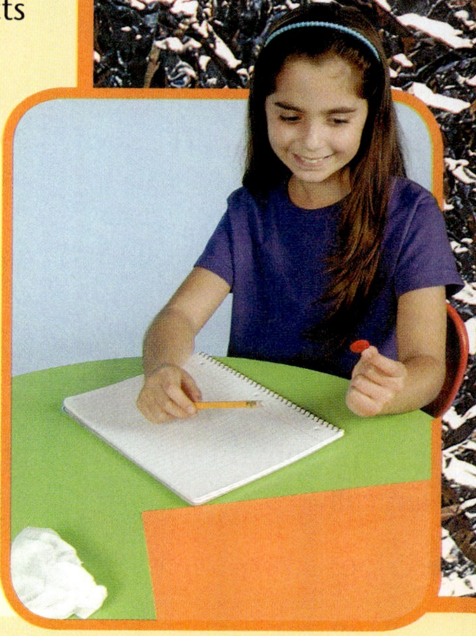

Draw Conclusions
Which physical properties could be altered by physical changes? Which physical properties could not be altered by physical changes?

Design Your Own Investigation

Demonstrate Basic Properties

Imagine that you are teaching a science class. Some students are having trouble understanding that air has mass and takes up space. Design an investigation that is different from the two procedures in Lesson 1 to demonstrate the concept. Gather materials and carry out the investigation.

Review and FCAT Preparation

Vocabulary Review

Write the term that fits each definition or description. The page numbers tell you where to look in the chapter if you need help.

- atom p. 66
- molecule p. 66
- element p. 68
- change of state p. 74
- physical change p. 76
- physical property p. 83
- chemical property p. 83
- chemical change p. 84
- chemical reaction p. 84
- compound p. 84

1. A substance having atoms of more than one element that are combined chemically.

2. Describes a substance by itself. phy. prop

3. Results in a new substance. chem ch

4. Describes how a substance reacts with other substances. chem prop

5. Process of melting or freezing.

6. Another name for *chemical change.*
   chem rxn

7. A particle made of two or more atoms.
   molec

8. Substance having just one kind of atom. elem

9. The smallest possible particle of matter.
   atom

10. Does not result in a new substance.
    phys ch

Check Understanding

Write the letter of best choice.

11. What is all matter made of?
    - A. atoms
    - B. oxygen
    - C. water
    - D. wood

12. Which statement about atoms is true?
    - F. They are all the same.
    - G. All substances are made of just one kind.
    - H. You can see them with your eyes.
    - I. They are too small to be seen with an ordinary microscope.

13. The diagrams show iron, oxygen, carbon dioxide, and hydrogen.

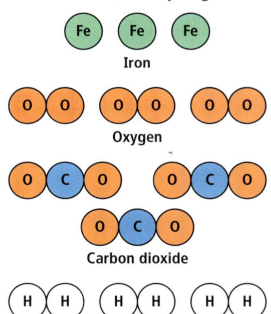

Which of these is a compound?
    - A. iron
    - B. oxygen
    - C. carbon dioxide
    - D. hydrogen

14. An element is made up of how many kinds of atoms?

  F. none

  G. one

  H. two

  I. two or more

15. MAIN IDEA AND DETAILS Which always happens during a chemical change?

  A. Matter disappears.

  B. A smell is produced.

  C. A gas is formed.

  D. A new substance is produced.

16. COMPARE AND CONTRAST How are physical properties and chemical properties similar?

  F. They both describe how one substance reacts with another.

  G. They both describe a substance.

  H. They both describe the size of a substance.

  I. They both describe a substance by itself.

Inquiry Skills

17. You're watching a chemist work. She mixes a green powder with a blue liquid and then heats the mixture. A yellow gas rises out of the beaker. When she is done, all that remains in the beaker is a crumbly orange solid. Do you think a chemical reaction took place? Explain your **conclusion**.

18. Next, the chemist places a whitish solid in a beaker and heats it. Before long, the solid has turned into a clear liquid. **Hypothesize** what might happen if she continues to heat the beaker.

 Read, Inquire, Explain

19. Do you think butter can have a change of state? Why or why not?

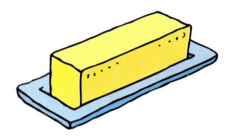

20. Suppose you leave a metal hand tool in a garden for a few weeks. Your area gets rain several times. When you finally pick up the tool, you see orange-brown spots on it.

  Part A What are the spots?

  Part B Explain what caused the orange-brown spots on the tool.

Energy

 The chapters in this unit address these Grade Level Expectations from the Florida Sunshine State Standards.

Chapter 3 Energy

SC.B.1.2.1.5.1	knows how to trace the flow of energy in a system (for example, electricity in a circuit to produce heat, light, sound, or magnetic fields).
SC.B.1.2.2.5.1	knows that energy can be described as stored energy (potential) or energy of motion (kinetic).
SC.B.1.2.5.5.1	extends and refines use of a variety of tools to measure the gain or loss of energy.
SC.B.1.2.6.5.1	knows that some materials conduct heat better than others.
SC.B.1.2.6.5.2	understands that convection, radiation, and conduction are methods of heat transfer.
SC.B.2.2.3.5.1	knows that the limited supply of usable energy sources places great significance on the development of renewable energy sources.

The investigations and experiences in this unit also address many of the Grade Level Expectations in Strand H, The Nature of Science.

PHYSICAL SCIENCE

Science in Florida

Miami

The Sunshine State

USA

Dear Brittany,

I'm having a great time on vacation in Miami. Yesterday mom took me to a show at the Gusman Center for the Performing Arts. There was so much energy all around us. The bright lights of the stage and the orchestra's beautiful music were better than I thought they would be. The actors filled the stage with song and dance. Maybe we can go see a show when I get back.

See you soon,

Sharday

FCAT Writing

Writing Situation
Think about how you use energy. Explain three ways that energy is important.

Experiment!

Changing Pitch Musicians in Florida have been entertaining visitors for many years. A good musician can tell if even one instrument in a band is out of tune. How does a guitar player tune a guitar? How can a piano play so many notes? Plan and conduct an experiment to find out.

3 Energy

Vocabulary

FCAT-Tested

energy	convection
kinetic energy	radiation
potential energy	reflection
energy transfer	fossil
light	resource
heat	nonrenewable resource
system	conservation
conduction	renewable resource

Other Terms

pollution

chemical energy

electric energy

mechanical energy

solar energy

Ice sailing began in the Netherlands in the 1700s. When lakes and rivers froze, people used ice boats to travel and move cargo across waterways. What gives an ice boat the energy to move?

What Are Kinetic and Potential Energy?

Fast Fact

Bull's-eye! The farther back an archer pulls the bow, the more energy the arrow has when it's released. Some Olympic archers can score a bull's-eye from 90 m (295 ft) away. The arrow must hit the target before it falls too far. In the Investigate, you'll explore factors that affect how objects fall.

Going Up!

Materials
- paper strip, 100 cm long
- tape measure
- tape
- colored pencils
- rubber ball

Procedure

1. Work with a partner. Tape the paper to the wall as shown. Using the tape measure, mark the paper strip at 10-cm intervals. Start with 0 cm at the floor, and end with 100 cm at the top.

2. Have your partner hold the ball next to the 50-cm mark. You should sit facing the paper, with your eyes at the level of the 50-cm mark.

3. Have your partner drop the ball while you observe how high it bounces. Record the height with a colored mark on the paper.

4. Repeat Steps 2 and 3 two more times. Record each height in a different color.

5. Switch roles with your partner. This time, drop the ball from the 100-cm mark. Repeat Step 4.

Step 1

Step 3

Draw Conclusions

1. How did your results change when you dropped the ball from 100 cm?

2. **Inquiry Skill** For this experiment, you dropped the ball from 50 cm and 100 cm. Draw conclusions about what was different when you dropped the ball from 100 cm.

Investigate Further

Write a **hypothesis** about how far the ball will bounce if you drop it from 200 cm. Then try it to check your hypothesis.

VOCABULARY

energy p. 100
kinetic energy p. 102
potential energy p. 102
energy transfer p. 104

SCIENCE CONCEPTS

▶ how kinetic energy differs from potential energy

READING FOCUS SKILL

COMPARE AND CONTRAST Look for similarities and differences between potential energy and kinetic energy.

| alike | different |

Energy

Sometimes a simple word can be hard to define. For example, how would you define the word *show*? You've probably used it often but haven't thought much about its meaning. A common word is often used in different ways.

Defining common words can be especially difficult in science. Some words are so ordinary that people use them without thinking. And the words used in science may have several everyday meanings. But scientists need specific definitions.

For example, think about the word *energy*. You might say after school that you don't have enough energy to do your chores. This personal feeling about energy is not based on the scientific definition. Scientists define **energy** as the ability to cause a change in matter.

The energy from this falling ice produces a big splash, a movement of the water.

One kind of change is movement, or a change in position. Does the glacier in the photograph have energy? Since part of it is moving, a scientist would say it has energy.

The race car in the photo is also moving, so it has energy. But where does its energy come from? A car can't just make the energy it needs. This is part of the *law of conservation of energy.* The law states that energy can never be made or destroyed, but it can change forms.

The race car's engine changes the energy stored in gasoline into movement. The car moves, or changes position, because one form of energy changes into another.

Now look at the volleyball player. He is giving energy to the ball, making it move. Where does the volleyball player get this energy? It comes from inside his body, from the food he eats. During a hard game, he may feel that he lacks energy because he is tired. In the scientific sense, however, he definitely has energy.

People use the energy stored in food to move, to talk, and even to sleep. Energy stored in food is used in the body for all life processes and also for making the body and objects move.

 COMPARE AND CONTRAST How is the everyday use of the word *energy* different from the way a scientist uses the word?

The volleyball player's muscles provide the energy for the ball to move. ▼

▲ **The car's engine provides the energy to move the car forward on the track.**

Kinetic and Potential Energy

There are many forms of energy and many ways to classify them. One way divides all forms into two groups: kinetic energy and potential energy.

Kinetic energy is the energy of motion. If something is moving, it has kinetic energy. The faster an object is moving, the more kinetic energy it has. An airplane flying through the air has more kinetic energy than a person riding a bicycle.

Potential energy is the energy an object has because of its condition or position. For example, the higher an object is, the more potential energy it has. So, a ball on the roof of a building has more potential energy than a ball on your desk, because it can fall farther.

Think about a book on a shelf. It has the potential to move down if it falls off the shelf, so it has potential energy. If it did fall and hit the floor, it would no longer have the same amount of potential energy.

An object can have potential and kinetic energy at the same time. As the book falls from the shelf, it loses potential energy and gains kinetic energy.

As the roller coaster car in the photo moves to the top of a hill, it gains potential energy. The higher the car rises, the more potential energy it has. When the car moves down, it has kinetic energy. As it falls, its kinetic energy increases and its potential energy decreases.

The other photo shows a boy jumping up and down on a pogo stick. When he first jumps onto the pogo stick, he is moving down, so he has kinetic energy. As he moves down, the spring inside the pogo

Is the roller coaster car gaining potential energy or using kinetic energy?

stick compresses. This adds potential energy to the spring.

At the bottom of the jump, the boy is not moving, so he has no kinetic energy. But the spring's potential energy transfers to him. It moves him up, so he has kinetic energy again.

At the top of the jump, the boy stops moving. He has no kinetic energy, but he has potential energy. As he moves down the potential energy changes back to kinetic energy.

COMPARE AND CONTRAST How is kinetic energy different from potential energy?

◄ As the boy goes up and down, sometimes he has potential energy, sometimes he has kinetic energy, and sometimes he has both.

Insta-Lab

Energy Release
Balance a ruler on top of a pencil. Place a small wad of paper on one end. Push the other end down quickly. When did you add potential energy? When did you see the effect of kinetic energy?

Energy Transfer

Energy can move between places or objects, as shown in this picture. In the picture, an acrobat is standing still on a teeterboard. He has no kinetic energy, and he doesn't have potential energy.

There is also a man flying through the air. He's moving, so now he has kinetic energy. What will happen when he lands on the teeterboard? His kinetic energy will be transferred to the other acrobat. When he drops, he will push his end of the teeterboard down. This will give potential energy to the first acrobat as the teeterboard raises up. He will also gain kinetic energy and be launched off the teeterboard.

Energy transfer is the movement of energy from one place or object to another. In the circus act, energy moved from the first acrobat to the second. Remember the boy on the pogo stick? His kinetic energy was transferred to the spring, where it changed into potential energy. As the spring expanded, that potential energy was transferred to the boy as kinetic energy, bouncing him into the air.

 COMPARE AND CONTRAST How is the circus teeterboard like the spring in the pogo stick?

What would happen if the acrobat dropped onto the side of the teeterboard that was on the ground? Would the teeterboard transfer any of the energy? ▼

Focus Skill

1. COMPARE AND CONTRAST Draw and complete this graphic organizer.

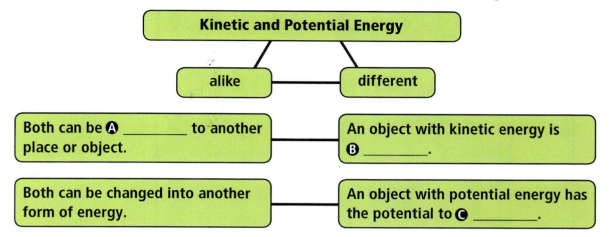

Kinetic and Potential Energy

alike — different

Both can be **Ⓐ** _____ to another place or object.

An object with kinetic energy is **Ⓑ** _____.

Both can be changed into another form of energy.

An object with potential energy has the potential to **Ⓒ** _____.

2. SUMMARIZE Write three sentences that summarize this lesson.

3. DRAW CONCLUSIONS If you throw a baseball, where does the ball's kinetic energy come from?

4. VOCABULARY Write a dictionary entry for each vocabulary word.

FCAT Prep

5. Read/Inquire/Explain Why does a book on a high shelf have more potential energy than a book on a low shelf?

6. Which has potential energy?
  A. a bike lying on a driveway
  B. a rock at the top of a cliff
  C. a chair sitting on the floor
  D. a baseball lost in the weeds

Links

Writing

Expository Writing

Your class is making a science video about energy. One part will show a girl playing with a yo-yo. Write the **narration** for this scene, describing the potential and kinetic energy in the yo-yo at any time.

Math 9÷3

Compare Numbers

When compressed fully and then released, Spring A sent a 10-kg mass 2 m into the air. Under the same conditions, Spring B sent the mass 8 m into the air. Which spring had more potential energy?

Language Arts

Definitions

Look up an everyday meaning of the word *potential*. Write a paragraph explaining that meaning and how it relates to potential energy.

 For more links and activities, go to **www.hspscience.com**

What Are Some Forms of Energy?

Fast Fact

Cool Lights! Neon tubes give off light in bright colors, but unlike some light bulbs, they don't get hot. The reaction that takes place in these tubes releases light energy but not much heat. In the Investigate, you'll test another reaction to see if it releases heat.

Warmer or Cooler?

Materials • measuring cup • water • thermometer • calcium chloride
• safety goggles • plastic cup • plastic spoon

Procedure

1. Make a table like the one shown.

2. **CAUTION: Put on safety goggles. Do not touch the calcium chloride.** Measure 50 mL of water, and pour it into the plastic cup.

3. Using the thermometer, measure the temperature of the water. Then record the temperature in your table.

4. Add 2 spoonfuls of calcium chloride to the water, and stir until the calcium chloride is dissolved. Wait 30 seconds.

5. Measure the temperature of the water, and record it in your table.

6. Repeat Step 5 one minute and two minutes after the calcium chloride has dissolved.

Step 4

Draw Conclusions

1. How did the temperature of the water change after you added the calcium chloride?

2. **Inquiry Skill** What energy change can you infer takes place when calcium chloride dissolves in water?

Temperature Changes	
Time	Temperature
Before dissolving calcium chloride	
30 seconds after dissolving	
1 minute after dissolving	
2 minutes after dissolving	

Investigate Further

Write a **hypothesis** about what would happen if you used 100 mL of water. Then **plan and conduct a simple investigation** to test your hypothesis.

Reading in Science

SC.B.1.2.5.5.1 tools to measure energy;
LA.A.2.2.1 main idea and details

VOCABULARY
solar energy p. 108
light p. 108
chemical energy p. 110
mechanical energy p. 110
electric energy p. 112

SCIENCE CONCEPTS
▶ how to identify and describe different forms of energy
▶ how energy can be changed from one form to another

READING FOCUS SKILL

MAIN IDEA AND DETAILS Look for details about the different forms of energy.

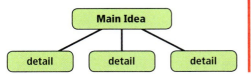

Solar Energy

You have read that all energy can be classified as potential energy or kinetic energy. Scientists also classify energy in other forms. However, the classification of energy you'll read about here isn't as simple as the main division into potential energy and kinetic energy. Sometimes two or more forms of energy overlap.

One form of energy is around you every day. Energy that comes from the sun is called **solar energy**. The word *solar* means "of the sun." People use solar energy in many ways. Do you have a calculator that doesn't need batteries? Many calculators have solar cells that change light energy from the sun into electricity. You'll learn more about electricity, or electric energy, later on.

Other forms of energy come from the sun directly. Energy from the sun travels as *radiation*. The sun produces several kinds of radiation. **Light** is radiation we see, and heat is radiation we feel. X rays and ultraviolet rays also come from the sun. The sun even produces radio waves, which we hear as static on radios.

On a warm, dry day you can feel radiation from the sun. You can also see the effects of radiation changing the temperature of the air.

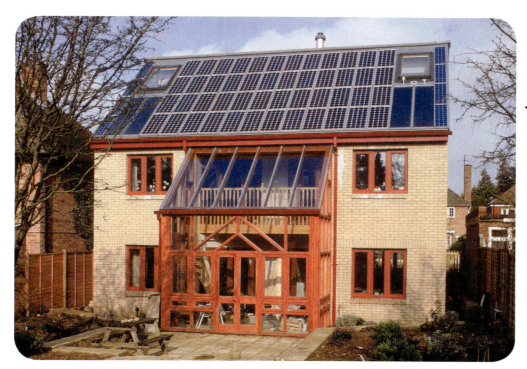

◄ Most of the heat and hot water for this home comes from the sun's energy, collected by the solar panels on the roof.

Without solar energy, Earth would be just a ball of frozen rock with no life. Heat from the sun allows Earth to support life forms. Light from the sun helps plants make food and oxygen. In fact, the sun is the source of almost all energy on Earth. Its energy is stored in fossil fuels—the coal, oil, and natural gas that come from long-dead plants and animals. The sun's energy is also the source of weather. Uneven heating of the Earth's surface produces winds and the water cycle.

Solar energy is useful in other ways, too. You know that light from the sun can provide electricity for tools such as calculators. Solar cells can also provide electricity for places that are hard to reach with standard power lines. Solar collector panels are used to absorb the sun's energy to heat water. The heated water can then be used to heat swimming pools or to provide hot water for home use.

However, although solar energy is free, solar cells and collectors can be expensive.

Another problem is that many places don't have enough sunny days to make solar energy practical.

MAIN IDEA AND DETAILS What forms of energy come directly from solar energy?

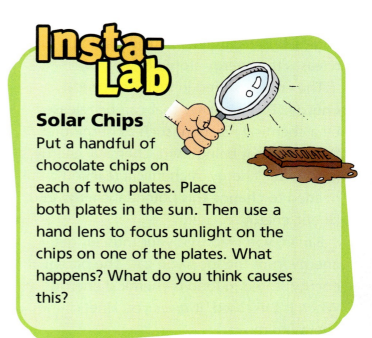

Insta-Lab

Solar Chips

Put a handful of chocolate chips on each of two plates. Place both plates in the sun. Then use a hand lens to focus sunlight on the chips on one of the plates. What happens? What do you think causes this?

Chemical energy in fuel is used to keep this remote-controlled model helicopter flying.

Chemical and Mechanical Energy

It takes a lot of energy to move something as heavy as a car. Where does that energy come from? In most cars, an engine burns gasoline, a fuel. Burning a fuel releases the energy stored in it.

The energy stored in fuel is **chemical energy**. This is energy that can be released by a chemical reaction, such as burning. When it is not being used, chemical energy is potential energy. A chemical reaction is needed to change this potential energy into kinetic energy.

Earlier, you read that your muscles get energy from the food you eat. The potential energy stored in food is chemical energy. When it's released, it gives you kinetic energy to move.

Have you ever used a heat pack to warm your hands or feet? The pack contains substances that have potential chemical energy. When you squeeze the pack, the substances mix, and a chemical reaction occurs. The heat from the reaction is what warms you up.

Many substances release energy in chemical reactions. For example, wood releases heat when it is burned. A glow stick releases light when a chemical reaction occurs. In the Investigate, you observed the release of chemical energy stored in a substance called calcium chloride.

Another form of energy that includes both potential energy and kinetic energy is mechanical energy. **Mechanical energy** is the combination of all the potential and kinetic energy that something has. The windup toy in the photo has a key attached to a spring. When you turn the key, you wind up, or tighten, the spring, giving the toy potential energy. The tighter the spring is wound, the more potential energy the toy has.

When the toy is moving, it has kinetic energy. Since the spring is still partly wound up, the toy also has some potential energy. The toy's mechanical energy is the combination of its potential energy and its kinetic energy.

The remote-control helicopter is moving, so you know that it has kinetic energy. The fuel in its tank has chemical energy, which is potential energy. The helicopter's mechanical energy is the combination of its kinetic and its potential energy.

 MAIN IDEA AND DETAILS Is chemical energy potential or kinetic energy?

Chemical energy is stored in fireworks. ▶

▲ A windup toy is operated by mechanical energy. Where does this toy get its kinetic energy?

Electricity and Sound

Have you ever experienced a blackout? Candles can help you see during a blackout, but they don't provide enough light to read easily. Televisions and computers don't work. Kitchen appliances don't either, so cooking is difficult. In a blackout, you realize how much you depend on electricity. Electricity, or **electric energy**, is energy that comes from an electric current. An electric current results from the movement of electrons. Electrons are particles in atoms.

You can see some effects of electric energy when you use appliances. You may have even felt electric energy. Have you ever walked across a rug on a dry day and then touched a doorknob? You probably felt electric energy in the form of a small shock.

People have invented a great many devices that use electric energy to make life better. These include all the basic things you'd miss in a blackout. They also include modern, battery-operated devices such as portable games, cell phones, and music players.

Another useful form of energy is sound. *Sound* is energy in the form of vibrations that travel through matter.

Sound vibrations pass through the particles of matter in a kind of domino effect. When a vibration reaches a particle of matter, that particle starts to vibrate, too. If it's close enough to other particles,

This band uses a lot of electric energy and produces a lot of sound energy. ▼

A megaphone focuses sound in one direction. Without the megaphone, the energy would spread out in all directions.

▲ Electric energy makes sound louder with this bull horn.

they also start to vibrate. In this way, sound vibrations can spread out, not just in a straight line, but in all directions.

Like light energy, sound energy can travel through many objects. Sound vibrations travel easily through air, so people can hear sounds—even quiet ones—at a distance.

Deep inside the ear is a thin membrane called the eardrum. Hearing begins with the vibration of the eardrum. When sound vibrations in the air reach the eardrum, it vibrates. These vibrations are transmitted deeper into the ear, where they are changed into nerve messages that travel to the brain. If the sound you are listening to is too loud, its vibrations can damage your ears and affect your hearing.

People can also experience sound energy in other ways. If you place your hands on the radio or television, you can feel the sound vibrations. Some people with hearing disabilities have been able to become dancers by feeling the vibrations of the music through their feet.

Another time you might be able to feel sound is at a fireworks show. Many fireworks produce not only bright colors, but also loud whistles, pops, and bangs. You can often feel the energy of these sounds on your body.

 MAIN IDEA AND DETAILS List three things in your classroom that use electric energy.

This emergency radio uses mechanical energy from a person to produce electric energy. News is available even if batteries are not.

▲ The batteries in a flashlight contain chemical energy. What happens to the chemical energy when you turn on the flashlight?

Changing Energy Forms

In this lesson, you've examined different energy forms and some of their uses. Often, one form of energy changes into another form.

The batteries in a flashlight contain chemical energy, but the flashlight bulb gives off light. Where does the light come from? The batteries' chemical energy changes into electric energy. Then the bulb in the flashlight changes the electric energy into light energy.

When you turn the crank of an emergency radio, you add potential energy to the radio. When you turn on the radio,

sound energy is produced. The potential energy you added was changed into electric energy. Then the electric energy was changed into sound energy.

Look again at the photo of the concert stage. The microphones change sound energy into electric energy, which is amplified, or increased. Then the speakers change the electric energy back into sound. In this situation and many others, energy is constantly being changed from one form to another in order to make it more useful to us.

 MAIN IDEA AND DETAILS Why do people change energy from one form to another?

1. MAIN IDEA AND DETAILS Draw and complete this graphic organizer.

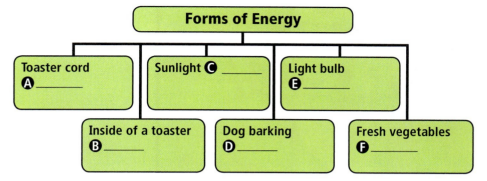

Forms of Energy

- Toaster cord **A** _____
- Sunlight **C** _____
- Light bulb **E** _____
- Inside of a toaster **B** _____
- Dog barking **D** _____
- Fresh vegetables **F** _____

2. SUMMARIZE Write a summary of this lesson by using each of the lesson vocabulary words in a sentence.

3. DRAW CONCLUSIONS A light bulb changes electric energy into two other forms of energy. What are they?

4. VOCABULARY Make a crossword puzzle, including clues, that contains all of this lesson's vocabulary words.

FCAT Prep

5. Read/Inquire/Explain Bess says that thunder produces sound energy. Her friend says kinetic energy comes from thunder. Who is correct? Explain.

6. Which of the following changes chemical energy directly into light energy?

 A. a candle **C.** a flashlight
 B. a car key **D.** a light switch

Links

Writing
Narrative Writing
Many forms of energy are around us and within us. Write two or three paragraphs **describing** some ways you use energy in a typical day.

Math
Compare Fractions
Battery A contains a full charge of chemical energy. Battery B has $\frac{3}{8}$ of a full charge, and Battery C has $\frac{2}{5}$ as much energy as Battery A. Which battery contains the least chemical energy?

Music
Composition
Write a one-minute song about energy. Include lyrics and, if possible, a melody.

 For more links and activities, go to **www.hspscience.com**

How Is Heat Transferred?

Fast Fact

Where's the Heat? A thermogram shows the heat patterns in a person's body. The colors show the different levels of heat that the body gives off. Red and yellow show the warmest areas, and green and blue show the coolest. In the Investigate, you'll observe some other heat patterns.

Hot Buttered Knives

Materials
- cold butter
- metal knife
- large plastic foam cup
- hot water
- plastic knife

Procedure

1 Place two pats of butter on the blade of the metal knife—one in the middle and one near the tip. Place the knife, handle first, in the cup to check that both pats are above the rim. Remove the knife.

2 **CAUTION:** **Be careful when pouring the hot water.** Fill the cup with hot water. Carefully place the knife, handle first, back in the cup.

3 Observe the knife and the pats of butter for 10 minutes. Record your observations.

4 Repeat Steps 1–3, substituting the plastic knife for the metal one. Record your observations.

Draw Conclusions

1. On which knife did the butter melt faster? On that knife, which pat of butter melted faster?

2. **Inquiry Skill** Draw a conclusion about which material—metal or plastic—transfers heat faster.

Step 1

Step 4

Investigate Further

Write a **hypothesis** about which knife would *lose* heat faster. Then **plan and conduct a simple investigation** to check.

Reading in Science

SC.B.1.2.1.5.1 energy flow in a system; **SC.B.1.2.6.5.1** conductors;
SC.B.1.2.6.5.2 conduction, convection, and radiation;
LA.A.2.2.1 main idea and details

Heat and Temperature

You probably know that the terms *heat* and *temperature* are related, but you may not know how. You also know that objects with a high temperature give off heat, but what exactly is heat?

Remember that all matter is made up of tiny particles that are always moving. Since they move, they have kinetic energy, also called *thermal energy.* The faster the particles move, the more thermal energy the matter has.

When particles of one substance come in contact with particles of another substance that are moving at a different rate, thermal energy is transferred. **Heat** is the transfer of thermal energy between objects with different temperatures.

Thermal energy travels from a warmer object to a cooler object. Energy from the stove burner flows through the pot and into the water, causing it to get hot. Energy doesn't travel from the low-temperature water to the high-temperature burner.

But what is temperature? *Temperature* is the measurement of the average kinetic energy of all the particles in a substance. You can measure temperature with a

Thermal Energy Transfer

 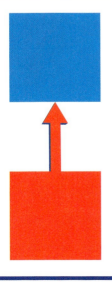

▲ The water in this pot is cool. Its particles don't have much kinetic energy, so its temperature is low.

▲ The particles of water in this pot have more kinetic energy than those in the first pot. This water's temperature is high.

Is the melting point of lead closer to the melting point of chocolate or the melting point of iron?

Substance	Melting Point
Ice	0°C
Chocolate	42°C
Lead	327°C
Iron	1535°C

◄ The particles of iron have so much heat energy that the iron has melted and become a liquid.

thermometer. The number shown on a thermometer is related to the amount of kinetic energy in a substance.

Some systems are very efficient at transferring thermal energy. A **system** is a set of parts acting together as a whole object. A burner, a pot, and water are a system through which thermal energy moves. The burner transfers thermal energy to the pot. The pot transfers thermal energy to the water. As the water receives more and more thermal energy, its particles move faster and faster.

The movement of particles helps explain changes in state. In ice, water particles are held together in a rigid pattern. They don't move around, but they vibrate in place. As thermal energy is added, they vibrate faster and faster. At a certain point, the particles have so much energy that they break out of the rigid pattern and flow easily around each other. The ice melts.

If you keep adding thermal energy, the water particles keep moving faster and faster. Finally, they have so much thermal energy they separate from each other and rise into the air. The water boils.

Some systems need more thermal energy than others to cause a change of state. For example, more energy is needed to make iron melt than to make chocolate melt. This is because it takes more energy to separate the particles in iron from each other than to separate the particles in chocolate.

MAIN IDEA AND DETAILS How is temperature related to heat?

Thermal Energy Transfer

There are three ways heat can move through a system. The first is by **conduction**, or the transfer of thermal energy from one object directly into another. In other words, if an object is touching a hotter object, thermal energy will flow from the hotter object directly into the cooler object.

The pot in the burner-pot-water system is heated by conduction. The pot is in contact with the burner, so thermal energy from the burner flows directly into the pot. The water is in contact with the pot, so thermal energy from the pot flows into the water.

Of course, only the water at the bottom and the sides is actually in contact with the pot. The water in the middle is heated by a process called convection. **Convection** is the transfer of thermal energy through the movement of a gas or a liquid. As a gas or a liquid is heated, the heat causes it to move upward, carrying heat to the area above the heat source.

That's how the water in the middle gets warm. Thermal energy from the pot flows into the water at the bottom by conduction. Then the heated water moves upward by convection, bringing thermal energy to the water above it.

▲ Heat from the iron moves directly into the clothing by conduction.

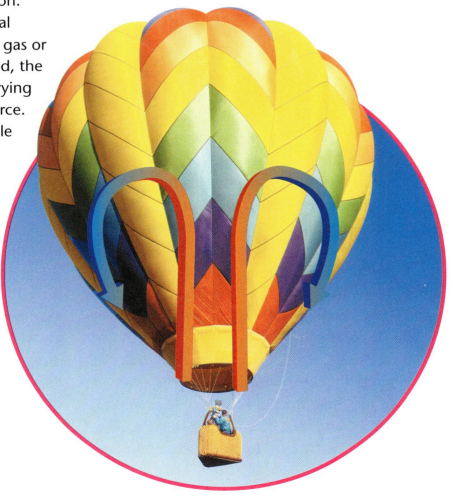

Inside the balloon, heated air moves up, carrying thermal energy to the air above it by convection. ▶

The meerkat is warming itself under the lamp. Radiation carries thermal energy from the lamp to the meerkat.

The third way thermal energy can be transferred is by radiation. **Radiation** is the transfer of energy by waves that move through matter and space. Remember that solar energy travels as light, X-ray, radio, and ultraviolet waves. It also travels as infrared waves. Infrared waves carry thermal energy from the sun and from heat sources such as campfires and toasters.

Unlike conduction and convection, radiation doesn't need matter for the heat to travel through. Conduction requires that two objects be in contact. Convection requires a gas or a liquid. Radiation can transfer thermal energy from the sun across 150 million km (93 million mi) of space to Earth.

Not all of this radiation from the sun reaches Earth's surface. Some of it is reflected back into space by the atmosphere. **Reflection** occurs when heat or light bounces off an object.

 MAIN IDEA AND DETAILS What are the three ways by which thermal energy can be transferred?

Insta-Lab

Distance and Heat
Hold a thermometer 40 cm from a light bulb. (Don't use a fluorescent light.) After two minutes, record the temperature. Repeat the procedure, holding the thermometer 30, 20, and 10 cm from the bulb. How does distance affect the transfer of thermal energy?

Insulators and Conductors

On a hot beach, the drinks inside an ice chest stay cold. It seems as if heat doesn't move from the air into the drinks. In fact, the heat does move, but it moves very slowly because the cooler is an insulator. Anything that slows the movement of thermal energy is an *insulator*.

Heat always moves from something warmer to something cooler. However, certain factors affect the rate at which heat moves from one object to another.

Not all insulators keep things cool. Thick coats keep us warm by trapping heat close to our bodies on winter days. Coats prevent warm air from escaping.

There are also things that allow heat to move through them very easily. If you use a metal spoon to eat hot soup, the handle may get very hot, even though it never touches the soup. Heat moves from the soup to and through the spoon by conduction. Anything that allows thermal energy to move through it easily is called a *conductor*. Have you ever seen a pan with a copper bottom? Copper is a good conductor of heat, so food in the pan cooks quickly and evenly. Many metals are good conductors of heat.

 MAIN IDEA AND DETAILS What are insulators and conductors?

◀ The lunch bag prevents heat in the air from moving into the bag. This keeps the food in the bag cool.

The cookie sheet is a conductor. The oven mitt is an insulator.

1. MAIN IDEA AND DETAILS Draw and complete the graphic organizer.

Heat can be transferred in three ways.

In **Ⓐ** ____, heat is transfered from one object to another.

In convection, heat causes a **Ⓑ** _____ or a **Ⓒ** _____ to move upward.

In **Ⓓ** _____, waves of energy move through matter and space.

2. SUMMARIZE Use the graphic organizer to write a summary of this lesson.

3. DRAW CONCLUSIONS When you face a campfire, why does your front feel warmer than your back?

4. VOCABULARY Use each lesson vocabulary term in a sentence.

FCAT Prep

5. Read/Inquire/Explain If you put one thermometer 10 cm (4 in.) above a flame and another one 10 cm to the side of the flame, which would show the higher temperature? Explain.

6. If you want heat to move from a light bulb to an object by conduction, where should you place the object?

A. above the light bulb

B. next to the light bulb

C. below the light bulb

D. touching the light bulb

Links

Writing

Expository Writing

Suppose you're tutoring a younger student in science. Write an **explanation** of how heat can be transferred within a system. Be sure to keep your explanation as simple as possible.

Math

Solve Problems

A substance in a beaker has a temperature of 22°C. At 1:00, you begin to heat it. After 14 minutes, its temperature reaches 48°C, and you stop heating it. By 2:03, it has cooled back down to 22°C. How long did it take to cool?

Language Arts

Word Usage

Use a dictionary to find as many words as you can that are related to the word *conduction*. List and define the words.

 For more links and activities, go to www.hspscience.com

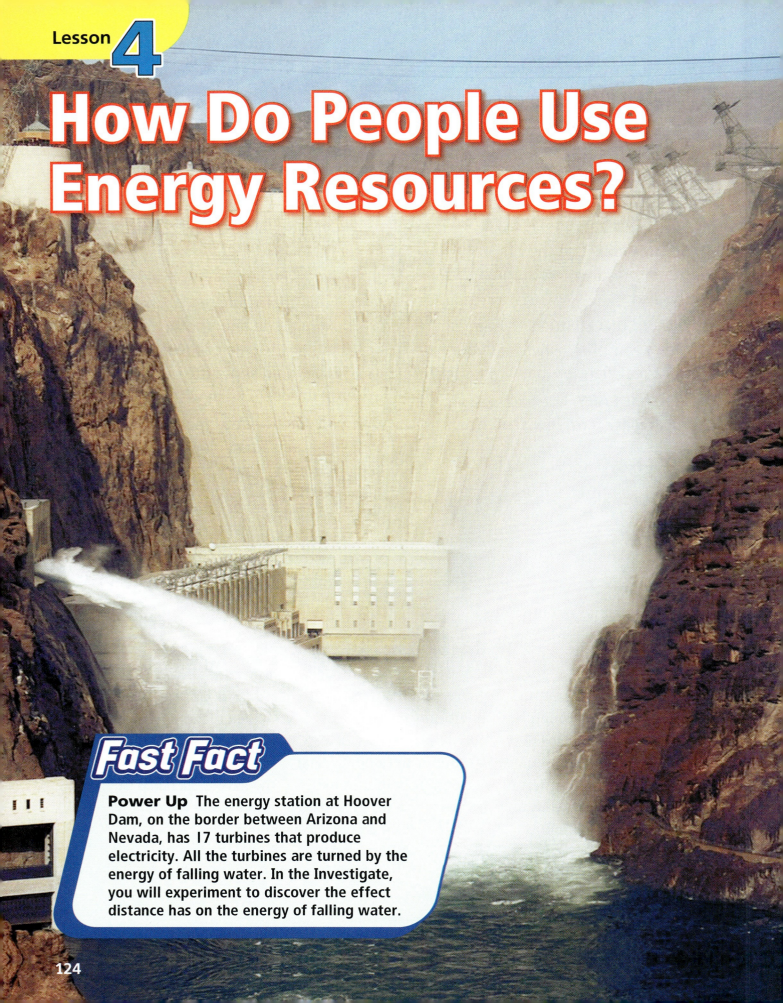

How Do People Use Energy Resources?

Fast Fact

Power Up The energy station at Hoover Dam, on the border between Arizona and Nevada, has 17 turbines that produce electricity. All the turbines are turned by the energy of falling water. In the Investigate, you will experiment to discover the effect distance has on the energy of falling water.

124

Water Power

Materials
- 2 plastic disks
- pencil
- string, 100 cm
- washers
- stapler
- masking tape
- 10-g mass (paper clip, weight)
- bottle of water
- scissors
- stopwatch
- meterstick
- basin

Procedure

1. **CAUTION:** Be careful with the scissors. Staple the disks together at their centers. Cut four 3-cm slits as shown. On the left side of each slit, fold the disks in opposite directions to form a vane.

2. Carefully pierce a small slit through the center of both disks. Insert the pencil.

3. Tape one end of the string to the pencil. Tie or tape the mass to the string.

4. Slide a washer onto each end of the pencil. Hold your water wheel by the washers so it can turn freely. Hold it horizontally over the basin, with the closed ends of the vanes away from you.

5. Have a partner slowly pour water from a height of 10 cm onto the vanes. Measure and record the time it takes for the mass to be wound up to the pencil. Repeat, pouring water from 15 cm and 20 cm.

Step 2

Step 5

Draw Conclusions

1. What variable did you control? What variable did you change?

2. **Inquiry Skill** What can you conclude about the effect of the distance the water fell on the speed at which the water wheel turned?

Investigate Further

Write a hypothesis about how the rate of the water's flow affects the speed of the water wheel. Then plan and conduct an experiment to check it.

SC.B.2.2.3.5.1 nonrenewable and renewable energy resources;
SC.D.2.2.1.5.1 reuse, recycle, reduce resources;
LA.A.2.2.7 compare and contrast

VOCABULARY
fossil p. 126
resource p. 127
nonrenewable resource
   p. 127
conservation p. 127
renewable resource p. 128
pollution p. 130

SCIENCE CONCEPTS
▶ why it is important to conserve energy resources
▶ how to conserve energy resources

READING FOCUS SKILL

COMPARE AND CONTRAST Look for similarities and differences between renewable energy sources and nonrenewable energy sources.

alike ——— different

Nonrenewable Energy Resources

Think about the hot water you use at home. Where does the energy that heats the water in your home come from? If your water heater is electric, it gets its energy, as your home's other electric appliances do, from an electric energy station. Some energy stations, such as the one at Hoover Dam, produce electricity by using the energy of falling water. Electricity made in this way is known as *hydroelectric energy*.

Most energy stations burn coal, oil, or natural gas as sources of energy to produce electricity. Burning these fuels changes their chemical energy to thermal energy, which is used to change water to steam. The steam, like the falling water in dams, powers the machines that produce electricity.

Coal, oil, and natural gas are *fossil fuels*. A **fossil** is the remains or traces of past life found in sedimentary rock. Fossil fuels are fuels that formed from the remains of once-living things.

This energy station in Australia burns coal to produce electricity. The coal comes from the remains of plants that lived and died millions of years ago.

It takes millions of years for coal, oil, and natural gas to form. When supplies are used up, there will be no more. This is why coal, oil, and natural gas are called nonrenewable resources. A **resource** is any material that can be used to satisfy a need. A **nonrenewable resource** is a resource that, once used up, cannot be replaced within a reasonable amount of time.

Does this mean that we will use up our nonrenewable resources? This will happen in time, but there are things we can do to keep from using them up before we find other resources to use in their place.

One thing people can do is use less of these fuels. Using less of something to make the supply last longer is called **conservation**. For example, if everyone uses less hot water, less fossil fuel will be burned to make electricity to heat the water. That will help make the world's supply of fossil fuel last longer.

Another thing people can do to conserve nonrenewable resources is switch to using resources that won't run out. Scientists are working to develop new ways to do this.

 COMPARE AND CONTRAST What do coal, oil, and natural gas have in common?

Since there is a limited supply of oil, the more gasoline we use now, the less we will have in the future for driving and manufacturing.

As oil resources are used up, it takes more work to get the oil that is left. This drilling platform pumps oil from under the ocean floor.

Renewable Energy Resources

Some resources are renewable. A **renewable resource** is a resource that can be replaced within a reasonable amount of time.

You may be wondering how an *energy* resource can be renewable. After all, once you burn a fuel, isn't it gone?

The key is that not all energy resources need to be burned in order to release energy. As you read at the beginning of this chapter, there are many different forms of energy.

One form of energy is solar energy, which can be changed directly into electric energy

by solar cells. Some highway signs use solar cells in the daytime to produce the electricity they need to light them at night. Since Earth gets sunlight every day, solar energy is a renewable energy resource.

Science Up Close

A Hybrid Car

A hybrid car runs on electricity at slow speeds and on gasoline at high speeds.

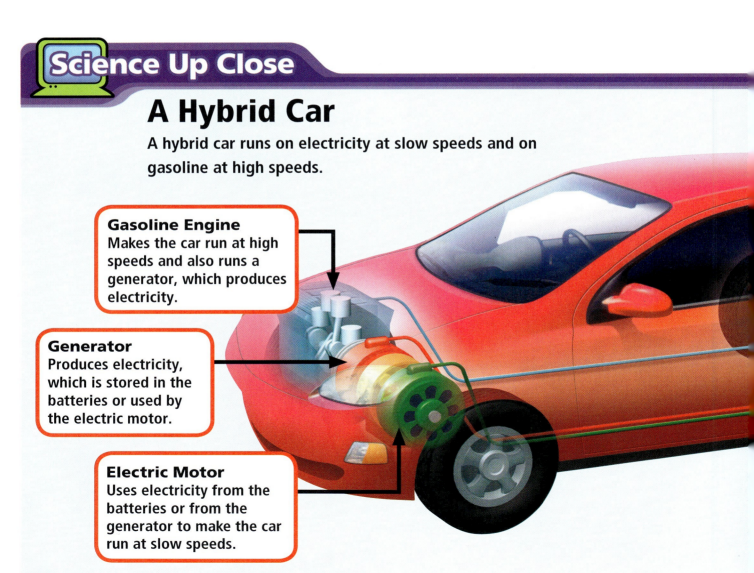

Gasoline Engine
Makes the car run at high speeds and also runs a generator, which produces electricity.

Generator
Produces electricity, which is stored in the batteries or used by the electric motor.

Electric Motor
Uses electricity from the batteries or from the generator to make the car run at slow speeds.

One windmill can produce only a small amount of electricity. That's why energy companies build "wind farms" that have hundreds of windmills.

You have just read about energy stations that use the energy of falling water to produce electricity. Falling water is a renewable energy resource, too. Water is constantly recycled and is not used up as fossil fuels are.

Wind is another renewable energy resource. Moving air can power windmill turbines that produce electricity, just as falling water powers turbines in dams.

Today, we still need nonrenewable resources. We don't yet have the technology to get enough energy from renewable resources at a reasonable cost. However, scientists are working to find lower-cost ways of using renewable energy resources in the future. An example is the research being done on windmills. Research also continues on ways to conserve nonrenewable resources, such as by using hybrid cars.

 COMPARE AND CONTRAST How are renewable energy resources the same as nonrenewable energy resources? How are they different?

Gas Tank
Holds the fuel for the gasoline engine.

Batteries
Store chemical energy, which is changed into electrical energy.

Insta-Lab

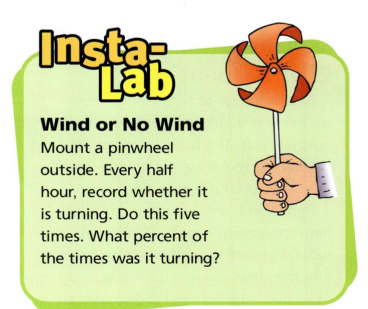

Wind or No Wind
Mount a pinwheel outside. Every half hour, record whether it is turning. Do this five times. What percent of the times was it turning?

For more links and activities, go to **www.hspscience.com**

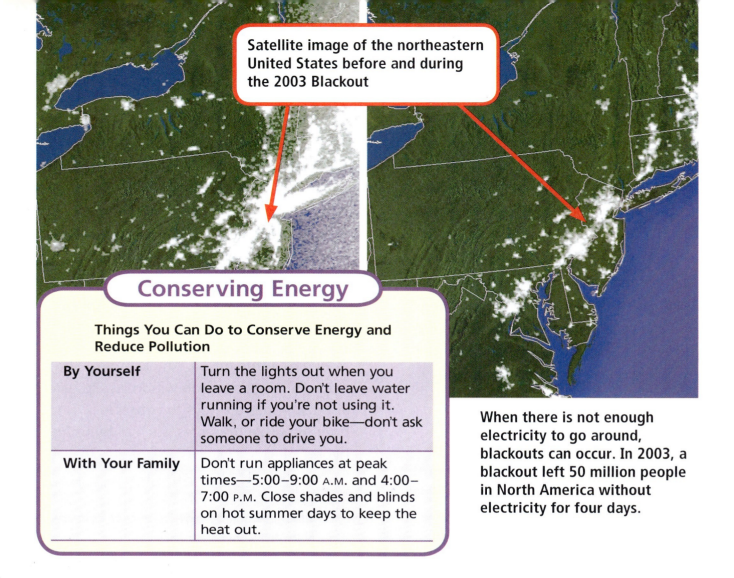

Satellite image of the northeastern United States before and during the 2003 Blackout

Conserving Energy

Things You Can Do to Conserve Energy and Reduce Pollution

By Yourself	Turn the lights out when you leave a room. Don't leave water running if you're not using it. Walk, or ride your bike—don't ask someone to drive you.
With Your Family	Don't run appliances at peak times—5:00–9:00 A.M. and 4:00–7:00 P.M. Close shades and blinds on hot summer days to keep the heat out.

When there is not enough electricity to go around, blackouts can occur. In 2003, a blackout left 50 million people in North America without electricity for four days.

Conservation and the Environment

An advantage of conserving energy resources is that it reduces harm to the environment. The burning of coal, oil, and natural gas to release the energy stored in them also produces pollution.

Pollution is anything that dirties or harms the environment. When coal, oil, and natural gas are burned, gases are released into the atmosphere. These gases are forms of *air pollution*. Some of these gases are poisonous. Others combine with water in the air to form acid, which harms plants and animals.

The conservation methods and the inventions you have read about not only save energy resources, they also reduce pollution. For example, a hybrid car runs on gasoline just part of the time. This means that when it travels the same distance as a regular car, it burns less fossil fuel. Driving a hybrid car can help conserve fossil fuel.

There are many other things people can do to conserve energy resources. The table above lists some of them.

 COMPARE AND CONTRAST How does conserving energy resources also help the environment?

1. COMPARE AND CONTRAST Draw and complete this graphic organizer.

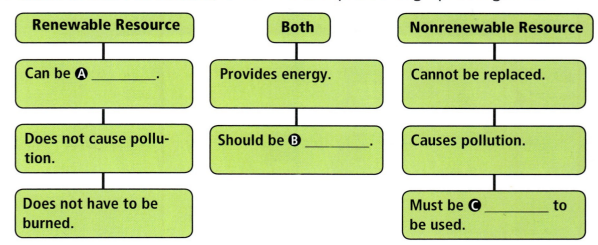

Renewable Resource	Both	Nonrenewable Resource
Can be Ⓐ _____.	Provides energy.	Cannot be replaced.
Does not cause pollution.	Should be Ⓑ _____.	Causes pollution.
Does not have to be burned.		Must be Ⓒ _____ to be used.

2. SUMMARIZE Write two sentences that tell what this lesson is mainly about.

3. DRAW CONCLUSIONS Solar panels on roofs produce electricity for homes. Why don't all homes have solar panels?

4. VOCABULARY Write a paragraph using all of the lesson vocabulary words.

FCAT Prep

5. Read/Inquire/Explain Suppose someone invented an inexpensive solar cell for producing electricity from sunlight. What drawback would the solar cell still have?

6. Which of the following is a renewable energy resource?
A. coal   **C.** oil
B. gasoline   **D.** wind

Links

Writing

Expository Writing
"Reduce, reuse, recycle" is a motto about protecting the environment. Find out what each of these words means. Then write a brief **definition** of each one.

Math

Find Area
An array of solar cells covers a rectangle that measures 450 m on two sides and 200 m on the other two sides. What is the area of the array?

Social Studies

Hydropower
Find out how long people have been using water power and what technologies they have used to capture it. Summarize your findings in a brief report with diagrams.

 For more links and activities, go to **www.hspscience.com**

Dream Machines

Welcome to the car showroom of the future. Step right up and take a look at some of our new models. If going fast is your thing, climb into this superfast car that can zip along at 405 km (252 miles) per hour! Say goodbye to smog with these cars. The AUTOnomy runs on clean-burning hydrogen instead of gasoline. The Hypercar runs on gasoline and hydrogen.

Zoom, Zoom, Zoom

A European car maker recently unveiled its 1001-horsepower, ultrafast supercar, which can reach a top speed of 405 km (252 miles) per hour. The car is made of lightweight materials. It also has specially made tires that won't melt when the car hits high rates of speed.

Engineers also designed the bottom of the car to create the venturi effect. The venturi effect is a downward pull that helps keep the car on the road.

H Is for Hydrogen Power

Can engineers design a car that doesn't cause pollution? An American carmaker thinks it can. The carmaker is working to build cars that operate on hydrogen-powered fuel cells.

Fuel cells, like batteries, store energy. But unlike batteries, fuel cells never lose power or need to be recharged as long as there is enough hydrogen fuel. Fuel cells create energy through the combination of hydrogen and oxygen. That energy can power an electric car motor.

The new AUTOnomy car runs on a series of hydrogen fuel cells. Instead of producing pollution, the AUTOnomy produces water vapor. Scientists expect AUTOnomy's hydrogen-powered system to get the equivalent of 161 km (100 miles) per gallon of gasoline.

Another type of hydrogen-powered car is the Hypercar, which will run on a gasoline- and hydrogen-powered fuel system. Scientists say the vehicle will be able to travel 482 km (300 miles) on a gallon of gas.

The design of the Hypercar is environmentally friendly, too. The vehicle is made from lightweight materials called composites—two or more substances that strengthen the individual properties of each material. The Hypercar is not as heavy as a typical vehicle, so it needs less energy to accelerate.

Think About It

1. How might cars powered by fuel cells help prevent pollution?
2. How might using lighter materials to build a car help with fuel efficiency?

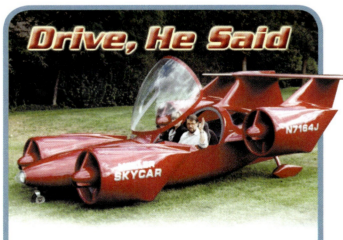

Drive, He Said

The cars of the future are already here as prototypes and might be available by the time you get your driver's license.

Spin-In

Find out more! Log on to www.hspscience.com

SC.H.3.2.1.5.1 technology has improved human lives; SC.H.3.2.1.5.2 some inventions lead to others

Fill'er Up With Grease

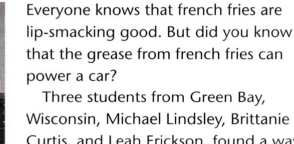

Everyone knows that french fries are lip-smacking good. But did you know that the grease from french fries can power a car?

Three students from Green Bay, Wisconsin, Michael Lindsley, Brittanie Curtis, and Leah Erickson, found a way to turn the grease from fast food into a clean burning fuel mixture used in diesel-powered cars and trucks.

The students made the new fuel, biodiesel, by combining 80 percent restaurant grease with 20 percent ethanol, an alcohol-based fuel made from fermented corn, fruits, and vegetables.

SC.D.2.2.1.5.1 reuse, recycle, reduce resources;
SC.H.3.2.1.5.1 technology has improved human lives

You Can Do It!

Materials
- rubber ball
- spring scale
- tape measure
- tape

Where Does a Ball Get Its Bounce?

Procedure

1. Work with a partner. You will need two tables or shelves of different heights.
2. Tape the ball to the end of the spring scale. Lift the ball from the floor to the lower shelf. Record how much force you use and how far you lift the ball.
3. Repeat, using the higher table or shelf.

Draw Conclusions

Did the ball have more potential energy in Step 2 or in Step 3? Could you have predicted that from earlier findings? If so, how?

Design Your Own Investigation

Follow the Bouncing Ball

You learned that a pogo stick has potential energy at the bottom of its bounce. You can see that a spinning yo-yo has kinetic energy at the bottom of its downward motion. Plan and conduct a simple investigation to see if a ball has any energy at the bottom of its bounce and, if so, which kind of energy.

135

Review and FCAT Preparation

Vocabulary Review

Use the terms below to complete the sentences. The page numbers tell you where to look in the chapter if you need help.

energy p. 100
kinetic energy p. 102
potential energy p. 102
solar energy p. 108
chemical energy p. 110
conduction p. 120
convection p. 120
radiation p. 121
conservation p. 127
renewable resource p. 128

1. Saving something so it doesn't get used up is _____.

2. Energy that comes from the sun as heat and light is _____.

3. The transfer of thermal energy between touching objects is _____.

4. The transfer of thermal energy within a hot-air balloon is _____.

5. Hydroelectric energy is an example of using a _____.

6. Energy released through a chemical reaction is _____.

7. The ability to cause changes in matter is _____.

8. The energy of an object because of its condition or position is _____.

9. The energy of motion is _____.

10. The transfer of energy in waves through matter and space is _____.

Check Understanding

Write the letter of the best choice.

11. **MAIN IDEA AND DETAILS** Which is a nonrenewable resource?

    A. natural gas   C. water
    B. sunlight   D. wind

Use the diagram to answer questions 12 and 13.

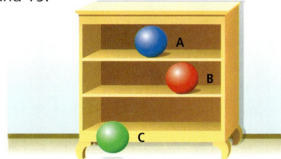

12. **COMPARE AND CONTRAST** Which statement is correct?

    F. Ball A has more potential energy than Ball B or C.
    G. Ball B has more potential energy than Ball A or C.
    H. Ball C has more potential energy than Ball A or B.
    I. All the balls have the same amount of potential energy.

13. Which ball has the most kinetic energy?
   A. Ball A
   B. Ball B
   C. Ball C
   D. They all have the same amount.

14. Which type of heat transfer does an oven mitt prevent?

   F. conduction
   G. convection
   H. radiation
   I. all of the above

15. Which kind of energy is stored in a battery?
   A. kinetic energy
   B. solar energy
   C. chemical energy
   D. light energy

16. Which change in form of energy occurs in a stereo speaker?
   F. sound energy to electrical energy
   G. chemical energy to sound energy
   H. potential energy to kinetic energy
   I. electrical energy to sound energy

Inquiry Skills

17. The Jenkinses' car can go 12 miles on a gallon of gasoline. The Guerreros' car can go 14 miles on a gallon of gasoline. The Watanabes' car can go 56 miles on a gallon of gasoline. What can you **infer** about the Watanabes' car?

18. If you leave a solar-powered flashlight in the sun for 8 hours, it will be able to stay lit for 3 hours. **Hypothesize** what would happen if you placed the flashlight under a bright light bulb for 8 hours.

 # Read/Inquire/Explain

19. A car is rolling down a hill. What determines how much potential energy and how much kinetic energy it has?

20. Energy changes form in many modern devices.
   Part A In a movie projector, how does energy change, and what forms of energy result?
   Part B Do the same changes happen in a TV set? Explain.

Forces and Motion

PHYSICAL SCIENCE

 The chapters in this unit address these Grade Level Expectations from the Florida Sunshine State Standards.

Chapter 4 Forces

SC.C.2.2.1.5.1	understands the relationship between force and distance as it relates to simple machines.
SC.C.2.2.3.5.1	knows the relationship between the strength of a force and its effect on an object.

Chapter 5 Motion

SC.C.1.2.1.5.1	uses scientific tools to measure speed, distance, and direction of an object.
SC.C.1.2.2.5.1	knows that waves travel at different speeds through different materials.
SC.C.2.2.2.5.1	knows that objects do not change their motion unless acted upon by an outside force.
SC.C.2.2.2.5.2	understands how friction affects an object in motion.
SC.C.2.2.4.5.1	knows that motion in space is different from motion on Earth due to changes in gravitational force and friction.
SC.C.2.2.4.5.2	understands how inertia, gravity, friction, mass, and force affect motion.

The investigations and experiences in this unit also address many of the Grade Level Expectations in Strand H, The Nature of Science.

Science in Florida

Daytona Beach

Dear Rick,

Today dad took me to watch a race at the Daytona International Speedway. The cars zoomed around the track at very high speeds. The turns of the track are sloped so the cars don't have to slow down as much when they go around the curves. I really enjoyed all of the excitement of the day.

See you soon,

Kathy

The Sunshine State

FCAT Writing

Writing Situation

Think about how you got to school. Explain how three types of transportation work.

Experiment!

Beach Protection Forces and motion are all around us, from the Daytona International Speedway to the nearby beaches. Waves and currents at the beach are constant forces that can move large quantities of sand. How can humans build artificial structures to affect the action of waves? For example, can building jetties stop the loss of beach sand? Plan and conduct an experiment to find out.

Lesson 1 What Forces Affect Objects on Earth Every Day?

Lesson 2 What Are Balanced and Unbalanced Forces?

Lesson 3 What Is Work, and How Is It Measured?

Vocabulary

FCAT-Tested
force
friction
gravity
gravitational force
magnetic
magnetic force
lever
fulcrum
inclined plane
pulley
wheel-and-axle
Other Terms
balanced forces
unbalanced forces
net force
buoyant force
work
simple machine

What do **YOU** wonder?

For 800 years, the Leaning Tower of Pisa has been tilted. Officials in Pisa, Italy, worried that it would fall over. In 1999, scientists were able to remove soil from one side of the building to stabilize the tower. What forces are acting on the Leaning Tower of Pisa?

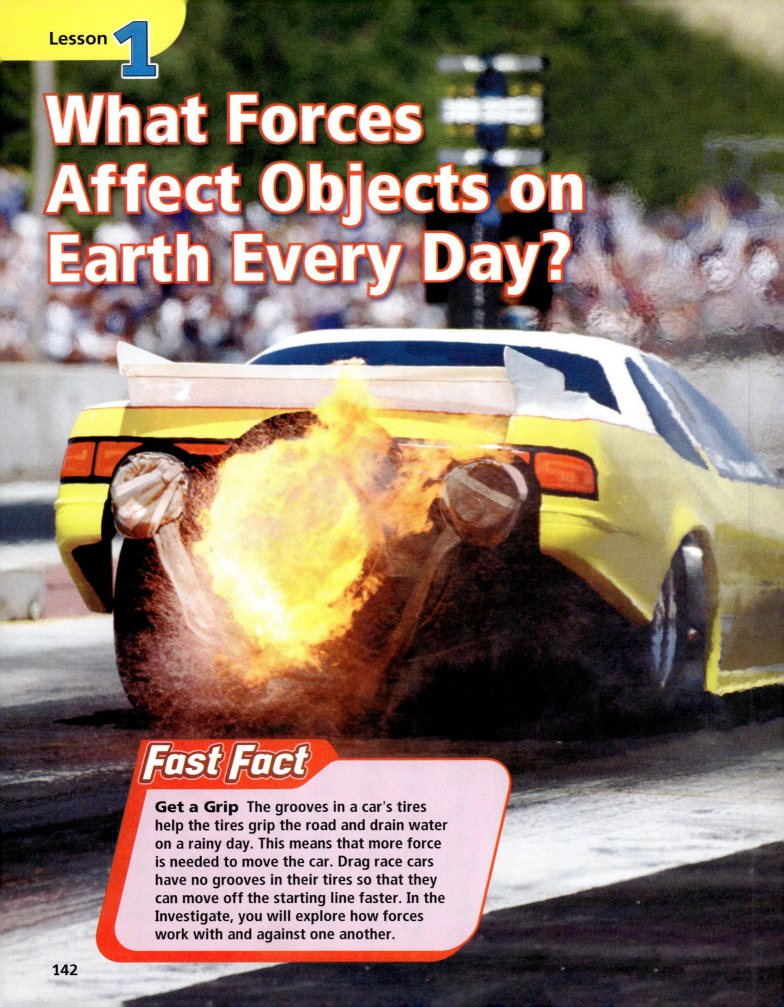

What Forces Affect Objects on Earth Every Day?

Fast Fact

Get a Grip The grooves in a car's tires help the tires grip the road and drain water on a rainy day. This means that more force is needed to move the car. Drag race cars have no grooves in their tires so that they can move off the starting line faster. In the Investigate, you will explore how forces work with and against one another.

On a Roll

Materials
- shoe box without a lid
- 20-cm piece of string
- blocks or other heavy objects
- unsharpened pencils
- spring scale

Procedure

1. Punch a small hole in one end of the box, near the center.

2. Thread the string through the hole. Tie the string to itself. You should be able to pull the box by the string.

3. Place some blocks, weights, or other heavy objects in the box.

4. Line up the pencils on a tabletop. The pencils should be close to one another but not touching. Keep the pencils parallel.

5. Place the box on a smooth, flat surface. Attach the string to the spring scale, and use the scale to pull the box. Observe the amount of force you use to move the box.

6. Place the box on the array of pencils. Pull the box again with the scale. Observe the amount of force you use this time.

Draw Conclusions

1. Is the box easier to move with the pencils or without them? Why?

2. **Inquiry Skill** Scientists communicate to share ideas. Why does putting wheels on heavy objects make them easier to move?

Step 5

Step 6

Investigate Further

Investigate to compare the amounts of force needed to move the box on different surfaces. What kind of surface makes the box easiest to pull?

SC.C.2.2.2.5.2 friction; SC.C.2.2.4.5.2 inertia, gravity, friction, mass, and force; SC.H.1.2.5.5.2 compare using models

143

Reading in Science

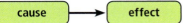

SC.C.2.2.2.5.2 friction; **SC.C.2.2.3.5.1** forces and mass;
SC.C.2.2.4.5.2 inertia, gravity, friction, mass, and force;
LA.E.2.2.1 cause and effect

VOCABULARY
force p. 144
friction p. 145
gravity p. 146
gravitational force p. 146
magnetic p. 148
magnetic force p. 148

SCIENCE CONCEPTS
▶ what the different kinds of forces are
▶ how motion is affected by weak and strong forces

READING FOCUS SKILL
CAUSE AND EFFECT Find out how different forces affect the objects around you.

| cause | → | effect |

Forces

What pushes you up in the air when you jump and then pulls you back down to Earth? What pulls magnets together or pushes them apart? What makes a skateboard roll, and what makes it stop? Forces do all these things.

A **force** is a push or a pull that causes changes in motion. A force speeds things up, slows things down, or makes them change direction.

Nothing changes its position, speed, or direction unless a force acts on it. For example, a book doesn't fall off a table by itself. Something has to push it. Can your backpack jump onto your back by itself? Of course not! You have to pull on it to lift it up. Without a force, the backpack can't move.

There are different kinds of forces. You will learn about some of them in this chapter. You are already familiar with the force from your muscles as you push or pull things. Other forces are just as important and just as easy to observe.

CAUSE AND EFFECT What are two forces that could cause a ball to roll down a hill?

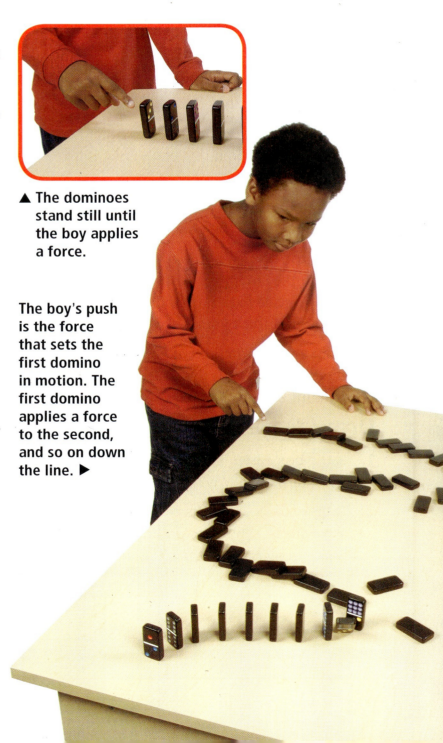

▲ The dominoes stand still until the boy applies a force.

The boy's push is the force that sets the first domino in motion. The first domino applies a force to the second, and so on down the line. ▶

144

Friction

When a soccer ball rolls across the grass, it slows down. Why? The ball slows mainly because of a force called friction. **Friction** is a force that works against motion. Friction can make things slow down or stop, or it can keep things from moving at all.

Friction is present whenever surfaces touch. When you erase a pencil mark, there is friction between the eraser and the paper.

Friction is greater between rough surfaces than between smooth ones. Have you ever walked on a newly waxed floor? It's not easy. There isn't much friction between your feet and the floor because the floor is smooth.

The speed skater in the picture glides across the ice because there is little friction between the skate blades and the ice. However, when she forces the blades of the skates against the ice, friction increases. The speed skater constantly changes the amount of friction between the skate blades and ice to control her direction and speed.

Friction has another important effect. It can make heat. Rub your hands together. Can you feel them getting warmer? Friction changes energy of motion to heat as objects rub together.

 CAUSE AND EFFECT How do you know there is friction when a saw cuts through wood?

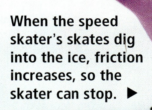

When the speed skater's skates dig into the ice, friction increases, so the skater can stop. ▶

A speed skater must learn how to control the amount of friction between the skates and the ice.

145

Gravity

Gravity is the attraction between you and Earth. Gravity pulls you to the floor if you fall off your chair. When you drop a ball, gravity pulls the ball to the ground.

Did you know that gravity causes falling objects to speed up as they fall? In the picture, the feather and the apple are falling in a vacuum, where there is no air. Photographs were taken at equal time intervals. At first, the objects fell a shorter distance per interval. Later, they fell a larger distance. This shows that objects move faster, or *accelerate*, as they fall.

The speed of any falling object is about 10 m/sec (33 ft/sec) after the first second. After another second, the object falls at a speed of about 20 m/sec (66 ft/sec). After the third second, it falls at about 30 m/sec (98 ft/sec). Can you see the pattern?

All objects in the universe pull on one another. That is, they exert a **gravitational force**. The gravitational force can be strong or weak, depending on the masses of the objects and the distances between them. The closer the objects are and the greater their mass, the greater the gravitational force between them is.

▲ Gravity pulls the apple and the feather downward. Their speeds increase as they fall. Both fall at the same rate in a vacuum because there is no air to slow down the feather.

Earth's gravity attracts objects near its surface, pulling them toward its center. ▶

force. The moon has less mass than Earth, so the moon pulls objects toward its center with less force.

There is a simple way to measure the gravitational force acting on an object. Find the object's weight. Weight is the measurement of gravitational force acting on an object.

Objects weigh more on Earth than they do on the moon. Earth has more mass and, therefore, more gravitational force than the moon. In other words, Earth pulls things harder, so they weigh more. Mass doesn't change, though, so an astronaut has the same mass on the moon as on Earth.

 CAUSE AND EFFECT You apply a force to your bike to move it uphill. Why don't you need to apply a force to make it go downhill?

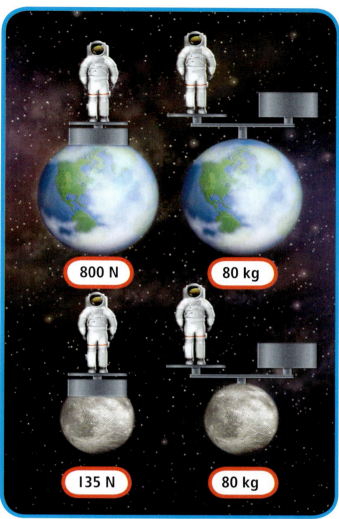

▲ The moon has less mass than Earth, so it has less gravitational force. On the moon, objects weigh about one-sixth of what they weigh on Earth.

All Fall Together?
See if objects really fall at the same rate. Drop a pencil and an eraser from the same height. Do they land at the same time?

Magnets and Compasses

For hundreds of years, people have used magnets to find direction. The first magnets used were made of a heavy natural mineral called *lodestone*. Today, scientists also call this mineral *magnetite*.

A compass needle points along an imaginary line connecting the North and South Poles. This is because Earth is like a giant magnet.

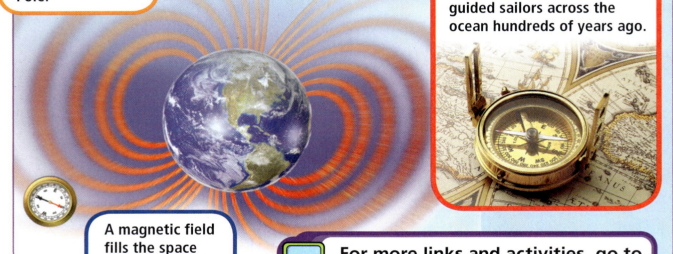

A compass needle is a magnet. Its north-seeking pole points toward Earth's magnetic North Pole.

This compass may have guided sailors across the ocean hundreds of years ago.

A magnetic field fills the space around Earth.

 For more links and activities, go to www.hspscience.com

Magnetic Force

Hold a magnet near some metal paper clips. What happens? The magnet pulls the paper clips, and they stick to the magnet. An object that attracts iron is <mark>magnetic</mark>.

The force exerted by a magnet is called <mark>magnetic force</mark>. The magnet is surrounded by a force field called a *magnetic field.* A magnet has two ends, called *poles.* The pulling force of the magnet is strongest at the poles. If a bar magnet can move freely, its *north-seeking pole* always points north,

and its *south-seeking pole* points south. A magnet's poles are often marked *N* and *S*.

You may have observed that magnets both attract each other and repel, or push away, each other.

If two magnets are held with their two *N* or two *S* poles near each other, they push away from each other. If the *N* pole of one magnet and the *S* pole of another are held near each other, they pull the magnets together.

Focus Skill **CAUSE AND EFFECT** How can you make two magnets repel each other?

148

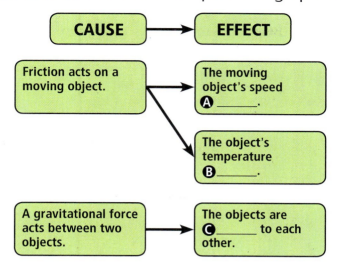

1. CAUSE AND EFFECT Draw and complete the graphic organizer.

CAUSE → EFFECT

Friction acts on a moving object.

The moving object's speed **A** _____.

The object's temperature **B** _____.

A gravitational force acts between two objects.

The objects are **C** _____ to each other.

2. SUMMARIZE Use the vocabulary terms in a paragraph to write a summary of this lesson.

3. DRAW CONCLUSIONS What forces act on a meteor as it falls toward Earth?

4. VOCABULARY Write a comic strip that uses each vocabulary term in this lesson.

FCAT Prep

5. Read/Inquire/Explain How is the force of gravity different from the force you apply when you push or pull something?

6. The gravitational force between two objects depends on their

A. colors. **C.** shapes.

B. masses. **D.** temperatures.

Links

Writing

Write to Describe

Describe the force of gravity. What factors affect the force of gravity? Is the force of gravity the same everywhere in the solar system?

Math

Use an Equation

The speed of an object can be written as:

speed = distance ÷ time

What is the speed of an object that travels 12 meters in 4 seconds?

Social Studies

History

Use library references to find out what Sir Isaac Newton contributed to our knowledge of gravity.

 For more links and activities, go to www.hspscience.com

What Are Balanced and Unbalanced Forces?

Fast Fact

A Delicate Balance What keeps these cards from falling? A house of cards is an example of forces in balance. The forces working to pull the cards down are balanced by the forces working to hold them up. If the forces change, the cards will fall. In the Investigate, you will explore how forces work with one another and against one another.

Picture the Force

Materials
- tape
- spring
- graph paper
- ring stand
- clipboard
- marker
- pencil
- weight

Procedure

1. Tape graph paper to a clipboard. Across the bottom of the paper, draw a line and label it *Seconds*. Starting at one end of the line, make a mark every 2.5 cm.

2. Tape a spring to a ring stand. Tape a weight to the free end of the spring. Tape a marker to the bottom of the weight so that it points toward the clipboard.

3. Have a partner hold the clipboard so that the marker touches the left edge of the graph paper. Pull the weight to stretch the spring all the way.

4. Have your partner slide the clipboard at a steady rate. As soon as the clipboard moves, let the weight go. As it bounces, the marker will trace its movements on the graph paper.

5. Identify along the line the direction (up or down) in which the weight moved.

Draw Conclusions

1. At what points did the weight not move? At what point did it move the fastest?

2. **Inquiry Skill** Scientists infer to explain events. What can you infer about the forces that made the spring go up and down?

Step 3

Step 4

Investigate Further

Plan and conduct a simple experiment to see what would happen if you used a heavier weight.

Reading in Science

SC.C.2.2.2.5.1 force and motion; **SC.C.2.2.3.5.1** forces and mass;
SC.C.2.2.4.5.2 inertia, gravity, friction, mass, and force;
LA.A.2.2.7 compare and contrast

VOCABULARY
balanced forces p. 152
unbalanced forces p. 152
net force p. 154
buoyant force p. 156

SCIENCE CONCEPTS
▶ how balanced and unbalanced forces affect motion
▶ what buoyant force is

READING FOCUS SKILL

COMPARE AND CONTRAST Look for the effects of balanced and unbalanced forces.

```
[ alike ]———[ different ]
```

Balanced and Unbalanced Forces

There is usually more than one force acting on an object. When you go down a slide, you apply a force to push yourself forward. Then gravity's pull takes over. At the same time, friction acts in the opposite direction. If friction is equal to your push, what happens? You don't move at all. The forces on you cancel one another. They are equally strong, but they act in opposite directions. Forces that act on an object but cancel each other are called **balanced forces**.

Suppose you are sitting at the top of the slide. The forces are balanced. Then you push forward with a force greater than the surface's friction. Now the forces are unbalanced. The forces in one direction are stronger, so they don't cancel each other.

When **unbalanced forces** act on an object, motion changes. The object may start, speed up, slow down, stop, or change its direction.

What force is acting on the dresser and is equal and opposite to the girls' pushes? ▼

The two teams' forces are balanced, so they cancel one another. ▶

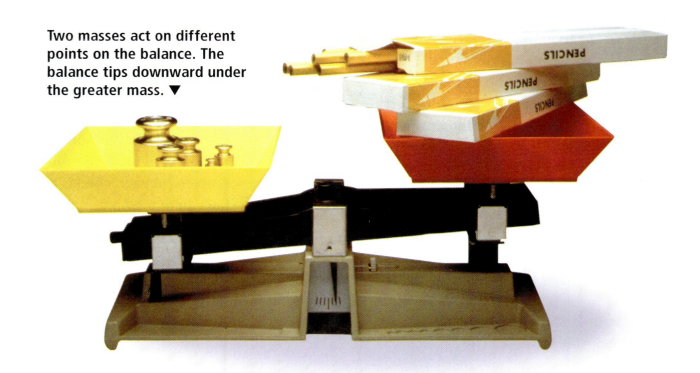

Two masses act on different points on the balance. The balance tips downward under the greater mass. ▼

When a tug of war starts and both teams pull the rope with the same force, the rope does not move one way or the other. The forces are balanced. When one team pulls harder, though, the rope and the other team move toward them.

A seesaw can show balanced and unbalanced forces. If the weight on one end of the seesaw is greater than the weight on the other end, the heavier end of the seesaw moves down. If the weights on both ends of the seesaw are the same, the forces are balanced, and the seesaw doesn't move.

 COMPARE AND CONTRAST Two people are arm wrestling, but neither one is winning. How do the forces acting on them compare?

Insta-Lab

Build an Instant Balance

Build a balance. Center a ruler on top of a pencil. Test coins or classroom objects to see how they compare on your balance. Can two nickels balance five dimes? What balances a quarter?

Net Force

The combination of all the forces acting on an object is called the **net force**. Net force affects an object's motion. To know how an object will move, you don't need to know the details of all the forces that are acting on the object. You just need to know the net force. When forces are balanced, the net force is zero.

In the picture, one elk is pushing to the right and the other to the left. Another force—friction—is pushing one elk to the right and the other to the left. The result is a net force of zero, so there is no change in the motion of either elk.

Have you ever watched two children trying to pull a toy in opposite directions? This is another example of a zero net force. If both children pull with equal strength, their forces are balanced. The net force on the toy is zero, so its motion doesn't change. The net force on each child is also zero, so they stay where they are.

Sometimes the net force on an object isn't zero. This happens when forces are unbalanced. For example, think about the

Forces are acting, but no change in motion results.

When wrestlers push in opposite directions with unequal strengths, a change in motion results. ▶

children pulling on the toy. What will the net force on the toy be if one child pulls harder?

To calculate net force, assign a plus (+) to the forces acting in one direction. Forces acting in the opposite direction get a minus (−). Add the strengths of the forces to get the net force. Usually, forces pushing or pulling to the right are given positive values. Forces pushing or pulling to the left are given negative values.

Suppose one child pulls the toy to the right with a force of 100 N. If the other child pulls to the left with a force of 50 N, the net force on the toy is 100 N + (−50 N) = 50 N. Since the net force is positive, the answer is that the net force on the toy is 50 N to the right.

If all the forces on an object push or pull in the same direction, the net force is easy to calculate. Simply add the forces together. In

the picture, both horses are pulling in the same direction, so their forces are added to calculate the net force. If one horse pulls with a force of 300 N and the other horse pulls with a force of 400 N, the net force on the sleigh is 700 N.

⭐ **Focus Skill**

COMPARE AND CONTRAST Compare the forces if one child pulls a chair to the left with a force of 100 N and another child pulls it in the opposite direction with a force of 200 N.

The net force is the sum of all the forces. When forces act in the same direction, find the net force by adding the individual forces. ▶

Buoyant Force

Why is lifting a heavy object in water easier than lifting the same object on land? The reason is that water pushes up on the object. This upward force is called a **buoyant force**. Because it pushes up on objects, they seem to weigh less.

The buoyant force isn't always equal to the *weight of an object*. It equals the *weight of the fluid* that the object displaces, or pushes aside. Large objects have a greater buoyant force acting on them, since they displace more water than smaller objects.

Buoyant force acts in the opposite direction from weight. As a result, buoyant force helps objects float. If the buoyant force on an object is equal to or greater than the object's weight, the object floats.

If the object's weight is greater than the buoyant force, the object sinks.

Ships are made of steel and are very heavy, yet they float. How is this possible? Ships are large, but they are not solid; they are filled with air. A ship's overall weight is the weight of its steel walls plus the air inside the ship. This total weight is less than the weight of the water the ship displaces. The buoyant force is greater than the ship's weight, so it floats.

 COMPARE AND CONTRAST Is the buoyant force greater on a cherry tomato or on a regular tomato? Why?

A ball of clay is heavier than an equal volume of water, so the ball of clay sinks. If the clay is reshaped so that it displaces enough water to equal its weight, the clay floats. ▼

buoyant force

weight

Buoyant force pushes the toy duck upward. The force is equal to the toy's weight, so the duck floats.

Focus Skill

1. COMPARE AND CONTRAST Draw and complete the graphic organizer.

Balanced Forces   **Unbalanced Forces**

add up to a zero net force

don't cause objects to change positions

in a floating object, weight and **Ⓐ** _____

can push or pull

can come from gravity, **Ⓒ** _____, or other combinations of forces

don't add up to zero

causes objects to **Ⓑ** _____

in a sunken object, weight is greater than buoyant force

2. SUMMARIZE Write sentences that tell the most important information in this lesson.

3. DRAW CONCLUSIONS Two balls of the same size are put in water. One floats and one doesn't. How is this possible?

4. VOCABULARY For each vocabulary term in this lesson, write a sentence that gives an everyday example of it.

FCAT Prep

5. Read/Inquire/Explain The forces on a parked car are balanced. If the car starts moving, what has happened to the forces?

6. The buoyant force works against the force of

  A. gravity.   **C.** pulling.

  B. magnetism.   **D.** pushing.

Links

Writing
Expository Writing
Write two paragraphs **describing** the balanced forces at work on a floating object.

Math
Solve a Problem
A girl pushes a crate along the floor with a force of 100 N. The force of friction on the crate is 1 N. What is the net force on the crate?

Physical Education
Design Exercises
Design exercises that use balanced forces. Include some exercises that stretch your muscles and some that raise your heart rate.

 For more links and activities, go to **www.hspscience.com**

What Is Work, and How Is It Measured?

Fast Fact

Machines for Play Machines help people do things as different as assemble cars, plow soil, design clothing, and animate cartoons! Long ago, catapults like this one were made for war. They were used to fling heavy stones at an enemy. This one was made to chuck pumpkins at a fall festival. In the Investigate, you will use a machine to lift a load.

Lifting Things the Easy Way

Materials   • several small books   • ruler   • 2 unsharpened pencils

Procedure

1. Stack several small books at one edge of your desk.

2. Slide your little finger under the stack.

3. Keep your hand on your desk, palm up, and move just your little finger to lift the stack of books as far as you can.

4. Add more books, and repeat until you can barely lift the stack with your little finger. Observe and measure how far you can raise the stack of books.

5. Now make a lever. To do this, put an unsharpened pencil under your stack. Put another unsharpened pencil under and at right angles to the first pencil.

6. Lift the books by pressing down on the outer end of the top pencil with your little finger. Observe and measure how high you can lift the books.

Draw Conclusions

1. Did you use more force when you lifted the books with only your finger or when you used your pencil lever?

2. **Inquiry Skill** Scientists predict to understand what might happen in a situation, based on observations. What do you predict would happen if you lifted the books with a meterstick?

Step 1

Step 2

Investigate Further

Explore how levers work by comparing distances between the load end and the other end of levers of different lengths.

VOCABULARY

work p. 160
simple machine p. 162
lever p. 162
fulcrum p. 162
wheel-and-axle p. 162
pulley p. 163
inclined plane p. 163

SCIENCE CONCEPTS

► the scientific meaning of *work*
► simple machines make work easier

READING FOCUS SKILL

MAIN IDEA AND DETAILS Look for things that make work easier to do.

Work

Some science terms are familiar words. However, their scientific definitions are more precise than their everyday meanings. *Work* is an example.

You might think you're doing work when you spend a couple of hours reading a book for a report. Scientifically speaking, however, you haven't done any work. In science, the only way to do work is to make something move. Unless something moves, no work is done.

In science, **work** is using a force to move an object through a distance. This equation shows that definition:

Work = Force × Distance.

Notice that work is a product of two things. The force applied to an object is multiplied by the distance it is moved.

Math in Science
Interpret Data

Work Needed to Lift Pails

Object to Be Moved	Force Needed (Weight of Object)	Distance	Work Done (Force × Distance)
Empty pail	5 N	3 m	5 N × 3 m = 15 J
Pail of water	40 N	3 m	40 N × 3 m = 120 J
Pail of nails	180 N	3 m	180 N × 3 m = 540 J

How much more work is done lifting the nails than lifting the water?

The boy has done work. He applied a force to the ball as he lifted it up.

Which is more work—rowing a boat 1 km (0.6 mi) or 10 km (6 mi)? Rowing 10 km (6 mi) is more work, since work depends on distance.

But force matters, too. It takes more force to lift a heavy object than it does to lift a light object. Lifting a brick is more work than lifting a feather.

Work is measured in units called *joules*. How much work is one joule (1 J)? A medium-size apple weighs about 1 N. If you lift that apple 1 m, you do 1 J of work.

 MAIN IDEA AND DETAILS What two things determine how much work is needed to lift your backpack onto your back?

Insta-Lab

Work and Weight

Weigh an object by using a spring scale. Record the weight in newtons. Measure the vertical height of a flight of stairs with a meterstick, and record it. Then carry the object up the stairs. Calculate how much work you did on the object.

Machines and Work

Moving a heavy object a long distance is a lot of work. One way to make work easier is to use a machine.

Machines don't actually reduce the amount of work. Remember, work is the product of force and distance. Machines make work easier by reducing the amount of force people must use to do the work. Most machines allow you to use less force, but you apply it over a greater distance. The product of force and distance remains the same.

Many machines are collections of several simple machines. A **simple machine** is a tool that makes a task easier by changing the strength or direction of a force or the distance over which the force acts.

A **lever** is a bar that makes it easier to move things. Levers have two parts. One part, the *lever arm,* moves. The other part is the balance point, or **fulcrum**. The fulcrum supports the arm but doesn't move. A rake is an example of a lever. This simple machine reduces the force needed to lift or move an object.

A **wheel-and-axle** helps you open a door. This simple machine is a wheel with a rod, or axle, in the center. When you turn the wheel (the doorknob), the axle inside the knob turns and pulls back the latch. Opening a door would be much harder if you had to turn just the axle.

Building a playhouse involves using many simple machines. Wedges, levers, a screw, and an inclined plane are some of the simple machines used here. ▶

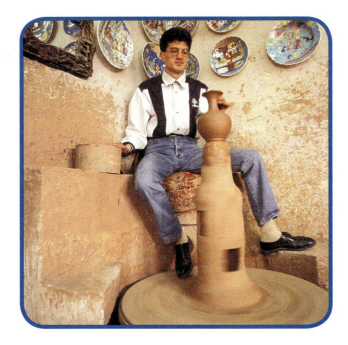

▲ Which simple machine do you think this potter's wheel uses?

▲ A dumbwaiter uses a pulley. You pull a load up by pulling down on a rope.

A **pulley** is a wheel with a groove for a rope. It works by changing the direction of a force. Pulleys allow you to lift things by pulling down on the rope rather than by pushing up on the object. Think back to the boy lifting the pail in the Interpret Data.

An example of an **inclined plane** is a ramp. It allows you to use less force over a distance to make work easier.

The *wedge* is made up of two inclined planes that form a cutting edge. A knife and a chisel are both wedges. An ax is a wedge that is used to chop wood.

 MAIN IDEA AND DETAILS What are the parts of a lever?

Compound Machines

Compound machines are made up of two or more simple machines. Like simple machines, compound machines make work easier. Most of them reduce the force you need to apply. Remember, machines don't reduce the work done. You usually push with less force through a greater distance when you use a machine.

A push lawn mower is a compound machine. It uses a wedge—the blade—to cut grass. The blades are attached to a wheel-and-axle, which turns them as the mower is pushed through the grass. The handle of the mower is a lever.

A hand-operated can opener is another compound machine. When cans were first invented, in the early 1800s, they had to be opened with a hammer and a chisel. That method was difficult and dangerous. A can opener uses two simple machines, a wedge and a wheel-and-axle, to change a small input force into an output force great enough to cut through the lid.

Sailors and movers often use a compound machine called a *block and tackle*. A block and tackle is made up of a series of pulleys. Heavy loads such as pianos and car engines can be lifted by one person using a block and tackle. That's because the combined pulleys reduce the force you need to lift the object.

 MAIN IDEA AND DETAILS Name a compound machine that you use and the simple machines it is made up of.

A hand-operated can opener is a compound machine made up of two levers, a wedge, and a wheel-and-axle.

effort force

effort force

A block and tackle is a system of pulleys used to lift heavy loads. Each pulley in the system makes the work a little easier. ▶

1. MAIN IDEA AND DETAILS Complete the graphic organizer.

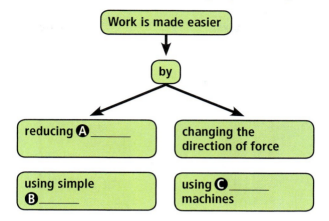

Work is made easier

by

reducing **A** _____

changing the direction of force

using simple **B** _____

using **C** _____ machines

2. SUMMARIZE Use the completed graphic organizer to write a lesson summary.

3. DRAW CONCLUSIONS Name two simple machines that make up a pencil sharpener.

4. VOCABULARY Make a crossword puzzle that uses the vocabulary terms for this lesson. Provide an answer key.

FCAT Prep

5. Read/Inquire/Explain How do machines make work easier?

6. Which of these is a simple machine that allows you to lift things by pulling down on a rope?

A. inclined plane **C.** pulley
B. lever **D.** wedge

Links

Writing

Write to Describe
Write a paragraph that **compares** three simple machines. Describe how they are similar and how they are different.

Math

Calculate Work
How much work does it take to move a cat weighing 20 N from the kitchen to the bedroom upstairs 12 m away? Does moving a 10-N cat 10 m take less or more work?

Social Studies

Research
Use library resources to research the Greek scientist Archimedes, who lived about 2,200 years ago. Write a few paragraphs about Archimedes and the ideas for which he is now famous.

 For more links and activities, go to **www.hspscience.com**

Have you perfected your ollie? Tried to goofy foot lately? Can you perform a grind or a varial? How's your caveman coming along? If you have no idea about what's going on, then you need to check out skateboarding. These are just a few of the dozens of gravity-defying moves in what is now one of America's biggest sports.

What makes the sport so cool? "It's like you have a sense of power over your board," said Andrew Vega, 17, of Lenexa, Kansas. "You can tell it what to do—and if it does it, then you've conquered it."

ON A ROLL

166

Grabbing Big Air

Skateboarding is hardly new. Surfers in southern California created the activity more than 50 years ago. The sport appeared to peak in the 1970s when polyurethane, or plastic, wheels replaced the old-fashioned metal wheels. Plastic wheels are lighter than metal wheels, so it takes less force to move the skateboard. Back then, skateboarding was about keeping your wheels on the ground.

But kids wanted to do more than just roll on a board from one place to another. So they began to skateboard in empty pools and in city parks. The curves and walls in a pool, for example, allowed a boarder to get up to speed quickly and make amazing jumps from the pool's edge.

To keep boarders off of city streets and out of city parks, skate parks began to appear around the country. They had ramps and half-pipes so that kids could try out their aerial moves. But most parks were hard to get to.

"Punks" No More

Before long, skateboarding lost

"Over the years, people have given skateboarding a bad reputation," said Seth Estes, 14, from Everett, Washington. "It's important that people not look at us like Punks."

momentum. Many skate parks closed because owners couldn't afford to insure riders against injury. Then, about six years ago, California, Washington, and other states started passing laws that classified skateboarding as a "hazardous activity." Although that sounds bad, the laws encouraged cities to build skate parks as long as skaters accepted all the risks involved.

Public officials hope that skate parks with rails and stairs will keep skaters off the streets and in a safer environment. Meanwhile, most skateboarders are working to improve the image of the sport.

Think About It

1. What forces of nature are at work when a skateboarder jumps clear of the edge of a half-pipe?
2. How does skating faster help a skateboarder jump higher?

Spin-In

Find out more! Log on to
www.hspscience.com

An Electrifying Discovery

Hans Oersted was a physics professor at the University of Copenhagen in Denmark more than 200 years ago. Oersted made a thin wire glow by sending an electrical current through it. He was the first to discover the link between electricity and heat.

Oersted was able to move a compass needle by placing an electrified wire near the compass. His experiment proved that electric currents create magnetic fields, which resulted in the development of electromagnets. Today, you can find electromagnets powerful enough to lift cars.

Career Electricians

Thanks to the work of electricians, you can watch TV, use a computer, keep your drinks cold in a refrigerator, and keep cool with an air conditioner. Electricians install, connect, test, and maintain electrical systems in houses and businesses.

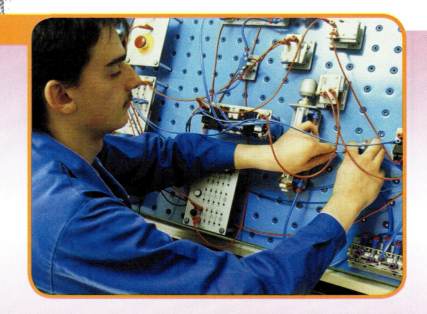

SC.H.3.2.1.5.1 technology has improved human lives;
SC.H.3.2.4.5.1 people can solve problems through science

You Can Do It!

Materials
- string
- block
- spring scale
- measuring tape
- books
- piece of cardboard
- tape

Inclined Planes Work for You

Procedure
1. Tie the string around the block.
2. Use the spring scale to lift the block 40 cm. Record the force the scale shows you used.
3. Stack books to make a tower 40 cm high. Tape the piece of cardboard to the books to make a ramp. Measure it.
4. Pull the block up the inclined plane with the spring scale. Record the force you used and the distance you pulled the block.

Draw Conclusions
1. How did using the inclined plane make lifting the block easier?
2. Did using the inclined plane reduce the amount of work you did to lift the block? Explain.

Make Your Work Easier

You have measured how much force raising the block 40 cm by yourself took. You have also measured the amount of force it took to do the same thing with an inclined plane. Use classroom materials to build another simple machine to lift the block. Measure the amount of force it takes. Compare your simple machine to the inclined plane. Which one makes the job easier?

Review and FCAT Preparation

Vocabulary Review

Use the terms below to complete the sentences. The page numbers tell you where to look in the chapter if you need help.

friction p. 145
gravity p. 146
balanced forces p. 152
net force p. 154
work p. 160
simple machine p. 162
lever p. 162
fulcrum p. 162
pulley p. 163
inclined plane p. 163

1. Using a force to move an object through a distance is called _____.

2. The balance point of a lever is the _____.

3. A machine that allows you to lift things by pulling down on a rope is a _____.

4. The combination of all the forces acting on an object is the _____.

5. Forces acting on an object that are equal and opposite are _____.

6. A force that works against motion is _____.

7. A bar that moves against a fulcrum is a _____.

8. A ramp is an example of a simple machine called an _____.

9. The force that Earth applies to objects near its surface is _____.

10. A machine that makes work easier is a _____.

Check Understanding

Write the letter of the best choice.

11. **MAIN IDEA AND DETAILS** A can opener is made up of several simple machines. One is the wedge. What is another one?
    A. wedge
    B. pulley
    C. incline plane
    D. wheel-and-axle

12. **CAUSE AND EFFECT** Which force causes a ship to float in water?
    F. air resistance
    G. buoyant force
    H. friction
    I. magnetism

13. Which simple machine is part of a screw?

    A. fulcrum   **C.** pulley
    B. inclined plane   **D.** wheel-and-axle

14. Which force makes a compass work?
    F. buoyant force   **H.** gravity
    G. friction   **I.** magnetic force

15. Which of these machines is a wheel-and-axle?

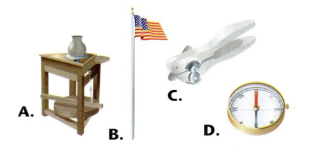

16. Which of these machines can be used to lift a piano into a second-story window?
    F. block-and-tackle   **H.** screw
    G. lever   **I.** wedge

Inquiry Skills

17. You use a shovel to dig. Identify and **communicate** the simple machines that make up a shovel.

18. As you go down a slide, your movement is not smooth. What can you **infer** about the forces acting on you?

Read/Inquire/Explain

19. You want to move a large, heavy box of toys up into your treehouse. It's too heavy and awkward to carry up the rope ladder. How can you move the box with a simple machine?

20. Think about the forces acting on the weight lifter and the weights.
Part A Are the forces acting on the weight lifter and the weights balanced or unbalanced? Explain.
Part B Identify the forces acting on the weight lifter and the weights.

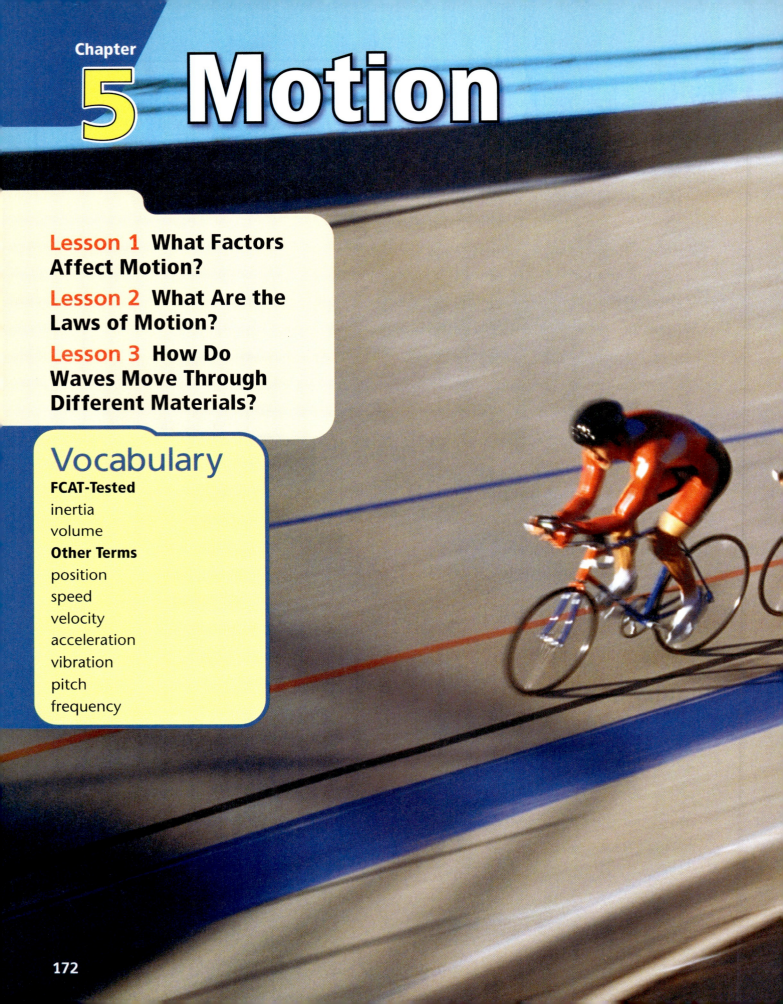

Vocabulary

FCAT-Tested

inertia

volume

Other Terms

position

speed

velocity

acceleration

vibration

pitch

frequency

What do YOU wonder?

These cyclists are racing around a track known as a velodrome. The sides of the velodrome are angled, which changes the forces acting on the cyclists. The angled sides allow them to go faster than 50 km/hr (30 mi/hr)! What other factors affect the cyclists' motion?

What Factors Affect Motion?

Fast Fact

Giant Tops This spinning-ring ride seems to defy gravity when it's moving. Carnival rides like this one are based on NASA training equipment. An astronaut trainee can turn in all directions: up and down, left and right, and sideways. In the Investigate, you will observe the way an air bubble moves when you apply force from different directions.

Changes in Motion

Materials • clear, 1-L plastic bottle with cap • water • small piece of soap

Procedure

1 Fill the bottle with water, but leave just enough space for a small air bubble. Add a small piece of soap. Cap the bottle tightly.

2 Lay the bottle on its side on a flat surface. You should see one small bubble in the bottle. Hold the bottle steady until the bubble moves to the center of the bottle and stays there.

3 Predict what will happen to the air bubble if you turn the bottle to the left or right. Turn the bottle, and observe what happens. Record your observations.

4 Repeat Step 3, but this time, move the bottle forward at a steady speed.

5 Repeat Step 4, but this time, increase the speed.

Draw Conclusions

1. Compare the results of all these types of movement with one another. Were they similar to or different from one another?

2. **Inquiry Skill** Scientists often form inferences to explain why something happened. Infer why the bubble moved the way it did.

Step 2

Step 4

Investigate Further

Hypothesize what will happen to the air bubble if the bottle is moving at a steady speed and its direction changes. Plan and conduct a simple investigation to test your hypothesis.

SC.C.1.2.1.5.1 speed, distance, and direction; SC.C.2.2.2.5.2 friction; SC.C.2.2.4.5.2 inertia, gravity, friction, mass, and force; LA.A.2.2.1 main idea and details

VOCABULARY
position p. 176
speed p. 178
velocity p. 178
acceleration p. 180

SCIENCE CONCEPTS
▶ how different kinds of force affect motion
▶ how motion is measured

READING FOCUS SKILL
MAIN IDEA AND DETAILS Look for details that describe forces and motion.

Main Idea
detail   detail   detail

Forces and Motion

Have you ever been sitting in an unmoving car when the car next to you started to move? Did you feel as if you were moving forward or backward? When you looked at the street you realized you weren't moving at all! In order to determine if an object is moving, you must have a *frame of reference.* Your frame of reference is the moving object and a background that isn't moving. If you were at the park watching the girls on the swings, the trees and ground would help you determine that the girls were changing their position.

You can tell the difference between a moving object and one that's still. But how would you *define* motion? An object is in motion when its position changes. **Position** is the location of an object in space, and it is always relative to a frame of reference. We use many words to express position, such as *east, west, above, below,* and *beside.*

Forces can make objects change their position. All forces—from gravitational force to magnetic force to friction—are pushes and pulls. What force is making the girls on the swings move?

You know these girls are moving, because their positions are changing.

Gravitational force is the force that attracts two objects. It increases as the objects' masses increase. Mass is the amount of matter in an object. If you get out of a chair and walk around the room, your chair stays where it is, because Earth is very large—the gravitational force it exerts is strong. Your chair doesn't move toward you because your mass is much smaller than Earth's mass.

Friction is a force that opposes motion. It either prevents motion or slows it down. Friction acts between two surfaces. The smoother the surface is between two objects, the less friction there usually is between them. This is why you slip on ice. The smooth ice and the soles of your shoes don't produce much friction when they slide past each other.

Often, several forces act together on an object. Think about an airplane in flight. Drag from the air slows the plane. Thrust works against drag. Thrust is the forward force produced by the plane's engine. Lift is the force that "pulls" the plane up, into the sky. Gravity opposes lift. For the plane to fly, the forces of lift and thrust must equal to or be greater than gravitational force and drag.

 MAIN IDEA AND DETAILS Why does a skydiver fall to the ground when she jumps out of a plane?

Gravity pulls the girls down the slide. Friction slows their motion.

A maglev train doesn't have wheels. It uses magnetic force—the pull between magnetic objects—to float above the track.

Speed and Velocity

What makes a roller coaster so much fun? Many people think that it's the roller coaster's speed. **Speed** is the distance an object travels in a certain amount of time. Speed tells you how quickly or slowly something is moving.

An object's speed is an important property of its motion. Suppose you read that a certain roller coaster zooms along 853 m (2800 ft) of track. Does that make you want to ride it? Maybe. You read on and learn that the top speed of the roller coaster is 193 km/hr (120 mi/hr). It's the fastest roller coaster in the world. Now, *that* sounds like fun!

You can calculate speed by using this formula.

$$\text{speed} = \frac{\text{distance}}{\text{time}}$$

If you walk 5 km (3.1 mi) in 1 hour, your speed is 5 km/hr. What is your speed if you walk 10 km in 2 hours?

Sometimes you need to know the *direction* of an object as well as its speed. Suppose some friends are meeting you at the park at 3:00. Will they be there on time? Yes—*if* they're moving fast enough *and* in the right direction. In other words, your friends must travel at the correct velocity. **Velocity** is the measure of an object's speed in a particular direction.

Suppose your friends are walking southeast at a speed of 5 km/hr. Their velocity is 5 km/hr, southeast. Now suppose they pass another group of people walking 5 km/hr in the opposite direction. The two groups are moving at the same speed but at different velocities.

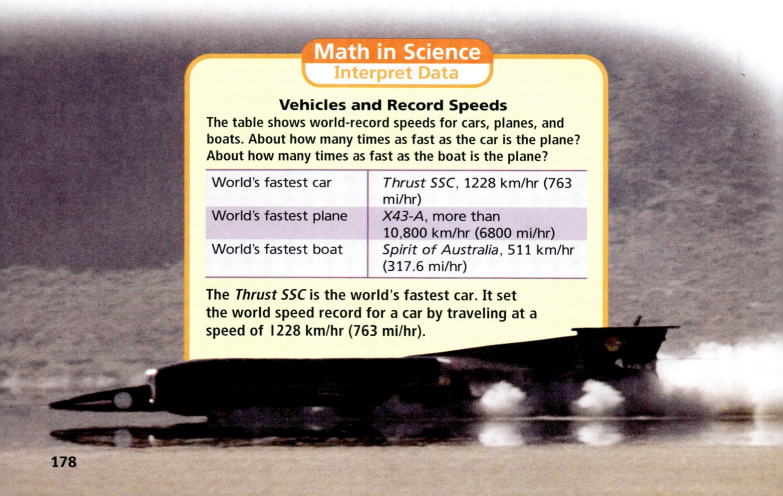

Math in Science
Interpret Data

Vehicles and Record Speeds

The table shows world-record speeds for cars, planes, and boats. About how many times as fast as the car is the plane? About how many times as fast as the boat is the plane?

World's fastest car	*Thrust SSC*, 1228 km/hr (763 mi/hr)
World's fastest plane	*X43-A*, more than 10,800 km/hr (6800 mi/hr)
World's fastest boat	*Spirit of Australia*, 511 km/hr (317.6 mi/hr)

The *Thrust SSC* is the world's fastest car. It set the world speed record for a car by traveling at a speed of 1228 km/hr (763 mi/hr).

Speed = 110 km/hr (68.4 mi/hr)
Velocity = 110 km/hr (68.4 mi/hr), east

Velocity is a more complete way to describe an object's motion. It includes the object's speed and its direction.

A car traveling down a straight highway at a constant speed has *constant velocity.* This means that the car is moving steadily in the same direction. It doesn't speed up or slow down. It doesn't turn. It only moves in a straight line.

We can also describe velocity as *changing.* In this case, the object's speed is changing *or* its direction is changing—or both. A car driving at a steady speed in a circle has a changing velocity. The car's speed is constant, but its direction changes every moment as it turns along the circle. When anything speeds up, slows down, stops, starts, or turns, its velocity changes.

 MAIN IDEA AND DETAILS What are four ways the friends walking to the park can change their velocity?

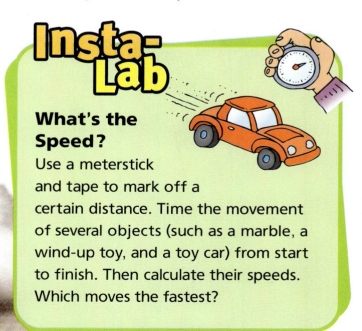

Insta-Lab

What's the Speed?
Use a meterstick and tape to mark off a certain distance. Time the movement of several objects (such as a marble, a wind-up toy, and a toy car) from start to finish. Then calculate their speeds. Which moves the fastest?

Acceleration

A car's velocity changes slowly as it backs out of a parking spot. But its velocity changes quickly if the driver slams on the brakes. Motion can be described by how quickly an object changes velocity, or *accelerates*. **Acceleration** is the rate at which velocity changes over time.

You can calculate acceleration by using this formula.

$$\text{acceleration} = \frac{\text{change in velocity}}{\text{time}}$$

Suppose you see an ad for a sports car that accelerates to 100 km/hr (62 mi/hr) in 5 seconds. What is its acceleration? Subtract the starting speed from the final speed to find the change in speed. Divide the change in speed by the time it takes for the speed to change. Use *a* for *acceleration*.

$$a = \frac{100 \text{ km/hr} - 0 \text{ km/hr}}{5 \text{ s}} = 20 \text{ km/hr/s}$$

The car is constantly accelerating by 20 km/hr during each second. At the end of one second, the car's speed is 20 km/hr (12.4 mi/hr). After two seconds,

▲ The whale thrusts the performer into the air with great force. As a result, the performer's velocity changes—he accelerates.

the car is going faster. Now its speed is 40 km/hr (24.9 mi/hr). What is the car's speed after three seconds?

The sports car also accelerates when it slows down or stops. Remember that acceleration is the rate of *change* in the velocity. Velocity involves speed and direction. So acceleration can happen through a change in either speed or direction—or both.

Several parts of a car control its acceleration. The gas pedal causes the car to gain speed. The brake slows down the car or stops it. The steering wheel changes the car's direction.

An object has a large acceleration when it changes its velocity quickly. For example, a motorcycle can have a lesser acceleration than a child's tricycle. Suppose the motorcycle is zipping down a highway in a straight line at a constant speed. Its acceleration is zero. But a tricycle in a driveway is accelerating as the rider slows down, speeds up, or turns.

MAIN IDEA AND DETAILS What two properties of an object's motion can change when it accelerates?

A roller coaster car is almost always accelerating during a ride because its speed and its direction are almost always changing. ▼

A jet plane has limited runway space to land on the deck of an aircraft carrier. The plane must come to a stop very quickly. So the acceleration of the plane is large. ▼

Momentum

A truck and a car are cruising down a highway. They have the same speed, the same velocity, and the same acceleration. Are the motions of the two vehicles the same?

The motion of the car differs from that of the truck in one important way—momentum. *Momentum* is a property of motion that describes how hard it is to slow down or stop an object. Momentum also describes how an object will affect something that it bumps into. Momentum depends on mass and velocity. You can calculate momentum by using this formula.

momentum = mass × velocity

In the example, the truck has a far greater mass than the car. So, the momentum of the truck is much greater than the momentum of the car. The truck will be harder to stop or slow down. If the truck bumps into something, it will cause more damage than the car would.

However, objects with different masses can have the same momentum if the object with less mass has more velocity. Momentum increases if either mass or velocity increases.

Consider two football players. One is big and heavy, and the other is small and light. Suppose the large player runs slowly and the smaller player runs quickly. They could each have the same momentum. Each player could be equally hard to stop. And each player could have an equally crushing effect on the other team!

 MAIN IDEA AND DETAILS What two factors determine an object's momentum?

A big truck moving at a fast speed has a lot of momentum. How much momentum does this small car have?

1. **MAIN IDEA AND DETAILS** Copy and complete this graphic organizer.

Ⓐ _____ are pushes and pulls.

Ⓑ _____ is defined as a change of position.

Ⓒ _____ is studied by analyzing its features.

Ⓓ _____ is the distance an object moves in a certain time.

Ⓔ _____ is a measurement of speed and direction.

Ⓕ _____ measures how hard it is to slow or stop an object.

Ⓖ _____ is the rate of change of velocity over time.

2. **SUMMARIZE** Use your completed graphic organizer to write a lesson summary.

3. **DRAW CONCLUSIONS** A car is moving in a straight line at a constant speed of 40 km/hr. Is it accelerating?

4. **VOCABULARY** Use the vocabulary terms in this lesson to create a crossword puzzle with answers.

FCAT Prep

5. **Read/Inquire/Explain** The speed of a ball falling from a high shelf to the floor is 9.8 m/sec. What is its velocity?

6. A motorcycle is accelerating at a rate of 1km/hr. If its speed is 20 km/hr after 5 seconds, what is its speed after 6 seconds?

   A. 20 km/hr   **C.** 100 km/hr
   B. 21 km/hr   **D.** 120 km/hr

Links

Writing

Narrative Writing
Write a **short story** that features world records for fast movers. You might choose animals, human runners, or vehicles. Use the vocabulary you have learned in this chapter.

Math

Solve a Problem
Find the speed of a motorcycle that travels 32 km in 16 minutes. Show the formula you used as well as your work.

Social Studies

Multicultural Studies
Compare the numbers of bicycles and cars in other countries with the numbers of these vehicles in the United States. Write a report explaining your findings.

For more links and activities, go to **www.hspscience.com**

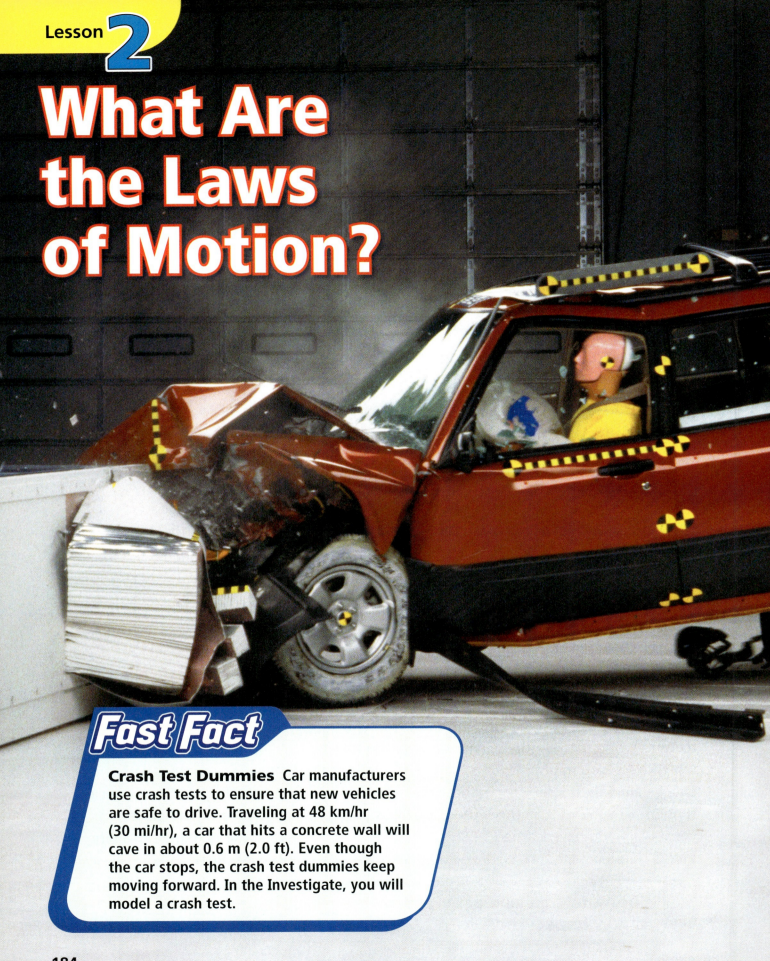

What Are the Laws of Motion?

Fast Fact

Crash Test Dummies Car manufacturers use crash tests to ensure that new vehicles are safe to drive. Traveling at 48 km/hr (30 mi/hr), a car that hits a concrete wall will cave in about 0.6 m (2.0 ft). Even though the car stops, the crash test dummies keep moving forward. In the Investigate, you will model a crash test.

Momentum Crash Test

Materials
- game board
- several books
- meterstick
- small toy car
- dime
- quarter

Procedure

1 Make a ramp by setting one end of the game board on a stack of books about 15 cm high. Place another book as a barrier about 10 to 15 cm from the bottom of the ramp. Be sure the barrier is lower than the front end of the car.

2 Put the car at the top of the ramp. Put the dime on the front end of the car. Let the car roll down the ramp and hit the barrier. Observe what happens to the dime. Measure and record the dime's distance from the barrier. Repeat several times.

3 Repeat Step 2, but use a quarter. Repeat several times.

4 Predict how the results will differ if you make the ramp higher. Add another book to the stack under the ramp. Repeat Steps 2 and 3 several times. Was your prediction correct?

Step 1

Step 3

Draw Conclusions

1. Put your data in a table. Compare data for the dime with data for the quarter. How does a coin's mass relate to the distance it travels?

2. What happened when you made the ramp higher? Infer why this happened.

3. **Inquiry Skill** What was the control variable in Steps 2 and 3? What was the test variable?

Investigate Further

Experiment with several methods of keeping the coin on the car when the car strikes the barrier. Conduct several trials for each method.

SC.C.1.2.1.5.1 speed, distance, direction;
SC.H.2.2.1.5.2 analyze patterns of change

Reading in Science

 SC.C.2.2.2.5.1 force and motion; **SC.C.2.2.3.5.1** forces and mass;
SC.S.2.2.4.5.1 motion in space; **LA.E.2.2.1** cause and effect

VOCABULARY
inertia p. 187

SCIENCE CONCEPTS
▶ how inertia affects motion
▶ how force, mass, and acceleration are related

READING FOCUS SKILL

CAUSE AND EFFECT Find out how forces affect motion.

| cause | → | effect |

Newton's First Law of Motion

A soccer ball doesn't roll across a field on its own. It takes a force, such as a kick from you, to get it moving. But once it's moving, the ball doesn't go on forever. Sooner or later, it stops.

You might think that the natural state of an object is to be still. You might also think that once it's moving, it stops only because the force that pushed it stops, too. In other words, the ball stops because you aren't kicking it anymore.

However, objects stop because a force acts on them. On Earth, gravity and friction stop moving objects. Gravity pulls objects toward Earth. If you throw a ball, it eventually curves and hits the ground. Suppose gravity didn't exist. The ball would keep moving through the air until drag stopped it.

Friction acts in the direction opposite to motion. The less friction between the ground and a rolling ball, the farther the ball will move. When pushed with the same force, the ball will roll farther down a paved street than down a grassy field.

◀ Isaac Newton (1641–1727) is a giant in the history of science. He is most famous for his three laws of motion, his law of gravitation, and his experiments with light and prisms.

▲ The ball doesn't move until a force hits it. Once the ball has been hit, will the ball keep moving forever? Why not?

186

▲ Inertia keeps you moving forward if the car stops suddenly. Safety belts apply the force needed to stop you.

When an ice hockey player hits a puck, the puck slides a long way because ice is very slippery. If the friction between the puck and the ice disappeared, the puck would slide forever. It would move in the same direction and at a constant speed.

Isaac Newton described the effects of forces in three laws of motion. Newton's first law of motion describes inertia. **Inertia** is the tendency of objects to resist a change in motion. Objects at rest don't move unless a force moves them. Objects in motion don't slow down, stop, or turn unless a force makes them do so. A simple way to state the first law of motion is *No acceleration can happen without a force.*

Have you ever seen a performer pull a tablecloth from under the dishes and silverware on a table? The dishes and

▲ The bulletproof vest is made of strong material that can absorb the force of a bullet, slowing it down.

silverware remain in place, amazing the audience. This trick works because of Newton's first law of motion. The inertia keeps the dishes and silverware in place. Only a small force is applied by snapping away the tablecloth. This force isn't large enough or long enough to move the table setting very far.

 CAUSE AND EFFECT Why are safety belts such an important safety feature in cars?

187

Newton's Second Law of Motion

Newton's first law tells you that when you kick a ball, the ball will move. Newton's second law tells you that if you kick the ball harder, it will move faster. It also tells you that a heavy ball is harder to move than a lighter ball.

The long row of empty shopping carts requires more force to accelerate than one empty cart requires. ▼

Newton's second law says that when a force acts on an object, the object accelerates. The law also tells you how much the object accelerates. Recall that acceleration is the rate at which velocity changes. In other words, the second law says *An object's acceleration depends on the object's mass and the force applied to it.*

Let's look at how force and mass affect acceleration. The larger the force is, the greater the acceleration is. Suppose you push a scooter gently. The scooter speeds up slowly. If you use more strength to push, the scooter's speed changes quickly. In both cases, the scooter moves in the direction in which it is pushed.

Let's take another example. A car will stop suddenly if the driver slams on the brakes. But if the driver applies the brakes gently, the car gradually slows down.

The ribbon requires only a little bit of force to accelerate because it has a small mass.

Science Up Close

Impact Between a Baseball and a Bat

When a bat and a baseball strike each other, acceleration results.

1 The baseball moves toward the bat as the bat moves toward the baseball.

2 The baseball applies a force to the bat as the bat applies a force to the baseball. The force from the bat gives different accelerations to individual particles of the baseball. This causes the baseball to change shape.

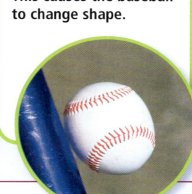

3 Both the baseball and the bat accelerate. The push of the bat on the baseball changes the baseball's speed and direction. The push of the baseball on the bat slows the bat.

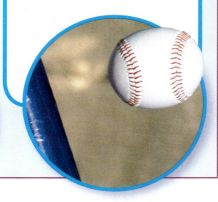

The less an object's mass is, the less force is needed to move it. It's much easier to push an empty shopping cart than a full one. Light cars are used in drag racing because a car with less mass accelerates faster than a car with more mass.

For a force to move an object, the force must overcome other forces. Suppose you want to pick up a box of books. The force you use to lift the box is the strength of your muscles. The force acting against your muscles is gravity.

Recall that weight is the measure of the force of gravity on an object. If the weight of the books is greater than your muscle strength, you can't move the box. However, you could take out some of the books to decrease the mass of the box. Or you could get someone to help you, increasing the force applied to the box. To lift an object, the lifting force must be equal to or greater than the weight of the object.

You can write the second law of motion as an equation.

$$\text{acceleration} = \frac{\text{force}}{\text{mass}}$$

The standard unit of force is the newton.

 CAUSE AND EFFECT What is the effect on a car's acceleration if six people ride in the car instead of one?

Newton's Third Law of Motion

Suppose you're running without watching where you're going. You run into a wall. Ouch!

Are you hurt because you hit the wall? No—you can't feel the force on the wall. You can feel forces only on your body. You're hurt because the wall hit you.

The wall didn't reach out and hit you, of course. But it did push you with the same amount of force with which you pushed it. If it hadn't, you would have moved the wall.

The third law of motion says *Whenever one object applies a force to a second object, the second object applies an equal and opposite force to the first object.*

A simple way to state this law is that forces always occur in pairs. For every action force, there is an equal and opposite reaction force. When your feet touch the ground, the ground touches your feet. When a hammer hits a nail, the nail hits the hammer. When Earth pulls on the moon, the moon pulls back on Earth—all with equal, but opposite, force.

Here's a way to make Newton's third law of motion easier to understand. Just remember that when one object pushes on another, the other object pushes back on the first.

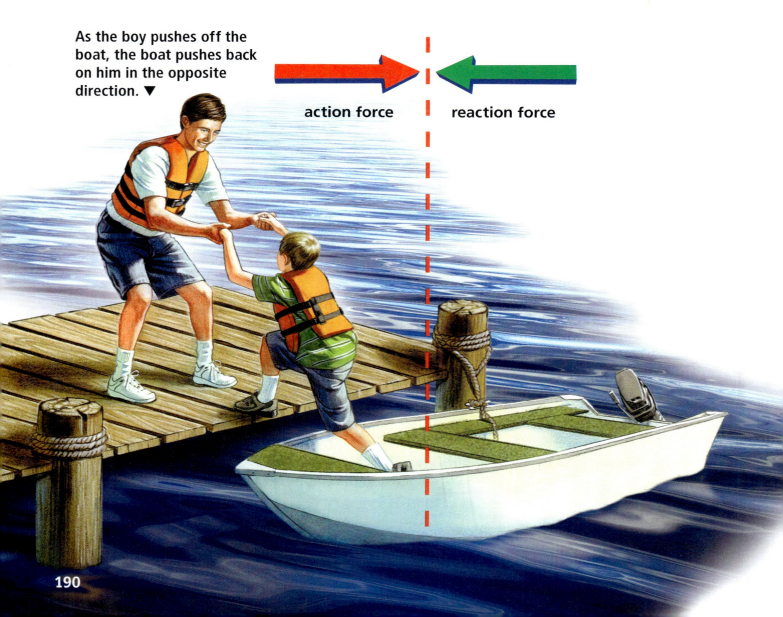

As the boy pushes off the boat, the boat pushes back on him in the opposite direction. ▼

action force   reaction force

As the runner's foot pushes against the starting block, the block pushes against the runner's foot.

action force

reaction force

A horse pulls a cart. Can you name the opposing forces? Just think of the rule. The horse pulls on the cart. So Newton's third law tells you that the cart pulls on the horse.

Newton's third law shows that forces always happen in pairs. An action force can't occur without an equal and opposite reaction force. The forces push with the same strength, but in opposite directions, at exactly the same time.

 CAUSE AND EFFECT You push a broom. What pushes on you, and in what direction?

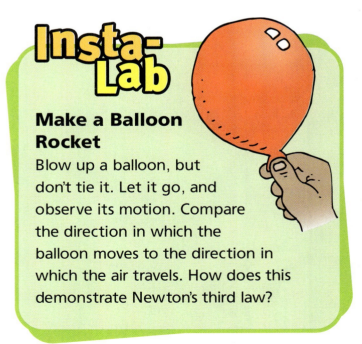

Insta-Lab

Make a Balloon Rocket

Blow up a balloon, but don't tie it. Let it go, and observe its motion. Compare the direction in which the balloon moves to the direction in which the air travels. How does this demonstrate Newton's third law?

Motion in Space

Astronauts inside the space shuttle float as if no gravity were acting on them. However, Earth's gravity at the shuttle isn't zero or even near zero. The shuttle's orbit is close enough to Earth that gravity is almost as strong there as it is on Earth.

Why do the astronauts seem to be weightless? After the shuttle reaches orbit, its engines shut down. Inertia carries the shuttle forward. Space near Earth has only a little drag to slow down objects. Gravity causes the shuttle to fall. The shuttle falls continuously toward Earth. But at the same time, it moves forward fast enough to keep from hitting Earth. The curve of the shuttle's path as it moves is the same as the curve of

Earth, so the shuttle doesn't get any closer to Earth's surface.

This same principle explains why planets and moons stay in orbit. Earth's moon, for example, moves forward because of inertia. At the same time, Earth's gravity pulls the moon toward Earth. The result is that the moon moves in a curved path around Earth. If gravity didn't pull the moon, it would continue moving forever in a straight line at a constant speed. If the moon didn't have inertia, it would crash into the Earth.

 CAUSE AND EFFECT What causes Earth to orbit the sun?

"Weightless" occurs in space as the shuttle orbits Earth. The astronauts don't feel the effects of Earth's gravity. ▼

▲ Drag acts on this space capsule as it reenters Earth's atmosphere.

▲ The satellite orbits Earth. It's pulled toward Earth by Earth's gravity.

192

1. CAUSE AND EFFECT Make a graphic organizer like the one shown. To fill out the chart, use Newton's laws to explain ❶ how inertia affects motion, ❷ how force affects acceleration, and ❸ how one object affects a second object that applies a force to it.

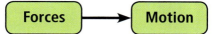

Forces → Motion

2. SUMMARIZE Write a summary of this lesson. Begin with the sentence *There are three laws of motion.*

3. DRAW CONCLUSIONS The first law of motion states that you don't have to apply a force to maintain motion. Why, then, do you have to keep pedaling your bike to keep moving?

4. VOCABULARY Make up a riddle or a quiz question about inertia. Provide the answer.

FCAT Prep

5. Read/Inquire/Explain Give an example from your everyday life of the third law of motion.

6. A girl throws a ball. If the ball's acceleration is 12 m/sec/sec and its mass is 0.5 kg, how much force did the girl apply to the ball?

A. 0.04 N   C. 6 N

B. 0.6 N   D. 12.5 N

Links

Writing

Narrative Writing
Find out how microgravity affects the daily activities of astronauts. Write a **skit** that describes a typical day in an astronaut's life.

Math

Solve Problems
Forces that act in the same direction add like regular numbers. A girl and a boy pull a wagon to the right. The girl applies 10 newtons. The boy applies 8 newtons. What's the total force on the wagon?

Social Studies

History of Science
Use library resources to research the life of Isaac Newton. Write a story for younger students that tells how he came up with the three laws of motion.

For more links and activities, go to **www.hspscience.com**

How Do Waves Move Through Different Materials?

Fast Fact

Dolphin Echoes Like bats, dolphins produce sound waves from their heads to help them find objects. The sound waves bounce off objects and travel back as echoes. The sound moves through their jawbone to their inner ears. In the Investigate, you will listen to sound traveling through water.

Sound Travels

Materials
- zip-top plastic bag
- water
- tuning fork
- solid object such as a wooden block or door

Procedure

1. Fill the zip-top plastic bag with water. Seal the bag.

2. Strike the tuning fork. Hold it a few inches from your ear. Listen to the sound.

3. Strike the tuning fork again. Hold it against one side of the bag. Put your ear against the other side of the bag. Listen to the sound of the tuning fork through the bag.

4. Strike the tuning fork once more. Hold it against one side of the solid object. Listen to the sound through the other side of the block.

Draw Conclusions

1. Could you hear the sound through the air, water, and wood? In each case, was there a difference in the loudness of the sound?

2. **Inquiry Skills** Scientists make hypotheses to try to explain observations. Hypothesize whether sound can travel through gases, liquids, and solids. What is the evidence to support your hypothesis?

Step 2

Step 3

Investigate Further

Plan and conduct an investigation to test whether sound travels better in liquids or in air.

Reading in Science

SC.C.1.2.2.5.1 knows that waves travel at different speeds through different materials; LA.A.2.2.1 main idea and details

VOCABULARY
vibration p. 196
volume p. 197
pitch p. 198
frequency p. 198

SCIENCE CONCEPTS
▶ what makes sounds vary
▶ how sounds travel

READING FOCUS SKILL

MAIN IDEA AND DETAILS Look for the characteristics of sound.

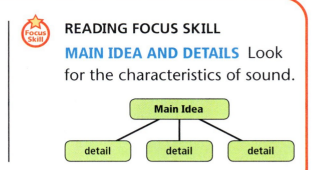

Sound Energy

Have you ever been to a Native American powwow? People dance and celebrate to the rhythm of a drum. The drum may be big—about 1 m (3 ft) in diameter. Eight or more people play the drum and sing. The sound gets very loud and can be heard far away.

Sound is a form of energy that travels through the air. Sound is made when something vibrates. A **vibration** is a back-and-forth movement of matter. When a drummer hits a drum's head, or covering, the head moves back and forth very quickly. These movements are vibrations. They cause the air nearby to vibrate, making the sound energy that you hear.

The head of a drum—a thin covering—is flexible and tight, so it vibrates when it is hit. ▶

196

Math in Science
Interpret Data

How Loud Are Some Sounds?

Sound	Decibel Level
Whisper	20 dB
Quiet radio	40 dB
Conversation	60 dB
Dishwasher	80 dB
Jackhammer	100 dB
Thunderclap	120 dB

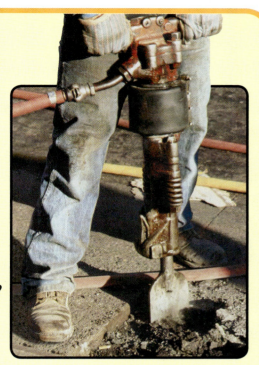

Why do factory workers and jack-hammer operators wear ear protection?

◀ These representatives at the United Nations are wearing headsets so they can listen to speeches in their own languages. Each person can adjust the volume of the sound for comfort and clarity.

Musical instruments make sounds in various ways. Some, like drums, vibrate when they're hit. A stringed instrument, like a violin, vibrates when the player plucks the strings or draws a bow across them. A woodwind instrument, like a clarinet, has a thin wooden reed attached to it. When the player blows into the instrument, the reed vibrates.

Some sounds are louder than others. If the drummers at the powwow hit the drum gently, the sound is soft. If they hit the drum harder, the sound gets stronger and louder. The loudness of a sound is called the **volume**. Can you think of a sound with a low volume and a sound with a high volume?

When a drummer hits a drum harder, more energy is transferred to the drum and to the sound. The more energy a sound has, the greater its volume is.

The volume of a sound is measured in units called *decibels* (DES•uh•buhlz), abbreviated *dB*. The softest sound a human can hear is 0 dB. A high-decibel sound is loud and has a lot of energy. Have you ever heard a sound that made your ears ring? Sounds above 100 dB can cause pain and can damage a person's ears. That's why people who work around loud sounds wear ear plugs or other ear protection.

 MAIN IDEA AND DETAILS Describe the ways in which three types of musical instruments make sound.

Sound Waves

Sound travels through the air as waves. When a jackhammer strikes the sidewalk, the sidewalk vibrates and pushes on the air directly above it. Molecules of air are *compressed,* or squeezed together. The compressed air pushes on the air next to it. This passes the compression along, like a wave at the beach.

You already know that some sounds are higher than others. If you've ever listened to a brass band, for example, you know that a trumpet makes a higher sound than a tuba does. The **pitch** of a sound is how high or how low it is. Changing the length of a guitar string alters the pitch of the sound you hear. That's because the length of the strings affects how fast they vibrate. A shorter string vibrates faster. There are more vibrations per second. The number of vibrations per second is the **frequency** of a sound.

A sound with a high frequency has a high pitch. A sound with a low frequency has a low pitch. Small objects often vibrate at higher frequencies than large objects do. In the Investigate, shortening the strings made them vibrate at a higher frequency. A trumpet is smaller than a tuba, so the trumpet makes sound waves with higher frequencies.

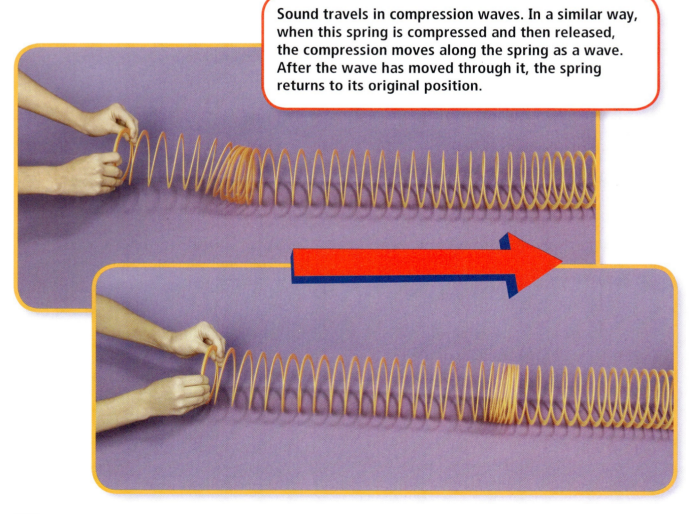

Sound travels in compression waves. In a similar way, when this spring is compressed and then released, the compression moves along the spring as a wave. After the wave has moved through it, the spring returns to its original position.

▲ If you shout toward a hard surface, such as a cliff, you may hear an echo of your voice. The echo isn't as loud as the original sound because the surface absorbs some of the energy.

Sound waves move out in all directions from an object that makes a sound. When a sound wave hits something, some or all of the energy is absorbed. Soft surfaces absorb more sound energy than hard surfaces. A sound that hits a hard surface bounces back—not much of it is absorbed. A sound that bounces off a surface is called an *echo.* If you stand at the foot of a cliff and shout, you may hear an echo of your voice. Some caves and canyons are famous for the echoes they produce.

 **MAIN IDEA AND DETAILS** How do sounds travel?

Playing the Glasses
You can make a sound by tapping on a drinking glass. If you put water in the glass, the pitch of the sound changes. Use water and several glasses to make different notes. How does adding water to the glasses affect the pitch of the sounds you make?

Sound Transmission

Have you ever set up a line of dominoes and then knocked them down? The first domino pushes over the second and so on. The wave of energy moves down the line, but the individual dominoes do not. Sound has energy just like the dominoes. Waves can carry energy a long distance. The energy travels from place to place, but the matter that carries the energy stays where it is.

In a similar way, sound waves move through air because particles in the air vibrate right where they are.

When you talk to a friend, vibrations move from you to your friend through the air. But the air doesn't have to move to your friend. If it did, a breeze blowing in your face would prevent your friend from hearing your words because they'd be blown back to you!

Science Up Close

How Sound Reaches You

Molecules of air carry sound waves from the source to the listeners.

When the performer sings, she produces vibrations that compress the air.

The sound moves through the air as compression waves.

Air is not the only matter that can carry sound waves. Any kind of matter can be made to vibrate and carry sound. Matter that carries sound waves is called a *medium.* Sound waves can't travel without a medium. That's why there's no sound in space, which has no air or other suitable medium.

The speed of sound depends on the medium through which it's moving. The speed doesn't depend on how loud or soft the volume is or how high or low the pitch is. All sounds travel through a certain kind of medium at the same speed.

If the medium changes, the speed of sound changes. Sound moves faster in warm air than in cold air. It travels faster in solids and liquids than it does in gases.

 MAIN IDEA AND DETAILS In reference to sound traveling, what is a medium?

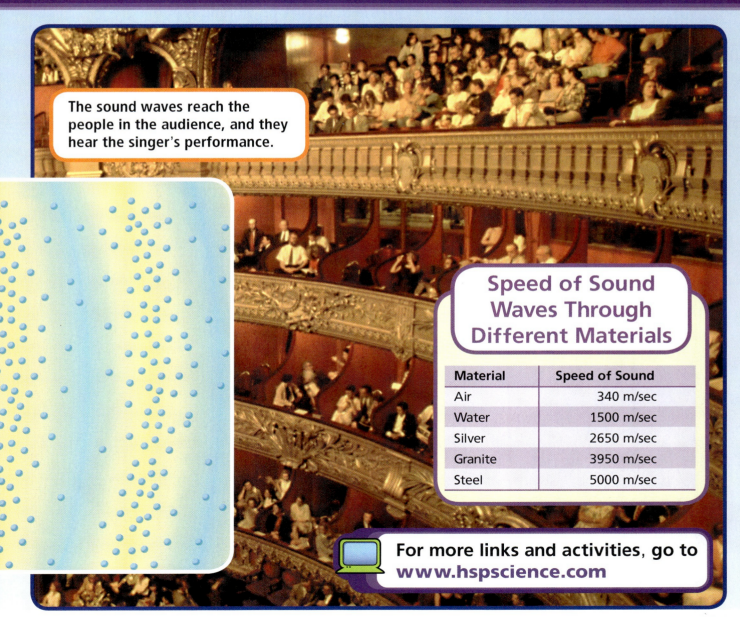

The sound waves reach the people in the audience, and they hear the singer's performance.

Speed of Sound Waves Through Different Materials

Material	Speed of Sound
Air	340 m/sec
Water	1500 m/sec
Silver	2650 m/sec
Granite	3950 m/sec
Steel	5000 m/sec

For more links and activities, go to www.hspscience.com

Animals and Sound

People can hear sounds over a wide range of frequencies. The highest sounds that people can hear have frequencies of about 20,000 vibrations per second.

Many animals can hear sounds that are outside the range of human hearing. Dogs can hear sounds with higher frequencies than people can hear—frequencies of 25,000 vibrations per second.

Bats have better hearing than most other animals. They can hear sounds with frequencies as high as 100,000 vibrations per second. Bats can also produce sounds with that frequency.

As a bat flies, it produces many short, high-frequency sounds. These bounce off objects in the bat's path, and the bat hears the echoes. The echoes help the bat fly at night by giving it information about its surroundings. They also help the bat hunt. Echoes that bounce from insects give information to the bat about where to find its next meal.

People, dogs, and bats have parts of their ears on the outside of their bodies. But this isn't true for all animals. Snakes and birds have no outside ear parts.

Grasshoppers pick up vibrations in several ways. A membrane near the leg picks up vibrations in the air. Hairlike structures on the body pick up vibrations in the ground.

 MAIN IDEA AND DETAILS What are two ways animals sense vibrations?

A bat uses echoes to find its prey in the dark.

A grasshopper picks up vibrations through structures near its hind legs.

A snake uses its lower jaw to sense vibrations from the ground.

1. MAIN IDEA AND DETAILS Draw and complete this graphic organizer.

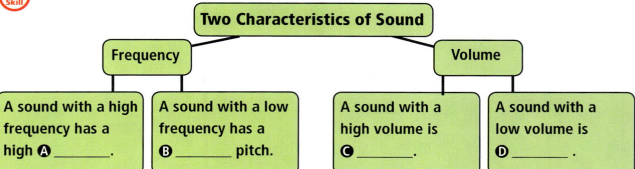

Two Characteristics of Sound

Frequency

Volume

A sound with a high frequency has a high **Ⓐ** _____ .

Ⓑ _____ pitch.

A sound with a high volume is **Ⓒ** _____ .

A sound with a low volume is **Ⓓ** _____ .

2. SUMMARIZE Write two sentences that tell what this lesson is mainly about.

3. DRAW CONCLUSIONS A guitar player changes the vibrating length of the strings by holding them down against the frets, which are ridges on the guitar. What does changing the length in this way do to the sound?

4. VOCABULARY Write a paragraph that uses the terms in this lesson.

FCAT Prep

5. Read/Think/Explain Why does carpet make a room seem quiet?

6. Which happens to a sound if the frequency of the vibrations increases?

   A. The volume decreases.
   B. The pitch increases.
   C. The sound echoes.
   D. The sound gets louder.

Links

Writing

Narrative Writing

Write a **story** about how a bat hunts for insects. Write your story from the bat's point of view.

Math

Construct a Graph

Research the speed sound travels through different materials. Make a bar graph to show your data. Be sure to include the materials listed in Science Up Close.

Social Studies

The Sound Barrier

A vehicle that travels faster than the speed of sound is said to break the sound barrier. Find out what kinds of vehicles have broken the sound barrier. Make a time line to show your findings.

 For more links and activities, go to www.hspscience.com

Building a Safer Race Car

Fasten your seat belt. The world's most dangerous sport just got safer. The car-racing world was shocked in 2001 when stock-car champion Dale Earnhardt died in a crash at the Daytona 500. Earnhardt died when his car struck the track's retaining wall during the last lap of the race.

The accident, which followed three other fatal accidents that year, showed just how dangerous car racing is. Now new equipment for both cars and drivers has made stock-car racing safer.

Strapped In

The most important safety change has been to improve the way drivers are strapped into their seats. NASCAR (National Association for Stock Car Auto Racing) now requires that all drivers wear head-and-neck restraints. These restraints keep a driver's head from violently slamming about during a crash. Other new restraints are designed to keep a driver's head and arms inside the car's cockpit during an accident.

Racing teams are also now experimenting with new seat materials and designs to keep a driver safe. For example, some new seats are being made from a carbon fiber material. This material is superstrong but is also lightweight.

The Black Box

After Dale Earnhardt's accident, NASCAR officials began installing "black boxes" on cars. A black box monitors a vehicle's motion throughout a race and records information on what goes on inside the car during a crash. Investigators use similar recorders to determine the causes of airplane accidents.

Other safety developments include these:

- NASCAR engineers have recommended that new kinds of fire extinguishers be built into cars.
- Since race car doors do not open, some have been equipped with rooftop escape hatches to let a driver out quickly.
- Engineers have developed a superstrong strap to keep a car's wheels from flying off during a crash.
- Mechanics have installed special air filters that keep deadly gases, such as carbon monoxide, from seeping into the cockpit of a race car.

Safety has not been limited to race cars. At many racetracks, engineers have begun installing "soft walls." These barriers are made of steel-and-foam cushioning. The soft walls help absorb energy when struck at high speeds by a 3,400-pound race car.

Think About It

1. Why does a race car driver need so much safety equipment?
2. How would "soft walls" at a race track absorb a car's energy?

Find out more! Log on to
www.hspscience.com

Speeds in NASCAR races can exceed 200 mi/hr.

SC.H.3.2.1.5.1 technology has improved human lives; **SC.H.3.2.1.5.2** some inventions lead to others; **SC.H.3.2.4.5.1** people can solve problems through science

205

Flipping Over Flip-Itz

Two once-bored boys from Illinois are now flipping out! They're the inventors of "Flip-Itz," the three-legged toys with human, animal, and alien faces that flip through the air. Matthew Balick and Justin Lewis, both 11 years old, got the idea while at a pizza party.

"We were bored, and the pizza wasn't even that good," said Justin. The boys began playing with the small three-legged pieces of plastic used to keep pizza cheese from sticking to the top of a delivery box.

The boys' fathers helped Justin and Matthew form their own company, 2 Bored Boys, Inc. Flip-Itz are headed for stores nationwide.

You Can Do It!

Materials
- index card
- cup or glass
- coin

Quick and Easy Project

Newton's First Law

Procedure

1. Balance the card on top of the cup or glass. Place the coin on the card, near the center.
2. With your fingers, flick the card away from the cup or glass.
3. Observe what happens to the coin.
4. Repeat Steps 1 and 2, but place the coin near the edge of the card. Observe what happens.

Draw Conclusions

1. What happened to the coin when the card was pushed off the rim of the glass?
2. Use the idea of inertia and Newton's first law of motion to explain your observations.

Design Your Own Investigation

Investigate Newton's Second Law

Design an investigation to show Newton's second law—force equals mass times acceleration. Use simple classroom materials. You could show the law with something as simple as a ball. The materials you use are up to you. Before you begin, write up your plan for the experiment and get your teacher's approval.

Vocabulary Review

Use the terms below to complete the sentences. The page numbers tell you where to look in the chapter if you need help.

position p. 176   acceleration p. 180
speed p. 178   inertia p. 187
velocity p. 178   volume p. 197

1. The speed and direction of a moving object are its _____.

2. The location of an object in space is its _____.

3. The distance an object travels in a certain amount of time is its _____.

4. The rate at which velocity changes is _____.

5. The tendency of objects to resist a change in motion is _____.

6. The loudness of a sound is also known as _____.

Check Understanding

Write the letter of the best choice.

7. When a boy lands on a trampoline, he pushes down on the trampoline. What is the reaction force?
   A. gravity pulling the boy down
   B. the boy pushing down
   C. the friction between the boy and the trampoline
   D. the trampoline pushing upward

8. In the diagram below, in which direction will the object move?

force → object

   F. in the direction opposite to the direction of the force
   G. in the same direction as the force
   H. at right angles to the force
   I. in any direction

9. What must happen in order for a sound wave to form?
   A. An electric current must flow.
   B. A certain frequency must be reached.
   C. Matter must vibrate.
   D. Volume must be absorbed.

10. A worm crawls 2 meters in 2 hours. What is the worm's speed?
    F. 1 m/hr   H. 4 m/hr
    G. 2 m/hr   I. 10 m/hr

11. A girl ice-skates in a circle at a constant speed of 10 km/hr. What part of her motion is changing?
    A. acceleration   C. speed
    B. friction   D. velocity

12. What is the result if someone hits a drum harder than it was hit before?
    F. The number of decibels increases.
    G. The pitch decreases.
    H. The frequency increases.
    I. The number of vibrations decreases.

13. A balloon rises at a rate of 2 km/hr. What is its velocity?

  A. 2 mi/hr, upward
  C. 2 km/sec/sec
  B. 2 km/hr, upward
  D. 2 km/hr

14. CAUSE AND EFFECT If you walk on a log that's floating in water, the log moves backward. Which of the following explains this?

  F. Newton's first law
  G. Newton's second law
  H. Newton's third law
  I. friction

15. A truck, a car, a motorcycle, and a train are all moving at the same speed. Which has the most momentum?

  A. car
  C. train
  B. motorcycle
  D. truck

16. MAIN IDEA AND DETAILS Which two factors determine momentum?

  F. mass and velocity
  G. force and mass
  H. mass and acceleration
  I. velocity and gravity

Inquiry Skills

17. Stephen is measuring the pitches of sound waves made by using strings of 12 different lengths. **Identify the variable** in Stephen's experiment.

18. How could a race-car driver keep the same engine (the same force) but increase the acceleration of the car? **Identify the control variable** and the **test variable** in the driver's test.

 # Read, Inquire, Explain

19. Look at the diagrams. For each one, state the reaction force.

  A.

  B.

  C.

  D.

20. Part A A cyclist travels at 40 km/hr going north. Another cyclist travels at 40 km/hr going south. Are the cyclists traveling at the same speed? The same velocity? Explain.

  Part B In what ways can the cyclists change their velocities? Name as many as you can.

Processes that Shape the Earth

EARTH SCIENCE

 The chapters in this unit address these Grade Level Expectations from the Florida Sunshine State Standards.

The investigations and experiences in this unit also address many of the Grade Level Expectations in Strand H, The Nature of Science.

Science in Florida

Blue Springs

Dear Alan,
I wish you could have been with us today at Blue Springs State Park. The crystal-clear spring water was flowing out of a big cave in the rocks. We talked to some scuba divers. They said that Florida is full of underground caves filled with flowing water. The water is purified as it flows underground, but the divers said they saw a lot of trash that people did not dispose of properly. We made sure to throw all of our trash into the dumpster.

Talk to you soon,

Terri

The Sunshine State

USA

FCAT Writing

Writing Situation
Think about litter and garbage. Explain why you should dispose of your trash properly.

Experiment!

Buffering Ability of Soils Acid rain is caused by pollution. It can change the soil and harm plants. Some soils are a good buffer for acid rain, which means the soil neutralizes the acids as the rain flows through the soil. Are soils in Florida a good buffer for acid rain? Plan and conduct an experiment to find out.

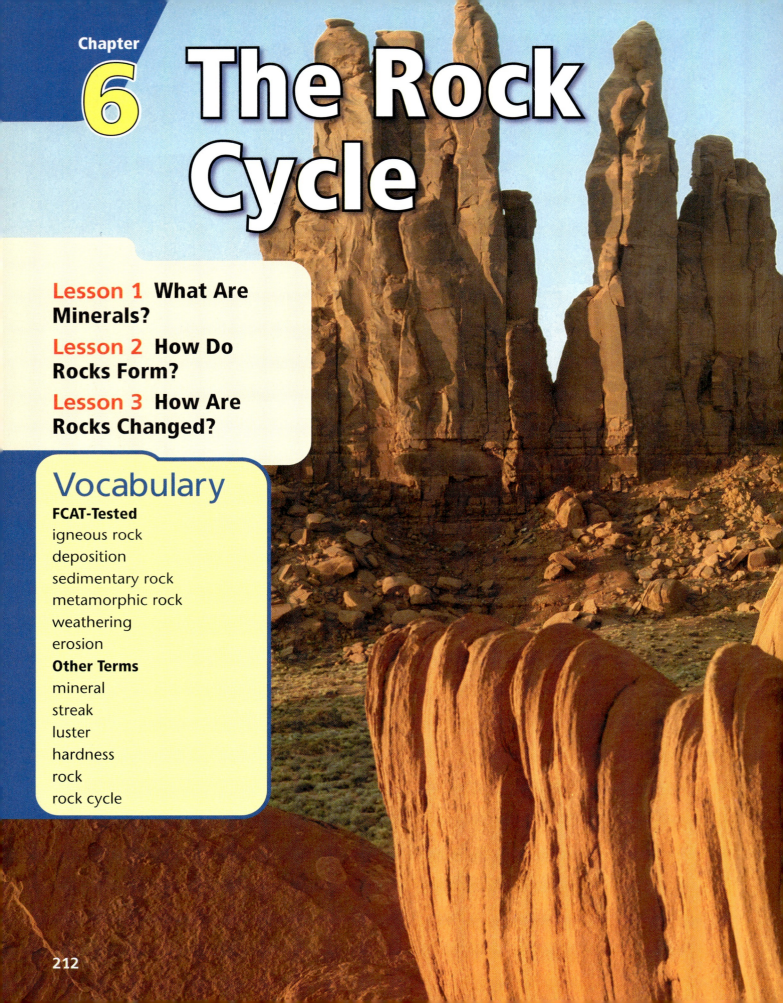

Chapter
6 The Rock Cycle

Lesson 1 What Are Minerals?

Lesson 2 How Do Rocks Form?

Lesson 3 How Are Rocks Changed?

Vocabulary

FCAT-Tested

igneous rock

deposition

sedimentary rock

metamorphic rock

weathering

erosion

Other Terms

mineral

streak

luster

hardness

rock

rock cycle

What do **YOU** wonder?

Joshua Tree National Park, in California, has rocks shaped like arches, soccer balls, and even skulls! What do you think could cause rocks to look like those in this photo?

What Are Minerals?

Fast Fact

Giant Gems! The Crown Jewels of Great Britain are set with thousands of diamonds, rubies, and sapphires. One diamond weighed 621.2 g (21.9 oz) before it was cut! A diamond is the hardest mineral known. That's one property that makes it a valuable gem. What property might make tanzanite, shown here, valuable? You'll learn about other mineral properties in the Investigate.

Mineral Properties

Materials
- 6 labeled mineral samples
- hand lens
- streak plate
- pre-1983 penny
- steel nail

Procedure

1. Copy the table.

2. Use the hand lens to observe each mineral's color. Record your observations in the table.

3. With each mineral, draw a line across the streak plate. What color is each mineral's streak? Record your observations.

4. **CAUTION: Use caution with the nail. It's sharp.** Test the hardness of each mineral. Try to scratch each mineral with your fingernail, the penny, and the steel nail. Then try to scratch each mineral with each of the other minerals. Record your observations in the table.

5. Classify the minerals by using the properties you tested: color, streak, and hardness. For each mineral, make a label that lists all three properties.

Step 3

Mineral Sample	Color of the Mineral Sample	Color of the Mineral's Streak	Things That Scratch the Mineral
A			
B			
C			
D			
E			
F			

Draw Conclusions

1. How are the mineral samples different from one another?

2. **Inquiry Skill** Scientists classify objects to make them easier to study. How do you think scientists classify minerals?

Investigate Further

Obtain five additional mineral samples. Classify each sample according to its color, streak, hardness, and one new property.

Reading in Science

SC.A.1.2.1 properties of materials can be compared and measured; **LA.A.2.2.1** main idea and details

VOCABULARY
mineral p. 216
streak p. 217
luster p. 217
hardness p. 218

SCIENCE CONCEPTS
▶ what minerals are
▶ how to identify minerals

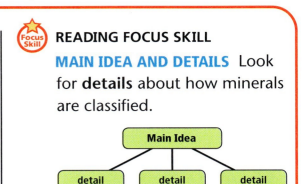

READING FOCUS SKILL

MAIN IDEA AND DETAILS Look for **details** about how minerals are classified.

Some Mineral Properties

You probably have heard the word *mineral* before. Foods that are healthful for you are full of vitamins and minerals. Bottled mineral water is often sold at the grocery store. Beautiful minerals such as diamonds and rubies are used in jewelry. But what exactly is a mineral? A **mineral** is a naturally occurring, nonliving solid that has a specific chemical makeup and a *crystalline*, or repeating, structure.

You may already be familiar with several kinds of minerals. Quartz, diamond, and salt are all minerals. So are the ores of metals such as copper, silver, and iron. There are hundreds of different minerals. So how do scientists identify all these minerals? Scientists use *mineral properties*, or characteristics, to identify and classify the more than 2000 different minerals that have been found on Earth.

One property of minerals that's easy to see is color. Minerals come in a rainbow of colors.

Mineral Color

Some minerals, such as quartz, are found in a variety of colors.

Rose quartz

Clear quartz

Amethyst quartz

Smoky quartz

216

Mineral Luster

Gypsum has a pearly luster.

Talc has a waxy luster.

Topaz has a glassy luster.

Pyrite has a metallic luster.

But color alone cannot be used to identify a mineral. For example, some minerals, such as quartz, are found in many different colors. Scientists need to use additional properties when classifying most minerals.

Another mineral property is streak. **Streak** is the color of the powder left behind when you rub a mineral against a rough white tile, or a streak plate. Many minerals make a streak that is the same color as the mineral. However, some minerals do not. For instance, hematite is silver, black, or dark brown. But its streak is red-brown. Streak is a better property for mineral identification than color, because—unlike color—streak does not vary. All colors of quartz make the same streak.

The way a mineral's surface reflects light is a property called **luster**. Many minerals have a metallic luster. Think of how light reflects off metals such as gold, silver, and copper. Pyrite, or fool's gold, has a metallic luster. Other minerals have a nonmetallic

luster. The luster of a nonmetallic mineral can be described as dull, glassy, pearly, waxy, and so on. For examples of different lusters, look at the minerals pictured above.

 MAIN IDEA AND DETAILS What are three visible properties of minerals?

Mineral Streak

The colors of these two pieces of hematite are different, but their streak is the same.

Mohs' Hardness Scale

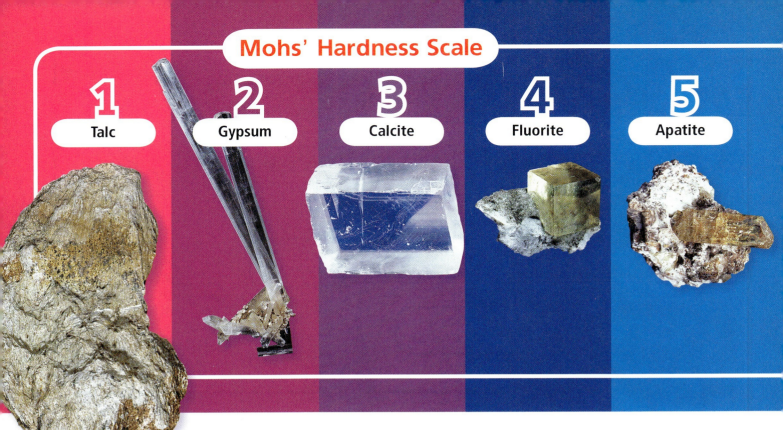

1 Talc

2 Gypsum

3 Calcite

4 Fluorite

5 Apatite

Pass the Salt, Please!

Most minerals are crystalline in structure. Examine some grains of table salt with a hand lens. Note whether individual grains look like tiny crystals. Describe their shape.

Mineral Hardness

Most people would agree that objects such as rocks, nails, and glass are hard. An important property of minerals is hardness. **Hardness** is a mineral's ability to resist being scratched. Some minerals are so hard that they can't be scratched by anything. Others scratch easily. A German scientist, Friedrich Mohs (MOHZ), found that minerals can be classified by how hard they are to scratch. He came up with a scale that ranks minerals from 1 to 10 according to their hardness.

The scale is called the *Mohs' hardness scale*. On this scale, the softest mineral—talc—is classified as a 1. Diamond, the hardest mineral, is classified as a 10. Any mineral higher on the scale can scratch any mineral lower on the scale.

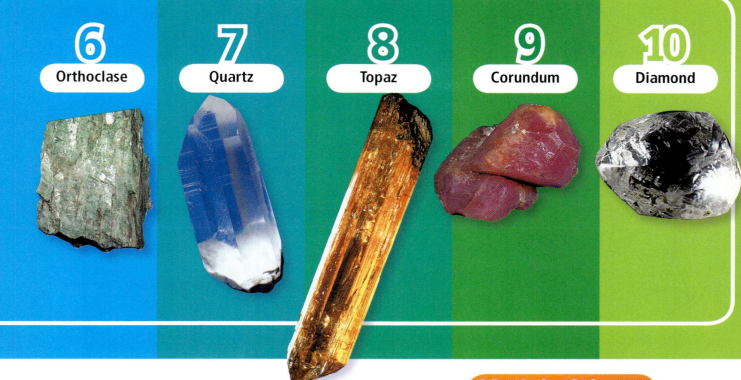

6	7	8	9	10
Orthoclase	Quartz	Topaz	Corundum	Diamond

The Mohs' scale is easy to use. If you have several minerals for which you know the hardness, you can use them to determine the hardness of an unknown mineral. You can also use common materials to test a mineral's hardness. For example, your fingernail has a hardness of about 2.5. That means your fingernail should be able to scratch any mineral that has a hardness of 1 or 2. A copper penny has a hardness of 3. (Be sure the penny was made before 1983. Pennies made after that are mostly zinc.) Steel nails have a hardness of about 5.5, and ordinary glass has a hardness of about 6.

 MAIN IDEA AND DETAILS How can you determine the hardness of a mineral?

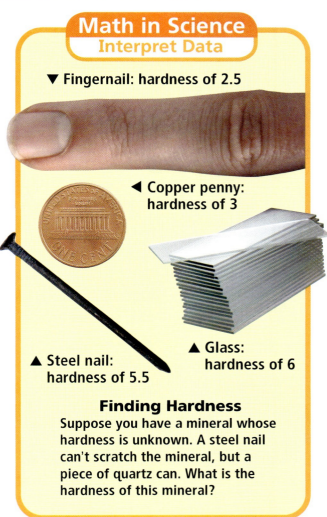

Math in Science
Interpret Data

▼ **Fingernail: hardness of 2.5**

◄ **Copper penny: hardness of 3**

▲ **Glass: hardness of 6**

▲ **Steel nail: hardness of 5.5**

Finding Hardness
Suppose you have a mineral whose hardness is unknown. A steel nail can't scratch the mineral, but a piece of quartz can. What is the hardness of this mineral?

Unique Properties of Minerals

You have unique characteristics that make you different from everyone else. Some minerals have unique properties that make them different, too. For example, the crystal structure of calcite (KAL•syt) refracts, or bends, light a certain way. If you place a picture behind a piece of calcite, you will see a double image of the picture.

The mineral magnetite (MAG•nuh•tyt) is magnetic. Magnetite is also called lodestone, after the word *lode*, which means "way." Lodestone can be used in a compass to help you find your way.

Some kinds of minerals glow under ultraviolet, or "black" light. Just as quartz can be found in many different colors, certain minerals glow in different colors. For example, corundum can glow red, yellow, green, or blue.

A few minerals—such as quartz—develop an electric potential when pressure is applied to them. This will also happen to quartz when the temperature changes. Because of this property, quartz is often used in computers, cell phones, radios, televisions, and watches.

 MAIN IDEA AND DETAILS What are four special properties of minerals?

◄ Calcite produces a double image.

◄ Fluorite glows, or fluoresces, under certain kinds of light.

Magnetite attracts materials containing iron. ▶

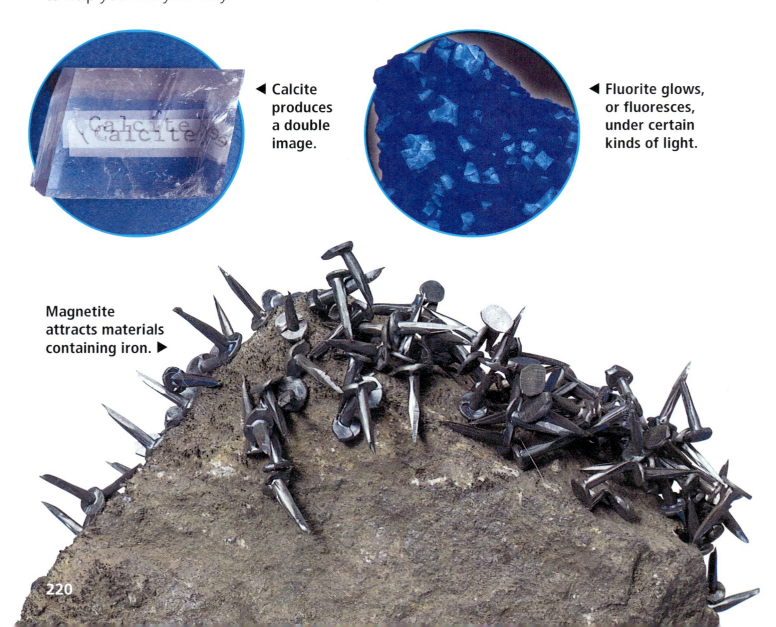

1. MAIN IDEA AND DETAILS Draw and complete the graphic organizer.

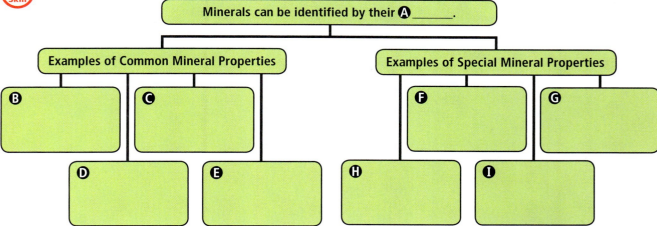

Minerals can be identified by their **Ⓐ** _____.

Examples of Common Mineral Properties

Ⓑ **Ⓒ**

Ⓓ **Ⓔ**

Examples of Special Mineral Properties

Ⓕ **Ⓖ**

Ⓗ **Ⓘ**

2. SUMMARIZE Use the graphic organizer to write a lesson summary.

3. DRAW CONCLUSIONS Suppose you have two mineral samples with the same hardness. What other mineral properties could you use to decide whether the two samples are the same mineral?

4. VOCABULARY Choose a mineral, and write a short paragraph describing its streak, luster, and hardness.

FCAT Prep

5. Read/Inquire/Explain What characteristic of a mineral does the term *luster* describe?

6. Which of the following mineral properties can be expressed by a number?

A. color **C.** luster

B. hardness **D.** streak

Links

Writing

Expository Writing
Write two paragraphs **comparing and contrasting** different ways minerals can be classified.

Math

Use Measuring Devices
Collect several mineral samples that are about the same size. Use a balance to find the mass of each sample. Explain why minerals that are the same size may have very different masses.

Social Studies

Mineral Collage
Cut out pictures of minerals from old magazines. You may find minerals shown in many things, such as buildings, jewelry, and coins. Use the mineral pictures to make a mineral collage.

 For more links and activities, go to **www.hspscience.com**

How Do Rocks Form?

Fast Fact

The Sands of Time This rock formation in Arizona is part of the famous Vermillion Cliffs. It is a 200-million-year-old sand dune that has turned to rock! In the Investigate, you'll identify some other kinds of rock.

Identifying Rocks

Materials
- hand lens
- 5 labeled rock samples
- safety goggles
- dropper
- vinegar
- paper plate

Procedure

1. Copy the table. In the column labeled *Picture,* make a drawing of each rock.

2. Use the hand lens to observe each rock. In the table, record each rock's color.

3. Look at the grains that make up each rock. Notice their sizes. Are their edges rounded or sharp? How do the grains fit together? Under *Texture* in the table, record your observations.

4. **CAUTION: Put on the safety goggles.** Vinegar makes bubbles form on rocks that contain calcite. Put the rocks on the paper plate. Use the dropper to slowly drop some vinegar onto each rock. Observe the results, and record your findings.

5. Classify the rocks into two groups so that the rocks in each group have similar properties.

Rock Sample	Color	Texture	Picture	Bubbles When Vinegar Added
1				
2				
3				
4				
5				

Step 4

Draw Conclusions

1. What properties did you use to classify the rocks?

2. **Inquiry Skill** Scientists classify objects to make them easier to study. One way scientists classify rocks is by how they form. Choose one of the rocks, and describe how it might have formed.

Investigate Further

Hypothesize about the best property to use to identify rocks. **Plan and conduct an investigation** to test your hypothesis.

SC.D.1.2.1.5.1 rocks change; **SC.D.2.2.1.5.1** reuse, recycle, reduce resources; **LA.E.2.2.1** cause and effect

VOCABULARY
rock p. 224
igneous rock p. 224
deposition p. 226
sedimentary rock p. 226
metamorphic rock p. 228

SCIENCE CONCEPTS
▶ how rocks form
▶ how people use rocks

READING FOCUS SKILL
CAUSE AND EFFECT Look for what **causes** rocks to form.

cause ⟶ effect

Igneous Rocks

What are mountains, valleys, hills, beaches, and the ocean floor made of? Rocks! Rocks are found almost everywhere on Earth. You've probably seen many different kinds of rocks. But all rocks have one thing in common— minerals. A **rock** is a natural solid made of one or more minerals. In fact, you might think of most rocks as mineral mixtures.

Rocks are classified into one of three groups depending on how they form. Rock that forms when melted rock cools and hardens is called **igneous rock** (IG•nee•uhs). Igneous rocks can form underground, or they can form on Earth's surface.

Igneous rocks that form underground cool much more slowly than those that form on the surface. Below ground, the surrounding rocks hold in the heat. On the surface, melted rock cools quickly.

This igneous rock, called *rhyolite*, forms above ground. It contains the same minerals as granite, but the mineral crystals are smaller.

This igneous rock, called *granite*, forms below ground. It has large mineral crystals.

224

When melted rock cools slowly, mineral crystals have time to grow. Because of this, igneous rocks that form underground have large crystals.

When melted rock cools quickly, it hardens before any mineral crystals can grow large. As a result, igneous rocks that form above ground have small or no crystals.

The size of mineral crystals is not the only difference among igneous rocks. Different igneous rocks contain different amounts or different kinds of minerals. That's because not all melted rock beneath Earth's surface is the same.

For example, igneous rocks that form from melted rock containing a lot of silica will also have a lot of silica. One way it shows up in the rocks is as the mineral quartz. Igneous rocks that form from melted rock with little silica will have other kinds of minerals and will be different rocks.

 CAUSE AND EFFECT What causes igneous rocks to form?

Igneous Rocks

▲ *Basalt* (buh•SAWLT) is the most common type of igneous rock. It forms above ground. It has small mineral crystals.

▲ *Gabbro* is made of the same minerals as basalt, but it forms below ground. It has big mineral crystals. Gabbro is sometimes used to make concrete.

▲ *Pumice* (PUHM•is) has a lot of air spaces and is very light. Some people use pumice stones to smooth their skin.

▲ *Obsidian* is also called volcanic glass. Surgeons once used blades made of obsidian because it breaks into sharp pieces.

Sedimentary Rocks

Picture a rock at the top of a hill. Every spring, rain falls on the rock, dissolving some of its minerals. In summer, the heat of the sun causes the rock to crack, and small pieces flake off. Fall arrives, and windblown dust slowly scratches the rock's surface. In winter, water seeps into cracks in the rock and freezes. The ice expands, breaking off more pieces of the rock. This rock is slowly being worn away.

What happens to all the little pieces of rock, called *sediment,* that have worn away? Sediment is carried off by water and wind. It is often set down, or *deposited,* in another place. This process in which sediment settles out of water or is dropped by the wind is called **deposition** (dep•uh•ZISH•uhn).

Over time, sediment piles up, one layer on top of another, pressing together tightly. Some minerals dissolved in water come out of solution, forming a kind of cement. This makes the sediment stick together. Cemented sediment forms a type of rock called **sedimentary rock** (sed•uh•MEN•tuh•ree).

Sedimentary rocks form from any rock that is worn down. Sediment of any size can be found in sedimentary rocks. Some sedimentary rocks have big pieces of sediment in them. Others contain grains of sand, or even smaller pieces. Some

Sedimentary Rocks

▲ A conglomerate (kuhn•GLAHM•er•it) rock is a sedimentary rock that is formed from sand, rounded pebbles, and larger pieces of rock.

▲ Sandstone is a sedimentary rock made up of sediment pieces the size of sand grains.

▲ Shale is a sedimentary rock made up of tiny, dust-size pieces of sediment.

▲ Limestone is a sedimentary rock that is usually formed in oceans from seashells, which are largely made of the mineral calcite. There is often more calcite between shells, cementing them together.

◀ As water moves through Florida Caverns, it dissolves minerals from the rocks. As this mineral-rich water drips, some of it forms icicle-like *stalactites* (stuh•LAK•tytz). Drops pile up on the floor and harden to form *stalagmites* (stuh•LAG•mytz).

sedimentary rocks have the remains of living things, such as shells, within the sediment. Other sedimentary rocks form when mineral-rich water evaporates. Try placing a pan of salt water in a warm area. When the water dries up, you will have salt. When this happens in nature, the mineral formed is called *halite*. Large deposits of halite are rock salt, a sedimentary rock.

After a sedimentary rock forms, it might be worn away. Sediment from the rock may be deposited in a different location or in a different way, forming a completely different sedimentary rock. This is one way that rocks are constantly changing. In the next section and in Lesson 3, you'll learn about other ways that rocks change.

 **CAUSE AND EFFECT** How do sedimentary rocks form?

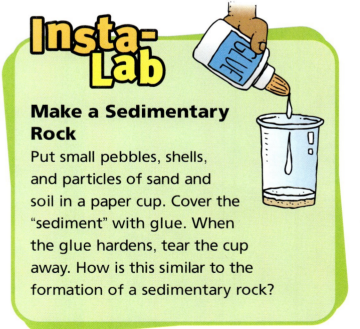

Insta-Lab

Make a Sedimentary Rock

Put small pebbles, shells, and particles of sand and soil in a paper cup. Cover the "sediment" with glue. When the glue hardens, tear the cup away. How is this similar to the formation of a sedimentary rock?

Metamorphic Rocks

Have you ever seen a caterpillar change into a butterfly? This process is called *metamorphosis* (met•uh•MAWR•fuh•sis), from the Greek words *meta*, meaning "change," and *morphosis,* meaning "form." Rocks, too, can change form under certain conditions. When rock is changed by heat and pressure, the new rock is called **metamorphic rock**. Metamorphic rocks can form from any other rock—including igneous rocks, sedimentary rocks, and other metamorphic rocks.

Where is there enough pressure and heat to change rocks? Metamorphic rocks are found in every mountain range on Earth. Picture the processes working there. Suppose you have a ball of clay. You place a book on top of the clay, and then another and another book. Soon you have a dozen books piled on top of the clay. What happens to the clay? As you can imagine, it becomes flat and very, very thin!

Now suppose the ball of clay is a rock somewhere in northern New Mexico. Instead of a pile of books on top of it, there is a huge mountain with a mass of millions and millions of kilograms. The weight of the mountain squashes the rock. The rock also gets very hot, because as pressure increases, temperature rises. All this heat and pressure changes the old rock into a new rock—a metamorphic rock.

Metamorphic rocks form in other places, too. Imagine an ocean floor where layers of sediment are constantly being piled on top

These layers of metamorphic rock, called Vishnu Schist, were formed in the Grand Canyon when sandstone was changed by pressure and heat. ▼

▲ Schist (SHIST) may form from sandstone. As mountains build up, they put a huge amount of pressure on sedimentary rocks.

▲ Gneiss (NYS) can form when granite, an igneous rock, is subjected to a lot of pressure.

▲ Slate is formed from a small-grained sedimentary rock such as shale.

▲ Quartzite is formed from sandstone that is made almost entirely of the mineral quartz.

Marble forms from calcite-rich limestone, so it is often white. Small amounts of other minerals give marble its colors. ▶

of one another. Stuck together by minerals that act as cement, sedimentary rocks form. In time, these rocks may be pushed under other rocks, causing them to change into metamorphic rocks.

Metamorphic rocks also form near some volcanoes. Volcanoes are places where melted rock rises above Earth's surface.

The melted rock is extremely hot—not hot enough to melt nearby rocks, but hot enough to change them into metamorphic rocks. Even igneous rocks can become metamorphic rocks.

 CAUSE AND EFFECT What causes metamorphic rocks to form?

How Rocks Are Used

Rocks have always been an important natural resource for people. Thousands of years ago, people used rocks called *flint* to make hand tools. Even today, rocks are used to make tools of many kinds—from sandpaper to surgical instruments.

People also use rocks such as sandstone, granite, limestone, and marble to build buildings and monuments. The Capitol building of the United States contains both sandstone and marble. The Great Pyramid of Giza in Egypt was made out of sandstone covered with limestone. In fact, everywhere in the world, you'll find important buildings and monuments made of rocks. Rocks are also used to make cement, glass, gravel, and other building materials.

Remember that rocks are made of minerals. Many minerals and the metals they contain are used in products such as cell phones, cars, and computers.

Rocks and minerals are natural resources, and so they must be conserved. People can conserve them by recycling metal products, such as cans, and by reusing rock from buildings. Recycling and reusing also protect the environment by reducing the need to dig into Earth for more resources.

CAUSE AND EFFECT How does the durability of rocks affect the way people use them?

Many things are made from granite, an igneous rock, including buildings, monuments, and kitchen countertops. ▼

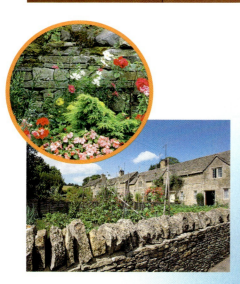

▲ This garden wall is made of limestone, a sedimentary rock. Pieces of the wall may have been used in an earlier wall or building.

The Taj Mahal in India, like many grand buildings and monuments, is made of marble, a metamorphic rock. ▶

Focus Skill

1. CAUSE AND EFFECT Draw and complete the graphic organizer.

CAUSE ⟶ EFFECT

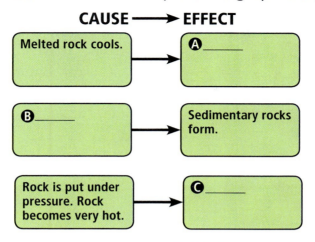

CAUSE		EFFECT
Melted rock cools.	→	Ⓐ _____
Ⓑ _____	→	Sedimentary rocks form.
Rock is put under pressure. Rock becomes very hot.	→	Ⓒ _____

2. SUMMARIZE Write a summary of this lesson by using the lesson vocabulary in a paragraph.

3. DRAW CONCLUSIONS You find an igneous rock with large crystals in it. Where was the rock formed? Explain your answer.

4. VOCABULARY Write three sentences that describe the three main types of rock. Give an example of each type.

FCAT Prep

5. Read/Inquire/Explain How can different kinds of igneous rocks be classified?

6. What kind of rock is gneiss?
- **A.** igneous
- **B.** marble
- **C.** metamorphic
- **D.** sedimentary

Links

Writing

Narrative Writing
Write a poem using as many adjectives as you can to **describe** how rocks form and change.

Math 9÷3

Use Mental Math
If it takes 150 years for a mountain to grow 2.5 cm, how many years will go by before the mountain is 10 cm taller?

Art

Stone Sculptures
Over the centuries, sculptors have made many beautiful works of art from rock. Choose a sculpture. Make a fact sheet listing who made the sculpture and when, where, and why.

 For more links and activities, go to **www.hspscience.com**

How Are Rocks Changed?

Fast Fact

A Window on the World North Window in Arches National Park, Utah, is a natural bridge—a hole worn through a rock. The hole was carved by water. In the Investigate, you'll see what it takes to change rocks!

Molding Rocks

Materials
- small objects—gravel, sand, pieces of paper, several fake gems
- 3 pieces of modeling clay, each a different color
- 2 aluminum pie pans
- water

Procedure

1. Suppose the small objects are minerals. Press two different kinds of "minerals" into each piece of clay. Now you have three different "igneous rocks."

2. What happens when wind and water wear down rocks? To model this process, break one of the rocks into pieces and drop the "sediment" into a pie pan filled with water.

3. On top of the sediment pile, drop pieces of the second rock. Then drop pieces of the third rock. Press the layers together using the bottom of the empty pie pan. Now what kind of rock do you have?

4. Squeeze and mold the new rock between your hands to warm it up. What is making the rock change? Which kind of rock is it now?

Draw Conclusions

1. How did the igneous rocks change in this activity?

2. **Inquiry Skill** Scientists often use models to help them understand processes that occur in nature. What process did you model in Step 4 of this activity?

Step 1

Step 4

Investigate Further

Can any type of rock change into any other type? Make a model to explore this question.

VOCABULARY
weathering p. 234
erosion p. 235
rock cycle p. 236

SCIENCE CONCEPTS
▶ how rocks change over time
▶ how rocks move through the rock cycle

 READING FOCUS SKILL

SEQUENCE Look for **sequences** in which rocks change.

Processes That Change Rocks

After a volcano erupts, molten rock hardens into igneous rock. But this isn't the end of the story for the newly formed rock. As you learned in Lesson 2, rocks are constantly being formed and worn away.

Igneous rocks, like all rock on Earth's surface, are exposed to wind, water, ice, sunlight, and more. All of these factors break down rocks into sediment. The process of wearing away rocks by natural processes is called **weathering**.

All rocks on Earth's surface are weathered. But not all rocks weather at the same rate. In Lesson 1, you discovered that minerals have different degrees of hardness. Some minerals, such as corundum and diamond, can't be easily scratched because they're hard. Others, such as talc, can be easily scratched because they're soft. Rocks that contain mostly hard minerals weather much more slowly than rocks that contain mostly soft minerals. So granite, which contains feldspar and quartz, weathers more slowly than limestone, which contains mostly calcite.

Weathering is only the beginning of a process that changes rocks on Earth's

After rock has been weathered, what remains may look unusual.

As soon as igneous rock cools, it begins to weather.

◄ The Colorado River erodes sediment from one area and moves it downstream. Some of the sediment is deposited at the river's mouth, forming a delta.

surface. The wind and water that weather rocks are part of another process. Wind and water move sediment from one place to another. The process of wearing away and removing sediment by wind, water, or ice is called **erosion**.

After erosion, sediment can be deposited, pressed together, and cemented, forming sedimentary rock. As more layers of sediment are deposited, processes that cement the sediment speed up.

Processes using pressure and heat, which form metamorphic rock, can take place where mountain ranges have formed. Rock layers in mountain ranges are often folded, broken, and upturned, showing that the rocks have been through many changes.

 SEQUENCE What happens to sediment after weathering?

The rock layers exposed by this road cut were bent and folded as this mountain formed.

235

The Rock Cycle

Weathering, erosion, deposition, heat, and pressure can all change rocks. Together, these processes make up the rock cycle. The ==rock cycle== is the continuous process in which one type of rock changes into another type. Study the Science Up Close feature to see how the rock cycle works.

 SEQUENCE What sequence of events would have to take place to change a metamorphic rock into an igneous rock?

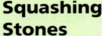

Squashing Stones

Use your metamorphic "rock" from the Investigate. Fold it in half and then in half again. Squeeze it tightly between your hands. Then cut through it with a plastic knife. How is this "rock" like the rock layers found in mountains?

The Rock Cycle

Just as you recycle aluminum cans and waste paper, Earth recycles rocks through the rock cycle.

Igneous Rock

Granite, an igneous rock, can be changed into sandstone, a sedimentary rock, through weathering and erosion. Heat and pressure can change granite into a metamorphic rock. With enough heat, granite can melt and harden into a new igneous rock.

Sedimentary Rock

Heat and pressure can change sandstone, a sedimentary rock, into gneiss, a metamorphic rock. If sandstone is melted, it hardens into an igneous rock when it cools. If sandstone is weathered and eroded, it can form a new sedimentary rock.

Metamorphic Rock

Gneiss (NYS), a metamorphic rock, can be weathered, eroded, deposited, and cemented into a sedimentary rock. If a metamorphic rock is melted and then hardens again, it will become an igneous rock. With heat and pressure, a metamorphic rock can become a new metamorphic rock.

For more links and activities, go to
www.hspscience.com

Soil Formation

The next time you're outside, take a close look at the soil under your feet. Soils around the world are very different from one another. They have many different colors and textures.

Some soils are good for farming. They contain the right amounts of both large and small particles. But some soils contain too much sand, which makes them dry out quickly. Other soils contain too much clay, which keeps them too wet. No matter how different soils are, though, they have one thing in common: they all come from weathered rock.

Soil can form from weathered rock right under it, or it can form from eroded sediment carried from far away. Because soils are made from rocks, they contain minerals. The kinds of minerals found in any soil depend on the kind of rock from which the soil formed. Certain minerals are needed for plant growth.

Most soil is made up of more than weathered rock. Rich farming soil also contains small pieces of decayed plant and animal matter, called *humus* (HYOO•muhs). Humus provides additional nutrients that plants need to grow. If these nutrients are missing, fertilizers must be added to the soil to meet the plants' needs.

 SEQUENCE **What must happen first for soil to form?**

Soil often forms layers, with the smallest particles and the most humus in the top layer, or topsoil. Layers below the topsoil have larger and larger pieces of weathered rock.▶

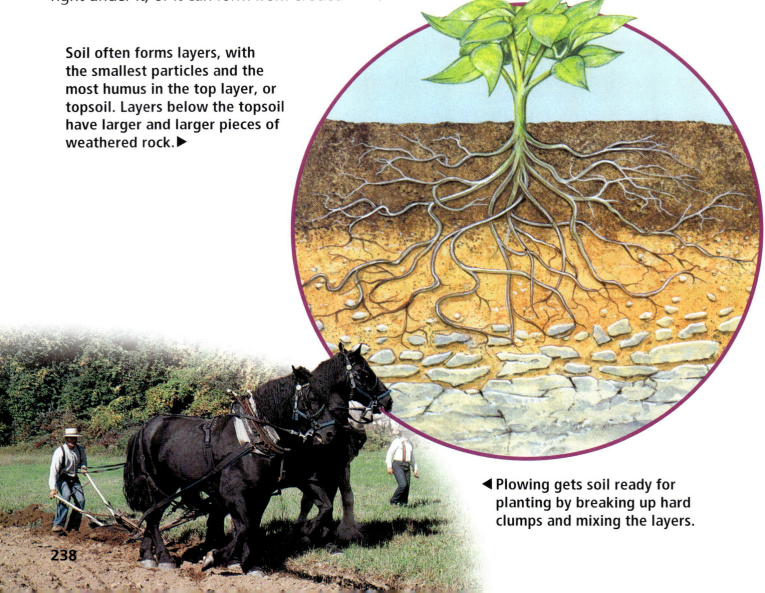

◀Plowing gets soil ready for planting by breaking up hard clumps and mixing the layers.

1. SEQUENCE Draw and complete the graphic organizer.

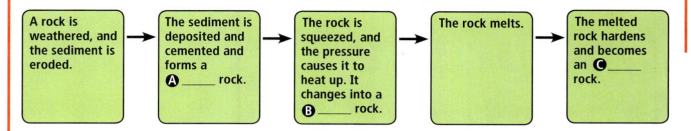

| A rock is weathered, and the sediment is eroded. | → | The sediment is deposited and cemented and forms a **A** _____ rock. | → | The rock is squeezed, and the pressure causes it to heat up. It changes into a **B** _____ rock. | → | The rock melts. | → | The melted rock hardens and becomes an **C** _____ rock. |

2. SUMMARIZE Draw a diagram that summarizes this lesson.

3. DRAW CONCLUSIONS How might a sedimentary rock change into another sedimentary rock?

4. VOCABULARY Write two or three sentences using terms from this lesson to explain how soil formation could be considered part of the rock cycle.

FCAT Prep

5. Read/Inquire/Explain What determines how quickly a rock is weathered?

6. Which of the following processes can change a metamorphic rock into a sedimentary rock?
   A. adding pressure
   B. increasing temperature
   C. melting
   D. weathering

Links

Writing

Expository Writing
Write a newspaper article **describing** the erosion of a local valley or river bank.

Math

Subtract Fractions
If $\frac{1}{4}$ of a granite rock is quartz, $\frac{5}{8}$ of the rock is feldspar, and the rest is mica, what fraction of the rock is mica?

Social Studies

Time Line
Research a famous landform. How old is it? How fast is it eroding? Make a time line showing the landform's changes.

For more links and activities, go to
www.hspscience.com

King of the Mountain

When Jerod Minich prepares to climb a mountain or scale a rock cliff, he makes sure he has all the right equipment. That equipment includes ropes, hammers, and his high-tech artificial legs and feet.

Minich is an experienced climber who had both his legs amputated below the knees when he was a child. He suffered from a disease called *diabetes,* and doctors had to cut off his legs to save his life.

In the past few years, Minich, of East Stroudsburg, Pennsylvania, has climbed some of the most dangerous and unforgiving rocks in the United States. He has scaled Devils Tower in Wyoming and, most recently, a 70-foot wall of rock called "the Column" in Minnesota.

Not Stopping

New technology has helped Minich do the sport he loves so much. Minich can hike with the help of new superstrong and lightweight carbon-fiber feet.

The feet are attached to artificial legs that are specially designed to reduce the pressure Minich feels when climbing up a rock face.

Minich isn't the only athlete who relies on high-tech artificial legs to climb mountains. In Nepal, a country in Asia, doctors fit climber Nawang Sherpa with an artificial leg after he was injured in a motorcycle accident.

Nawang received his first artificial leg in 2001. After getting used to that for a year, Nawang later received an artificial climbing leg. Nawang's climbing leg is lighter than his regular leg, which allows him to climb farther and more comfortably.

Nawang brought two of these legs with him when he attempted to climb Mount Everest, Earth's tallest mountain. Nawang changed the leg when he lost weight during the climb, which is normal. The foot that was attached to the leg was designed so that it would allow Nawang to get traction on the rough terrain of Everest.

Using the high-tech leg worked so well that Nawang became the first amputee to climb Mount Everest.

Think About It

1. What do you think engineers had to keep in mind when designing an artificial climbing foot?
2. What is the toughest challenge you have ever had to overcome?

Find out more! Log on to
www.hspscience.com

KID ROCKS!

Using nimble skills that would make Spider-Man proud, Scott Cory inches his way along a craggy rock face high above Yosemite National Park in California. From a distance, Scott looks like an ant against the massive wall of granite known as El Capitán.

Scott pays close attention to each step, reaching for any type of tiny ledge or crack to grab on to. He pulls upward with his fingers and uses his feet to stay steady. Scott knows that one mistake could cause him to slip. Without a safety line, such an error would mean a long, deadly plunge.

What might surprise you is that Scott is just 13 years old. He was the youngest person to scale *El Capitán* and *Half Dome,* another of Yosemite's famous peaks, in one day each.

You Can Do It!

Materials
- 3 soil samples
- 3 sheets of white paper
- hand lens
- toothpicks

Observing Soil

Procedure

1. Obtain soil samples from three different places.
2. Pour each sample onto a separate sheet of paper.
3. Examine each sample with the hand lens. Record your observations.
4. Use the toothpicks to separate the grains in each sample into piles of soil particles, rock, and plant matter.
5. Classify each sample by its contents.

Draw Conclusions

Compare and contrast the three soils. What do the contents of soil tell you about its formation? Which of the three soil samples would be best to grow plants in? Explain your answer.

Weathering Rocks

Decide how you can test which agent of weathering erodes rocks the fastest. For example, you may decide to place some rocks in water, freeze them, and then thaw them out again. You might place other rocks in a container and shake it. Collect small rocks to use for your experiment. Remember that different rocks weather at different rates, so be careful to collect rocks of the same type. Record your observations. You may want to present your findings to the class.

6 Review and FCAT Preparation

Vocabulary Review

Use the terms below to complete the sentences. The page numbers tell you where to look in the chapter if you need help.

mineral p. 216
streak p. 217
luster p. 217
igneous rock p. 224
deposition p. 226
sedimentary rock p. 226

metamorphic rock p. 228
weathering p. 234
erosion p. 235
rock cycle p. 236

1. The way a mineral reflects light is its _____.

2. Rocks are broken down into sediment during _____.

3. Rock changed by heat and pressure is known as _____.

4. Rocks continually change into other types of rocks in the _____.

5. Pieces of sediment settle out of water or wind during _____.

6. You can rub a mineral against a white tile to see its _____.

7. A naturally occurring solid with a crystalline structure is a _____.

8. Pieces of sediment that have been pressed and cemented together form _____.

9. Melted rock cools to form _____.

10. Wind and water carry sediment from one place to another during _____.

Check Understanding

Write the letter of the best choice.

11. What property describes a mineral's ability to resist being scratched?
    A. erodibility   C. luster
    B. hardness   D. streak

12. Which of the following is a good definition of the word *rock*?
    F. A rock is any nonliving solid found in nature.
    G. A rock is anything found in the ground.
    H. A rock is a hard object.
    I. A rock is a mineral mixture.

13. You find an igneous rock with no visible mineral crystals. Where did this rock most likely form?
    A. deep underground
    B. in a cave
    C. on Earth's surface
    D. under a mountain

14. MAIN IDEA Look at the picture below. What kind of rock is this an example of?

    F. basalt rock
    G. igneous rock
    H. metamorphic rock
    I. sedimentary rock

15. CAUSE AND EFFECT Which of the following lead to weathering?
    A. high temperatures
    B. mineral type and color
    C. pressure and light
    D. wind and rain

16. Which of the following are the main ingredients of soil?
    F. humus and weathered rock
    G. minerals and water
    H. sedimentary and igneous rocks
    I. soft minerals and cement

Inquiry Skills

17. Explain some ways in which minerals are **classified**.

18. What changes might you **observe** in a rock as it is weathered?

Read, Inquire, Explain

19. Monica found a clear mineral crystal. She wanted to identify its hardness. She tried to scratch it with her fingernail, a penny, and a steel nail. But none of these worked. Then she tried topaz, which did leave a scratch. The mineral was able to scratch glass. What mineral could Monica have found? Explain your answer.

20. Examine the pictures of the two rock samples.
Part A How did Rock A form? Where did Rock A form? Explain your answer.
Part B How did Rock B form? Could Rock B have formed from Rock A? Explain your answer.

ROCK A   ROCK B

Chapter 7

Changes to Earth's Surface

Lesson 1 What Are Some of Earth's Landforms?

Lesson 2 What Causes Changes to Earth's Landforms?

Lesson 3 How Do Movements of the Crust Change Earth?

Vocabulary

FCAT-Tested

topography
earthquake
volcano

Other Terms

landform
glacier
sand dune
delta
sinkhole
plate
epicenter
fault
magma
lava

What do **YOU** wonder?

In 1931, a young Navajo girl was exploring the countryside near her home in Arizona. She noticed a small slit in the ground. That small slit led to a canyon 40 m (130 ft) deep and more than 5 km (3 mi) long! Today, the canyon is called Antelope Canyon. What do you think could have made this landform?

247

What Are Some of Earth's Landforms?

Fast Fact

Mitten of Rock The landform shown here is called Right Mitten. Its unusual shape made it a popular location for car commercials. Vehicles were flown in by helicopter and placed on the top. How did Right Mitten form? Earth's surface seems to stay the same, but wind and water change landforms into interesting shapes. You can model some of these changes in the Investigate.

Modeling Earth's Landforms

Materials • clay • plastic tray • forceps • cup

Procedure

1. With a partner, form the clay into pea-size balls. Use the balls to model a landform, such as a mountain or a plain, in the tray.

2. One partner should close his or her eyes. Then the other partner should change the landform by removing one clay ball with the forceps and putting the ball into the cup.

3. After the ball is removed, the partner whose eyes were closed should observe the landform carefully. Can that person see any change? Switch roles and repeat Step 2.

4. Take turns removing clay balls and observing until one of you can describe a change in the landform.

5. Count the clay balls in the cup. If each ball represents a change that takes place in 1000 years, how long did it take before a change was observed?

Draw Conclusions

1. Why might changes in hills and mountains be seen sooner than changes in plains?

2. **Inquiry Skill** Scientists often use models to help them understand natural processes. Why might a model be useful for understanding how landforms change?

Step 1

Step 3

Investigate Further

Build a model of a landform. Then show how the landform may look in 10,000 years.

Reading in Science

SC.D.1.2.4.5.1 erosion and deposition;
LA.A.2.2.1 main idea and details

VOCABULARY
landform p. 250
topography p. 250
glacier p. 252
sand dune p. 253

SCIENCE CONCEPTS
▶ what landforms are
▶ what makes each landform different from others

READING FOCUS SKILL

MAIN IDEA AND DETAILS Look for examples and details for each type of landform.

Mountains, Hills, and Plains

What is the land around your town like? Is it wide and flat? Does it have rolling hills or steep mountains? Land has many different shapes. A natural land shape or feature is called a **landform**. When you describe the landforms around your town, you're describing the area's topography. **Topography** is all the kinds of landforms in a certain area.

The jagged peaks of the Rocky Mountains are many thousands of feet higher than the surrounding land. ▼

Look at the pictures below. How would you describe the topography of the two areas? Both areas have mountains. A *mountain* is a landform that is much higher than the surrounding land. Often, mountains occur in groups called ranges. Mountain ranges can be very different from each other. The Rocky Mountains, for example, form tall, jagged peaks that rise thousands of feet above the surrounding land. The Appalachian Mountains are lower and more rounded. They are still thousands of feet high, but much lower than the Rocky Mountains.

The Appalachians are mountains, too, but their peaks are lower and more rounded than the peaks of the Rockies. ▼

▲ The Great Plains covers much of the middle of the United States. Because plains are flat, they are often good farming areas.

So, although these two areas have similar landforms—mountains—their topographies are very different.

The topography of volcanic areas differs in another way. Volcanoes usually occur as individual mountains, not in ranges. They may have steep sides or rounded slopes.

Hills are landforms that are like mountains, but not as high. Most have rounded slopes.

Not all landforms have slopes. A *plain* is a large, flat landform with little relief. *Relief* is the difference in elevation between high and low places. In the middle of the United States is a very large plain known as the Great Plains. Plains form in different ways, but all plains have the same topography. Right Mitten is flat on top, but the top is small and elevated, so it's not a plain.

Hills are lower than mountains and have gentle slopes. ▶

MAIN IDEA AND DETAILS List details that describe mountains, hills, and plains.

▲ Mount Etna, a volcano on the island of Sicily, is a single mountain.

Landforms from Ice

Look at the landforms shown below. They look different from each other, but they have one thing in common—they were both formed by glaciers. A **glacier** is a large, thick sheet of ice. As glaciers move, they change the land around and beneath them. For example, *moraines* (muh•RAYNZ) are long, low hills formed by materials carried by a glacier. As moving ice scrapes the land beneath it, rocks and other materials are picked up and carried along. This material is deposited when the glacier melts.

How can you tell a moraine from an ordinary hill? A moraine contains rocks, sand, and clay. If you dig into a moraine, you find these things deposited together. You do not find them together in most hills. There are many moraines in the northern part of the United States. Some are more than 200 km (120 mi) long!

Other landforms produced by glaciers are *glacial grooves*. These features form when a glacier scrapes and scratches the rock beneath it. As the glacier melts, grooves can be seen in the rock.

 MAIN IDEA AND DETAILS What detail tells you how a moraine is different from an ordinary hill?

In this glacier, you can see a moraine between ice flows. ▼

These glacial grooves on Kelley's Island, in Ohio, formed when ice scarred the rock. ▼

▲ Captiva is a barrier island on Florida's west coast. Because of currents, many shells wash up on the island's beaches in winter.

◄ Sand dunes form where the wind is strong and the sand deposits are plentiful. These sand dunes are in the Oregon Dunes Recreation Area.

Landforms of Sand

Some landforms are made of sand and small bits of rock. These landforms move and are shaped by both wind and water. Landforms of sand are more easily changed than landforms of rock.

A <mark>sand dune</mark> is a sand hill that is made and shaped by wind. As wind blows over a dune, the sand moves. This can change the dune's shape or even move the whole dune. Some dunes move as much as 30 m (100 ft) a year.

Like wind, water can also move sand. Water waves and currents reshape beaches, forming barrier islands and sand spits extending out into the water from the ends of many islands. *Sand spits* and *barrier islands* are long, narrow piles of sand that help protect the mainland from wave erosion. They are found all along the Atlantic coast and the Gulf of Mexico.

Rivers, too, can make sand landforms. Rivers carry sand from the land they flow through. When the flow of a river slows, the sand settles. This makes a landform called a *sandbar*. The Pacific coast has many sandbars where rivers flow into the ocean.

Focus Skill **MAIN IDEA AND DETAILS** What details about sand dunes make them different from moraines?

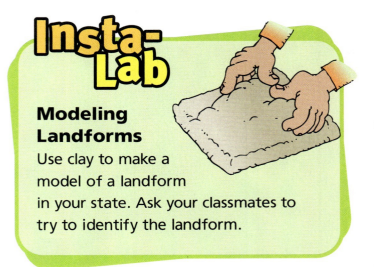

Insta-Lab

Modeling Landforms

Use clay to make a model of a landform in your state. Ask your classmates to try to identify the landform.

253

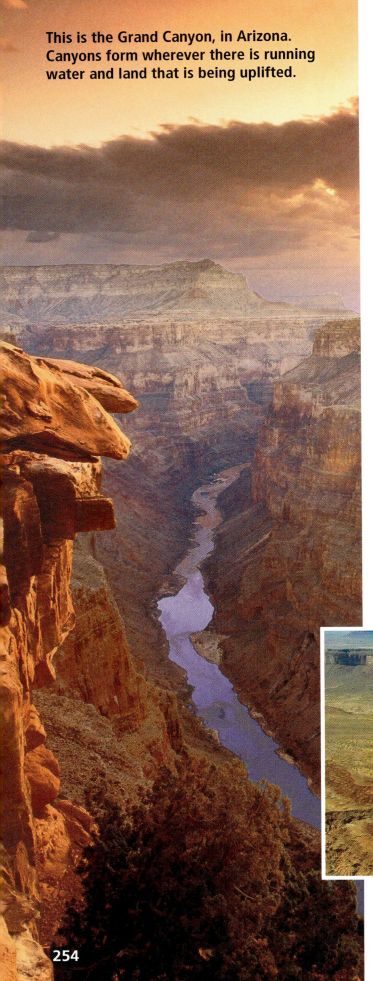

This is the Grand Canyon, in Arizona. Canyons form wherever there is running water and land that is being uplifted.

Landforms from Water

The topography of the southwestern United States is beautiful and varied. There you will find landforms such as Mesa Verde (green mesa). A *mesa* is a tall, flat-topped rock feature. *Mesa* is a Spanish word meaning "table." A mesa forms as running water erodes the surrounding rock. The Southwest is also home to many canyons and unusual rock formations, like those in Monument Valley.

Canyons are deep valleys with steep sides. They are found throughout the Southwest. The Grand Canyon, in Arizona, is the largest land canyon in the world. The rushing water of the Colorado River carved through many layers of rock to make this mile-deep canyon. Much of the topography of the Southwest resulted from erosion by the Colorado River and streams that flow into it.

Not all landforms made by water are as dramatic as those in the Southwest. However, landforms that water has made are found almost everywhere in the world.

MAIN IDEA AND DETAILS What types of landforms in the Southwest were formed by running water?

▲ Monument Valley, along the Arizona-Utah border, was made by water and wind.

1. MAIN IDEA AND DETAILS Draw and complete the graphic organizer by listing details that describe each landform.

Landforms are features on Earth's surface.

Mountains: Are higher than surrounding land; they form ranges.

B Plains:

D Glacial grooves:

F Sand spits and barrier islands:

H Canyons and mesas:

A Hills:

C Moraines:

E Sand dunes:

G Sandbars:

2. SUMMARIZE Make an outline that summarizes the main idea and details of the lesson.

3. DRAW CONCLUSIONS How is the way a mesa forms similar to the way a canyon forms?

4. VOCABULARY Explain how the term *landform* is related to the term *topography*.

FCAT Prep

5. Read/Inquire/Explain Suppose you find a hill containing a jumble of small and large rocks. What kind of landform might it be? Explain.

6. What makes sand dunes and moraines similar?
   A. Both are formed by ice.
   B. Both are formed by rivers.
   C. Both are found in the Southwest.
   D. Both are kinds of hills.

Links

Writing

Expository Writing
Research the geography of your state. Use the information to write a **narration** for a tour of landforms in your state.

Math

Solve Problems
Suppose a sand dune travels 100 m in a year. At that rate, how long would it take for the dune to travel 1 km? How far would the dune travel in 15 years and 2 months?

Social Studies

Topographic Maps
Find a topographic map of your area, and compare it to your area's landforms. Record your observations about how various landforms are shown on the map.

 For more links and activities, go to **www.hspscience.com**

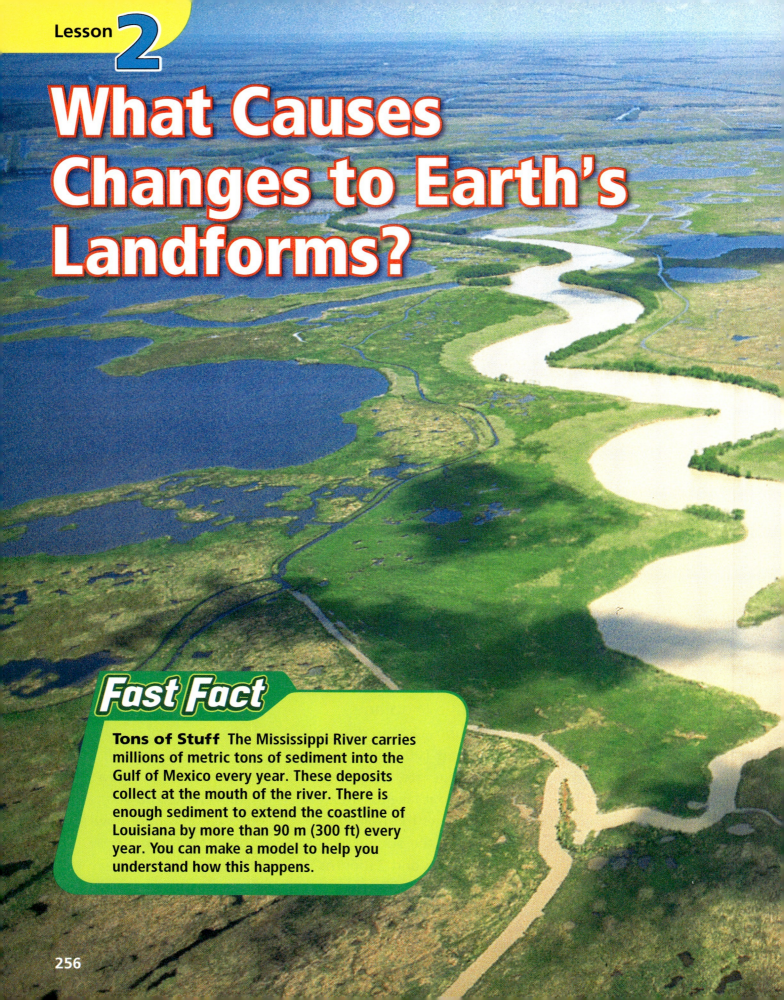

What Causes Changes to Earth's Landforms?

Fast Fact

Tons of Stuff The Mississippi River carries millions of metric tons of sediment into the Gulf of Mexico every year. These deposits collect at the mouth of the river. There is enough sediment to extend the coastline of Louisiana by more than 90 m (300 ft) every year. You can make a model to help you understand how this happens.

Rivers and Sand

Materials
- paint tray
- clay
- plastic cup
- clean sand
- water
- spoon
- kitchen baster

Procedure

1. Cover the slope of the paint tray with a thin layer of clay. Press and mold the clay to form a shoreline and a beach. Form a channel in the clay to model a riverbed.

2. Add equal amounts of sand and water to the cup. Stir the mixture so the sand becomes suspended in the water. Then fill the kitchen baster with the mixture.

3. Place the baster at the top of the river channel. Squeeze the bulb to release a flow of the sand-and-water mixture.

4. Release the mixture several times, changing the speed of the flow. Observe the behavior of the sand and water as the mixture runs down the channel.

Draw Conclusions

1. What happened to the sand when it reached the mouth of the river in your model?

2. How was the speed of the mixture related to the deposition of the sand?

3. **Inquiry Skill** Scientists learn by observing. You observed how sand is deposited in water. What does this tell you about the way water changes land?

Step 1

Step 3

Investigate Further

How do continuing deposits of sediment affect a river? Plan and conduct a simple investigation that answers this question.

SC.D.1.2.4.5.1 erosion and deposition;
SC.H.1.2.5.5.2 compare using models   **257**

Reading in Science

SC.D.1.2.4.5.1 erosion and deposition; SC.D.1.2.5.5.1 Earth's features change slowly or quickly; LA.E.2.2.1 cause and effect

VOCABULARY
delta p. 261
sinkhole p. 262

SCIENCE CONCEPTS
► what causes weathering, erosion, and deposition
► how wind, water, ice, and plants cause Earth's landforms to change

READING FOCUS SKILL
CAUSE AND EFFECT Look for the causes of change in Earth's landforms, and their effects.

cause → effect

Changes Caused by Wind

Imagine yourself standing on a beach with your face to the wind. Sand hits your skin so hard that it begins to sting.

Now imagine this blowing sand hitting a rock. Over time, the sand wears away the rock by breaking it into smaller pieces. Recall from an earlier chapter that the process of wearing away rocks by natural means is known as weathering.

The weathered pieces of rock, some as large as sand grains, are carried away by the wind. The pieces keep moving as long as the wind is blowing. But when the wind slows down, the large pieces fall to the ground.

Over a long time, the wind leaves small piles of sand in some areas. These piles grow as more and more sand is blown into the pile. Slowly, they become sand dunes.

Sand dunes are found in many places, such as in deserts, at beaches, and on lakeshores. Some desert dunes are as high as a 30-story building! Many beaches along the Atlantic coast have long lines of dunes. These dunes help protect the land during storms. But they can also damage nearby buildings and roads as they move inland, pushed by strong winds from the ocean.

CAUSE AND EFFECT
How can wind change landforms?

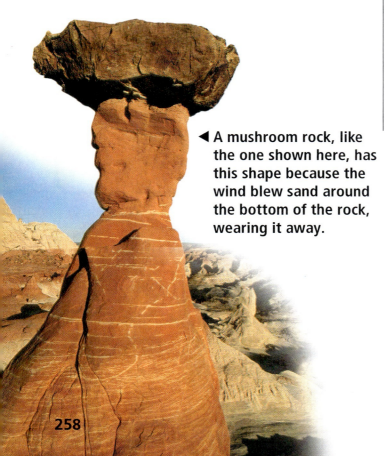

◄ A mushroom rock, like the one shown here, has this shape because the wind blew sand around the bottom of the rock, wearing it away.

Changes Caused by Moving Water

Suppose your hands are dirty after working in the garden. Rinsing your hands removes most of the soil. The water flows over your hands, picks up the soil, and carries it away. In a similar way, moving water can change Earth's surface by carrying soil and small pieces of rock away from landforms.

Water is an important cause of change for Earth's landforms. Moving water can dig a mile-deep canyon or change the path of a river.

For example, a rapidly flowing river erodes its banks and its bottom. Eroding the banks makes the river wider. Eroding the bottom makes the river deeper. The moving water then carries sediment downstream. When the flow of water slows down, sediment is deposited. Deposits on a river's banks make it narrower. Deposits on the bottom make the river shallower.

 CAUSE AND EFFECT How can water cause a river's banks to change?

Canyons along the Colorado River are examples of changes made by moving water. For millions of years, the river has been wearing away rocks and carrying sediment downstream. The river has carved deeper and deeper into the landforms of the Southwest.

Erosion and Deposition

Moving wind or water has energy, which enables it to move sediment. The faster the wind or water moves, the more energy it has. Fast water, with a lot of energy, can erode a lot of sediment. Slow water, with little energy, can erode only a small amount of sediment. But all moving water, even a gentle rain, can erode some sediment.

Rain doesn't seem very powerful, but it can cause erosion. When rain falls on a bare hill or mountain, it splashes away soil. As it runs downhill, the water increases its speed and gains energy. The moving water carries away sediment. Over time, water erosion may leave gullies, or ditches, in the ground.

Ocean waves also cause erosion. Constant wave action can change sloping shorelines into cliffs. Waves crashing against the shore carry away broken bits of rock. Piece by piece, the cliffs get steeper. In many places, there is so much erosion that the top of a cliff overhangs the bottom. When this happens, the entire cliff can collapse into

▲ **The channels and gullies in this hillside were caused by rain.**

the ocean. Then waves begin eroding the collapsed rock and forming new cliffs.

Ocean waves change landforms in another way, too. If you stand on a beach and watch the waves, you see that each wave brings more sand onto the beach. Remember, the process by which sediment drops out of water is called deposition.

Why does deposition occur? You've read that sediment is carried in water as long as the water flows fast. Fast-flowing water has a lot of energy.

Crashing waves can change the face of a cliff.

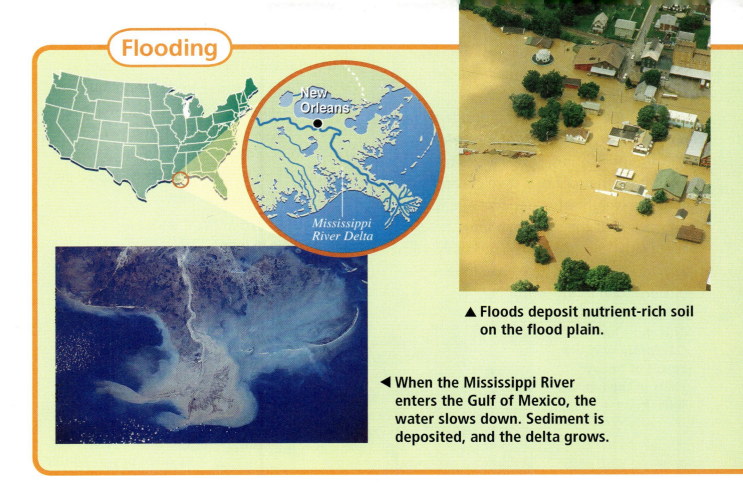

Flooding

New Orleans

Mississippi River Delta

▲ Floods deposit nutrient-rich soil on the flood plain.

◀ When the Mississippi River enters the Gulf of Mexico, the water slows down. Sediment is deposited, and the delta grows.

When water slows down, it loses energy. Larger pieces of sediment drop out of the water first and settle to the bottom. As the water slows down more, smaller and smaller particles sink to the bottom.

A river often deposits sediment at its *mouth,* the place where it empties into the ocean. The flow of water slows as a river reaches the ocean. As a result, much of the sediment the river carries is deposited, forming a delta. A ==delta== is an area of new land at the mouth of a river

Flooding can deposit sediment near a river. During heavy rains, a flooding river sends water over its banks. When the rains end, the water slowly returns to the river, but the sediment it carried is deposited on the land. This sediment is rich in nutrients that plants need. As a result, *flood plains,* as these areas are called, are usually good for

farming. But living on a flood plain can be dangerous. Rapidly flowing water can move houses as well as sediment.

 CAUSE AND EFFECT What causes a delta to form?

Settle Down

You'll need a clear container, some water, and a mixture of soil and sand. Fill the container half full of water. Put the mixture in your hand, and slowly drop it into the container. How does the mixture settle out of the water?

Sinkholes and Landslides

Water can change not only landforms on Earth's surface but also features underground. For example, groundwater can weather and erode soft rocks. Underground erosion causes caves to form. Often, the roof of a cave collapses due to the weight of material above it. If the cave is near the surface, a large hole, called a **sinkhole**, may open suddenly. Most sinkholes are found where limestone is common, such as in Florida.

As you learned, water isn't the only factor that causes erosion and deposition. Gravity can also cause these land-changing processes to happen. Gravity can make soil, mud, and rocks move quickly down a slope. This form of erosion is called a *landslide*. Landslides can happen suddenly, especially after heavy rains or earthquakes.

 CAUSE AND EFFECT What causes a sinkhole to form?

This mudflow in California was the result of heavy rains in the nearby hills. ▶

This sinkhole opened up suddenly in Winter Park, Florida, in 1981. It swallowed a city block. ▼

The Columbia ice field, in Canada, includes many glaciers.

▲ Glaciers carve deep U-shaped valleys as they flow slowly down a mountain.

Ice

Ice can change landforms in several ways. One way is by weathering rocks. The surfaces of most rocks have tiny cracks and holes that fill with water when it rains. If the weather is cold, the water turns to ice. As the water freezes, it expands, making the cracks bigger. The next time it rains, more water gets in, and the process continues. Over time, the rocks break into smaller and smaller pieces, until there is little more than a pile of sand.

Ice can change landforms in other ways, too. As you read in Lesson 1, glaciers can shape landforms by erosion and deposition. Glaciers often follow a river valley down a mountain. As they move, they change the V-shaped valley eroded by the river into a U-shaped valley.

Glaciers deposit their loads of sediment as they begin to melt. The result can be a huge moraine, such as Long Island in New York. Glacier deposits can also form small, round hills.

 CAUSE AND EFFECT What changes to landforms can ice cause?

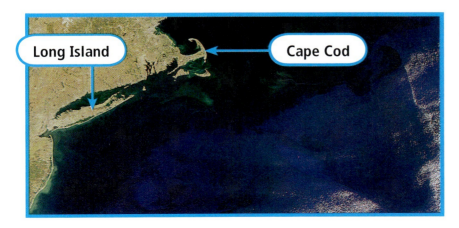

Long Island   Cape Cod

◀ Long Island, NY, and Cape Cod, MA, are huge moraines left by glaciers that once covered most of the northeastern United States.

Plants

Plants can also cause weathering and erosion. When a seed germinates on a rocky slope, it sends roots into tiny cracks or holes in the rock. The roots grow and may eventually become large enough to break the rock into smaller pieces. Some plants also release chemicals into the soil. These chemicals help weather rock by dissolving certain minerals.

Plants don't just weather rock. They also help preserve and protect Earth's landforms. Plant roots hold soil and sand in place. This helps prevent erosion by wind and water.

Farmers often plant clover or other *cover crops* in fields they aren't using to grow food crops. Cover crops help return nutrients to the soil and help prevent erosion. In some areas, farmers plant rows of trees to slow wind erosion of nearby fields.

This protection works naturally as well. Along many beaches, plants grow on dunes. The roots of these plants help hold the sand in place when the wind blows. That's why people should always use beach crossovers instead of walking across the dunes and damaging the plants.

 CAUSE AND EFFECT How do plants affect Earth's landforms?

Plant roots help hold sand in place. This preserves dunes that might otherwise blow away. ▼

▲ The growth of plant roots can weather rock.

1. CAUSE AND EFFECT Draw and complete the graphic organizers.

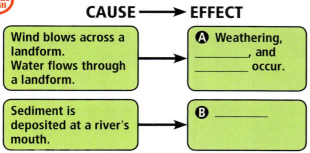

CAUSE ⟶ EFFECT

| Wind blows across a landform. Water flows through a landform. | ⟶ | Ⓐ Weathering, _____, and _____ occur. |

| Sediment is deposited at a river's mouth. | ⟶ | Ⓑ _____ |

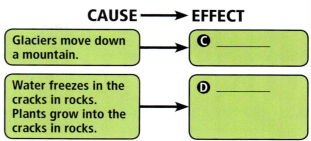

CAUSE ⟶ EFFECT

| Glaciers move down a mountain. | ⟶ | Ⓒ _____ |

| Water freezes in the cracks in rocks. Plants grow into the cracks in rocks. | ⟶ | Ⓓ _____ |

2. SUMMARIZE Write a short paragraph summarizing the factors that change Earth's surface.

3. DRAW CONCLUSIONS How are wind erosion and water erosion alike?

4. VOCABULARY Describe the formation of deltas and of sinkholes.

FCAT Prep

5. Read/Inquire/Explain Tell how snowdrifts and sand dunes are formed in similar ways. Then describe differences in how they are formed.

6. A 3-kg (7-lb) rock is placed on a hill. What do you hypothesize will happen to the rock in 100 years?

   A. will get heavier due to deposition

   B. will get lighter due to weathering

   C. will disappear completely

   D. will become a different rock

Links

Writing

Narrative Writing

Write a **description** of the events that made a landform look the way it does. You might tell about a mesa, a sand dune, or a moraine.

Math

Use Mental Math

Suppose a weathered rock breaks into two pieces. Then each piece breaks in two. How many pieces will there be? How many pieces will there be if the process occurs five more times?

Social Studies

Map Works

Draw a map showing places in the United States where you might find sand dunes, moraines, and deltas. On your map, color these places differently and include a key.

 For more links and activities, go to www.hspscience.com

How Do Movements of the Crust Change Earth?

Fast Fact

No End in Sight Since 1823, Kīlauea, a volcano on the island of Hawai`i, has erupted 59 times. On January 3, 1983, Kīlauea began erupting again, and it hasn't stopped since. That's more than 20 years of continuous eruption! In the Investigate, you can make a model to help you understand volcanoes like Kīlauea.

Modeling a Volcanic Eruption

Materials
- newspaper
- pie pan
- safety goggles
- plastic gloves
- film canister with lid
- effervescent antacid
- teaspoon
- potting soil
- red food coloring
- light maple syrup

Procedure

1. Cover your workspace with newspaper, and place the pie pan on the paper. **CAUTION: Put on the safety goggles and the plastic gloves.**

2. Fill the film canister halfway with antacid.

3. Add some potting soil to the canister. Put the lid on, and shake the canister.

4. Open the canister, and add 10 drops of food coloring to the mixture.

5. Put the canister in the center of the pan. Add several handfuls of clean potting soil to the pan. Heap the soil against the canister to model the sides of a volcano.

6. Add some corn syrup to the canister. Observe what happens. It may take a few moments for the "lava" to start flowing.

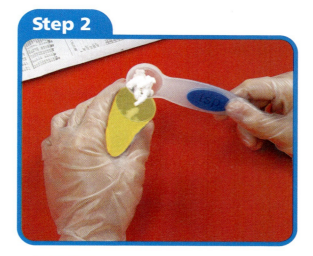

Step 2

Step 6

Draw Conclusions

1. Did you observe clear paths in the lava flow? Explain.

2. **Inquiry Skill** Scientists use models to help them understand the dangers of certain natural processes. How might your model help communicate the potential danger of living near volcanoes?

Investigate Further

To protect against lava flows, people often construct barriers. Hypothesize how a barrier might help protect a community.

SC.D.1.2.4.5.2 movements of Earth's crust; **SC.D.1.2.5.5.1** Earth's features change slowly or quickly; **LA.E.2.2.1** cause and effect

VOCABULARY
plates p. 269
earthquake p. 270
epicenter p. 270
fault p. 270
magma p. 272
lava p. 272
volcano p. 272

SCIENCE CONCEPTS
▶ how movements of Earth's crust change the surface
▶ how quickly Earth's landforms can change

Focus Skill
READING FOCUS SKILL
CAUSE AND EFFECT Look for what causes earthquakes, volcanoes, and mountains.

cause → effect

Earth's Structure

Imagine you're a miner digging for gold or gems. You dig deep into Earth, maybe 2 or 3 km (1 or 2 mi) down. But even at this depth, you've barely scratched Earth's surface. You'd need to dig down about 6000 km (4000 mi) to reach the center of Earth! What do you think you'd find at the center? Rock? The whole Earth seems to be rock, but it isn't.

Earth has four layers—the crust, the mantle, the outer core, and the inner core. If you could dig a hole to the center of Earth, you'd find that the layers are different from one another. The thin *crust* is solid rock. So is most of the next layer, the *mantle*. But some rock within the mantle is soft, like melted candy.

If you continued toward the center, the deeper you'd go, the hotter things would

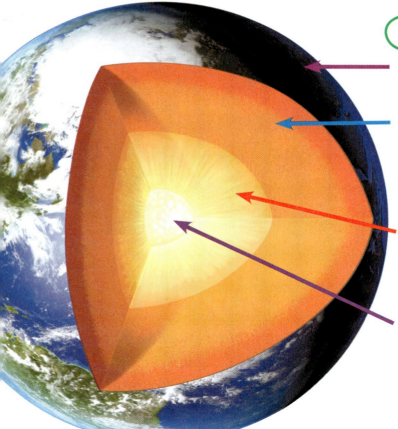

Earth's Layers

Crust 5–70 km (3–43 mi)
The crust is the surface layer of Earth.

Mantle 2885 km (1790 mi)
The mantle has two parts: The upper mantle and the lower mantle. Most of the mantle is solid rock, but some mantle rock is soft.

Outer Core 2270 km (1410 mi)
The hot outer core is liquid iron.

Inner Core 1210 km (750 mi)
The inner core is iron and nickel. Even though the core is very hot, great pressure at the center of Earth keeps the inner core solid.

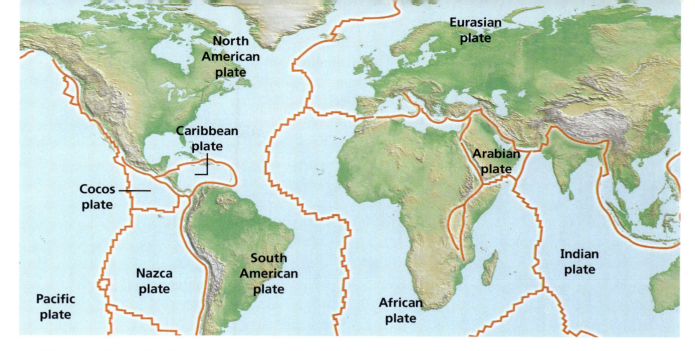

▲ This map shows Earth's major plates.

get. The *outer* core is liquid, but it's iron, not rock. The inner core is also metal, but it's solid due to intense pressure.

Earth's crust and uppermost mantle are divided into sections, called plates. **Plates** are blocks of crust and upper mantle rock that fit together like puzzle pieces.

Look at the map above. There are 10 major plates. Most of North America, Greenland, and part of the Atlantic Ocean are on the North American plate. Part of California and most of the Pacific Ocean are on the Pacific plate.

Plates "float" on the softer rock of the mantle. As this rock flows, plates move. Because plates fit together so closely, the movement of one plate affects other plates.

At different places, plates move toward each other, away from each other, or next to each other. These plate movements cause many changes in Earth's surface.

(Focus Skill) **CAUSE AND EFFECT** What causes Earth's plates to move?

Thick continental crust and thin oceanic crust rest on the mantle. ▼

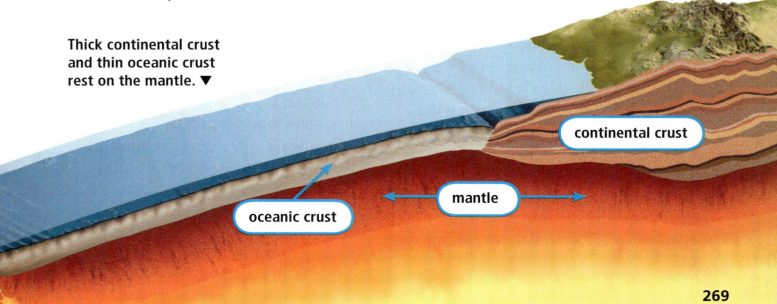

continental crust

oceanic crust

mantle

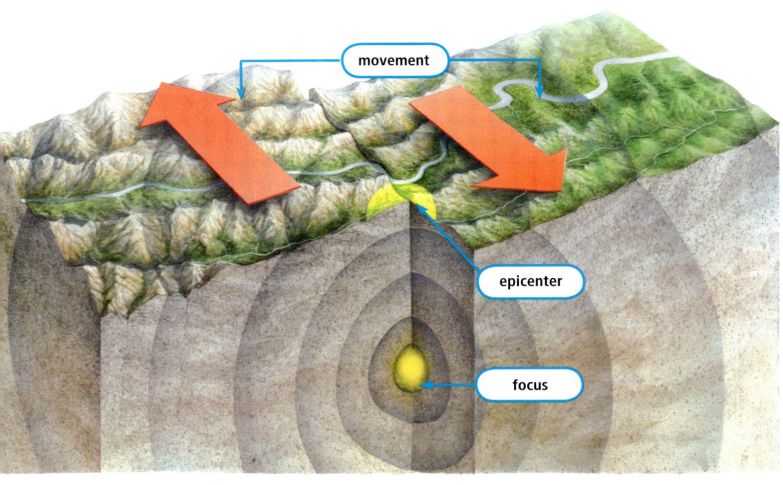

movement

epicenter

focus

▲ An earthquake occurs when Earth's crust moves and releases energy. The energy of an earthquake spreads out like ripples on a pond. Places farther from the epicenter are likely to experience less damage than places near the epicenter.

Earthquakes

Suppose you press your palms together as hard as you can. If one hand slips, energy is released suddenly and your hands move past each other. When two of Earth's plates move suddenly past each other, energy is also released and the ground shakes.

An **earthquake** is movement of the ground caused by a sudden release of energy in Earth's crust. The place within the crust where energy is released during an earthquake is called the *focus*. The release of energy may hardly be noticed, or it may cause a lot of damage. The greatest damage is likely to occur directly above the focus. The point on Earth's surface directly above the focus is called the **epicenter**.

Earthquakes are caused by three different types of plate movement. Plates pushing together, plates sliding past each other, and plates pulling apart all produce earthquakes.

Most earthquakes occur along a **fault**, or break in Earth's crust. Some faults occur in the middle of plates, but most are found near the edges of plates. Faults develop as plate movements bend and crack the crust.

Earthquakes caused by plates or pieces of crust pushing together or sliding past each other are usually very strong. Earthquakes caused by plates or pieces of crust pulling apart are usually weak. Scientists classify earthquakes by estimating their *magnitude,* or amount of energy released. This is reported using a scale of magnitude,

Major Earthquakes

Read the information in the table. Then, on a world map, mark the areas where these major earthquakes occurred. Using the information in the text below, estimate how many times stronger the 1964 Alaska earthquake was than the 1976 China earthquake.

Measurement on the Richter Scale	Year	Location
9.5	1960	Chile
9.2	1964	Alaska
9.0	2004	Indonesia
8.9	1933	Japan
8.2	1976	China
8.1	1979	Indonesia
8.1	1985	Mexico
7.9	2001	India
7.9	2002	Alaska

▲ An earthquake in Seattle in 2001 measured 6.8 on the Richter scale and caused a lot of damage.

The pattern of the rocks after an earthquake clearly show the San Andreas Fault. The map shows the location of this fault. ▶

such as the *Richter scale*. An earthquake measuring 2.0 on the Richter scale is too small to be felt. There are millions of earthquakes like this every year.

An earthquake measuring 6.0 or higher on the Richter scale can cause a great deal of damage. This is because a 6.0 earthquake is not 3 times stronger than a 2.0 earthquake. It's more than 1,000,000 times stronger. Each increase of 1 on the Richter scale is an increase in strength of about 32 times. About 20 earthquakes of magnitude 6.0 or greater occur each year.

CAUSE AND EFFECT What causes an earthquake?

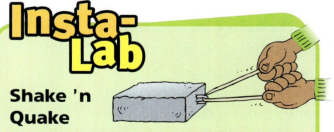

Shake 'n Quake

Push a paper clip most of the way into a block of clay. Tie a rubber band to the paper clip. Then use the rubber band to pull the clay across your desk. If the clay and the desk both represent plates, how does the clay's movement model an earthquake?

Volcanoes

You know that there are places in Earth's mantle where solid rock melts. Melted, or *molten,* rock beneath Earth's surface is known as ==magma==. Magma forms in places where plates push against each other or pull away from each other. Magma is less dense than solid rock, so it's pushed upward through the mantle and crust.

As magma travels upward, it sometimes reaches an opening, or *vent,* in the crust. Magma that has flowed out of a vent is called lava. ==Lava== is molten rock that reaches Earth's surface. As more and more lava flows from a vent, a volcano begins to form. A ==volcano== is a mountain made of lava, ash, or other materials from eruptions.

Lava may ooze slowly out of a vent. Or it may explode from a vent with tremendous force. The 1883 eruption of Krakatoa in Indonesia blew lava and ash 27 km (17 mi) into the air!

Some volcanoes form above an especially hot column of magma. This column is called a *hot spot.* A hot spot supplies a steady flow of magma that rises to the surface. As a plate moves slowly over a hot spot, volcanoes form in new locations. Eventually, a hot spot can produce a chain of volcanoes. This is how the Hawaiian Islands were formed. Hawai`i is the youngest island. Kure Atoll, about 2600 km (1620 mi) to the northwest, is the oldest.

 CAUSE AND EFFECT What causes a chain of volcanoes to form?

Types of Volcanoes

Volcanoes have different shapes depending on the ways the volcanoes form. Some volcanoes are mostly hardened lava. Others are mostly ash, or they are a combination of lava and ash.

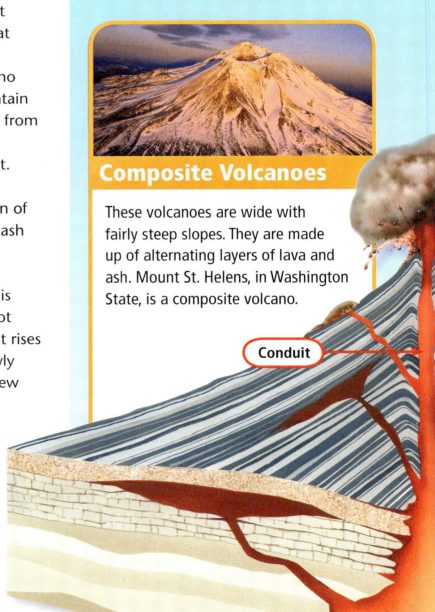

Composite Volcanoes

These volcanoes are wide with fairly steep slopes. They are made up of alternating layers of lava and ash. Mount St. Helens, in Washington State, is a composite volcano.

Conduit

Shield Volcanoes

These are broad volcanoes with gentle slopes. They form from lava that flows easily from vents, surface openings that lead to lava conduits. The island of Hawai`i is made up of five different shield volcanoes. One of them, Mauna Loa, is the most massive mountain on Earth. Mauna Loa contains about 85 percent of the mass of all the Hawaiian Islands combined.

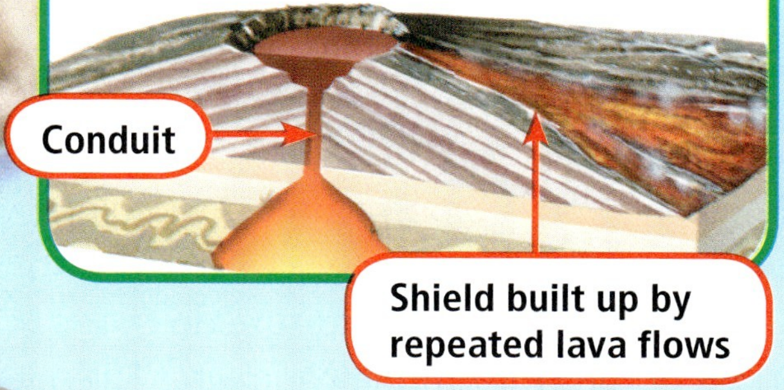

Conduit

Shield built up by repeated lava flows

Cinder Cone Volcanoes

These are tall and narrow with steep slopes. They are made of rock, ash, and other solid materials from volcanic eruptions. They are not made of lava. Paricutín, which formed very quickly in Mexico in 1943, is an example of a cinder cone volcano.

Conduit

Cone built up by rocks, ash, and cinders

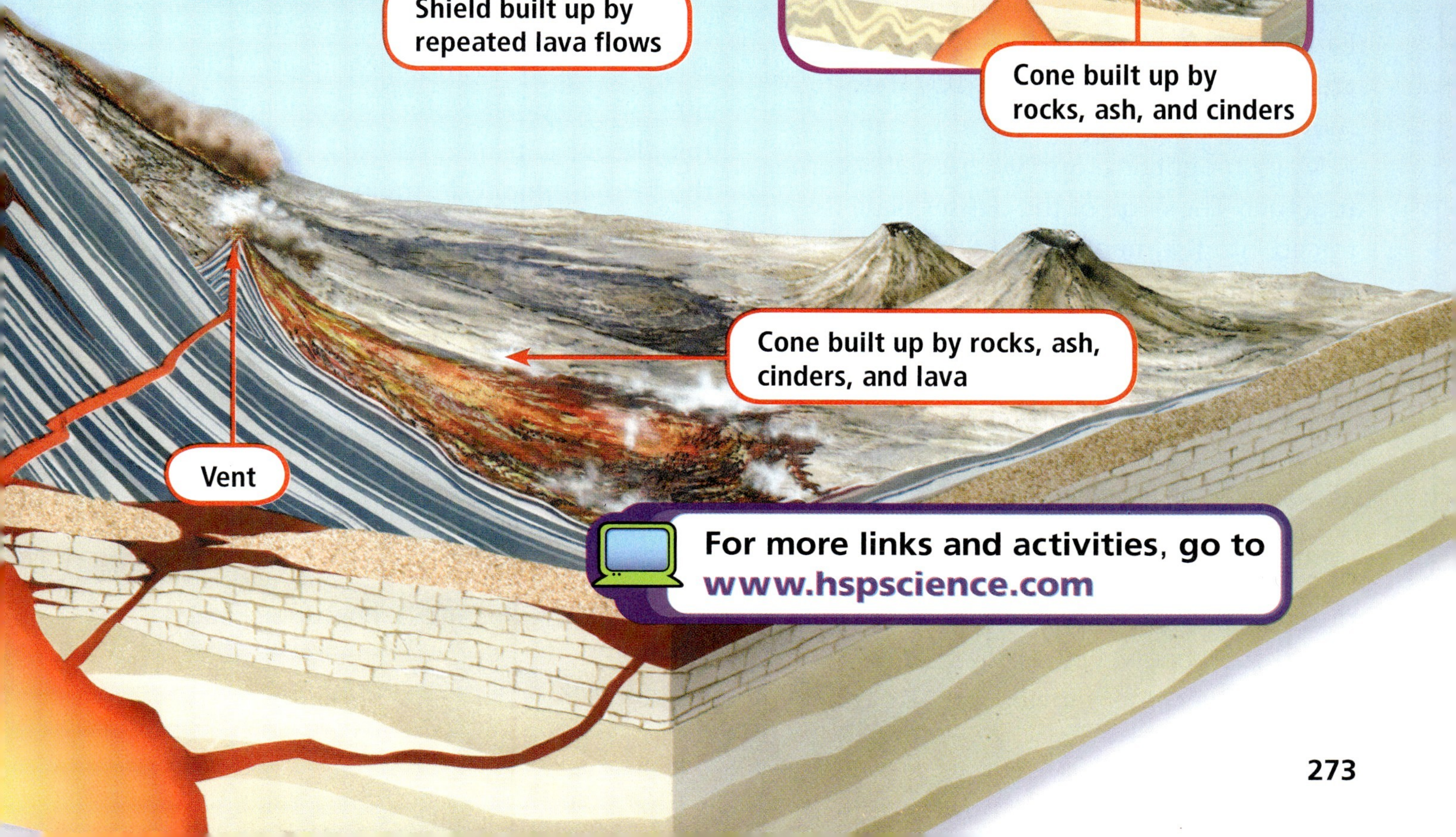

Cone built up by rocks, ash, cinders, and lava

Vent

For more links and activities, go to
www.hspscience.com

273

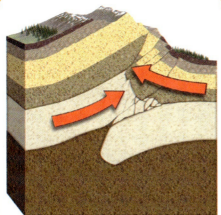

Because continental plates have the same density, they crumple up. Neither is forced into the mantle.

▲ The Himalayas formed when the Indian plate crashed into the Eurasian plate. They are still growing.

How Mountains Form

Mountains are the tallest landforms on Earth. They form where the crust is crumpled and pushed upward by the movements of plates.

Many mountains form where plates come together. The edge of the denser plate is forced into the mantle, while the less dense plate is pushed up. If the plates are the same density, both plates are pushed up. The Himalayas, an Asian mountain range that is the tallest on Earth, formed this way. Mountains in the Himalayas continue to rise about 1 cm (2 in.) each year.

Mountains may also form in the middle of a plate. Suppose you hold a cracker and push down on opposite edges. The cracker would soon break, with jagged, broken edges in the center moving up. This is how the Grand Teton Mountains, in Wyoming, formed. Millions of years ago, surrounding plates put tremendous pressure on the edges of the North American plate. The pressure snapped a block of rock in the middle of the plate. That rock rose up from the land around it, forming mountains.

Plates that move apart leave gaps between them. When this happens, mantle rock moves in to fill the gaps. Magma builds up along plate boundaries, forming a ridge. The mountains in this ridge are volcanoes, since they are made of lava that has cooled. The underwater ridge formed as the North American and Eurasian plates pulled apart is known as the Mid-Atlantic Ridge.

 **CAUSE AND EFFECT** How do mountains form?

1. CAUSE AND EFFECT Draw and complete this graphic organizer.

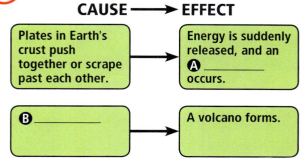

CAUSE ⟶ EFFECT

| Plates in Earth's crust push together or scrape past each other. | ⟶ | Energy is suddenly released, and an **A** _____ occurs. |

| **B** _____ | ⟶ | A volcano forms. |

CAUSE ⟶ EFFECT

| Plates push together. | ⟶ | Gradually, **C** _____ . |

| Pressure is put on the sides of a plate. | ⟶ | **D** _____ |

2. SUMMARIZE Draw a series of illustrations that summarize the lesson.

3. DRAW CONCLUSIONS How are earthquakes related to the formation of mountains?

4. VOCABULARY Explain how the terms in each pair are related: *faults* and *earthquakes; plates* and *mountains; volcanoes* and *magma.*

FCAT Prep

5. Read/Inquire/Explain How might a volcanic eruption cause both slow changes and rapid changes to landforms?

6. Which is a cause of earthquakes and volcanic eruptions?
  A. weathering
  B. the mantle
  C. plate movement
  D. cinder cones

Links

Writing

Narrative Writing

Pompeii, an ancient Roman city, was destroyed in A.D. 79. Find out what happened to Pompeii. Write a **description** of the events as though you were there.

Math

Organize Data

Mountain	Height in Meters
Mauna Kea	4600
Mount McKinley	6775
Mount Olympus	320
Mount Rainier	4800

Make a bar graph of this data. How does the graph help you compare these mountains?

Social Studies

Time Line

Use library references to make a time line showing the largest volcanic eruptions of the last 100 years.

 For more links and activities, go to **www.hspscience.com**

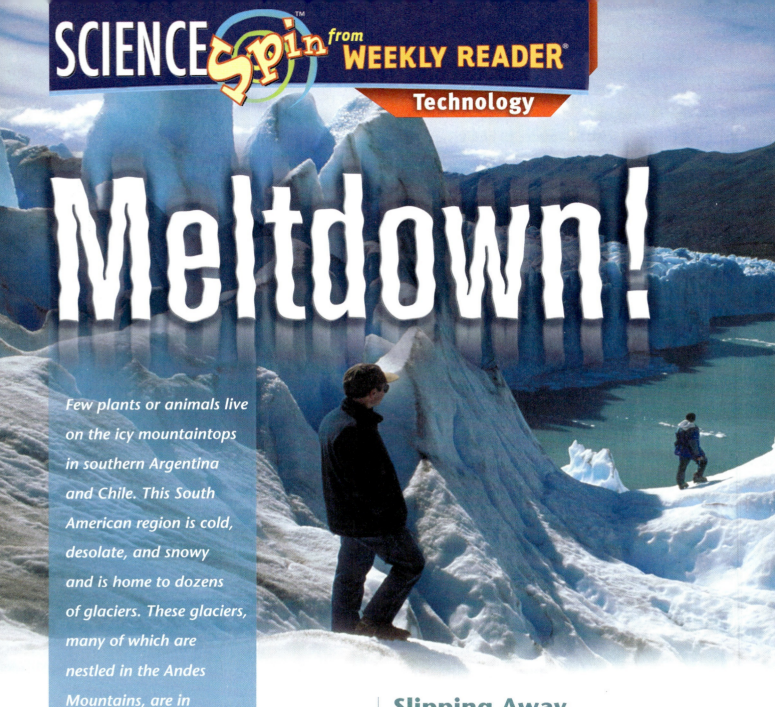

Meltdown!

Few plants or animals live on the icy mountaintops in southern Argentina and Chile. This South American region is cold, desolate, and snowy and is home to dozens of glaciers. These glaciers, many of which are nestled in the Andes Mountains, are in danger of melting away.

The glaciers in South America are some of the largest outside of the polar regions. Because of the region's rough terrain and harsh weather, scientists have trouble reaching the area by foot. To study the melting of the South American glaciers, scientists recently used satellite technology.

Slipping Away

Scientists used satellites to take pictures of the glaciers. Those pictures were compared with earlier information. What scientists found was that the glaciers in this area are rapidly wasting, or melting. In fact, they are melting twice as fast as they were just a few years ago. Erik Rignot, an expert who studied the glaciers, referred to the South American ice fields as the "fastest area of glacial retreat on Earth."

As the glaciers in South America, and in other parts of the world, retreat, their water flows into lakes or oceans. As a result, the meltdown is causing levels of Earth's oceans to rise. If ocean levels rise by even a foot, coastal cities around the world could be flooded.

The Heat Is On

What is causing the glaciers to pull a disappearing act? Warmer temperatures and less snowfall are to blame for the meltdown, say scientists. The warmer temperatures cause some glaciers to break off into the ocean as icebergs. That process, called calving, has increased in recent years. It's not just the South American glaciers that are on thin ice. Scientists warn that about 90 percent of the world's glaciers are melting from global warming.

Think About It

1. How do you think a glacier might shape the Earth's surface?
2. What other surface features of Earth could scientists use satellites to study?

FROSTY FACTS

Glaciers are large sheets of snow and ice that move slowly over land. Glaciers are found in the polar regions around the world and in mountain valleys.

Spin-In

Find out more! Log on to
www.hspscience.com

SC.H.2.2.1.5.2 analyze patterns of change; **SC.H.3.2.1.5.1** technology has improved human lives; **SC.H.3.2.3.5.1** solving problems may create others

Looking Beneath the Surface

Florence Bascom was one of the first women in the United States to enter the field of geology. Geology is the study of rocks, rock formations, and the structure of Earth.

In 1896, Bascom became the first woman to be hired by the United States Geological Survey. Bascom studied how mountains formed, and she became an expert in the study of crystals, minerals, rock composition, and landforms. She focused a lot of her attention on the Piedmont—foothills—east of the Appalachian Mountains, some of the oldest mountains in North America.

Bascom was also one of the first American geologists to use microscopes to study the composition of rocks and minerals.

Career Geologist

Geologists study the makeup, changes, and history of Earth. They also try to understand how rocks were formed and what has happened to rocks since their formation. Many geologists are involved in searching for oil and gas, and others work closely with environmental scientists in preserving and cleaning up the environment.

You Can Do It!

Quick and Easy Project

Make a Topographic Map

Materials
- paint tray
- modeling clay
- ruler
- water
- sheet of paper
- pencil

Procedure

1. Use modeling clay to make several landforms at the bottom of the paint tray. You may want to include mountains, valleys, hills, and so on.

2. Using the ruler, mark centimeters on an inner side of the paint tray, starting from the bottom.

3. Pour enough water into the tray to reach the 1-cm mark.

4. Look at where the water line hits the landforms. Draw an outline of these water lines, viewed from above, on your paper.

5. Repeat Steps 3 and 4 for each higher centimeter mark until the water reaches the top of all the landforms.

Draw Conclusions

How does your topographic map show the landforms you made? What do the lines you drew on your paper represent? Do any of the lines cross each other?

Design Your Own Investigation

A Change in the Neighborhood

Find a place in your neighborhood to observe changes that might be taking place due to weathering or erosion. Decide how to keep a record of the changes. Draw conclusions about what may be causing the changes. Present your findings at a school science fair or community event.

Review and FCAT Preparation

Vocabulary Review

Use the terms below to complete the sentences. The page numbers tell you where to look in the chapter if you need help.

landform p. 250   sinkhole p. 262
topography p. 250   earthquake p. 270
glacier p. 252   fault p. 270
sand dune p. 253   magma p. 272
delta p. 261   volcano p. 272

1. A natural shape or feature of Earth's surface is a _____.

2. A _____ is a sheet of ice.

3. Molten rock beneath Earth's surface is _____.

4. The collapse of an underground cave may produce a _____.

5. A movement of the ground, caused by the sudden release of energy in Earth's crust, is an _____.

6. The landform of sand and other material deposited at the mouth of a river is called a _____.

7. A sand hill formed and shaped by wind is a _____.

8. A mountain made of lava and ash is a _____.

9. _____ is all the kinds of landforms in a certain place.

10. A break in Earth's crust is called a _____.

Check Understanding

Write the letter of the best choice.

11. In which order are the processes listed below most likely to occur?
    A. erosion—deposition—weathering
    B. deposition—erosion—weathering
    C. weathering—deposition—erosion
    D. weathering—erosion—deposition

12. **CAUSE AND EFFECT** Samantha made a display about changes on Earth. She made labels for a cause-and-effect table. Her brother tried placing the labels. These are his results.

Cause	Effect
Volcano	Sand Dune
Earthquake	Delta
Mountain	Deposition
Glacier	Moraine

Which of the causes is correctly paired with its effect?
    F. earthquake
    G. glacier
    H. mountain
    I. volcano

13. Which landform is most likely to be produced by windblown sand?
    A. canyon   C. mesa
    B. delta   D. sand dune

14. MAIN IDEA AND DETAILS Rita made this sketch of Echo Canyon. Which of the following most likely formed the canyon?

F. lava   **H.** water erosion
G. ice erosion   **I.** wind erosion

15. Look at the picture below. How were these landforms most likely produced?

A. earthquake   **C.** water erosion
B. ice erosion   **D.** wind erosion

16. If you wanted to make a model of how a delta forms, which of the following materials might be useful?
  F. a pile of cornflakes and a fan
  G. ice with dirt frozen inside
  H. mud and a bicycle pump
  I. water and fine sand in a bottle

Inquiry Skills

17. What can you **observe** about these pieces of rock that shows one was probably weathered by water?

18. How would you **make a model** of an earthquake?

Read, Inquire, Explain

19. Martin wants to put his pictures of landforms in order by how quickly the landforms were produced, from slowest to fastest. He has pictures of a fault after an earthquake, a cinder cone volcano, and a canyon. In what order should he put his pictures?

20. Rocks that form from ash are very light and can almost float in water. Rocks that form from lava are heavy. Terry and her class take a trip to a volcano that no longer erupts. She wants to know what kind of volcano it is. She collects some rocks and finds a mixture of light rocks and heavy rocks.
Part A What kind of volcano has Terry visited?
Part B How can she use the rocks to support her conclusion in class?

Weather and the Water Cycle

Lesson 1 **What Causes Weather?**

Lesson 2 **What Conditions Affect the Water Cycle?**

Lesson 3 **How Can Patterns in Weather Be Observed?**

Vocabulary

FCAT-Tested

atmosphere

water cycle

evaporation

condensation

Other Terms

troposphere

air pressure

local wind

prevailing wind

humidity

precipitation

air mass

front

climate

In 2004, the state of Florida was hit by four hurricanes. Hurricanes are tropical storms with winds of at least 119 km/hr (74 mi/hr). More hurricanes hit Florida that year than had hit any single state for more than 100 years! Why do hurricanes form over tropical waters, and why do so many of them strike the East Coast of the United States?

What Causes Weather?

The Uneven Heating of Earth

Materials
- 2 tin cans (lids removed)
- water
- dry soil
- 2 thermometers

Procedure

1. Fill one can about three-fourths full of water and the other can about three-fourths full of soil.

2. Place one thermometer in the can of water and the other in the can of soil. Put the cans in a shady place outside. Wait 10 minutes, and then record the temperature of the water and of the soil.

3. Put both cans in sunlight. Predict which can will heat faster. Record the temperature of each can every 10 minutes for 30 minutes.

4. Put the cans back in the shade. Predict which can will show the faster temperature drop. Again, record the temperature of each can every 10 minutes for 30 minutes.

5. Make line graphs to show how the temperatures of both materials changed as they heated and cooled.

Step 1

Step 3

Draw Conclusions

1. How did your results match your predictions?

2. Which would you predict heats faster— oceans or land? Which would you predict cools faster? Explain.

3. **Inquiry Skill** Scientists learn by predicting and then experimenting to test their predictions. How did you test your predictions in this Investigate?

Investigate Further

Predict how fast moist soil, sand, and salt water heat up and cool down. Then plan and conduct an investigation to test your prediction.

Reading in Science

VOCABULARY
atmosphere p. 286
troposphere p. 286
air pressure p. 287
local wind p. 289
prevailing wind p. 290

SCIENCE CONCEPTS
▶ what the atmosphere is like
▶ how the sun affects weather conditions

READING FOCUS SKILL

MAIN IDEA AND DETAILS Look for details about how uneven heating of Earth's surface leads to wind.

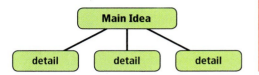

The Atmosphere

You probably know that Earth is surrounded by a blanket of air called the **atmosphere**. The atmosphere is very thin compared to the size of Earth. In fact, if Earth were the size of a peach, the atmosphere would be thinner than the peach's fuzz!

The atmosphere is made up of several layers. Each layer has a different temperature. The layer closest to Earth's surface is called the **troposphere**. It's about 13 km (8 mi) thick, on average. Even the highest mountains on Earth are within it. The troposphere contains about 90 percent of the gases in the atmosphere. It also contains water, dust, and other tiny particles. Most of Earth's weather occurs there.

The stratosphere is the next higher layer. Most of Earth's ozone is in the stratosphere. Ozone is a gas that protects Earth from

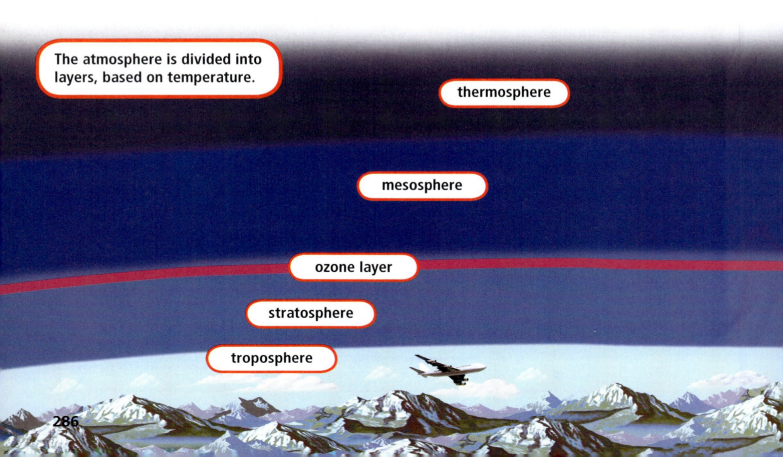

The atmosphere is divided into layers, based on temperature.

thermosphere

mesosphere

ozone layer

stratosphere

troposphere

the sun's harmful ultraviolet rays. The air in the stratosphere is very dry, so clouds are rare. Above the stratosphere, the air is very thin—there is less air. The outermost layer of the atmosphere extends into space.

Gas molecules in the atmosphere are constantly moving. Gravity pulls them toward Earth's surface. As a result, air near the surface is dense and has considerable weight. **Air pressure** is the weight of the atmosphere pressing down on Earth.

Air pressure is greater at sea level than it is on a mountain. That's because there is more air closer to Earth's surface than away from the surface. Temperature also affects air pressure. Cold air is more dense than warm air, so it is heavier than warm air.

 MAIN IDEA AND DETAILS What is the atmosphere made of?

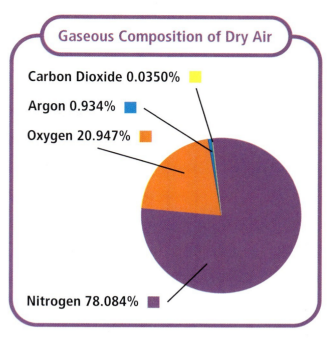

Gaseous Composition of Dry Air

Carbon Dioxide 0.0350%

Argon 0.934%

Oxygen 20.947%

Nitrogen 78.084%

▲ This circle graph shows the percentages of gases in dry air. However, most air in the troposphere is about 1 percent to 4 percent water vapor.

The lower you are in the atmosphere, the greater the air pressure is, because air molecules higher up in the atmosphere press down on all the air molecules below them.

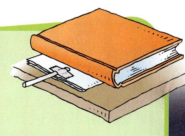

How Strong Is Air Pressure?

Put one end of a straw in a plastic bag. Use tape to seal the bag. Put the bag on a table, and lay a book on the bottom half of the bag. Blow through the straw. Observe what happens. In what ways might you use air pressure?

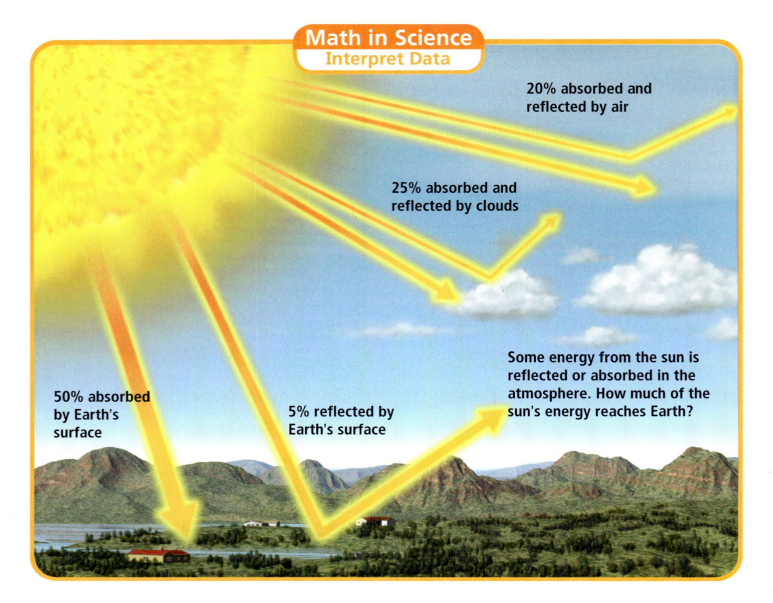

20% absorbed and reflected by air

25% absorbed and reflected by clouds

Some energy from the sun is reflected or absorbed in the atmosphere. How much of the sun's energy reaches Earth?

50% absorbed by Earth's surface

5% reflected by Earth's surface

Uneven Heating

When you left home this morning, how did the air feel? Was it hot or cold? Was it windy, or was it calm? If you were to go outside right now, would the air feel the same? It probably wouldn't. That's because the air around you is always moving and changing. Why is this so?

When the sun's energy reaches Earth, some of the energy bounces off objects such as clouds. Earth absorbs the rest of the energy. Different types of surfaces absorb different amounts of energy. For example, you learned in the Investigate that water can absorb more heat than an

equal amount of soil. That means if you're spending the day at the beach and you want to cool off, your best bet would be to take a swim. The sand is hotter than the water, so it gives off more heat. Because of this, the air over the beach will be hotter, too. The air over the water will be cooler.

Remember, cool air is denser than warm air. Dense air is heavy, so it sinks. Air that is warm—and less dense—is pushed up. This sinking and rising of air causes wind. In other words, wind is the result of uneven heating of the atmosphere.

 MAIN IDEA AND DETAILS Why does air in the atmosphere move?

Local Winds

Air is always moving. Winds result from air moving from areas of high air pressure to areas of low air pressure. Because cool air has a higher pressure than warm air, wind blows from cooler places toward warmer places.

Sometimes, two places in the same area have slightly different temperatures. This produces a <mark>local wind</mark>, a wind that results from a local difference in temperature. Local winds often occur on lakeshores or seashores. During the day, the air over the land is warmer than the air over the water. Air over the water becomes more dense. The result is a wind that blows from the water toward the land. This wind is known as a sea breeze.

In the evening, the wind blows the opposite way. Remember, land cools off more quickly than water does. Once the land becomes cooler than the water, a wind blows from the land toward the water. This wind is called a land breeze.

 MAIN IDEA AND DETAILS What are the directions of a local wind along a shoreline?

During the day, the land heats up faster than the sea. Cooler sea air moves toward the land. This is called a *sea breeze.* ▼

At night, the land loses heat faster than the sea does. Cooler air over the land moves toward the sea. This is called a *land breeze.* ▼

Prevailing Winds

Local winds move short distances and can blow from any direction. But there are other, more constant winds. <mark>Prevailing winds</mark> are global winds that always blow from the same direction. Uneven heating of large areas of Earth's surface causes prevailing winds. Earth's rotation affects prevailing winds, too.

Earth's poles are covered with ice. Depending on the time of year, the poles receive indirect sunlight or no sunlight at all, so they're always cold. By contrast, Earth's equator gets direct sunlight all year long, so it's always warm. As a result, cold air above the poles sinks and moves toward the equator. At the same time, air at the equator moves up and goes toward the poles. But air doesn't just move in one big circle. As warm air at the equator moves up, it begins to cool. Some of the cooling air sinks before it reaches the poles. Air in the atmosphere travels in many circles as it continually warms and cools.

You might expect air moving within these circles to move straight north or south. Instead, air moves in curved paths. For example, over the United States, winds moving north curve to the east. Winds moving south curve to the west. The curving is due to Earth's rotation. This rotation causes the prevailing winds to blow mainly from the east or the west.

 MAIN IDEA AND DETAILS What two factors cause prevailing winds?

The global winds that blow over most of the United States are called the prevailing westerlies. They blow from the west to the east. ▼

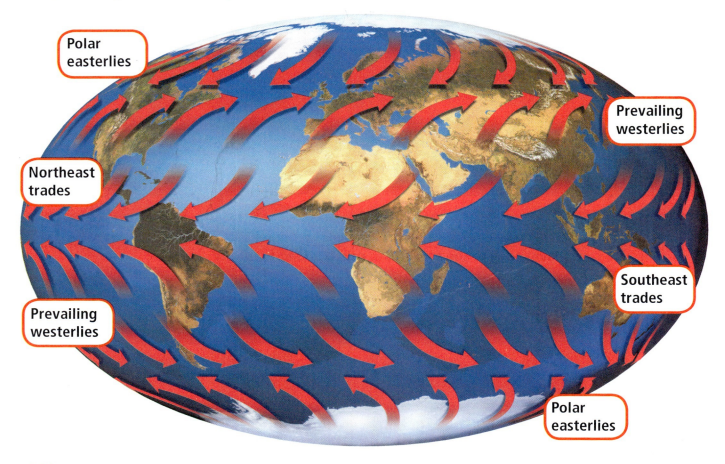

Polar easterlies

Prevailing westerlies

Northeast trades

Southeast trades

Prevailing westerlies

Polar easterlies

Focus Skill

1. MAIN IDEA AND DETAILS Draw and complete the graphic organizer.

The atmosphere has several layers of air.

The layer closest to Earth is the **A** _____.

Almost all of Earth's **B** _____ happens in this layer.

The second layer of the atmosphere is called the **C** _____.

This layer contains the protective gas **D** _____.

2. SUMMARIZE Summarize the ways that the sun's energy affects Earth's atmosphere.

3. DRAW CONCLUSIONS How does the troposphere affect everyday living?

4. VOCABULARY Choose three vocabulary terms from this lesson. Draw diagrams that illustrate the meanings of the three terms.

FCAT Prep

5. Read/Inquire/Explain Suppose you're going fishing on a lake. Describe the winds that might occur along the lakeshore.

6. Which of the following is the most common gas in the troposphere?
   A. carbon dioxide
   B. nitrogen
   C. oxygen
   D. water vapor

Links

Writing

Expository Writing

Suppose you're on vacation. Write a postcard **describing** the weather to a friend. Include temperature, wind speed, and wind direction.

Math

Solve Problems

About 20 percent of the sun's energy that reaches the air is reflected back into space. Another 25 percent is absorbed or reflected by the clouds. What percent of the sun's energy reaches Earth's surface?

Health

Sunscreen

Research how the sun affects human skin. Then make a brochure that explains how people can keep their skin healthy and why they should use sunscreen.

 For more links and activities, go to **www.hspscience.com**

What Conditions Affect the Water Cycle?

Fast Fact

Blizzard! The United States has an average of 105 snowstorms each year. A snowstorm can last from just a few hours to many days. During one snowstorm in Buffalo, New York, 96 cm of snow fell in 24 hours! In the Investigate, you'll see how water for rain or snow gets into the air.

Water, Water Everywhere

Materials
- graduate
- water
- small plastic cup
- zip-top plastic bag

Procedure

1. Using the graduate, measure and pour 100 mL of water into the cup.

2. Open the plastic bag and carefully put the cup inside. Then seal the bag. Be careful not to spill any water from the cup.

3. Place the sealed bag near a sunny window. Predict what will happen to the water in the cup.

4. Leave the bag near the window for 3 to 4 days. Observe the cup and the bag each day. Record what you see.

5. Remove the cup from the bag. Measure the water in the cup by pouring it back into the graduate. By using the numbers you recorded, find any difference in the amount of water poured into the cup and the amount of water removed from the cup.

Draw Conclusions

1. What did you observe during the time the cup was inside the bag?

2. What happened to the water in the cup?

3. **Inquiry Skill** Scientists often infer the cause of what they observe. What can you infer about where the water in the bag came from?

Step 1

Step 3

Investigate Further

Is the amount of water in the bag the same as the amount of water missing from the cup? Plan and conduct a simple investigation to find out.

VOCABULARY
water cycle p. 294
evaporation p. 295
condensation p. 295
humidity p. 296
precipitation p. 296

SCIENCE CONCEPTS
► how water moves through the water cycle
► how the water cycle relates to weather

READING FOCUS SKILL

SEQUENCE Look for the order of steps in which water moves through the water cycle.

The Water Cycle

In Lesson 1, you learned that air always moves. Water is always moving, too. In fact, water continuously moves from Earth's surface to the atmosphere and back to Earth in a process called the **water cycle**.

The water cycle is important because people, plants, and animals need fresh water to live. Without rain and snow, we wouldn't have drinking water. We also wouldn't have water to grow crops.

Science Up Close

The Water Cycle

The water cycle is driven by heat energy from the sun. The sun's rays warm water on Earth's surface. The water evaporates, leaving behind the salt in sea water. The sun also heats the atmosphere unevenly. This causes the air, containing water vapor, to move from one place to another.

As moist air rises, it cools. If it cools enough, the water vapor in it condenses, forming clouds.

Water vapor mixes with dust and other particles in the air.

Every day, tons of water evaporate from Earth's oceans, lakes, rivers, and moist soil.

294

How does the water cycle work? You may remember that water on Earth exists in three states. Water is a liquid in oceans, lakes, and rivers and in rain. If water is heated, it turns into a gas—water vapor. If water is cooled enough, it changes to a solid—ice.

During part of the water cycle, liquid water changes to a gas by the process of **evaporation**. As a gas, water molecules are too spread out to be seen. You can observe the results of evaporation if, for example, you leave a glass of water uncovered for a long time. The water just seems to disappear. Water in the air remains a gas as long as the air is warm. If the air cools, the water becomes a liquid. Water changes from a gas to a liquid in the process of **condensation**. When a large amount of water vapor condenses, a cloud forms. If the drops of water in the cloud become heavy enough, the water falls as rain.

When rain falls on the land, the water runs into streams, rivers, and lakes. Some of it soaks into the ground. Rivers carry the water back to the ocean. Water under the ground, called *groundwater,* also flows back to the ocean or into streams and rivers.

 SEQUENCE What steps in the water cycle must occur before rain can fall?

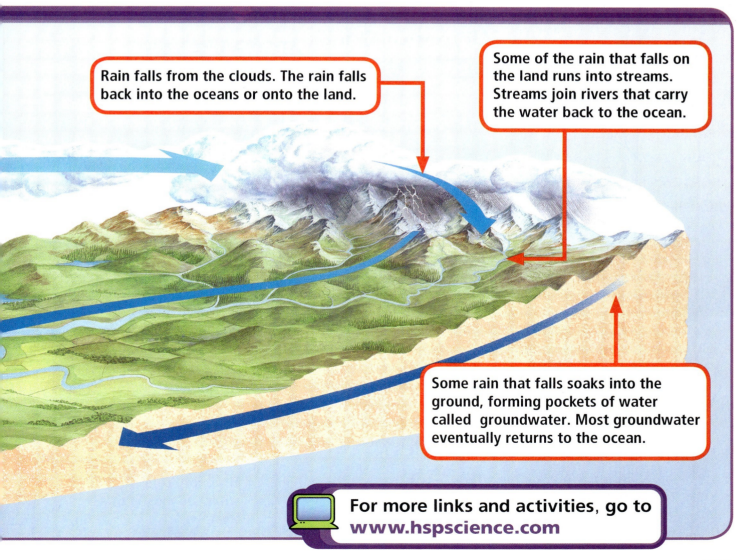

Rain falls from the clouds. The rain falls back into the oceans or onto the land.

Some of the rain that falls on the land runs into streams. Streams join rivers that carry the water back to the ocean.

Some rain that falls soaks into the ground, forming pockets of water called groundwater. Most groundwater eventually returns to the ocean.

For more links and activities, go to **www.hspscience.com**

Clouds and Precipitation

Much of what you may call weather is actually part of the water cycle. A large part of the water cycle occurs in the atmosphere. Water enters the atmosphere when it evaporates and becomes water vapor. Some areas of the atmosphere have more water vapor than other areas. The amount of water vapor in the air is **humidity**. The more water vapor in the air, the more humid the air is.

Humidity is limited by air temperature. Warm air can have more water vapor in it than cold air can have. Suppose you're on an island near the equator. The air over the island is warm, so it will contain a lot of water that has evaporated from the ocean. As warm air is forced up, it cools. Some of the water vapor begins to condense on dust and other particles in the air. As more and more water condenses, a cloud forms. A cloud is basically dust and condensed water.

Small water droplets inside the cloud join to form larger droplets. The larger droplets then join to make water drops. Water drops are too heavy to stay in the atmosphere. They fall from the clouds as precipitation (pree•sip•uh•tay•shuhn). **Precipitation** is water that falls from the atmosphere to Earth's surface. Rain is liquid precipitation.

Types of Clouds

CUMULUS CLOUDS

Cumulus (KYOO•myuh•luhs) clouds are puffy. They indicate fair weather, but as a cumulus cloud grows, rain can develop.

STRATUS CLOUDS

Stratus (STRAT•uhs) clouds form low in the atmosphere. They usually cover the sky. Heavy precipitation does not usually fall from stratus clouds, but moderate rainfall or snowfall is possible.

CIRRUS CLOUDS

Cirrus (SIR•uhs) clouds form high in the atmosphere, where the air is very cold. They are made mostly of ice crystals.

Several kinds of precipitation fall from cumulus clouds. This cloud is a cumulonimbus cloud. Cumulonimbus clouds produce moderate to heavy rain, hail, or snow.

Rain

Snow

Sleet

Hail

The other forms of precipitation—snow, sleet, and hail—are solid. Snow forms when water vapor turns directly into ice crystals. Sleet and hail form when liquid water passes through air that is cold enough to freeze water drops.

Water vapor doesn't always form precipitation as it condenses. Have you ever found dew on the ground after a cool night? Car windows and other objects may also be covered with dew. Why does dew form? The ground loses heat more quickly than the air does. When the ground becomes cold enough, water vapor in the air directly above the ground condenses. If the temperature is very cold, frost forms on the ground or on car windows. Frost is water vapor that turns directly into ice.

A similar weather condition can form fog. Fog is water vapor that has condensed into small water droplets near ground level.

 SEQUENCE What is the first step in the formation of a cloud?

Insta-Lab

Making Raindrops

Use a spray bottle to mist a piece of wax paper with water. This models a cloud. Move the wax paper around so that the small water droplets start to join into larger droplets. What process are you modeling? If this were a real cloud, what would happen?

Factors That Affect the Water Cycle

Many factors affect the water cycle. One factor is how close a place is to Earth's poles or the equator. Places close to the poles are always cold. Because of this, they're much more likely to get snow or sleet than places close to the equator.

Another factor that affects the water cycle is the shape of the land. Air must move around and over landforms such as mountain ranges. When air is pushed up the side of a mountain, it cools. Much of the water in the air condenses. This causes rain to fall, usually on one side of the mountain. If the mountain is high enough, snow may fall instead of rain. The snow stays on the mountain until spring. In spring, the snow melts, sending huge amounts of water flowing down the mountain in streams and rivers. This is called the spring melt.

Landforms such as coastlines also affect the water cycle. You've read about how sea breezes form along coastlines. A sea breeze usually carries humid air. As the air rises over the land, clouds form. If the drops of water in the clouds get large enough, rain falls.

Landforms and temperature affect the water cycle because they change the pressure of the air. Remember, warm air has lower pressure than cold air. And warm air can have more water in it than cold air can. Any factor that causes a change in air pressure can also cause a change in the water cycle.

 SEQUENCE What events on a mountain lead to the spring melt?

Fog is a stratus-like cloud that forms at ground level. Fog often forms on hills and mountains when humid air moves up a slope to the point where the water vapor in the air condenses and forms a cloud.

1. SEQUENCE Draw and complete the graphic organizers.

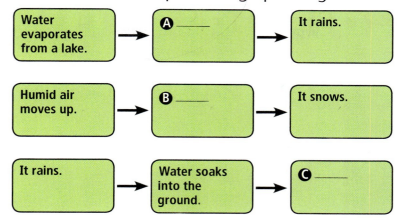

Water evaporates from a lake.	→	Ⓐ ____	→	It rains.
Humid air moves up.	→	Ⓑ ____	→	It snows.
It rains.	→	Water soaks into the ground.	→	Ⓒ ____

2. SUMMARIZE Write a paragraph describing a sequence of events that happens to a water molecule during the water cycle.

3. DRAW CONCLUSIONS What would happen to the water cycle if the sun heated the atmosphere evenly?

4. VOCABULARY Compare and contrast the two terms within each pair: *evaporation* and *condensation*; *humidity* and *precipitation*.

FCAT Prep

5. Read/Inquire/Explain You see cirrus clouds in the sky. Will it rain soon? Explain your answer.

6. You heat an ice cube, and it melts. What will happen to the water if you continue to apply heat?
  A. It will condense.
  B. It will evaporate.
  C. It will freeze.
  D. It will precipitate.

Links

Writing

Narrative Writing
Write a **description** of how the water cycle varies in your area during the year. Include the seasons in your description.

Math

Draw Conclusions
Make a graph showing types and amounts of precipitation in 10 cities around the United States. What conclusions can you draw about snowfall amounts by comparing your graph to a map?

Social Studies

Monsoons
Monsoons are weather systems that produce dry and wet seasons in some parts of the world. Research monsoons, and write a report about them.

For more links and activities, go to **www.hspscience.com**

Lesson 3

How Can Patterns in Weather Be Observed?

Fast Fact

Blowing the Horn During heavy fog, operators of the Golden Gate Bridge—in San Francisco—sound a horn. This helps ships avoid the bridge. From July through October, there's so much fog that the horn sounds for about five hours nearly every day! In the Investigate, you'll observe other predictable weather patterns.

Measuring Weather Conditions

Materials • weather station

Procedure

1 Copy the table titled Weather Station Daily Record. You'll use it to record the weather each day for five days. Try to gather data about weather conditions at the same time each day.

2 Place the weather station in a shady spot, about 1 m above the ground. Be sure the rain gauge will not collect runoff from buildings or trees. Put the wind vane where wind from any direction can reach it.

3 Record the amount of rain or snow, if any.

4 Record wind direction and speed. Identify wind by the direction from which it's blowing.

5 Observe and record the cloud conditions. Draw a circle, and shade part of it to show the fraction of the sky that is covered with clouds.

6 Record the temperature. Make a line graph showing how the temperature changes from day to day.

Draw Conclusions

1. Compare weather conditions you observed on two different days.

2. **Inquiry Skill** Scientists learn about the weather by measuring and gathering data. From the data you gathered, how might you predict the weather for tomorrow?

Step 2

Weather Station Daily Record			
Date			
Time			
Temperature			
Rainfall or snowfall			
Wind direction and speed			
Cloud conditions			

Investigate Further

Can clues about tomorrow's weather be found in today's weather data? Plan and conduct an investigation to find out if specific observations can help you predict upcoming weather.

Reading in Science

SC.H.3.2.1.5.1 technology has improved human lives; LA.E.3.2.2 cause and effect

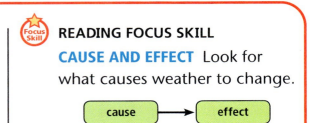

VOCABULARY
air mass p. 304
front p. 305
climate p. 306

SCIENCE CONCEPTS
▶ how weather conditions are measured
▶ how weather can be predicted

READING FOCUS SKILL

CAUSE AND EFFECT Look for what causes weather to change.

cause ⟶ effect

Measuring Weather

You use a ruler to measure length. You use a spring scale to measure weight. And you use a graduate to measure volume. What do you use to measure weather? Because there are many different kinds of weather data, you need many different instruments.

You're probably familiar with one kind of weather instrument—a thermometer. A thermometer measures air temperature. A *hygrometer* measures humidity—the amount of water in the air. Another kind of weather instrument is the *barometer*. A barometer measures air pressure.

barometer

hygrometer

A weather station has many different kinds of instruments. Hundreds of weather stations similar to this one are used to collect weather data around the world. ▼

▲ In the past, people relied on simple observations to help them forecast the weather. Sayings such as "Red sky at night, sailors' delight" and "When the dew is on the grass, rain will never come to pass" helped people remember what their observations might predict about the weather.

Remember, air temperature and air pressure are related. A rising barometer, which shows increasing air pressure, often precedes the arrival of colder air. Since cold air has less water in it than warm air does, a rising barometer also means less humidity and less chance of rain.

There are several instruments that measure wind. An *anemometer* measures wind speed. *Windsocks* and *wind vanes* both measure wind direction. It's important to measure wind because changes in wind often bring changes in the weather. Knowing from which direction the wind is blowing helps people predict the weather. For example, if it's winter and a wind starts blowing from the south, you can predict that the weather will soon be warmer. Any change in wind direction or speed usually means a change in the weather.

Weather changes can also be predicted, although less accurately, just by observing the sky. For example, observing the clouds can tell you a lot. There's a saying that goes "Red sky at night, sailors' delight. Red sky in the morning, sailors take warning." A red sky in the morning occurs when the rising sun reflects on storm clouds coming from the west. This often means it will rain later in the day. A red sunset means that no storms are approaching from the west, so the next day should be sunny. Different cloud types are also associated with different types of weather.

 CAUSE AND EFFECT How can rising air pressure lead to a prediction about temperature?

303

Air Masses and Fronts

You read in Lesson 1 that Earth's atmosphere heats unevenly. This causes the air in the atmosphere to move. Air doesn't move around Earth randomly in small amounts. Instead, air moves in regular ways in air masses. An **air mass** is a large body of air that has the same temperature and humidity throughout. In the United States, air masses often move from west to east, pushed along by the prevailing winds.

Air masses can be warm or cold. They can also be humid or dry. What determines an air mass's characteristics? An air mass takes on the characteristics of the region over which it forms. For example, an air mass that forms over the Caribbean Sea will be humid and warm. An air mass that forms over northern Canada will be dry and cold.

Look at the map. As you can see, there are four kinds of air masses that affect weather in the United States. Continental polar air masses (cP) bring cool, dry weather. Continental tropical air masses (cT) bring hot, dry weather. Maritime polar air masses (mP) bring cold, humid weather. Finally, maritime tropical air masses (mT) bring warm, humid weather.

When the weather changes in an area, it means that the air mass over the area is changing. That is, the current air mass is being replaced by a different air mass.

A continental air mass forms over land, so it is dry. A maritime air mass forms over water, so it is humid. A polar air mass forms over cold areas, so it is cold. A tropical air mass forms over warm areas, so it is warm. ▶

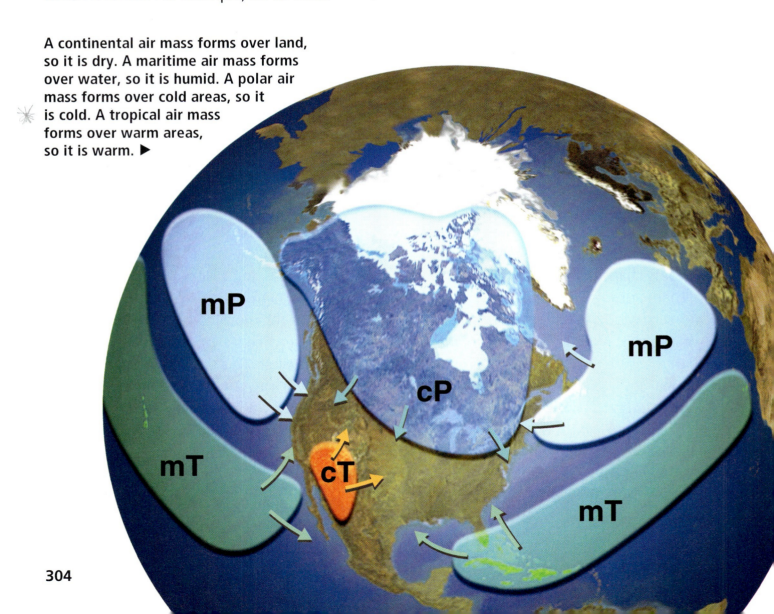

▲ After a cold front passes (left), the weather is cooler and drier. After a warm front passes (right), the weather is warmer and more humid.

The border where two air masses meet is called a **front**. Most weather changes occur along a front. For example, if a cold, dense air mass pushes into a warm, light air mass, the warm, light air begins to move up. As that air moves up, it cools. Water vapor in it condenses, and clouds form. There is usually precipitation along a front.

There are two main kinds of fronts: cold fronts and warm fronts. A *cold front* forms where a cold air mass moves under a warm air mass (left side of diagram above). The warm air mass is less dense, so it is pushed up. Cumulonimbus clouds form, producing heavy rain, thunderstorms, or snow near the front. Cold fronts usually move quickly, so the precipitation doesn't last long.

On weather maps, cold fronts are shown by blue lines with triangles. Warm fronts are shown by red lines with half circles. ▶

A *warm front* forms where a warm air mass moves over a cold air mass (right side of diagram above). As the warm air slides up and over the cold air, stratus clouds form ahead of the front. This causes rain or snow that can last for hours.

 CAUSE AND EFFECT What kind of air mass causes hot, humid weather?

Weather Patterns and Climates

Weather in most locations occurs in regular patterns. You already know several factors that produce weather patterns. Local winds produce weather patterns in a small area. Prevailing winds produce weather patterns over large areas.

In addition to wind patterns, there are temperature patterns. For example, on most days, it's cool in the morning and warmer in the afternoon. The air warms up as the sun's energy heats the Earth. When the sun sets, the air begins to cool off again.

Over a longer time, there are seasonal patterns. Every year, much of the United States has different weather during winter, spring, summer, and fall. The weather is coldest during winter and warmest during summer.

Like daily patterns, seasonal weather patterns are driven by the sun. Fall and winter are cool in the United States because the Northern Hemisphere receives sunlight that is less direct and for fewer hours. Spring and summer are warmer because the Northern Hemisphere receives sunlight that is more direct and for more hours.

The pattern of weather an area experiences over a long time is called **climate**. There is a difference between weather and climate. Weather is the condition of the atmosphere at a particular time. Climate is the average of weather conditions over many years. Average temperature and precipitation are the main characteristics of climate.

Because the sun heats Earth unevenly, areas close to the equator get more energy from the sun than areas closer to the poles do. As a result, the farther a place is from the equator, the colder its climate is. How wet or dry a climate is usually depends on how close a place is to large bodies of water. Therefore, coastal areas are often wetter than areas in the interior of a continent.

⭐ **CAUSE AND EFFECT** What causes seasonal weather patterns?

Earth takes a year to revolve around the sun. Because Earth tilts on its axis, the intensity of sunlight reaching the Northern Hemisphere and the Southern Hemisphere varies during the year. This causes the seasons. ▶

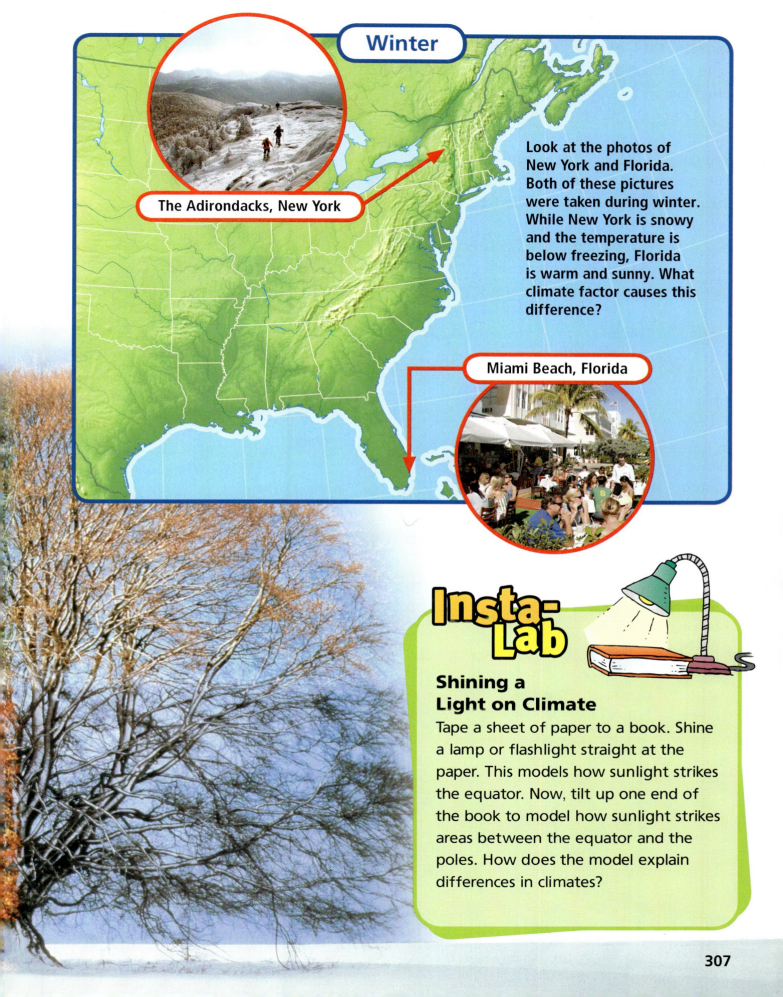

Winter

The Adirondacks, New York

Look at the photos of New York and Florida. Both of these pictures were taken during winter. While New York is snowy and the temperature is below freezing, Florida is warm and sunny. What climate factor causes this difference?

Miami Beach, Florida

Insta-Lab

Shining a Light on Climate

Tape a sheet of paper to a book. Shine a lamp or flashlight straight at the paper. This models how sunlight strikes the equator. Now, tilt up one end of the book to model how sunlight strikes areas between the equator and the poles. How does the model explain differences in climates?

Landforms Affect Climate

In addition to distance from the equator, other factors affect an area's climate.

In Lesson 2, you read that a mountain affects the water cycle by forcing air to rise and cool. As the air cools, clouds form. This causes rain or snow on the side of the mountain that faces the wind. By the time the air reaches the other side of the mountain, it has lost most of its water. And since the air is sinking, its humidity goes down even more. For these reasons, there is little or no rain on the downwind side of the mountain. This is known as the *rain shadow effect*. A rain shadow effect can cause one side of a mountain to have a wet climate while the other side has a dry climate.

Large bodies of water, such as an ocean or a very large lake, can affect an area's climate. Remember, water heats up and cools down more slowly than land does.

▲ Grapes can be grown here despite its northern location. This is because of the warming effect of the nearby lake.

So land near a large body of water tends to have a milder climate than other areas. This land is usually cooler in summer, warmer in winter, and more humid all year than areas farther inland.

 CAUSE AND EFFECT What factors affect an area's climate?

The climates on opposite sides of a mountain range can be very different because of the rain shadow effect.

Moist air blown from Pacific Ocean

Dry air moving toward desert

308

1. CAUSE AND EFFECT Draw and complete the graphic organizer.

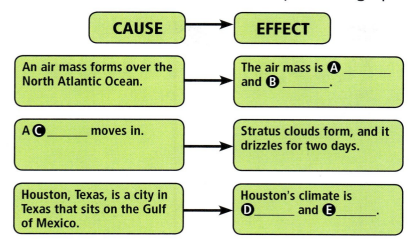

| CAUSE | → | EFFECT |

An air mass forms over the North Atlantic Ocean. → The air mass is **Ⓐ** _____ and **Ⓑ** _____ .

A **Ⓒ** _____ moves in. → Stratus clouds form, and it drizzles for two days.

Houston, Texas, is a city in Texas that sits on the Gulf of Mexico. → Houston's climate is **Ⓓ** _____ and **Ⓔ** _____ .

2. SUMMARIZE Summarize several types of weather patterns.

3. DRAW CONCLUSIONS If Earth's oceans were much smaller, how do you think climates on Earth would be affected?

4. VOCABULARY In your own words, write definitions for the following terms: *air mass, front,* and *climate*.

FCAT Prep

5. Read/Inquire/Explain Suppose you feel strong winds, see dark clouds forming, and hear thunder. What could cause this weather?

6. Which of the following affects climate by causing air to move up?
  A. Earth's revolution
  B. large lakes
  C. mountains
  D. nearness to the poles

Links

Writing

Expository Writing
Write a **letter** that could be sent to a pen pal in another country to describe what the climate is like where you live.

Math

Display Data
Find the average precipitation for your area for each month of the year. Also find the average temperature. Make bar graphs to display the data.

Social Studies

Mountain Effects
Locate a mountain range with a rain shadow effect. Research the different kinds of plants and animals that live on the wet side and the dry side of the mountains.

 For more links and activities, go to **www.hspscience.com**

On the Lookout

Weather forecasters have one of the toughest jobs around. Millions of people rely on weather forecasts to make their plans. But if a weather forecast is wrong, you can bet the weather experts hear about it.

Weather forecasting isn't easy, though. Forecasters can't use a crystal ball or flip a coin to predict the weather. They have to rely on data from different sources and use computers to be as accurate as possible in their predictions.

Pictures from Space

Satellites are some of the most important tools weather forecasters use. Satellites orbit about 35,000 kilometers (21,748 miles) above Earth. They give forecasters a bird's-eye view of clouds and how they are moving across land and water.

One pair of weather satellites, called GOES, is used by the National Weather Service. The satellites send weather data and pictures to forecasters on the ground. Using the images from the satellites, forecasters can track the movements of storm clouds.

Doppler Radar

Doppler radar also helps forecasters determine whether clouds hold snow, sleet, hail, or rain. The radar provides color-coded images that identify each type of precipitation. Precipitation is any form of water that falls to Earth from the clouds.

The various colors show the intensity of the precipitation. Light and dark blue colors usually indicate areas of light precipitation. Areas of red and pink colors usually indicate strong to severe thunderstorms. So if a radar image shows a broad band of pink moving toward a town, forecasters can warn people in the town of incoming severe weather.

Up, Up, and Away

The National Weather Service releases weather balloons twice a day from 100 different locations around the United States. The balloons can rise 32 kilometers (20 miles) high and have a transmitter, called a radiosonde, attached. The radiosonde sends temperature, humidity, wind, and air pressure data back to the scientists on the ground.

Reliable Technology

Weather balloons have been used by forecasters for decades. The balloons show forecasters what is happening high in the atmosphere.

THINK ABOUT IT

1. Why might the National Weather Service still use weather balloons?
2. Why are accurate weather forecasts important to people and to businesses?

Spin-In Find out more! Log on to www.hspscience.com

SCD.D.1.2.3.5.1 atmospheric pressure; SC.H.2.2.1.5.1 analyze patterns of change; SC.H.3.2.1.5.1 technology has improved human lives

Watching the Weather

Rain? Clouds? Snow? Thalya Cruz and Yesenia Zapata watch and know. Each day the girls follow a cool, weather-watching routine.

First, they log on to a classroom computer to find things like temperature, wind speed, wind direction, and air pressure. Next, they record those findings. In time, they will look back for weather patterns that take place.

Then, the girls add to a bar graph they made, which shows the number of days having rain or clouds. Their work with maps helps them learn about kinds of climate and weather. The best thing, they say, is working with weather maps. Why? It's like a guessing game to try and predict what the weather will be like the next day or even next week.

SC.H.3.2.3.5.1 solving problems may create others;
SC.H.3.2.4.5.1 people can solve problems through science

You Can Do It!

Materials
- 50 mL of water
- large plastic cup
- 15 g of salt
- small plastic cup
- crushed ice
- stirring stick

Quick and Easy Project

Making Hail

Procedure

1. Put 50 mL of water into the large plastic cup. Stir in about 15 g of salt.
2. Put 15 mL of cold water into the small cup.
3. Fill the large cup with crushed ice. Put the small cup inside the large cup. Be sure not to get any ice in the small cup.
4. Stir the ice in the large cup for 7 minutes.
5. Remove the small cup from the large cup. Drop a small piece of ice into the small cup, and observe what happens.

Draw Conclusions

Describe what you observed. Based on your observations, what conditions in the atmosphere cause hail to form?

Design Your Own Investigation

Predicting Weather

Can you predict the weather with the instruments you used in the Investigate? Use them to record weather data for a week. Compare the previous day's measurements with the current measurements. What patterns do you observe? Record weather data during a second week. Each day, predict the weather for the next day by applying the patterns you observed the week before. What other data might you need in order to make your predictions accurate?

Review and FCAT Preparation

Vocabulary Review

Use the terms below to complete the sentences. The page numbers tell where to look in the chapter if you need help.

atmosphere p. 286   condensation p. 295
air pressure p. 287   evaporation p. 295
local wind p. 289   precipitation p. 296
prevailing   air mass p. 304
  wind p. 290   climate p. 306
water cycle p. 294

1. Water that falls from the air to Earth is _____.

2. Global winds that blow constantly in the same direction are _____.

3. The weight of the atmosphere pressing down on Earth is _____.

4. Water changes from a gas to a liquid in the process of _____.

5. The pattern of weather an area experiences over many years is _____.

6. The blanket of air surrounding Earth is the _____.

7. Water changes from a liquid to a gas in a process known as _____.

8. A large body of air is an _____.

9. A wind that results from local changes in temperature is a _____.

10. The movement of water between the atmosphere, the land, and the ocean is known as the _____.

Check Understanding

Write the letter of the best choice.

11. MAIN IDEA AND DETAILS In which layer of Earth's atmosphere does most weather occur?
  A. hydrosphere
  B. stratosphere
  C. thermosphere
  D. troposphere

12. CAUSE AND EFFECT Which of these is a common effect of a warm front?
  F. cold, clear weather
  G. many hours of rain
  H. strong, blowing winds
  I. violent thunderstorms

13. Of the following processes, which most likely left the moisture on the outside of the glass below?
  A. condensation
  B. evaporation
  C. humidification
  D. precipitation

14. Examine the diagram of a seashore. Why do sea breezes form?

    F. Air heats more slowly than land.
    G. Earth's surface is heated evenly.
    H. Land heats more slowly than water.
    I. Water heats more slowly than land.

15. What is shown in the picture below?

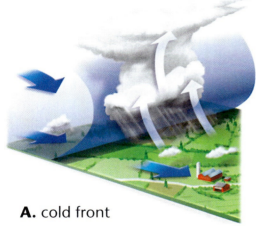

    A. cold front
    B. evaporation
    C. rain shadow
    D. warm front

16. Which of these is liquid precipitation?
    F. dew
    G. fog
    H. hail
    I. rain

Inquiry Skills

17. Which do you **predict** will heat up faster on a sunny day—a pond or a meadow? Explain your answer.

18. What two instruments are most important for the **measurements** of a region's climate? Explain your answer.

Read, Inquire, Explain

19. What type of weather should you expect when you see this type of cloud?

20. Suppose it is sunset on a warm, humid day. After dark, the temperature is predicted to drop.
Part A How does air temperature relate to the amount of water vapor in the air?
Part B What will happen to the water vapor in the air if the temperature drops as predicted?

Earth and Space

 The chapters in this unit address these Grade Level Expectations from the Florida Sunshine State Standards.

Chapter 9 Earth, Moon, and Beyond

SC.E.1.2.1.5.1 knows the orbit of the Earth is slightly elliptical and the Earth is closest to the Sun in the Northern Hemisphere in winter.

SC.E.1.2.1.5.2 knows that the angle that the rays of the Sun strike the surface of the Earth determines the amount of energy received and thus the season of the year.

SC.E.1.2.1.5.3 knows the effect of the tilt of the Earth on polar climates.

SC.E.1.2.2.5.1 knows the relative positions of the Moon, Earth, and the Sun during each of the phases of the Moon.

SC.E.1.2.4.5.1 knows that the planets differ in size, characteristics, and composition and that they orbit the Sun in our Solar System.

SC.E.1.2.5.5.1 knows the arrangement of the planets and the asteroid belt in our Solar System.

The investigations and experiences in this unit also address many of the Grade Level Expectations in Strand H, The Nature of Science.

EARTH SCIENCE

Science in Florida

Orlando

Dear Katrina,

Today my class took a field trip to the Crosby Observatory at the Orlando Science Center. We got to look through their telescope into space, and we saw all kinds of neat stuff. I learned that there are many things that look like stars but really are not. We saw Saturn, Jupiter, and entire galaxies that are so far away they look like stars. I would love to have my own telescope to gaze at the stars.

Sincerely,

Jacques

The Sunshine State

USA

FCAT Writing

Writing Situation

Think about traveling into space. Write a story about your journey into space.

Experiment!

Modern Rocket Stages Scientists study the universe from Earth and space. Studying the universe from space requires rockets that can send heavy materials into space. What rocket design will carry heavy payloads the farthest? For example, is one large rocket more powerful than several smaller rockets? Plan and conduct an experiment to find out.

9 Earth, Moon, and Beyond

Lesson 1 How Does Earth's Orbit Affect the Seasons?

Lesson 2 How Do Earth and the Moon Compare?

Lesson 3 What Makes Up Our Solar System?

Vocabulary

FCAT-Tested

sun	star
axis	solar system
equator	constellation
moon	planet
moon phase	universe
refraction	galaxy

Other Terms

rotate

revolve

orbit

crater

eclipse

What do YOU wonder?

The world's largest single-dish radio telescope is in Arecibo, Puerto Rico. Scientists use the telescope—whose dish is 305 m (1000 ft) wide—to study deep space. In what other ways do scientists study objects in space?

319

How Does Earth's Orbit Affect the Seasons?

Sunrise from Space Astronauts in space may see 16 sunrises and 16 sunsets every day as they travel around Earth. In the Investigate, you'll learn about movements of Earth and the moon and why, here on Earth, we see only 1 sunrise and 1 sunset each day.

Moving Through Space

Materials   ● beach ball   ● baseball   ● table-tennis ball

Procedure

① Work in a group of four. You will use a model to show the time and space relationships among Earth, the moon, and the sun. One person should hold the beach ball (the sun). Another should stand far away and hold the baseball (Earth). A third person should hold the table-tennis ball (the moon) near the baseball. The fourth person should record the movements.

② For the model, Earth should move around the sun in a circle and spin at the same time. The real Earth spins about 365 times during each complete path around the sun.

③ While the model Earth moves, the model moon should move around Earth in a nearly circular path. The real moon spins once during each complete path around Earth. Earth spins about $29\frac{1}{2}$ times from one new moon to the next.

Draw Conclusions

1. One movement in the model represented a year. Which movement was that?

2. **Inquiry Skill** Use your understanding of time and space relationships to compare the moon's and Earth's movements. How are they alike? How are they different?

Step 1

Step 3

Investigate Further

Make a model to show how you think the amount of sunlight reaching different parts of Earth changes during the year.

Reading in Science

VOCABULARY

sun p. 322
rotate p. 322
axis p. 322
revolve p. 324
orbit p. 324
equator p. 324

SCIENCE CONCEPTS

▶ how the movements of Earth and the sun result in day and night and the seasons

▶ why we have time zones

READING FOCUS SKILL

MAIN IDEA AND DETAILS Look for the details about Earth's movements.

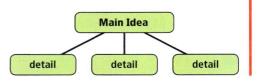

Day and Night

Every day the **sun**, the star at the center of our solar system, appears to rise in the east. It appears to reach its highest point around noon, and to set in the west. After a period of darkness, this process repeats.

This cycle of day and night occurs because Earth **rotates**, or spins on its axis. Earth's **axis** is an imaginary line that passes through the North and South Poles. When a place on Earth faces the sun, it is day in that place. When that place faces away from the sun, it is night.

Our system of time is based on Earth's 24-hour cycle of daylight and darkness. Because of Earth's rotation, sunrise and sunset occur at different times in different places. Long ago, people didn't need to know the exact time. And each place used local time—time based on sunrise and sunset in that place. This changed in the late 1800s. Trains were starting to travel long distances. If each train station had kept its own time, there would have been confusion. People needed to develop standard times.

The sun appears to rise and set. Of course it actually doesn't. Earth's rotation causes what appear to be a sunrise and a sunset.

▲ It's 7 A.M. in Seattle, on the west coast.

▲ Much of the United States is within one of four time zones. Time zone lines aren't perfectly straight, partly because of state boundaries.

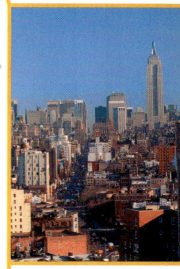

▲ In New York City, on the east coast, it's 10 A.M.

In 1884, standard times were set up in 24 time zones around the world. Each time zone represents one of the hours in the day. All the places within a time zone have the same time. If you travel east from one time zone to the next, the time becomes one hour later. If you travel west from one time zone to the next, the time becomes one hour earlier. In the middle of the Pacific Ocean is the International Date Line. If you go west across that line, you travel into the next day. Crossing the line eastward, you travel into the previous day. For example, if it's 3 A.M. Tuesday and you cross the International Date Line while going west, the time becomes 2 A.M. Wednesday, not Tuesday.

The United States has seven time zones, from Puerto Rico in the east to Hawai`i in the west. If you're just about to have dinner at 6 P.M. in Florida and you call a friend in Oregon, it will be 3 P.M. there. Your friend may be just getting home from school.

 MAIN IDEA AND DETAILS Explain why officials needed to set up time zones in the late 1800s.

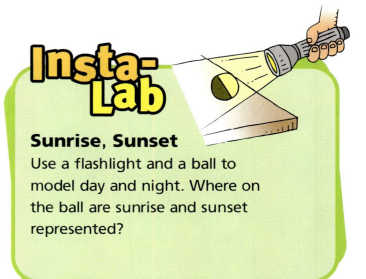

Insta-Lab

Sunrise, Sunset
Use a flashlight and a ball to model day and night. Where on the ball are sunrise and sunset represented?

Earth's Seasons

You probably know that most places on Earth have seasons. During the summer, there are more hours of daylight than hours of darkness. The temperature is usually higher, too. During the winter, there are fewer hours of daylight and the temperature is lower. These seasonal changes are a result of the tilt of Earth's axis.

In addition to rotating on its axis, Earth **revolves**, or travels in a path around the sun. The path Earth takes as it revolves is its **orbit**. One orbit takes about 365 days, or one year.

Some people think we have seasons because Earth is closer to the sun in the summer than in the winter. This isn't so. (Earth is actually closer to the sun during our winter.) The shape of Earth's orbit is only slightly elliptical; that is, it's nearly circular. It's the tilt of Earth's axis that produces seasons.

Earth's axis is not straight up and down in relation to its orbit. If it were, the angle of the sun's rays when they hit Earth would be the same all year long. There would be no seasons. But Earth's axis is tilted about 23.5°. During part of the year, half of Earth is tilted toward the sun. On that part of Earth, it is summer. On the part tilted away from the sun, it is winter.

Earth is divided into Northern and Southern Hemispheres by the equator. The **equator** is an imaginary line going all the way around Earth halfway between the North and South Poles. When the Northern Hemisphere is tilted toward the sun, the Southern Hemisphere is tilted away.

To see this process, follow the seasons shown in the diagram. When the Northern Hemisphere is tilted toward the sun, it is summer there. The number of hours of daylight is greater than the number of hours of darkness. The sun's rays strike part

When it is summer in the Northern Hemisphere, . . .

. . . it is winter in the Southern Hemisphere.

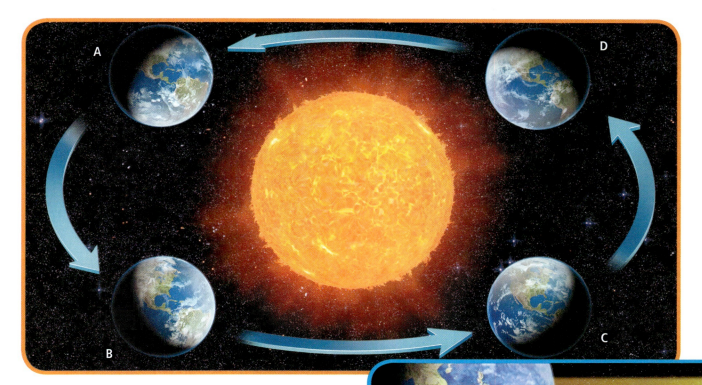

▲ The position of Earth in relation to the sun changes, depending on where the Earth is in its orbit. During summer in the Northern Hemisphere (C), that hemisphere points toward the sun. During spring (B) and fall (D), neither hemisphere points toward the sun.

of the hemisphere directly, so the weather is warm. Even in Alaska, summer temperatures can reach 30°C (86°F).

As Earth continues in its orbit, the Northern Hemisphere is tilted away from the sun. There are fewer hours of daylight and more hours of darkness in that hemisphere. The rays of the sun strike the Northern Hemisphere at more of an angle. The weather is much cooler, even in Florida.

The day when the amount of daylight is the greatest is called the *summer solstice* (SAHL•stis). In the Northern Hemisphere, it's June 20 or 21, depending on the year. The winter solstice, the day with the least amount of daylight is December 21 or 22.

Halfway between the solstices, neither hemisphere is tilted toward the sun. The

▲ During the Northern Hemisphere's summer, the number of hours of daylight is at its highest. During summer also, the sun's rays hit the Northern Hemisphere more directly, not at as great an angle as in winter. This causes more heating because the sun's rays don't spread out as much.

hours of daylight and darkness are about equal. These days are called the *equinoxes* (EE•kwih•nahks•uhz). In the Northern Hemisphere, the autumn equinox is September 22 or 23. The spring equinox is March 20 or 21.

 MAIN IDEA AND DETAILS What are the days called that have the most and the least hours of daylight?

325

Highs and Lows

Seasons at the North and South Poles are very different from seasons everywhere else. In the summer, the poles get six months of daylight and no darkness. Winter brings six months of darkness, with no daylight.

Even though the South Pole has a summer of nonstop daylight, it's never very warm. Sunlight that reaches Antarctica, even in the summer, is at a low angle and more spread out. This results in low temperatures all year.

At the equator, halfway between the poles, days and nights are about 12 hours each all year. Temperatures stay about the same all year, too. The warmest places in the world are just south and north of the equator. Rain at the equator keeps temperatures from reaching highs like those in deserts such as the Sahara.

 MAIN IDEA AND DETAILS In Antarctica, why is it cold even in the summer?

The lowest temperature ever recorded on Earth, −89°C (−129°F), was at Russia's Vostok Station, in Antarctica in 1983.

The highest temperature ever recorded on Earth, 58°C (136°F), was in Al Aziziyah, Libya, in the Sahara in 1922.

1. MAIN IDEA AND DETAILS Draw and complete these graphic organizers.

Day		Night

Day and night happen because of Ⓐ _____.

Earth is divided into 24 time zones.

	Earth's Seasons	

Seasons happen because of Earth's orbit and the Ⓑ _____.

A solstice is Ⓒ _____.

2. SUMMARIZE Write a summary by answering the question in the lesson title.

3. DRAW CONCLUSIONS If Earth were not tilted on its axis, how would life be different?

4. VOCABULARY Use the words *revolve* and *rotate* to explain Earth's movements in space.

FCAT Prep

5. Read/Inquire/Explain A friend lives where there are 12 hours of daylight every day. Where does this person live, and how do you know?

6. What season is it in the Northern Hemisphere when the Southern Hemisphere points toward the sun?
   A. fall   **C.** summer
   B. spring   **D.** winter

Links

Writing

Narrative Writing
Living at a research station in Antarctica would be an unusual experience for most of us. Write a **story** telling what a week of summer vacation there would be like.

Math

Solve Problems
Use the highest and lowest temperatures ever recorded on Earth (see previous page) to determine the range of temperatures on Earth.

Social Studies

Maya Calendar
Research the Maya calendar. Write a paragraph comparing that calendar with the calendar we use today. Draw a picture of the calendar to go with your paragraph.

 For more links and activities, go to **www.hspscience.com**

How Do Earth and the Moon Compare?

Fast Fact

The Moon Rocket The Saturn V launch vehicle shown here is 36 stories high. Powered by the Saturn launch vehicle, six Apollo missions landed on the moon. In 1969, Neil Armstrong was the first person to walk on the moon's cratered surface. In the Investigate, you'll make a model of craters being formed.

Making Craters

Materials
- newspaper
- aluminum pan
- apron
- large spoon
- $\frac{1}{2}$ cup water
- 1 cup flour
- safety goggles
- marble
- meterstick

Procedure

1. Copy the table.

2. Spread the newspaper on the floor. Place the pan in the center of the newspaper.

3. Put on the apron. Use the spoon to mix the water and most of the flour in the pan. Spread out the mixture. Lightly cover the surface of the mixture with dry flour to make a model of the moon's surface.

4. **CAUTION: Put on the safety goggles** to protect your eyes from flour dust. Drop the marble into the pan from a height of 20 cm. Carefully remove the marble.

5. Measure the width of the crater, and record it in the table. Repeat Step 4 two more times. Measure and record each time.

6. Now drop the marble three times from each of the heights 40 cm, 80 cm, and 100 cm. Measure and record the crater's width after each drop. Compare your results with those of your classmates.

Making Craters		
Trial	Height	Width of Crater
1	20 cm	
2	20 cm	
3	20 cm	
1	40 cm	
2	40 cm	
3	40 cm	

Step 3

Draw Conclusions

1. How did height affect crater size?

2. **Inquiry Skill** Scientists use models to study space. From using a model, what did you learn about how the moon's craters may have been formed?

Investigate Further

How would dropping objects of different sizes affect the size and shape of the craters? Plan and conduct a simple investigation to find out.

VOCABULARY
moon p. 330
crater p. 330
moon phase p. 333
eclipse p. 334
refraction p. 334

SCIENCE CONCEPTS
▶ how the moon and Earth are alike and different
▶ how the phases of the moon and solar and lunar eclipses happen

READING FOCUS SKILL

COMPARE AND CONTRAST Look for ways the phases of the moon are alike and different.

| alike | | different |

The Moon and Earth

If you stare at the moon at night, you may wonder what the surface of this silent, round object is like. A **moon** is any natural body that revolves around a planet. Earth and its moon are similar in several ways. Both are rocky and fairly dense. Both are made of many of the same elements, including aluminum, oxygen, calcium, silicon, and iron. Both the moon and Earth have craters. A **crater** is a low, bowl-shaped area on the surface of a planet or moon.

However, there are also important differences between the moon and Earth. One clear difference is size. The moon's diameter is about 3476 km (2160 mi), only about one-fourth of Earth's diameter.

The moon's pull of gravity is only about one-sixth that of Earth. A person who weighs 800 newtons (180 lb) on Earth would only weigh 133 newtons (30 lb) on the moon. The moon, unlike Earth, has almost no atmosphere and no liquid water. Temperatures on the moon can range

From space, the moon looks gray because of its rocks and dust. ▼

From space, Earth looks blue because of its oceans. There is no liquid water on the moon.

▲ Astronauts need spacesuits on the moon to provide air to breathe and to protect them from the extreme temperatures. The heavy suits and other equipment feel much lighter on the moon than on Earth because of the weaker gravitational pull of the moon.

from more than 100°C (212°F) during the day to –155°C (–247°F) at night. Earth's temperatures are much less extreme.

The moon's surface is covered with craters, many more than on Earth. The craters were made by objects falling from space, like the marbles in the Investigate.

Most objects that fall from space toward Earth burn up in the atmosphere before they reach the ground. The craters that do form on Earth are usually worn down by weathering. Objects that fall to the moon, though, do not burn up, because there is hardly any atmosphere. And there is no erosion, because of the lack of atmosphere and lack of water. As a result, craters on the moon last indefinitely.

COMPARE AND CONTRAST How is the moon's surface different from that of Earth?

A footprint on Earth doesn't last long, but a footprint on the moon could last millions of years due to lack of erosion.

Insta-Lab

Astronaut Moves

To work on the moon or in space, astronauts need to wear spacesuits to protect themselves. Try to thread a nut on a bolt while wearing heavy gloves. How difficult do you think it would be to work on the moon or in space?

Phases of the Moon

On some nights, you may notice that the moon seems to have disappeared. On other nights, you see a large, white moon shining brightly. The moon, though, has not changed at all. Instead, the moon and Earth have moved.

In the Investigate in Lesson 1, you learned how Earth travels around the sun and how the moon travels around Earth at the same time. Earth orbits the sun in a slight ellipse. The moon's orbit around Earth is a slight ellipse, too. When the moon is closest to Earth, it is about 356,400 km (221,000 mi) away.

Both Earth and the moon rotate as they revolve, though at different speeds. The moon rotates more slowly. It completes a rotation every $29\frac{1}{2}$ Earth days. So a day on the moon is $29\frac{1}{2}$ Earth days long.

The moon rotates as it orbits Earth, but the same side of the moon always faces Earth. That's because one lunar cycle, from new moon to new moon, takes $29\frac{1}{2}$ days, the same amount of time the moon takes to complete one rotation.

The side of the moon we can't see from Earth was once called the dark side of the moon. A better name is the far side of the moon. Although we can't see the far side of the moon, the sun shines on that side as often as on the side we see.

The moon is often bright at night, but it doesn't give off its own light. As the moon orbits Earth, its position in the sky changes. The part of the moon that is exposed to the sun reflects the sun's light.

The Apollo 8 mission, in 1968, was the first mission to carry people in orbit around the moon. While in orbit, the crew took pictures like this one of the moon's far side.

Phases of the Moon

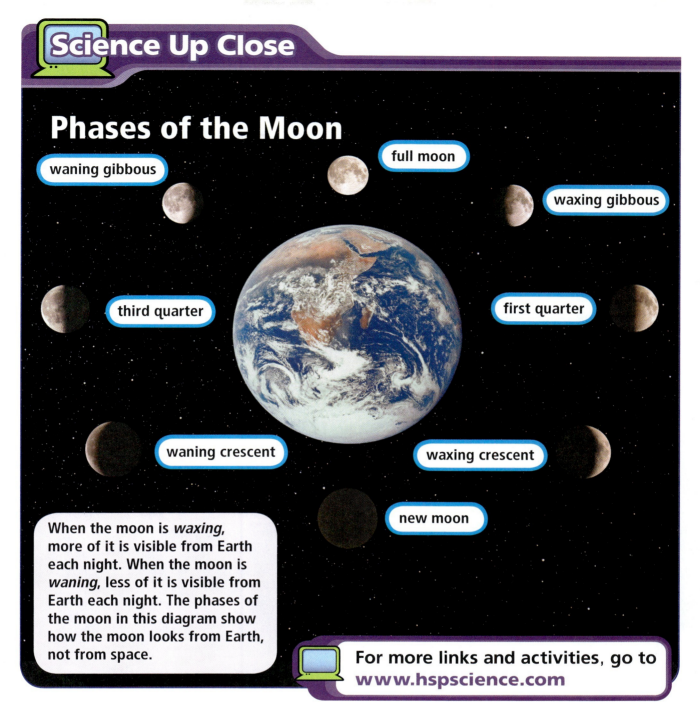

waning gibbous

full moon

waxing gibbous

third quarter

first quarter

waning crescent

waxing crescent

new moon

When the moon is *waxing*, more of it is visible from Earth each night. When the moon is *waning*, less of it is visible from Earth each night. The phases of the moon in this diagram show how the moon looks from Earth, not from space.

 For more links and activities, go to **www.hspscience.com**

The way the moon looks from Earth changes daily. At any time, half of the moon is lit by the sun. But how much you see depends on the moon's phase. A ==moon phase== is one of the shapes the moon seems to have as it orbits Earth. When Earth is between the moon and the sun, you see a full moon. When the moon is between Earth and the sun, you can't see the moon at all. This is called a new moon.

The cycle of phases of the moon takes $29\frac{1}{2}$ days. During the cycle, the visible portion of the moon changes gradually. Starting with a new moon, you see more and more of the moon each day until the full moon. Then you see less and less each day until the next new moon.

COMPARE AND CONTRAST Contrast the appearance of the moon during a full moon and a new moon.

333

Eclipses

Objects in space block some of the sun's light, producing shadows. An **eclipse** occurs when one body in space blocks light from reaching another body in space.

Eclipses we see on Earth are solar eclipses and lunar eclipses. They are alike because both occur when Earth, the sun, and the moon line up. However, solar and lunar eclipses also differ.

A solar eclipse occurs when the moon—always a new moon—casts a shadow on Earth. In some places the moon seems to cover the sun, and the sky gets dark. Only the outer atmosphere of the sun is visible, as a bright glow around the moon. At other places, only part of the sun is covered.

A lunar eclipse occurs when the moon—always a full moon—passes through the shadow of Earth. Earth blocks the sun's light from reaching the moon, but the moon does not look black. Instead, it looks red. This is because Earth's atmosphere bends red light, which then reflects off the moon. Scientists call this bending of light **refraction**.

You might think that eclipses happen with every new or full moon. But the moon and Earth are not always in the proper alignment. Sometimes only a partial eclipse occurs. Partial solar and lunar eclipses each occur two to four times a year.

 COMPARE AND CONTRAST How do solar and lunar eclipses differ?

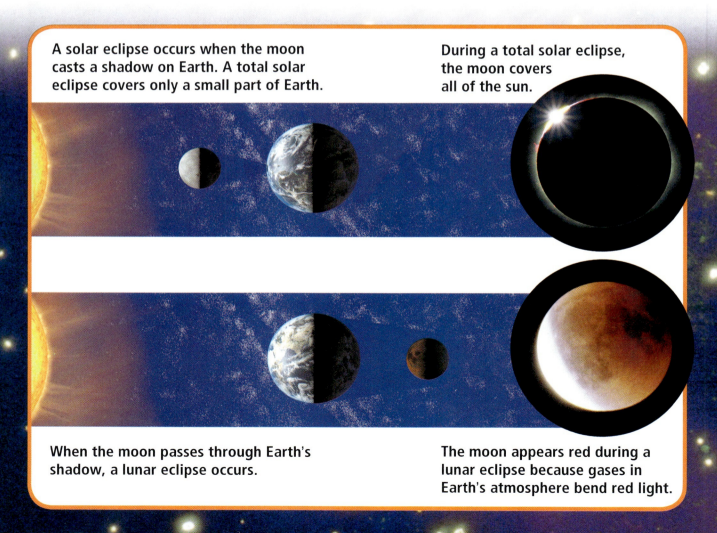

A solar eclipse occurs when the moon casts a shadow on Earth. A total solar eclipse covers only a small part of Earth.

During a total solar eclipse, the moon covers all of the sun.

When the moon passes through Earth's shadow, a lunar eclipse occurs.

The moon appears red during a lunar eclipse because gases in Earth's atmosphere bend red light.

1. COMPARE AND CONTRAST Complete the diagram.

	Different	Alike
Earth and moon	atmosphere: Earth has an atmosphere. The moon does not. size: **Ⓐ** _____ gravity: **Ⓑ** _____ temperature: **Ⓒ** _____	materials: **Ⓓ** _____ surface features: Both the moon and Earth have craters.
New moon and full moon	appearance: **Ⓔ** _____	phases: Both are phases of the moon.
Solar eclipse and lunar eclipse	positions of bodies in space: **Ⓕ** _____	causes: Both pass through shadows of bodies in space.

2. SUMMARIZE Write two sentences that tell what this lesson is mostly about.

3. DRAW CONCLUSIONS How would the moon be different if it had liquid water?

4. VOCABULARY Explain in a sentence what a moon phase is.

FCAT Prep

5. Read/Inquire/Explain On a night when you see a full moon, where are the moon, sun, and Earth relative to each other in space?

6. Which of these are on the surfaces of both the moon and Earth?
  A. craters
  B. liquid water
  C. oxygen
  D. windstorms

Links

Writing

Narrative Writing

Think about the differences between the moon and Earth. Then write a **story** that describes the differences. Use as many descriptive words as you can.

Math 9÷3

Use Fractions

During a full moon, you can see half of the moon's surface. During a first quarter, what fraction of the moon's surface can you see on a clear night?

Physical Education

Running to the Moon

The moon is about 221,000 mi from Earth at its closest point. To get an idea of how far that is, run or walk 221 steps. Each step represents 1000 miles.

 For more links and activities, go to **www.hspscience.com**

Lesson **3**

What Makes Up Our Solar System?

Fast Fact

Deep Space Close-Up Since the launch of the Hubble Space Telescope in 1990, people have studied and enjoyed many of the Hubble's amazing images, like this one of the Cone Nebula. Some of the objects shown in Hubble images are at a distance greater than 10 billion light-years (60 billion trillion mi). In the Investigate, you'll make your own telescope—though you won't see as far as with a telescope like the Hubble.

The Cone Nebula

Make a Telescope

Materials
- 2 sheets of construction paper
- tape
- modeling clay
- 2 convex lenses

Procedure

1. Roll and tape a sheet of construction paper to form a tube slightly larger in diameter than the lenses. Make a second tube just large enough for the first tube to fit inside it.

2. Slide most of the smaller tube into the larger tube.

3. Use some of the clay to hold one of the lenses in one end of the smaller tube. This will be the telescope's eyepiece.

4. Use clay to hold the other lens in the far end of the larger tube. This will be the lens closer to the object you are viewing.

5. Choose three distant objects to view. **CAUTION: Do not look at the sun.** Slide the smaller tube to focus on each object.

6. Observe each object twice, once without the telescope and once with it. Record each observation in a drawing.

Draw Conclusions

1. Compare the drawings made with and without the telescope. Why do they differ?

2. **Inquiry Skill** How was your observing similar to using a space telescope?

Step 1

Step 3

Investigate Further

Use your telescope to observe the brightest object in the eastern night sky. List details you can see with the telescope but not without it.

Reading in Science

SC.E.1.2.4.5.1 differences in planets; **SC.E.1.2.5.5.1** arrangement of planets; **LA.A.2.2.1** main idea and details

VOCABULARY

star p. 338
solar system p. 338
constellation p. 339
planet p. 341
universe p. 344
galaxy p. 344

SCIENCE CONCEPTS

▶ what objects make up our solar system
▶ what other objects are in the universe

 READING FOCUS SKILL

MAIN IDEA AND DETAILS Look for main ideas about planets and stars.

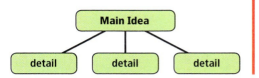

Main Idea

detail · detail · detail

The Sun and Other Stars

One object that you can see in the sky without a telescope is the sun. But you should NEVER look directly at the sun. The sun is a **star**, a huge ball of very hot gases in space. The sun is at the center of our solar system. A **solar system** is made up of a star and all the planets and other objects that revolve around that star.

The sun is the source of much of the energy on Earth. Plants use energy from the sun to make food and store energy. Animals eat plants to use that food energy. When plants and animals die, they decay, or rot. Some that died long ago became fossil fuels, such as oil, that people use today.

The sun's features make it different from everything else in our solar system. The sun is huge: a million Earths could fit inside it.

The energy in one solar flare is greater than any explosion ever produced by humans.

Scientists use this solar furnace to experiment with the sun's energy. The furnace temperatures range from 800°C (1470°F) to 2500°C (4530°F). ▼

▲ There are many ways to classify stars. A star can be classified according to its size, its brightness, its temperature, and its color.

The constellation Ursa Major, or the Great Bear, was named by the ancient Greeks. It contains a more familiar star pattern—the Big Dipper.

The glowing surface of the sun is what we see from Earth. On the sun's surface are sunspots visible from Earth. Sunspots are darker, cooler areas of the sun. They can produce brief bursts of energy called solar flares. Above the sun's surface is the corona. This area of hot gases extends about 1 million km (600,000 mi) from the surface of the sun.

The sun is important to us because of its energy. But the sun is just one of billions of stars in the universe. Among all those stars, the sun is average. It's a yellow star of medium size, medium brightness, and medium heat.

One way scientists classify stars is by color. Star colors range from blue, white, and yellow to orange and red. The color of a star is a clue to its surface temperature. Blue stars are the hottest, and red stars are the coolest.

Another way scientists classify stars is by brightness. How bright a star appears depends on two factors. One is how far it is from Earth. The other is how bright it actually is.

Since ancient times, people have grouped stars into constellations. A **constellation** is a pattern of stars that is named after a religious or mythical object or animal. One set of constellations is visible from the Northern Hemisphere. Another set is visible from the Southern Hemisphere.

 MAIN IDEA AND DETAILS What are two ways scientists classify stars?

Mercury
diameter: 4900 km
(about 3040 mi)
distance from sun:
58,000,000 km
(about 36,000,000 mi)
length of year:
88 Earth days

Venus
diameter: 12,100 km
(about 7500 mi)
distance from sun:
108,000,000 km
(about 67,000,000 mi)
length of year:
225 Earth days

Earth
diameter: 12,700 km
(about 7900 mi)
distance from sun:
150,000,000 km
(about 93,000,000 mi)
length of year:
365.25 Earth days

Math in Science
Interpret Data

Weight on Different Planets

The pull of gravity at a planet's surface depends on the planet's diameter and on how much mass the planet has. The greater the planet's pull of gravity, the more you would weigh on its surface. Here are the weights on different planets for a person who weighs 100 pounds on Earth.

Note: Diagrams not to scale.

Planet	Weight (lb)
Mercury	37.8
Earth	100.0
Venus	90.7
Mars	37.7

Does Venus have a stronger or weaker pull of gravity than Earth?

The Inner Planets

Our solar system includes nine planets. A ==planet== is a body that revolves around a star. A planet is held in its orbit by the gravitational force between the planet and the star.

Scientists divide the nine planets that orbit the sun into four inner planets and five outer planets. These groups are separated by the huge asteroid belt between Mars and Jupiter. The *asteroid belt* is a ring-shaped area where many small, rocky bodies, or asteroids, are located.

The four inner planets are rocky and dense. Mercury, which is closest to the sun, is about the size of Earth's moon. Like the moon, Mercury has almost no atmosphere and a surface covered with craters and dust. The side of Mercury facing the sun is hot—about 430°C (810°F). The side not facing the sun can become very cold, however—about −180°C (−290°F).

Venus is the brightest object in the night sky, after the moon. This planet is about the same size as Earth, and it is rocky. The similarities end there. Venus can become very hot, reaching about 460°C (860°F). It is even hotter than Mercury because Venus's thick atmosphere keeps heat from escaping.

Earth is the only planet to support life, because of its liquid water and atmosphere. Earth's atmosphere maintains temperatures in which living things can survive.

Mars is called the red planet because of its reddish soil. Its atmosphere is mostly carbon dioxide. Its valleys are evidence that Mars once had liquid water. Mars has the largest volcano in the solar system, and it has dust storms that can last for months.

Mars
diameter: 6800 km
(about 4200 mi)
distance from sun:
228,000,000 km
(about 142,000,000 mi)
length of year:
687 Earth days

 MAIN IDEA AND DETAILS What separates the inner planets from the outer planets?

The Outer Planets

Beyond the asteroid belt are the five outer planets. In their order from the sun, they are Jupiter, Saturn, Uranus, Neptune, and Pluto. The first four of these planets are called gas giants, because they are composed mostly of hydrogen and helium.

Jupiter is the largest planet in the solar system. It has rings and dozens of moons, including Ganymede, the largest moon in the solar system. There is a huge storm on Jupiter that has lasted for about 400 years. The storm, like a hurricane, has a name, and its name describes its appearance—the Great Red Spot.

Saturn is best known for its rings, made of ice, dust, boulders, and frozen gas. The rings stretch about 136,200 km (84,650 mi) from the center of the planet. Like Jupiter, Saturn has dozens of moons.

Uranus also has many moons and rings. This planet rotates on an axis that is tilted much more than those of other planets. Compared with the other planets, Uranus looks like a top that has fallen over but is still spinning.

Neptune has several rings and moons and the fastest winds in the solar system. The winds can reach 2000 km/hr (1200 mi/hr)!

Pluto, unlike the other outer planets, is small and rocky. It also has an unusual orbit. Part of its orbit passes inside the orbit of Neptune, so sometimes Neptune is the farthest planet from the sun. Pluto's single moon, Charon, is about half as big as the planet itself.

 MAIN IDEA AND DETAILS What are some characteristics of the gas giants?

Jupiter
diameter: 143,000 km
(about 89,000 mi)
distance from sun:
778,000,000 km
(about 483,000,000 mi)
length of year:
11.9 Earth years

Note: Diagrams not to scale.

asteroid Ida

Pluto
diameter: 2300 km
(about 1400 mi)
distance from sun:
5,890,000,000 km
(about 3,660,000,000 mi)
length of year:
249 Earth years

Saturn
diameter: 120,000 km
(about 74,000 mi)
distance from sun:
1,427,000,000 km
(about 886,000,000 mi)
length of year:
29.5 Earth years

Uranus
diameter: 51,000 km
(about 32,000 mi)
distance from sun:
2,869,000,000 km
(about 1,783,000,000 mi)
length of year:
84 Earth years

Neptune
diameter: 49,000 km
(about 30,000 mi)
distance from sun:
4,505,000,000 km
(about 2,799,000,000 mi)
length of year:
165 Earth years

Asteroids and Comets

Both asteroids and comets orbit the sun. Asteroids are chunks of rock less than 1000 km (621 mi) in diameter. Comets have a small, solid, frozen core. As a comet nears the sun, however, its core begins to melt, forming a cloud of gas that is pushed into a long tail by energy from the sun. A comet's tail can be tens of millions of kilometers long.

comet Hale-Bopp

Beyond the Solar System

Look up on a clear night, and you may think you can see the universe. But what you see is only a small fraction of it. The **universe** is everything that exists—all the stars, the planets, dust, gases, and energy.

If it's dark enough where you live, you may see what look like ribbons of stars overhead. These ribbons are part of the Milky Way Galaxy, the galaxy that includes our solar system. A **galaxy** is gas, dust, and a group of stars, including any objects orbiting the stars. The Milky Way Galaxy has more than 100 billion stars and is one of the largest galaxies in the universe. Scientists estimate that the universe contains more than 100 billion galaxies.

Galaxies are classified by shape. There are four basic types: spiral, barred spiral, elliptical, and irregular. The Milky Way Galaxy is a spiral galaxy with a bulge of stars in the center and rotating arms around a disk. The sun is in one of the Milky Way Galaxy's spiral arms. The sun makes one complete turn around the center of the galaxy in about 200 to 250 million years.

A spiral galaxy can look like a giant pinwheel spinning through space. The arms wind around the center as the galaxy turns. ▼

The Hubble Space Telescope produced this image. Each bright spot is a galaxy containing countless stars. But even this image shows just one relatively small region of space. There are billions of galaxies in the universe.

A barred spiral galaxy is similar to a spiral galaxy, but the spiral arms extend from a bar of stars that stretches across the center. Elliptical galaxies make up about half of all galaxies. Their shapes range from almost a sphere to a flattened football shape. They do not seem to rotate. Irregular galaxies are groups of stars with no obvious shape.

Galaxies form groups known as clusters. The Milky Way Galaxy is one of about 30 galaxies in a cluster called the Local Group. There are thousands of galactic clusters in the universe.

Astronomers hypothesize that stars form in a nebula. A nebula is a huge cloud of hydrogen, helium, and tiny particles of dust. The matter of a nebula may clump together to form a *protostar*, a collection of gas clouds that starts reacting chemically. When a protostar is hot enough, it forms a star and begins to release energy in the form of heat and light.

Black holes are other, less understood parts of the universe. A black hole is an object of extremely intense gravity. Black holes are so dense that even light gets pulled into them. Scientists have concluded that a black hole forms when a large star collapses.

 MAIN IDEA AND DETAILS Describe the sun's position and movement in the Milky Way Galaxy.

A nebula may be composed of matter shed by an aging star. ▶

Rolling in Space
With supervision, sit in a desk chair that has wheels, lift up your feet, and try to move to another part of the room without touching the floor. How is the feeling you get the same as how you'd feel in space?

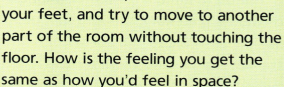
The Hubble Space Telescope took this image in 1994 of a huge spiral of dust being pulled into a black hole.

Space Exploration

In ancient times, people observed the sky and asked questions about what they saw. With the invention of the telescope in 1609, people first got a closer look into space. Early telescopes allowed astronomers to see details of the moon's surface, as well as moons around Jupiter. It was not until the mid-twentieth century, though, that people could launch vehicles into space.

The Russian satellite *Sputnik 1* was launched into Earth's upper atmosphere in 1957. A *satellite* is any body that orbits another. In the 1960s, Russian and United States spacecraft carried the first humans into space. In 1969, U.S. astronaut Neil Armstrong became the first person to walk on the moon.

Since the Apollo missions that flew astronauts to the moon from 1969 to 1972, much of space exploration has focused on other parts of the universe. In 1977, the United States launched the *Voyager 1* and *Voyager 2* space probes to study deep space. These robot vehicles have traveled to the edge of the solar system, past all the planets, and are still sending back information to Earth.

In 2004, the *Cassini* spacecraft reached Saturn. From its orbit around Saturn, *Cassini* has given scientists a wealth of information about the planet's famous rings.

Today's scientists use telescopes, satellites, and space probes to continue to explore space. All these devices are helping scientists understand more about our universe.

 MAIN IDEA AND DETAILS How has space exploration changed since the Apollo missions?

Two *Mars Rovers* landed on Mars in 2003. The six-wheeled rovers traveled over the surface of Mars collecting data, taking photographs, and analyzing Martian rocks and soil. ▶

In 1976, *Viking 1* and *Viking 2* became the first space probes to successfully land on Mars.

1. MAIN IDEA AND DETAILS Draw and complete the graphic organizer.

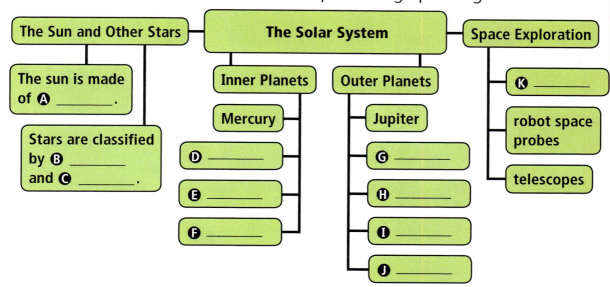

The Sun and Other Stars

The sun is made of **A** _____.

Stars are classified by **B** _____ and **C** _____.

The Solar System

Inner Planets

Mercury

D _____

E _____

F _____

Outer Planets

Jupiter

G _____

H _____

I _____

J _____

Space Exploration

K _____

robot space probes

telescopes

2. SUMMARIZE Using the graphic organizer, write a lesson summary.

3. DRAW CONCLUSIONS Why is Pluto considered an odd planet?

4. VOCABULARY How are *star, solar system,* and *galaxy* related?

FCAT Prep

5. Read/Inquire/Explain Why haven't scientists found life on other planets in the solar system?

6. Where is the asteroid belt?
   A. in the nebula
   B. in Saturn's rings
   C. between Jupiter and Mars
   D. between Earth and Venus

Links

Writing

Persuasive Writing
Should the United States increase the money spent for space exploration? Write a **letter** that tells your point of view. Include reasons that support your position.

Math

Multiply Numbers
An astronomical unit (AU) is about 149,600,000 km, the distance between Earth and the sun. If an object is 4 AU from Earth, how far away is it?

Literature

Space Poetry
Myra Cohn Livingston writes poetry about space. Read a book of her poetry, and write a paragraph about the poem you liked best.

 For more links and activities, go to www.hspscience.com

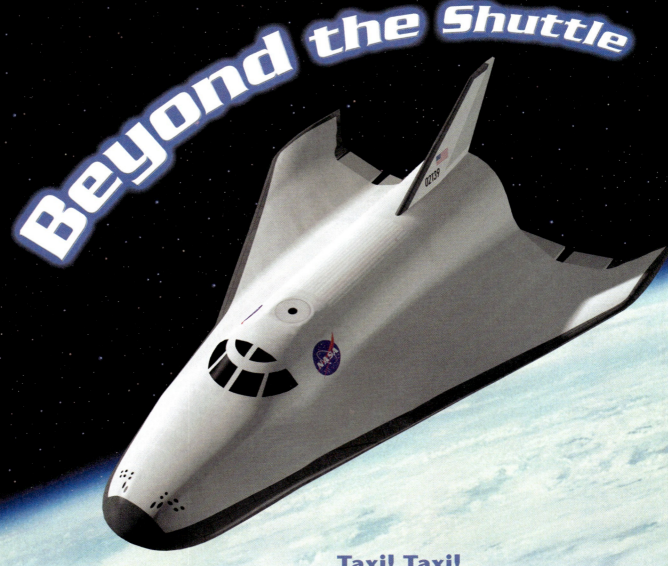

Beyond the Shuttle

An elevator to space? A spaceship with engines so powerful that the vehicle can take off like an airplane and fly—not blast off—into orbit? Those might sound like the basis of an episode of Star Trek, but the ideas are currently under development by the National Aeronautics and Space Administration (NASA).

Taxi! Taxi!

On the top of NASA's list is a space taxi. The vehicle would ferry ten astronauts at a time to and from the International Space Station (ISS) beginning in 2010. NASA is spending $882 million to design a craft called the Orbital Space Plane.

The space plane is a shuttlelike craft that would sit on top of a rocket. The rocket would blast the plane into orbit. "It would not be a space shuttle replacement," Barry

Davidson of Syracuse University said of the space plane. "It would be the next-generation vehicle out there."

Within the next 15 years or so, scientists say, NASA will have to replace the three space shuttles—*Discovery*, *Atlantis*, and *Endeavour*—which were all built in the 1970s and early 1980s.

NASA might also replace the shuttles with a spacecraft that would be attached to the back of a large aircraft. Once both vehicles are airborne, the spacecraft would release itself and speed into orbit using a super-powerful jet engine called a ramjet or a scramjet. The ramjet or scramjet engine would propel the craft into orbit at ten times the speed of sound.

Sound Byte

Sound travels through air at about 340 meters (1100 feet) per second.

Next Stop, Space

Some scientists say the easiest way to get into space might just be by elevator. NASA scientists are currently working on a plan that would put a large satellite in orbit about 35,000 kilometers (21,748 miles) above the equator. The satellite would be programmed to constantly hover over the same spot on Earth's surface.

Scientists would attach to the satellite a very long cable and an elevator that could then be used to transport people and equipment into space. "We think we can have it up and operational in about 15 years," said scientist Bradley C. Edwards.

Think About It

1. Why is it a good idea to have a space plane that is easy to reuse?
2. Do you think it's important for people to keep exploring outer space? Why or why not?

Spin-In

Find out more! Log on to
www.hspscience.com

Flying High

Franklin Chang-Diaz knew from the age of 7 that he wanted to fly in outer space. Chang-Diaz was born in Costa Rica and moved to the

United States when he was 17. He studied hard in high school and college to become an expert in a type of rocket propulsion called plasma physics.

Chang-Diaz became an astronaut in 1980 when he joined the National Aeronautics and Space Administration (NASA). Since then, he has flown on seven space-shuttle missions. Some of Chang-Diaz's missions have involved launching new types of satellites into orbit around Earth. The satellites give NASA information about our planet and the solar system.

Career | Aerospace Engineer

Aerospace engineers produce amazing machines and engines that propel those machines. The engineers design, develop, and test every kind of flying machine, from an airplane the size of a warehouse, to a spacecraft that travels almost 20,000 miles an hour.

SC.H.1.2.2.5.1 scientists use different types of investigations;
SC.H.3.2.1.5.1 solving problems may create others

You Can Do It!

Materials
- 15-cm cardboard square
- protractor
- drinking straw
- tape
- 20-cm piece of string
- metal washer

Quick and Easy Project

Navigating by the Stars

Procedure

1. At one corner of the cardboard square, draw a line at an angle of 10° from an edge. Use the protractor to do this. Then draw lines at 20°, 30°, and so on.
2. Tape the straw to the cardboard as shown.
3. At the point where all the lines meet, make a hole in the cardboard. Push the string through the hole, and tie a knot. Tie the washer to the other end of the string.
4. Look at a star through the straw. Measure the angle of the star by noting the angle of the string.

Draw Conclusions

The angle at which you see the North Star tells the latitude of where you are on Earth. What is the angle of the North Star where you live? What is the latitude where you live?

Design Your Own Investigation

A Change in the Days

You know that the seasons result from the tilt of Earth's axis as Earth moves around the sun. Design an investigation to find out how the amount of daylight changes because of Earth's movement. Plan to keep track of the amount of daylight each day for one week. Include a graph or table comparing the days.

Review and FCAT Preparation

Vocabulary Review

Use the terms below to complete the sentences. The page numbers tell you where to look in the chapter if you need help.

revolve p. 324	**eclipse** p. 334
orbit p. 324	**solar system** p. 338
equator p. 324	**constellation** p. 339
moon p. 330	**universe** p. 344
crater p. 330	**galaxy** p. 344

1. The path that Earth takes as it moves around the sun is its _____.

2. The sun is the center of our _____.

3. Everything that exists, including planets, stars, dust, and gases, is the _____.

4. Stars, gas, and dust make up our _____.

5. To travel in a path around another object is to _____.

6. Earth is divided into Northern and Southern Hemispheres by the _____.

7. When one body in space blocks light from reaching another body, there is an _____.

8. A bowl-shaped low place on a surface is a _____.

9. A natural body that revolves around a planet is a _____.

10. A pattern of stars is a _____.

Check Understanding

Write the letter of the best choice.

11. **MAIN IDEA AND DETAILS** Which detail explains why summers at the North Pole are cold?
    - **A.** Winters are long at the poles.
    - **B.** The North Pole is covered with ice.
    - **C.** Earth's orbit around the sun is elliptical.
    - **D.** The sun's rays are indirect at the North Pole.

12. **COMPARE AND CONTRAST** Which is a correct comparison of the moon and Earth?
    - **F.** They have similar gravitational force.
    - **G.** They both undergo weathering.
    - **H.** They both are rocky and dense.
    - **I.** They have similar atmospheres.

13. What does this illustration show?

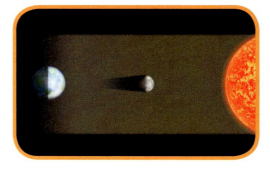

    - **A.** a full moon
    - **B.** a new moon
    - **C.** a waning moon
    - **D.** a waxing moon

14. Which is correct during summers in the Northern Hemisphere?

   F. Earth has its winter equinox.

   G. The Southern Hemisphere is tilted away from the sun.

   H. The Northern Hemisphere is not tilted toward the sun.

   I. Rays of the sun hit the equator more intensely than during the winter.

15. Which planet is labeled X?

   A. Earth

   B. Mars

   C. Mercury

   D. Venus

16. What determines the seasons on Earth?

   F. Earth's orbit and tilt

   G. the sun's speed and the orbit of the sun

   H. changing directions of Earth's orbit

   I. the position of the moon in relation to Earth

Inquiry Skills

17. How could you **use a model** to learn more about eclipses?

18. What tools do scientists use to **observe** deep space?

Read/Inquire/Explain

19. Explain how Saturn and Jupiter differ from Pluto.

20. The moon is Earth's only natural satellite. We know now about many of the moon's characteristics.

Part A Why do people sometimes refer to "the dark side of the moon"? Explain why this phrase is incorrect.

Part B Think about the differences between Earth and the moon. Then make a plan for a settlement on the moon. Explain what settlers will need to take to the moon or change on the moon to make it suitable for life.

Processes of Life

 The chapters in this unit address these Grade Level Expectations from the Florida Sunshine State Standards.

LIFE SCIENCE

Chapter **10** Cells to Body Systems

SC.F.1.2.1.5.1	understands how body systems interact.
SC.F.1.2.4.5.1	uses magnifying tools to identify similar cells and different kinds of structures.
SC.F.1.2.4.5.2	knows the parts of plant and animal cells.
SC.F.1.2.4.5.3	understands how similar cells are organized to form structures.

Chapter **11** Animal Growth and Heredity

SC.F.2.2.1.5.1	knows that many characteristics of an organism are inherited from the genetic ancestors of the organism.
SC.F.2.2.1.5.2	knows that some characteristics result from the organism's interactions with the environment.

The investigations and experiences in this unit also address many of the Grade Level Expectations in Strand H, The Nature of Science.

Science in Florida

Sarasota

Dear Aunt Gloria,

Today mom and dad took my friend and me to the Selby Botanical Gardens in Sarasota. They have thousands of plants in their gardens, which were the most beautiful I have ever seen. My favorite plants were the orchids. Orchids are called "epiphytes" because they grow in trees and do not need soil. I am going to plant my own colorful garden in the spring.

Love,

Kim

The Sunshine State

USA

FCAT Writing

Writing Situation

Think about a green garden. Write a story about starting a garden at home.

Experiment!

Plant Growth Living things respond to certain factors in their environments. A plant's roots grow toward the ground because they respond to gravity. Another environmental factor that plants respond to is light. How do plants respond to light? For example, will plants grow toward a light source? Plan and conduct an experiment to find out.

Chapter

10 Cells to Body Systems

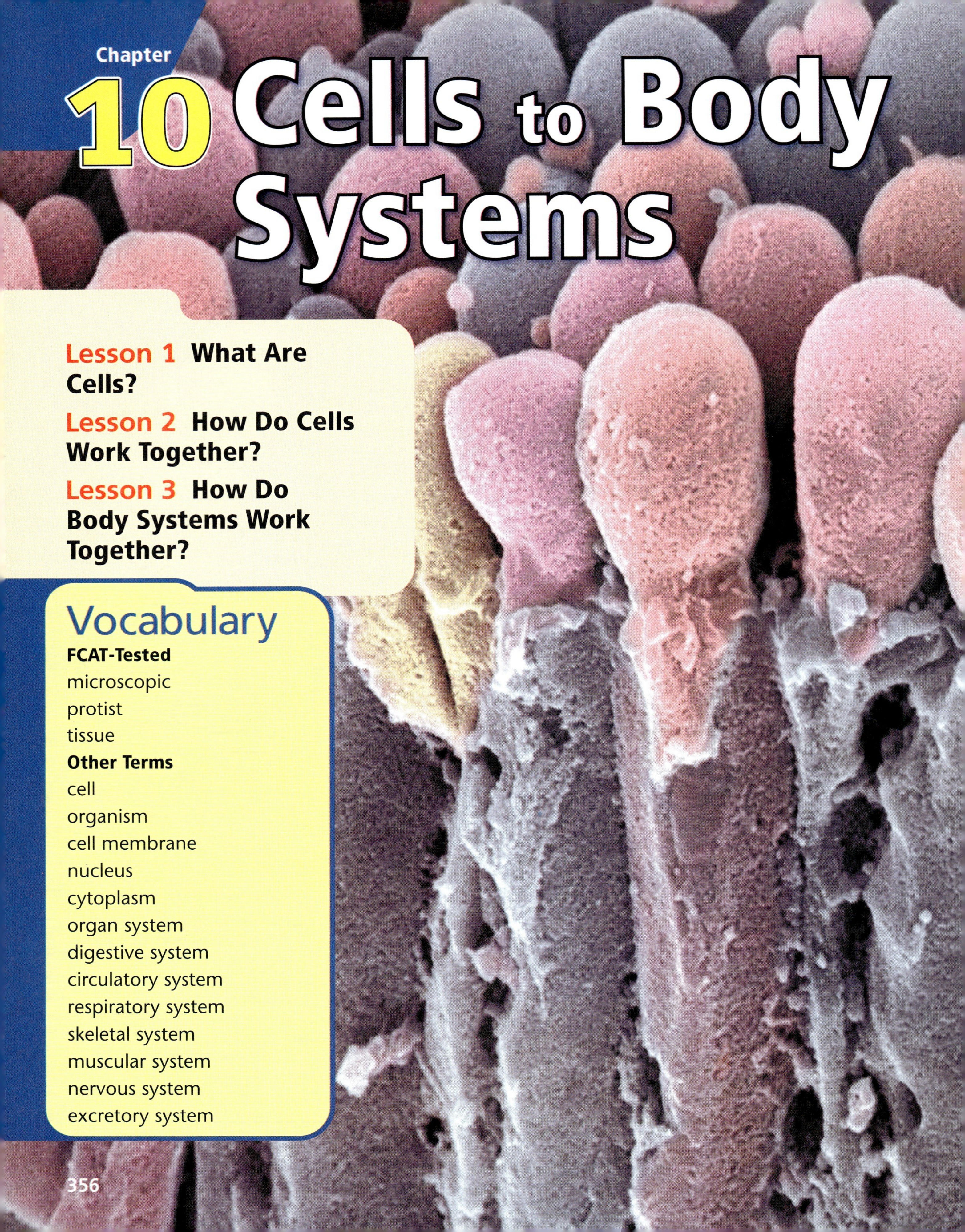

Lesson 1 **What Are Cells?**

Lesson 2 **How Do Cells Work Together?**

Lesson 3 **How Do Body Systems Work Together?**

Vocabulary

FCAT-Tested

microscopic
protist
tissue

Other Terms

cell
organism
cell membrane
nucleus
cytoplasm
organ system
digestive system
circulatory system
respiratory system
skeletal system
muscular system
nervous system
excretory system

What do YOU wonder?

The human body has many different kinds of cells. The cells shown here, called secretory cells, are found in most of the body's glands. They are also found in the skin and in the digestive system. What do you think secretory cells do?

357

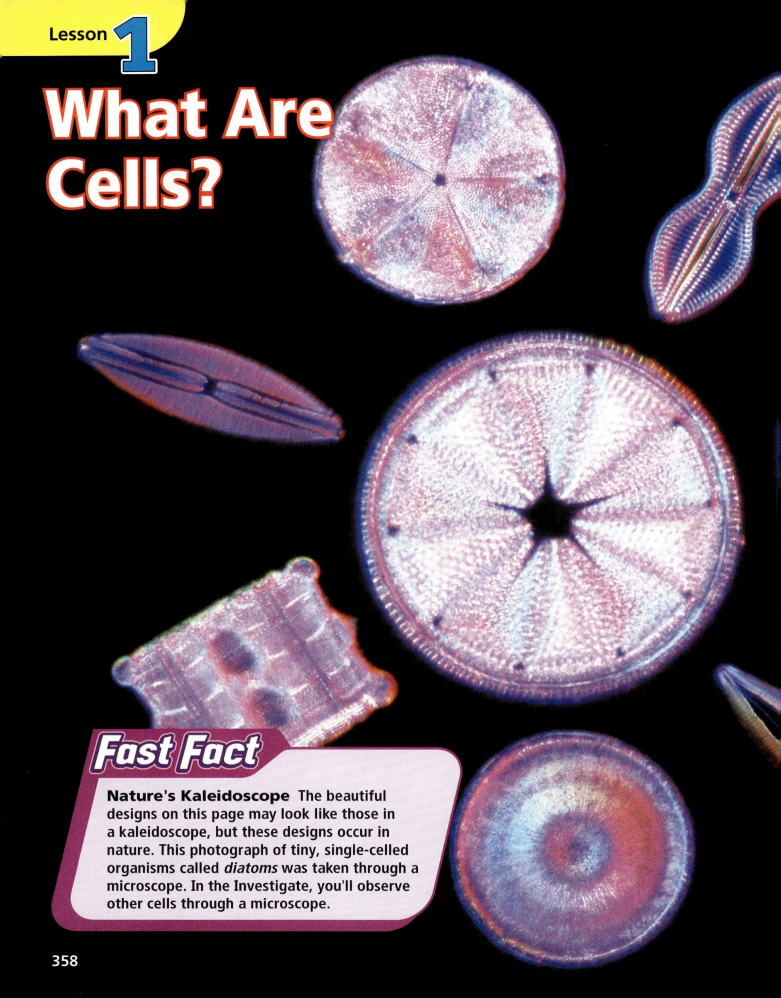

What Are Cells?

Fast Fact

Nature's Kaleidoscope The beautiful designs on this page may look like those in a kaleidoscope, but these designs occur in nature. This photograph of tiny, single-celled organisms called *diatoms* was taken through a microscope. In the Investigate, you'll observe other cells through a microscope.

Observing Cells

Materials
- dropper
- red food coloring
- microscope slide
- slice of onion
- coverslip
- paper towels
- microscope
- colored pencils
- prepared slide of animal skin

Procedure

<mark>CAUTION:</mark> **Food coloring stains. Avoid getting it on your clothing.**

1 Use the dropper to place one drop of food coloring in the center of the slide. Break the onion slice, and pull off a piece of onion skin. Put the onion skin in the drop of food coloring. Gently lower the coverslip at an angle so that it spreads the food coloring. Use a paper towel to remove any excess food coloring.

2 Observe the onion skin cells under the microscope. Use the colored pencils to record your observations in a drawing.

3 Observe the prepared slide of the animal skin cells. Use colored pencils to record your observations in another drawing.

Draw Conclusions

1. Compare the onion skin cells and the animal skin cells.

2. **Inquiry Skill** When scientists observe, they use their senses to learn about objects and events. In the center of most cells are structures that direct how the cells function. Look for these structures. Based on what you observe, how many directing structures do you think each cell has?

Step 1

Step 2

Investigate Further

In what ways do you think all plant cells are alike? **Design and conduct a simple experiment** to test your ideas.

Reading in Science

SC.F.1.2.4.5.1 use magnification to identify cell structures;
SC.F.1.2.4.5.2 plant and animal cells;
LA.A.2.2.1 main idea and details

VOCABULARY

cell p. 360
microscopic p. 360
organism p. 360
cell membrane p. 362
nucleus p. 362
cytoplasm p. 362
protist p. 364

SCIENCE CONCEPTS

▶ how living things are made of cells

▶ why different cells have different jobs

READING FOCUS SKILL

MAIN IDEA AND DETAILS Once you understand cells, look for details about each cell type.

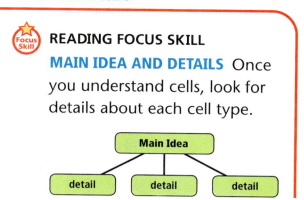

Cells

You've probably seen cork stoppers in jars and cork bulletin boards. But did you know that cork comes from the bark of an oak tree? In 1665, Robert Hooke, an English scientist, observed a layer of cork through a microscope. He saw the same kind of structures you observed in the onion skin. Because the structures he saw looked like tiny rooms, Hooke named them cells.

The microscope you used in the Investigate enabled you to observe and compare cells from an animal and a plant. A **cell** is the basic unit of structure and function in living things. Most cells are **microscopic**—they can be seen only with a microscope. Hooke's description of cells encouraged scientists to learn more about them. Using microscopes, they found that all cells share some characteristics. And that different cells do different jobs. They also know that all organisms are made up of cells. An **organism** is any living thing that maintains vital life processes.

Robert Hooke's seventeenth-century microscope looks much different from a modern microscope. But both can show cells in a layer of cork.

◀ The single cell of this amoeba carries out all the functions the organism needs to stay alive.

▲ The outer cells of this plant's leaf help keep the plant from losing too much water. Inner cells of the leaf make food for the plant. Each plant cell also carries out life functions for itself.

▲ A salamander's skin cells don't look like a plant's outer cells, but they also help keep the organism from drying out. As in the plant, each cell carries out life functions for itself.

You may see hundreds of different organisms each day. Each of these is made up of cells. Some simple organisms are just a single cell. But most plants and animals are made up of huge numbers of cells.

Plants and animals have different types of cells, each with its own job. For example, your body has digestive cells, which help you break down food, and nerve cells, which help you sense and respond to your surroundings. Different types of cells work together to carry out functions that keep an organism alive. To carry out its own functions, each cell has structures called *organelles*, which help keep the cell alive.

 MAIN IDEA AND DETAILS How do cells keep organisms alive and healthy?

A Cell Model
Carefully use a plastic knife to cut a peeled hard-boiled egg in half. Compare it to the animal skin cells you observed in the Investigate. Why is an egg a good model for animal cells?

Plant and Animal Cells

All cells have similar structures and organelles. Every cell is surrounded by a thin covering called the ==cell membrane==. This structure protects the cell, holds its contents together, and controls what goes in and out of the cell. Most organelles are also surrounded by membranes. Each type of organelle has a specific function that helps the cell.

Most cells have a nucleus. The ==nucleus== directs all of a cell's activities, including reproduction. Inside the nucleus are *chromosomes* (KROH•muh•sohmz), threadlike structures that contain information about the characteristics of the cell. When a cell reproduces, the nucleus divides and each new cell gets identical chromosomes.

Between the cell membrane and the nucleus is a jellylike material called ==cytoplasm== (SYT•oh•plaz•uhm). Cytoplasm contains chemicals that help keep a cell healthy.

Several kinds of organelles are suspended in the cytoplasm. *Mitochondria* are the "powerhouses" of a cell. They release energy from nutrients. *Vacuoles* store nutrients, water, or waste materials in plant cells. Smaller *vesicles* have a similar function in animal cells.

Plant cells have structures not found in animal cells. A thick *cell wall* helps support a plant cell. The cell wall lies outside the cell membrane. In the cytoplasm of many plant cells are *chloroplasts*. Chloroplasts make food for plant cells.

 MAIN IDEA AND DETAILS What purposes does the cell membrane serve?

Comparing Plant and Animal Cells

Plant and animal cells have certain structures in common. They have a nucleus, cell membrane, cytoplasm, and organelles. Study the differences between plant and animal cells.

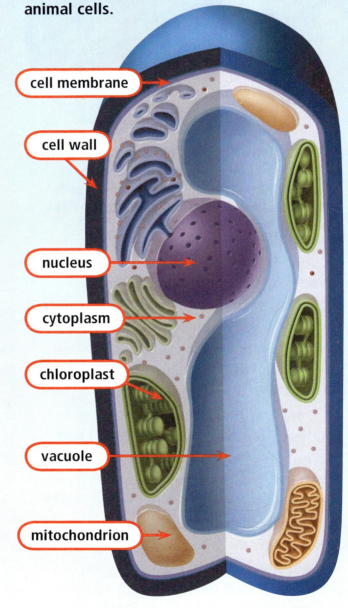

cell membrane

cell wall

nucleus

cytoplasm

chloroplast

vacuole

mitochondrion

Plant cells have different sizes, shapes, and functions, but most have the same organelles.

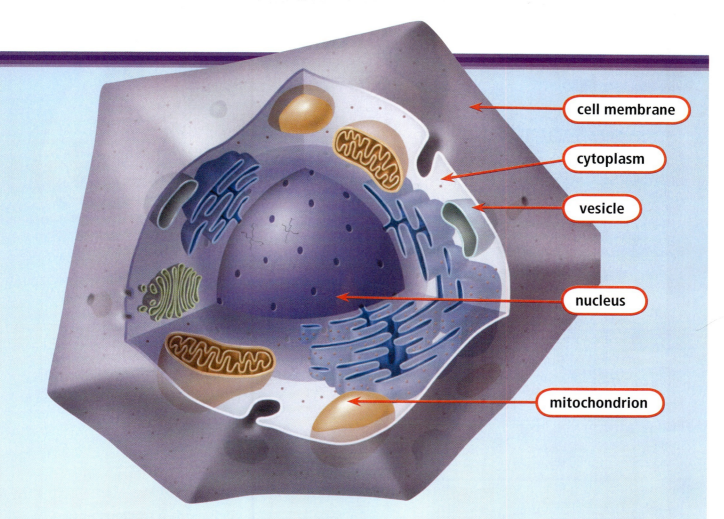

cell membrane

cytoplasm

vesicle

nucleus

mitochondrion

Like plant cells, animal cells have different sizes, shapes, and functions. They also have most of the same organelles. How is an animal cell different from a plant cell?

Cell Structures

Organelle	Function	Kind of Cell
Nucleus	directs a cell's activities	plant and animal
Chromosome	inside nucleus; contains information about cell	plant and animal
Cell membrane	holds a cell together and separates it from its surroundings	plant and animal
Cell wall	supports and protects a plant cell	plant
Cytoplasm	a jellylike substance containing chemicals that help the cell stay healthy	plant and animal
Chloroplast	makes food for the cell	plant
Vacuole	stores food, water, or wastes	plant
Mitochondria	release energy from nutrients	plant and animal

 For more links and activities, go to **www.hspscience.com**

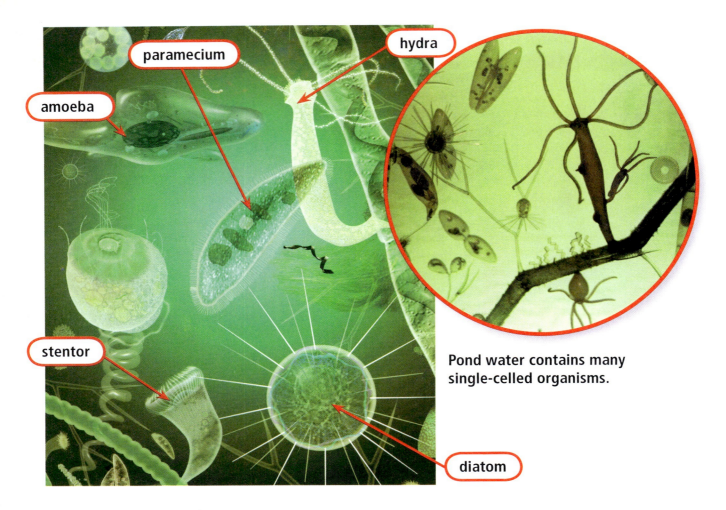

paramecium

hydra

amoeba

stentor

diatom

Pond water contains many single-celled organisms.

Single-Celled Organisms

What do you think of when you hear the word *bacteria*? Many people think of "germs." But not all bacteria are harmful. Many of these single-celled organisms are helpful. Some enrich the soil by breaking down dead plants and animals. Others help animals digest food. Still others help make food! Cheese and yogurt are foods that form when certain bacteria mix with milk.

Bacterial cells are different from plant and animal cells. Like plant cells, bacterial cells are surrounded by cell walls. But bacteria do not have a nucleus or membrane-bound organelles. Instead, their chromosomes and other materials are in the cytoplasm.

Another kind of single-celled organism makes up most of the group called protists. A **protist** (PROHT•ist) is a simple organism, usually a single cell, with a nucleus and organelles. Some protists have cell walls and chloroplasts. These protists are plantlike. Other protists have no cell walls or chloroplasts and are animal-like.

The diatoms shown at the beginning of this lesson are plantlike—they have chloroplasts and make their own food. They are part of a group of protists called *algae* (AL•jee). Algae live mostly in water, and produce a lot of Earth's oxygen. They also produce a lot of food for ocean life.

Animal-like protists are called *protozoa*. They get food by "eating" other small organisms, such as algae and bacteria.

 MAIN IDEA AND DETAILS How do bacterial cells differ from plant and animal cells?

1. MAIN IDEA AND DETAILS Draw and complete the graphic organizer.

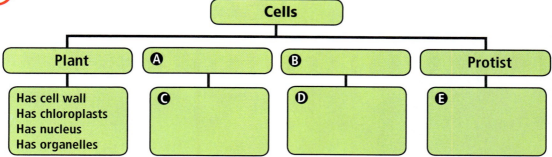

2. SUMMARIZE Use your graphic organizer to write a lesson summary.

3. DRAW CONCLUSIONS You're looking at a slide through a microscope, and you see cells with cell walls but without chloroplasts. What kind of cells are you probably looking at? How do you know?

4. VOCABULARY Use lesson vocabulary and other lesson terms to make a crossword puzzle.

FCAT Prep

5. Read/Inquire/Explain Suppose you observe cells through a microscope. How might you infer whether the cells are animal cells?

6. What is the function of a cell's nucleus?
   A. to make food
   B. to direct the cell's activities
   C. to protect the cell
   D. to keep the cell healthy

Links

Writing

Expository Writing
Imagine a cell as being a city. Write a **description** of how each part of the cell helps carry out a task important for the maintenance of the city.

Math 9÷3

Extend a Pattern
Imagine that a single cell divides into two cells every 15 minutes. If each of these cells also divides in two, and so on, how long will it take for a single cell to produce 500 cells?

Language Arts

Word Parts
The word *cytoplasm* contains the word parts *cyto-* and *-plasm*. Use a dictionary to find the meanings of the parts. How do those meanings relate to the meaning of the whole word *cytoplasm*?

 For more links and activities, go to **www.hspscience.com**

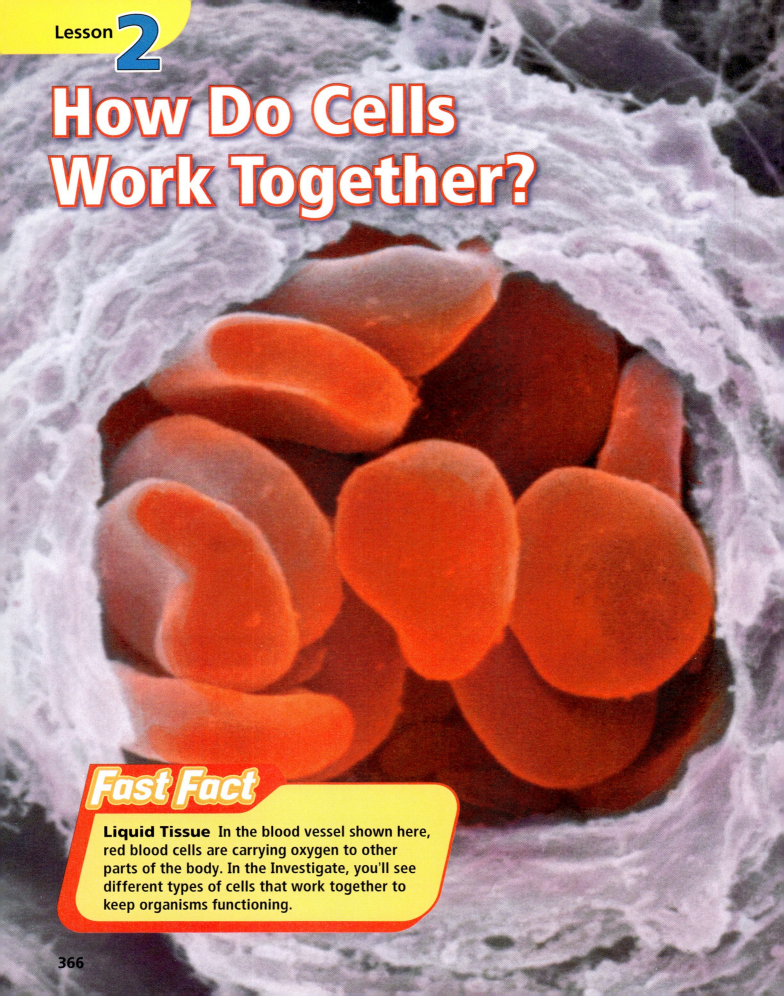

How Do Cells Work Together?

Fast Fact

Liquid Tissue In the blood vessel shown here, red blood cells are carrying oxygen to other parts of the body. In the Investigate, you'll see different types of cells that work together to keep organisms functioning.

Cells and Tissues

Materials
- prepared slides of a plant root, a plant leaf, and a plant stem
- microscope
- colored pencils

Procedure

1 Place the slide of the plant root on the stage of the microscope. Turn the focus knob until you can see the cells clearly. Observe the root cells. Use the colored pencils to record your observations in a drawing.

2 Repeat Step 1, using the slide of the plant leaf. Again, use the colored pencils to record what you observe.

3 Repeat Step 1, using the slide of the plant stem. Record your observations.

4 Compare the cells from the different parts of a plant. What similarities did you observe? What differences?

Draw Conclusions

1. You observed cells from three different parts of a plant. Based on your observations, what conclusion can you draw about cells that look similar in all three parts?

2. **Inquiry Skill** When scientists compare objects, they often infer reasons for any differences. What can you infer about why leaf cells contain more green structures than do stem cells?

Step 1

Step 2

Investigate Further

Form a **hypothesis** about similarities and differences among animal cells. Using prepared slides of animal cells, test your hypothesis.

VOCABULARY

tissue p. 368
organ p. 369
organ system p. 370
digestive system p. 370

SCIENCE CONCEPTS

▶ how tissues are formed of similar cells

▶ how tissues work together in organs

▶ how body systems are groups of organs that work together

READING FOCUS SKILL

COMPARE AND CONTRAST Look for ways that tissues, organs, and organ systems are alike and different.

| alike | — | different |

Cell, Tissue, Organ

Your body is made up of trillions of cells. Each cell is able to carry out its own life functions. But your body's cells—like those in other organisms made up of many cells—also work together. Cells that work together to perform a certain function form a **tissue**. There are four kinds of tissue in your body.

Your body is covered and lined with *epithelial* (ep•ih•THEE•lee•uhl) *tissue*. Epithelial tissue is in your skin. It also lines your internal organs.

Most of your body mass is *muscle tissue*. Whenever you move, muscle tissue contracts and relaxes to move your skeleton. The bones and cartilage of your skeleton are made of *connective tissue*. Tendons and ligaments are connective tissue, too. Tendons connect bones to muscles. Ligaments connect bones to bones.

Signals from another kind of tissue, *nervous tissue*, "tell" muscles when to contract. Nervous tissue is found in the brain, spinal cord, and nerves.

Muscle tissue is made up of cells that contract when they receive signals from the brain. The contraction and relaxation of muscle tissue moves the skeleton. ▶

The heart is an organ made up of muscle tissue, epithelial tissue, nervous tissue, and connective tissue. These tissues work together to pump blood to all parts of your body. ▼

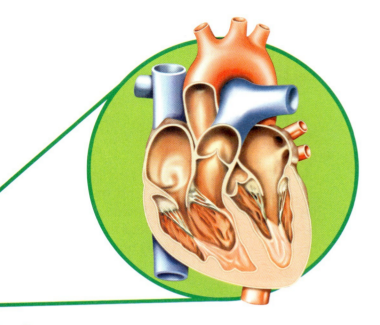

Just as cells work together to form tissues, tissues work together to form organs. An **organ** is several kinds of tissue working together for the same function. Your skin is an organ. It is made up of many layers of epithelial tissue. It also has muscle tissue, nervous tissue, and a layer of connective tissue. These tissues work together to protect your body.

Your heart is an organ that pumps blood to all parts of your body. It contains each of the different kinds of tissue. The heart is mostly muscle tissue, but it also has connective tissue. It is lined and covered with epithelial tissue. Nervous tissue in the heart receives signals from the brain to make it beat faster or slower.

The lungs are organs that take in oxygen from the air. They are made up of epithelial tissue and connective tissue.

The lungs, the heart, and all other organs rely on a very special kind of connective tissue—blood. The red cells in blood deliver oxygen to all other cells of the body. The liquid part of blood, called *plasma*, delivers nutrients and helps remove wastes from body cells. White blood cells help your body fight diseases. And platelets help blood clot if you get cut.

 COMPARE AND CONTRAST How are muscle tissue and connective tissue alike? How are they different?

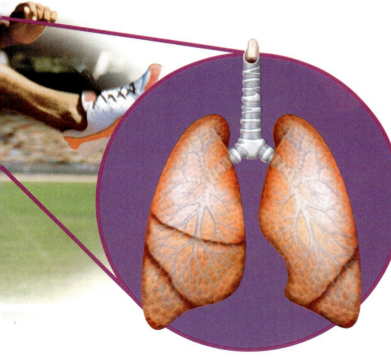

◀ The lungs are made up of epithelial tissue and connective tissue. These tissues work together to take in oxygen from the air and move it into the blood.

The Digestive System

Organs that work together to do a job for the body are called an **organ system**. There are ten major organ systems in your body. One of the major systems is the **digestive system**. The digestive system breaks food down into chemical nutrients that body cells need for energy, growth, and repair.

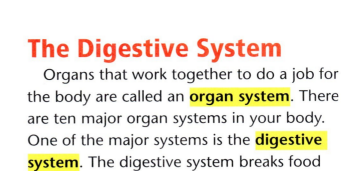

◀ As food passes through the digestive system, chemicals made in the stomach, pancreas, and small intestine break the food down. Nutrients from the food help the body's cells grow and stay healthy.

For a more detailed look at the digestive system, see the Health Handbook.

Nutrients pass into the blood through the walls of the villi in the small intestine. ▼

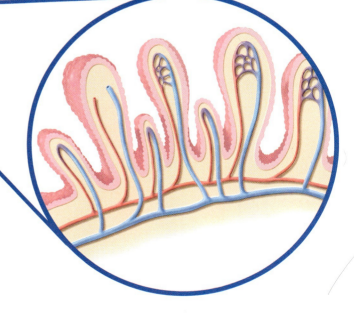

The digestive system helps the body get the nutrients it needs from food. First, chemicals break food down into nutrients. Then, nutrients are moved into the blood. Blood moves the nutrients to each of the body's cells.

Most people think the stomach is the first body organ involved in digestion. But digestion of certain foods starts as soon as you take a bite! As you chew, food is broken into smaller pieces. Glands in your mouth produce saliva. Saliva contains chemicals that begin breaking down some carbohydrates. Together, chewing and saliva begin digesting starchy foods. Starchy foods, like breads and pasta, begin to break down into sugars. You can investigate this yourself. Try chewing an unsalted cracker for a minute or two. You'll notice that its starchy taste soon becomes sweet.

From the mouth, food travels down the *esophagus*, a long tube that leads to the stomach. In the stomach, strong muscles churn the food with acid and other chemicals that break down proteins.

From the stomach, partly digested food moves into the *small intestine*. Chemicals produced there, along with chemicals from the pancreas and the gallbladder complete digestion.

Once digestion is complete, nutrients are absorbed into the blood. The small intestine is lined with finger-like bumps called *villi* (VIL•eye). Villi have many blood vessels. Nutrients move from the small intestine into the blood vessels of the villi. Then they are carried by the blood throughout the body.

 COMPARE AND CONTRAST How are villi like the roots of a plant? How are they different?

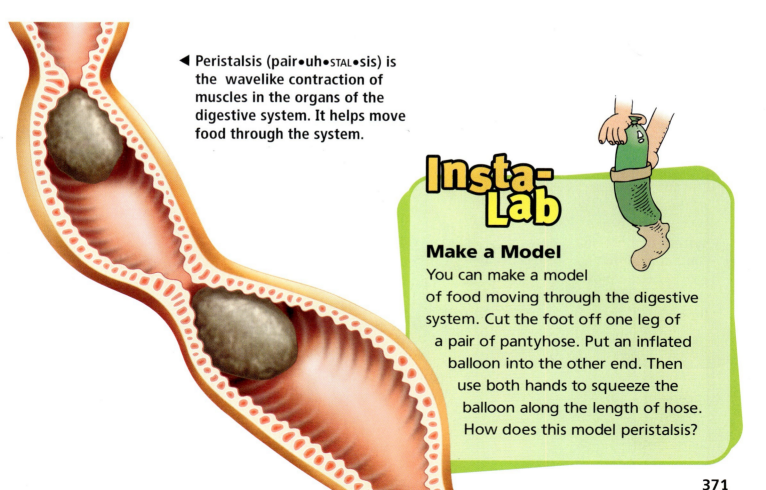

◀ **Peristalsis (pair•uh•STAL•sis) is the wavelike contraction of muscles in the organs of the digestive system. It helps move food through the system.**

Insta-Lab

Make a Model
You can make a model of food moving through the digestive system. Cut the foot off one leg of a pair of pantyhose. Put an inflated balloon into the other end. Then use both hands to squeeze the balloon along the length of hose. How does this model peristalsis?

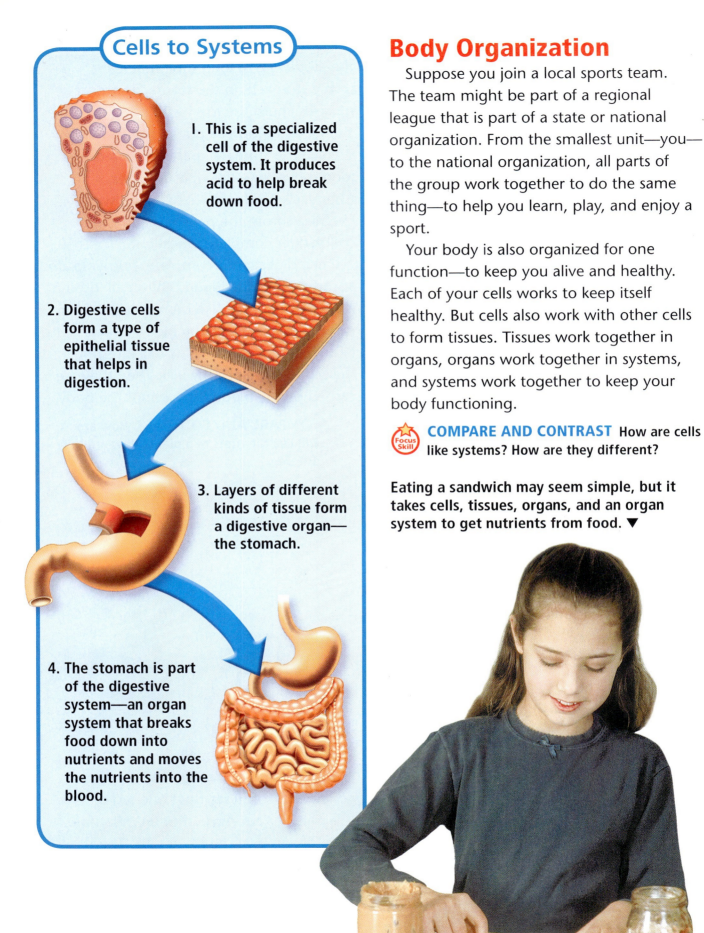

Cells to Systems

1. This is a specialized cell of the digestive system. It produces acid to help break down food.

2. Digestive cells form a type of epithelial tissue that helps in digestion.

3. Layers of different kinds of tissue form a digestive organ—the stomach.

4. The stomach is part of the digestive system—an organ system that breaks food down into nutrients and moves the nutrients into the blood.

Body Organization

Suppose you join a local sports team. The team might be part of a regional league that is part of a state or national organization. From the smallest unit—you— to the national organization, all parts of the group work together to do the same thing—to help you learn, play, and enjoy a sport.

Your body is also organized for one function—to keep you alive and healthy. Each of your cells works to keep itself healthy. But cells also work with other cells to form tissues. Tissues work together in organs, organs work together in systems, and systems work together to keep your body functioning.

COMPARE AND CONTRAST How are cells like systems? How are they different?

Eating a sandwich may seem simple, but it takes cells, tissues, organs, and an organ system to get nutrients from food. ▼

1. COMPARE AND CONTRAST Draw and complete the graphic organizer by writing *Yes* or *No* in place of the circled letters.

Body Organization				
	Cell	**Tissue**	**Organ**	**Organ System**
Carries out its own life processes	Ⓐ	No	Ⓑ	Ⓒ
Works with other structures to perform a function	Yes	Ⓓ	Ⓔ	Ⓕ
Is made up of many kinds of cells	Ⓖ	No	Ⓗ	Ⓘ

2. SUMMARIZE Use the graphic organizer to write a lesson summary.

3. DRAW CONCLUSIONS What part of the digestive system isn't working properly in people who cannot absorb nutrients? Explain.

4. VOCABULARY Use the lesson vocabulary and other lesson terms to write a paragraph about the digestive system.

FCAT Prep

5. Read/Inquire/Explain What is the relationship between the digestive system and the circulatory system?

6. Which is an example of a tissue?
   A. the heart
   B. a nucleus
   C. a muscle
   D. a vacuole

Links

Writing

Narrative Writing
Write a creative story **describing** an adventure through the digestive tract. Tell about the "stops" you make along the way, including the various organs.

Math

Calculate
Count how many times your heart beats in 15 seconds. Multiply by 4 to find how many times your heart beats in a minute. Run in place for two minutes and repeat. How much faster is your heartbeat rate now?

Health

Lifeblood
Blood is a vital tissue. When a person loses a lot of blood due to an injury, a transfusion can save his or her life. Contact your local blood bank to learn about blood transfusions.

For more links and activities, go to
www.hspscience.com

How Do Body Systems Work Together?

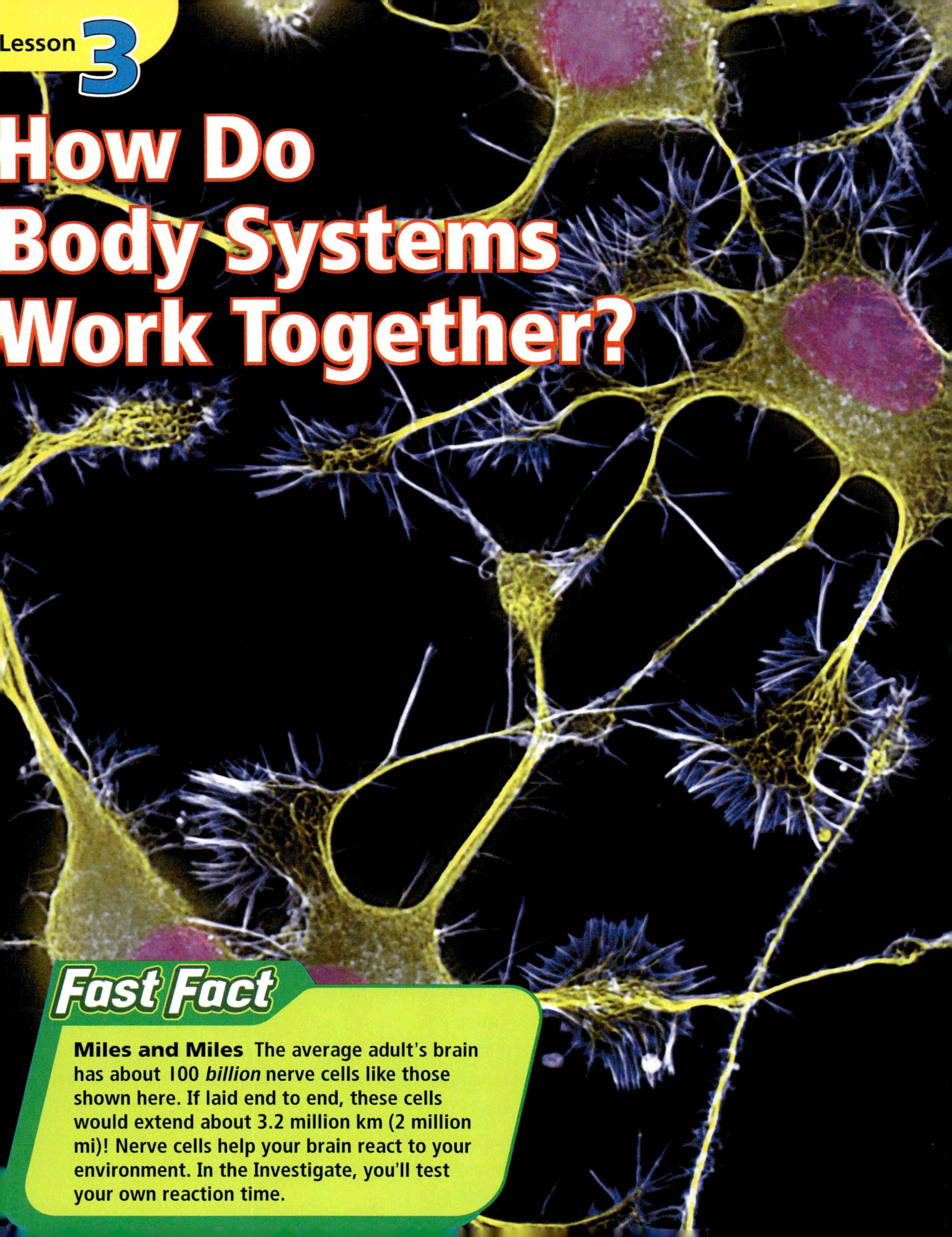

Fast Fact

Miles and Miles The average adult's brain has about 100 *billion* nerve cells like those shown here. If laid end to end, these cells would extend about 3.2 million km (2 million mi)! Nerve cells help your brain react to your environment. In the Investigate, you'll test your own reaction time.

Testing Reaction Time

Materials • metric ruler • reaction time chart

Procedure

1. Sit with your arm resting on a table and your wrist hanging over the edge. Hold your hand sideways, ready to catch the ruler with your fingers.

2. Have your partner hold the ruler above and perpendicular to your hand, so you'll be able to catch it.

3. Have your partner let go of the ruler. Try to catch it as quickly as possible.

4. Note the measurement on the ruler, at the place where you caught it. Compare this number to the reaction time chart to find out how long it took you to catch the ruler. Record your results.

5. Repeat Step 4 three times, and then trade places with your partner. Make graphs to compare your results.

Draw Conclusions

1. How did your reaction time change with each trial? Why?

2. **Inquiry Skill** What can you infer about the messages your brain receives and sends to enable you to catch the ruler?

Reaction Time Chart	
Distance on Ruler (cm)	Reaction Time (sec)
5	0.10
10	0.14
15	0.18
20	0.20
25	0.23
30	0.25

Step 2

Investigate Further

Now you know how to measure reaction time. Hypothesize how you might improve yours. Plan and conduct an experiment that would test your hypothesis.

VOCABULARY

circulatory system p. 376
respiratory system p. 378
skeletal system p. 380
muscular system p. 380
nervous system p. 382
excretory system p. 384

SCIENCE CONCEPTS

▶ that the body has different systems with different roles

▶ how body systems interact

READING FOCUS SKILL

SEQUENCE Look for ways to organize in steps the processes described in this lesson.

Circulatory System

If you were asked to identify the most important system in the body, which would you choose? Though all of the body's systems perform important functions, the circulatory system is one of the most vital. It pumps blood to all parts of the body.

The **circulatory system** is made up of the heart, the blood vessels, and the blood. Together, these parts of the circulatory system transport oxygen, nutrients, and wastes through the body.

Blood is a connective tissue made up of several parts. The liquid part, called plasma, is mostly water. Nutrients from food and waste products from cells dissolve in plasma. Nutrients and other chemicals are carried to the body's cells. Waste products, which result from cell functions, are carried away from the cells so they can be removed from the body.

The solid part of blood includes red blood cells, white blood cells, and platelets. Red blood cells carry oxygen to all body cells. White blood cells help fight infection. Platelets help the blood clot, and stop bleeding from wounds.

Blood leaves the heart through blood vessels called *arteries*. Arteries lead to small blood vessels called *capillaries* (KAP•uh•lair•eez). Capillaries are so tiny that blood cells move through them in single file. Capillaries lead to larger blood vessels called *veins*. Veins return blood to the heart.

Blood is a kind of connective tissue that is part of the circulatory system. It travels through blood vessels, carrying oxygen and nutrients to body cells and carrying wastes away from body cells. Blood vessels are one kind of organ of the circulatory system. ▼

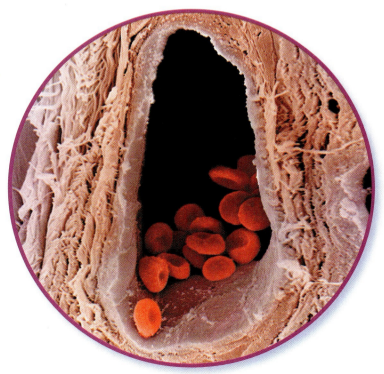

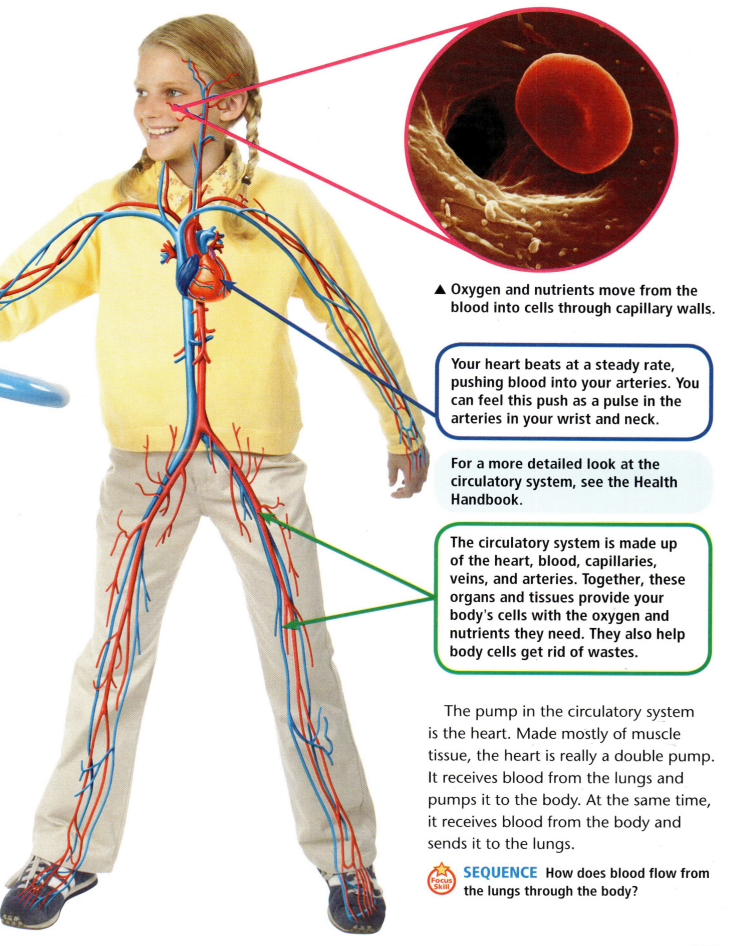

▲ Oxygen and nutrients move from the blood into cells through capillary walls.

Your heart beats at a steady rate, pushing blood into your arteries. You can feel this push as a pulse in the arteries in your wrist and neck.

For a more detailed look at the circulatory system, see the Health Handbook.

The circulatory system is made up of the heart, blood, capillaries, veins, and arteries. Together, these organs and tissues provide your body's cells with the oxygen and nutrients they need. They also help body cells get rid of wastes.

The pump in the circulatory system is the heart. Made mostly of muscle tissue, the heart is really a double pump. It receives blood from the lungs and pumps it to the body. At the same time, it receives blood from the body and sends it to the lungs.

SEQUENCE How does blood flow from the lungs through the body?

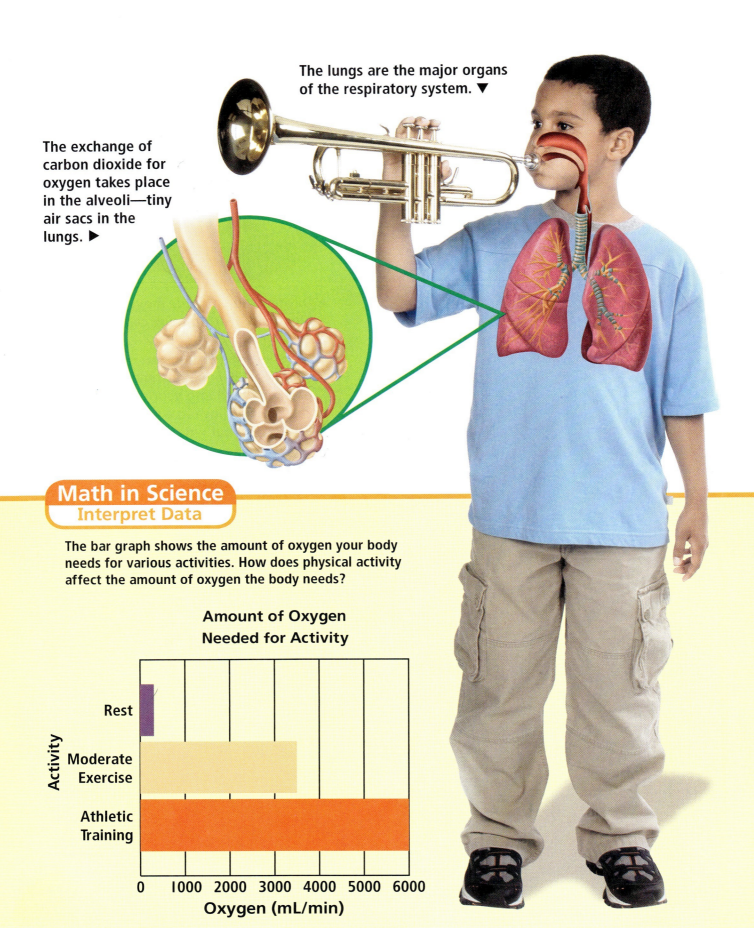

The lungs are the major organs of the respiratory system. ▼

The exchange of carbon dioxide for oxygen takes place in the alveoli—tiny air sacs in the lungs. ▶

Math in Science
Interpret Data

The bar graph shows the amount of oxygen your body needs for various activities. How does physical activity affect the amount of oxygen the body needs?

Amount of Oxygen Needed for Activity

Activity (vertical axis)

- Rest
- Moderate Exercise
- Athletic Training

Oxygen (mL/min): 0 1000 2000 3000 4000 5000 6000

Respiratory System

Think of all the things you do each day. You go to school, you might play on a sports team, you participate in clubs, you play outdoors, and you do homework. You need a lot of energy! So your cells need a lot of oxygen. The **respiratory system** is a group of organs and tissues that exchange oxygen and carbon dioxide between your body and the environment.

When you breathe, your body gets the oxygen it needs. Tiny hairs in your nose filter the air you inhale. Next, capillaries in your nasal passages warm the air. Warm, clean air then travels down your *trachea*, or windpipe. In your chest, the trachea branches into two large tubes called *bronchi* (BRAHNG•ky). Each bronchus leads to a lung.

The lungs are the main organs of your respiratory system. In the lungs, the bronchi branch into smaller and smaller tubes. At the end of the smallest tubes are tiny air sacs called *alveoli* (al•VEE•uh•ly). The walls of the alveoli are only one cell thick and are surrounded by capillaries. Gases are exchanged between the air in the alveoli and blood in the capillaries.

The capillaries of the alveoli receive oxygen-poor blood from the heart. This blood contains a lot of carbon dioxide (CO_2). Your body produces CO_2 as a waste product of cell functions. CO_2 passes from the blood plasma into the alveoli. Your body gets rid of the CO_2 when you exhale. Oxygen from the air you inhale passes into the blood, and red blood cells pick up the oxygen. Oxygen-rich blood travels back to the heart. From the heart, it is pumped throughout the body, to every body cell.

 SEQUENCE How does oxygen get from the air into your blood?

Pulmonary Circulation

The heart pumps oxygen-poor blood through the pulmonary arteries to the lungs. There, the blood picks up oxygen. The oxygen-rich blood travels back to the heart through the pulmonary veins. The circulatory system has blood vessels that provide blood for the heart muscle itself.

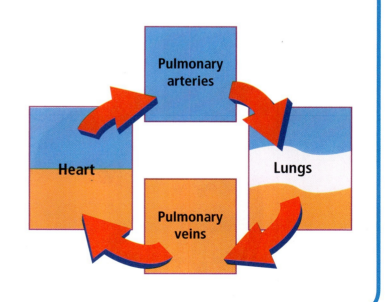

Skeletal and Muscular Systems

Imagine a mammal with no skeleton. Do you picture a shapeless blob on the ground? That's probably what the mammal would look like!

Your **skeletal** **system**, which includes mainly bones, gives your body its form and protects many of your organs. The skeletal system works with your muscular system. The **muscular** **system** includes muscles and tendons that move bones.

The skeletal system includes bones, cartilage, and ligaments. An adult's skeleton is made up of 206 bones. *Cartilage* is spongy connective tissue that cushions the ends of many bones. Bands of connective tissue called *ligaments* hold bones together.

Without your skeleton's well-organized bony structure, you would not be able to sit, stand, or move. Your brain, heart, and lungs would be at risk of injury, and your circulatory system would lack blood cells. That's because blood cells are produced inside your largest bones.

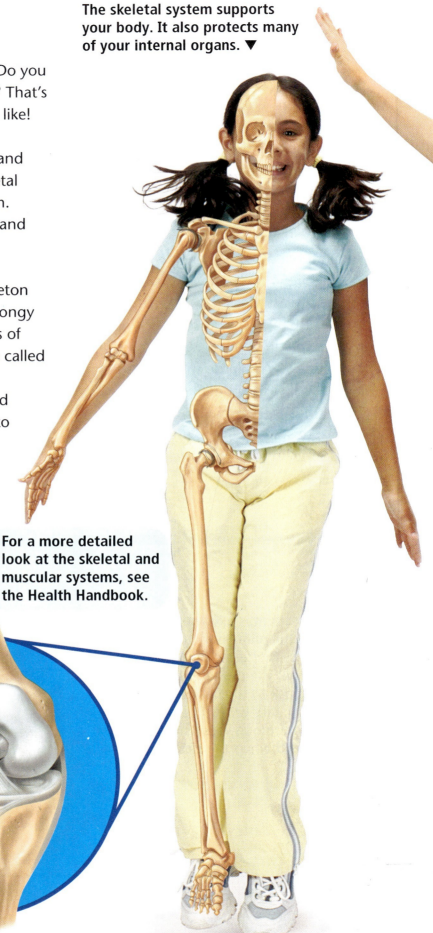

The skeletal system supports your body. It also protects many of your internal organs. ▼

For a more detailed look at the skeletal and muscular systems, see the Health Handbook.

The bones at this joint are held together by ligaments. Muscles are attached to bones by tendons. ▶

Skeletal muscles work with the skeletal system to help you move your body. ▼

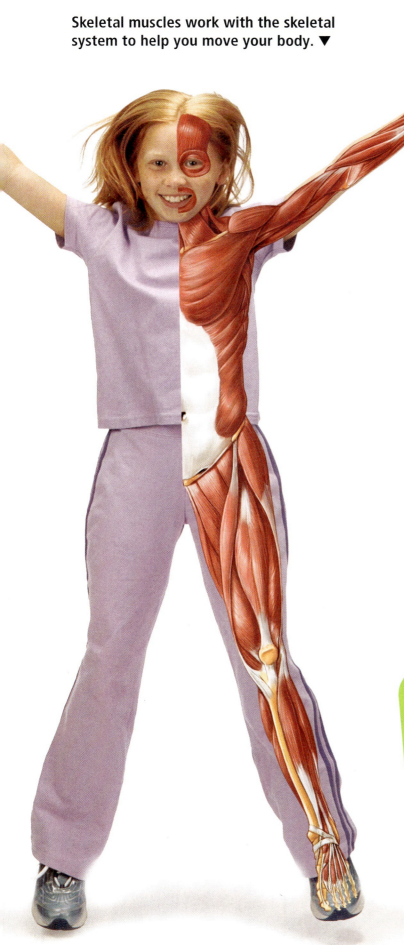

You're probably aware of the muscles that support and move your body. These muscles are *skeletal muscles*. They are made of groups of muscle tissue held together by connective tissue. Skeletal muscles usually are attached to bones, either directly or by bands of connective tissue called tendons.

Skeletal muscles often work in pairs. This means that one muscle contracts to bend a joint and another muscle contracts to straighten it. Skeletal muscles are voluntary muscles, because you can control them.

There are two other kinds of muscle. *Smooth muscle* makes up most of the walls of the body's organs, including blood vessels and digestive organs. There, contractions help move blood or food through tubes. *Cardiac muscle* makes up the walls of the heart. It contracts strongly to pump blood to all parts of the body. These two types of muscles are sometimes called *involuntary muscles*—you can't control their movements.

⭐ **Focus Skill** **SEQUENCE** How do opposing muscles cause movement at a joint?

Insta-Lab

Muscle Contraction

Measure around your upper arm when your elbow is straight and when it's bent. Record and compare the measurements. Describe the muscle that you infer controls the bending of your arm. Explain your reasoning.

Nervous System

Your <mark>nervous system</mark> enables you to sense your environment and to react to it. The nervous system directs other systems' activities, and it connects all the tissues and organs in your body to your brain. It is amazing, but it is the least-understood part of your body.

The nervous system has two parts. The *central nervous system* is made up of the brain and spinal cord. The spinal cord is a bundle of nerves, about as thick as a pencil, that extends from the brain all the way to the hips. The central nervous system receives and interprets signals from the nerves throughout the body. The central nervous system sends signals up and down the spinal cord and determines responses that are needed. The brain sends signals through nerves that direct all of the body's voluntary muscles. It also controls the body's automatic functions, like contraction of cardiac muscle, respiration, digestion, and circulation.

The *peripheral* (puh•RIF•uh•ruhl) *nervous system* is made up of sensory organs, such as your eyes and ears, and touch sensors in your skin.

For a more detailed look at the nervous system, see the Health Handbook.

A *synapse* (SIN•aps) is a connection between nerve cells. Chemical signals travel across synapses, helping to send messages to and from the brain. ▲

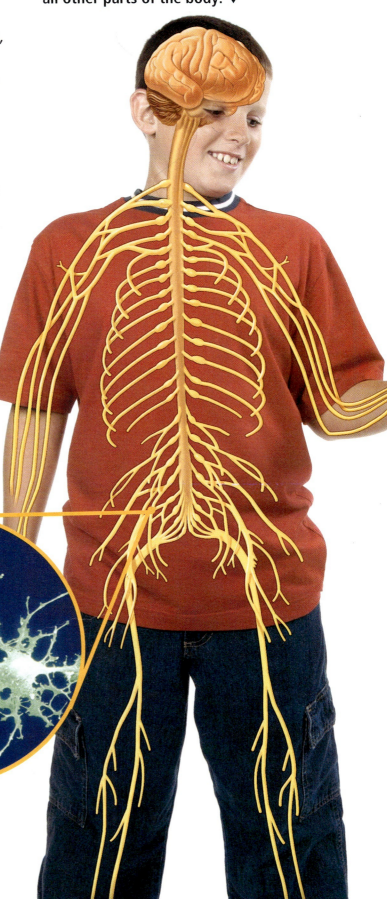

Nerves connect the central nervous system—the brain and spinal cord—and all other parts of the body. ▼

▲ If you accidentally prick your finger on a thorn, your hand pulls back in a reflex action. This happens even before the information travels to your brain. The nerve signal triggered by the thorn takes a "shortcut," signaling the spinal cord to "tell" the muscles in your arm to pull your hand out of danger.

Sensory organs have special nerves called *sensory receptors*. The receptors detect changes in your surroundings and send signals along nerves to the central nervous system. Sensory receptors in your ears, for example, detect vibrations. They "tell" your brain about the vibrations, and the brain interprets them as sounds.

Has your doctor ever struck your knee with a small rubber mallet? If so, you likely experienced a reflex response. *Reflexes* are automatic responses to certain stimuli. When the doctor struck your knee, a nerve signal traveled to your spinal cord, where

it took a "shortcut." Before traveling on to your brain, the signal in your spinal cord triggered a nerve in your muscles to jerk your leg. You kicked *before* your brain was even aware there was a tap!

Reflexes often occur in response to stimuli that cause pain. The brain is bypassed at first. Your vulnerable body part is quickly pulled from the source of the pain. Eventually, your brain senses the pain—but not until after your body has responded to it.

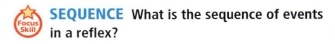 **SEQUENCE** What is the sequence of events in a reflex?

Excretory System

You know that body systems work together to carry out life functions. They digest food and release nutrients. They carry oxygen and nutrients to body cells, and they remove wastes from body cells. Carbon dioxide is eliminated when you exhale. But other wastes, such as ammonia, are removed from the body by the <mark>excretory system</mark>.

Ammonia, a waste product of certain cell functions, enters the blood. It is carried by blood plasma to the liver. The liver converts ammonia into *urea*, which travels through the blood to the kidneys. As blood flows through the *kidneys*, the main organs of the excretory system, urea and other wastes are filtered from the blood. The result is urine. Urine flows through tubes called *ureters* to a muscular organ called the *bladder*. When the bladder is full, urine is then eliminated from the body.

SEQUENCE How is ammonia removed from the body?

Cell wastes are removed from the blood through capillaries in the kidneys. Materials the body needs, mostly water and salts, are returned to the blood. ▶

For a more detailed look at the excretory system, see the Health Handbook.

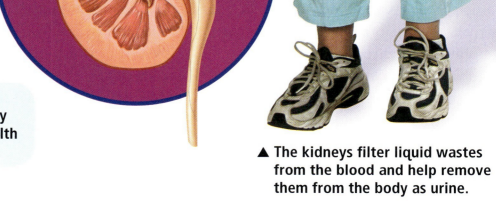

▲ The kidneys filter liquid wastes from the blood and help remove them from the body as urine.

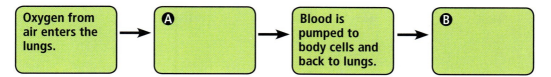

Focus Skill

1. **SEQUENCE** Draw and complete the graphic organizer.

| Oxygen from air enters the lungs. | → | Ⓐ | → | Blood is pumped to body cells and back to lungs. | → | Ⓑ |

2. **SUMMARIZE** Use the graphic organizer to write two or three sentences about the movement of oxygen in the respiratory system.

3. **DRAW CONCLUSIONS** Between the trachea and the esophagus is a flap of tissue that closes when you swallow. What is its function?

4. **VOCABULARY** Use the information in the lesson to write a clue for each vocabulary term. Then hide each term in a grid of letters to make a word-search puzzle.

FCAT Prep

5. **Read/Inquire/Explain** In what ways do the digestive and circulatory systems work together?

6. Tendons are connective tissues that
   A. make blood cells.
   B. carry signals from nerves.
   C. connect bones to bones.
   D. connect muscles to bones.

Links

Writing

Expository Writing

Write a **narrative** about the "travels" of a nerve signal. Explain how the signal causes movement in an arm or a leg.

Art

Pointillism

In the nineteenth-century style of painting called pointillism, pictures are painted with small dots of color. The brain interprets the many dots as smooth forms. Make a picture of your classroom using the pointillism style.

Physical Education

Circulatory System

You can improve the health of your circulatory system by lowering your resting heartbeat rate. Measure your heartbeat rate at rest. Then exercise for 30 minutes a day for a month. How much does your resting heartbeat rate drop?

 For more links and activities, go to **www.hspscience.com**

Saving Stephanie

Most kids love to eat pizza, hamburgers, and french fries. But until she was 8 years old, Stephanie Singh couldn't eat any of those foods. In fact, she couldn't eat any solid foods. Stephanie could be fed only through a tube inserted in her arm. Then an amazing operation changed Stephanie's life.

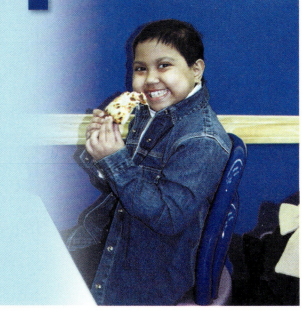

Stephanie's Favorite Foods

pizza

macaroni and cheese

homemade soups

Eating Through a Tube

Stephanie was born with visceral myopathy, a rare condition that doesn't allow the intestine to develop properly. The intestines are a long tube made up of two main parts. The first part, the small intestine, is connected to the stomach at one end. Partially digested food flows from the stomach into the small intestine. The small intestine absorbs nutrients from the food. Food that cannot be digested further flows into the large intestine. The large intestine then eliminates the undigested food waste from the body.

Because of her condition, Stephanie's small intestine couldn't break down food into nutrients. Stephanie would have starved, even if she had eaten plenty of food. To keep her alive,

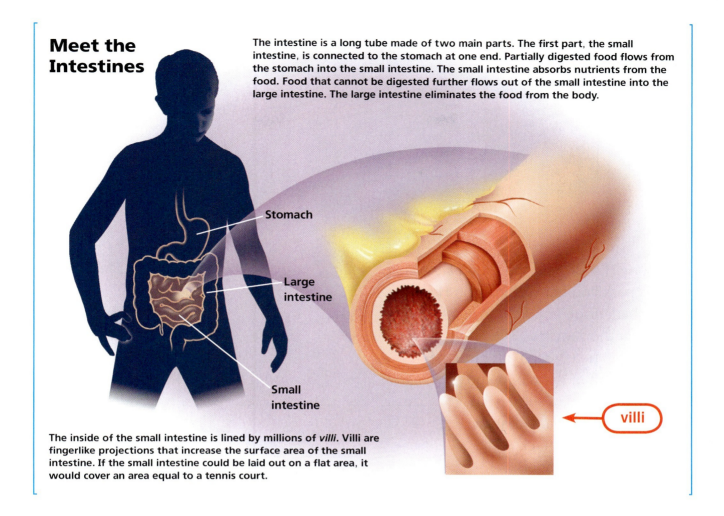

Meet the Intestines

The intestine is a long tube made of two main parts. The first part, the small intestine, is connected to the stomach at one end. Partially digested food flows from the stomach into the small intestine. The small intestine absorbs nutrients from the food. Food that cannot be digested further flows out of the small intestine into the large intestine. The large intestine eliminates the food from the body.

Stomach

Large intestine

Small intestine

The inside of the small intestine is lined by millions of *villi*. Villi are fingerlike projections that increase the surface area of the small intestine. If the small intestine could be laid out on a flat area, it would cover an area equal to a tennis court.

villi

Stephanie's doctors connected a tube to her arm. The tube delivered nutrient-rich fluids directly into her bloodstream.

A Lifesaver

To help Stephanie, doctors performed an intestine transplant. Doctors perform many different types of transplant operations, including heart, liver, and kidney transplants. However, an intestine transplant is a risky and dangerous operation.

The intestine has special cells that protect a person's body from bacteria in food. When a healthy intestine is put into a patient's body, the patient's immune system attacks the transplanted organ. But those special bacteria-fighting cells in the intestine fight the body's immune system. The cells fight one another, often causing the patient's body to reject the transplanted organ.

After performing the operation, doctors gave Stephanie drugs to keep her immune system from attacking the transplanted intestine. Since the operation, Stephanie has been able to eat anything she wants.

THINK ABOUT IT

1. How else is your immune system at work in your body?
2. Why would the human body fight to reject a transplanted organ?

Spin-In

Find out more! Log on to
www.hspscience.com

Back on BOARD

Bethany Hamilton is one tough kid. While she was paddling her surfboard in Hawai`i, a tiger shark ripped off Bethany's left arm below the shoulder. The 13-year-old Hawaiian nearly died after losing more than half of her blood and undergoing hours of surgery.

Doctors told Bethany that she survived the shark attack because she was in good physical condition. All she remembers is lying on her board in clear water off the island of Kaua`i. She did not see the 14-foot-long shark lurking nearby.

"My arm was hanging in the water, and [the shark] just came and bit me," Bethany said. "I just held on to my board, and then it let go."

Doctors fitted Bethany with a prosthetic, or artificial, arm. Soon after, she learned to snowboard in Colorado. Amazingly, less than three months after the attack, the young surfing champion was back on the water in a local surfing competition. She reached the finals of her age group finishing in fifth place.

SC.H.3.2.1.5.1 technology has improved human lives;
SC.H.3.2.4.5.1 people can solve problems through science

You Can Do It!

Materials

- plastic spoon
- zip-top plastic bag
- unflavored gelatin, prepared
- small rubber ball
- raisins
- marbles

Quick and Easy Project

Model an Animal Cell

Procedure

1. Use the plastic spoon to fill the bag about two-thirds full of gelatin.
2. Add the ball to the bag. What cell structure do you think the ball represents? What is this structure's function in the cell?
3. Add raisins and marbles. Seal the bag tightly.

Draw Conclusions

Which cell structures do you think the raisins and marbles represent? What are these structures' functions in the cell?

Design Your Own Investigation

Model a Plant Cell

Think about the differences between animal cells and plant cells. How might you change your model of an animal cell so that it represents a plant cell? Choose materials, and make a plant-cell model.

Vocabulary Review

Use the terms below to complete the sentences. The page numbers tell you where to look in the chapter if you need help.

cell p. 360
nucleus p. 362
tissue p. 368
organ p. 369
organ
   system p. 370

digestive system p. 370
respiratory
   system p. 378
skeletal system p. 380
muscular system p. 380
nervous system p. 382

1. Cells that work together to carry out a function make up a _____.

2. The group of organs and tissues that exchanges oxygen and carbon dioxide in the lungs is the _____.

3. A group of organs that work together to carry out life processes is an _____.

4. Tissues that work with your skeleton to help you move make up the _____.

5. A group of tissues working together to perform a function is an _____.

6. Structures that support and protect your body are in the _____.

7. The basic unit of structure and function of living things is the _____.

8. The organelle that directs a cell's activities is the _____.

9. The mouth, esophagus, stomach, and intestines are parts of the _____.

10. Organs and tissues that work together to help you sense your environment make up the _____.

Check Understanding

Write the letter of the best choice.

11. What is the purpose of a cell membrane?

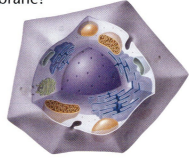

A. to keep the cell dry
B. to keep the cell warm
C. to hold the contents of the cell together
D. to provide a sticky surface for the cell

12. SEQUENCE How does oxygen-rich blood travel from the heart to capillaries around the body?

    F. through arteries

    G. through cardiac muscle

    H. through pulmonary veins

    I. through veins

13. MAIN IDEA AND DETAILS Which is **not** a kind of connective tissue?

    A. nerve   **C.** cartilage

    B. bone   **D.** blood

14. Which term describes **both** a diatom and an amoeba?

    F. animal   **H.** plant

    G. bacteria   **I.** protist

15. How are plant cells different from animal cells?

 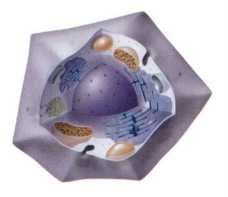

    A. Plant cells have membranes and a nucleus, but animal cells do not.

    B. Plant cells have cell walls and chloroplasts, but animal cells do not.

    C. Plant cells have cell walls and organelles, but animal cells do not.

    D. Plant cells have no nucleus or organelles, but animal cells do.

16. Which systems work together to provide the body's cells with oxygen?

    F. circulatory and digestive

    G. respiratory and digestive

    H. respiratory and circulatory

    I. respiratory and excretory

Inquiry Skills

17. Compare bacteria cells to plant cells.

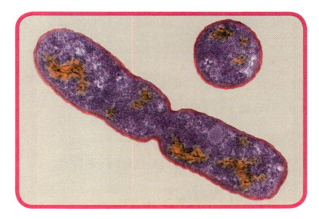

18. Describe the **sequence** of events that takes place to remove ammonia from the body.

 Read/Inquire/Explain

19. The large bones work with the circulatory system to produce blood cells. Why is this important?

20. Jamie is helping his mother cook. As he adds pepper to the food, he sneezes.

Part A What kind of action is his sneezing? Why?

Part B Which two systems act together to cause Jamie's sneeze? Explain.

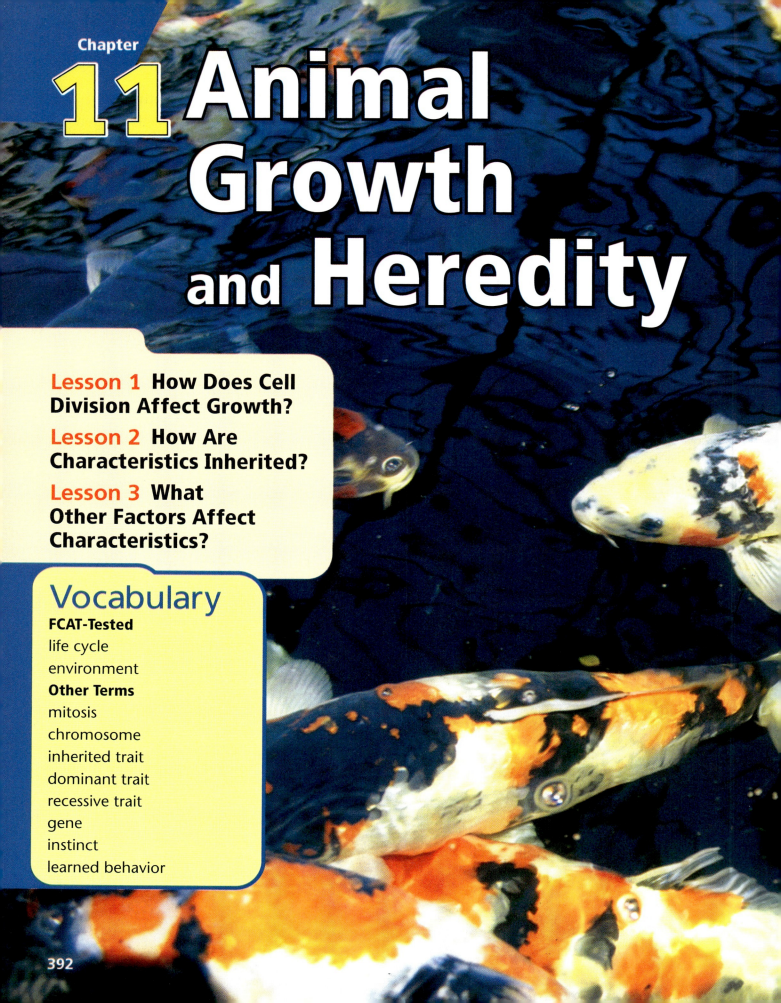

Lesson 1 How Does Cell Division Affect Growth?

Lesson 2 How Are Characteristics Inherited?

Lesson 3 What Other Factors Affect Characteristics?

Vocabulary

FCAT-Tested

life cycle

environment

Other Terms

mitosis

chromosome

inherited trait

dominant trait

recessive trait

gene

instinct

learned behavior

What do YOU wonder?

Though they look like giant goldfish, these colorful fish are called koi. The color patterns of koi are hereditary. That means the patterns are passed from the parents to their young. What other kinds of characteristics are passed from parents to offspring?

393

Lesson 1

How Does Cell Division Affect Growth?

Fast Fact

Doubling Up When a cell divides, the two new cells are identical to the original cell. Some single-celled organisms, such as certain bacteria, can divide as often as every 30 minutes. In 5 hours, a bacterial cell can become 1024 cells! In the Investigate, you'll see how different types of cells divide.

Animal-cell division

Cell Reproduction

Materials
- prepared slide of plant mitosis
- prepared slide of animal mitosis
- microscope

Procedure

1. Put the plant mitosis slide on the microscope stage. Focus until you see cells clearly. Observe the cells that show division.

2. Make drawings to record what you see in different cells.

3. Replace the plant mitosis slide with the animal mitosis slide. Observe the cells that show division.

4. Make drawings to record what you see in different cells.

5. Compare your drawings of plant cell division with your drawings of animal cell division. How are they alike? How are they different? Record your comparisons.

Step 1

Draw Conclusions

1. What part of a cell changes as the cell divides? What changes take place?

2. How many new cells does each cell division produce?

3. **Inquiry Skill** Scientists observe and ask questions based on their observations. What questions do you have about cell division, based on your own observations?

Step 3

Investigate Further

Now that you've observed cells dividing, make models showing the stages of cell division.

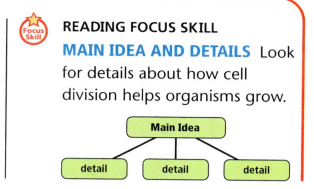

VOCABULARY
life cycle p. 397
mitosis p. 398
chromosome p. 398

SCIENCE CONCEPTS
▶ how cells that already exist make new cells
▶ how cell division helps organisms grow

READING FOCUS SKILL
MAIN IDEA AND DETAILS Look for details about how cell division helps organisms grow.

Main Idea

detail detail detail

Growth and Development

All organisms start life as a single cell. In plants and animals, the cell then begins dividing. The one cell divides into two cells. The two cells divide into four cells, and so on. By the time a plant or an animal is complete, its body is made up of trillions of cells.

Even in a complete organism, like you, cells continue to divide. Your bone cells divide, building more bone tissue. Your skin cells divide, producing new skin tissue. You grow and change.

Sometimes the changes are obvious. For example, you get taller and outgrow your clothes. But sometimes you can't see the changes, especially when they happen to tissues inside the body. By the time you're an adult, your body will be made up of about 100 trillion cells!

As you know, each type of cell has a special function. During cell division, most body cells make exact copies of themselves. When bone cells divide, they make new bone cells. When muscle cells divide, they make new muscle cells. The new cells have the same functions as the old cells. This enables body organs and systems to function properly as you grow.

A chick begins life as a single cell—a fertilized egg.

After 7 days, the single cell has divided into many cells. Blood vessels begin to form.

By Day 14, the skeleton and most organs have formed.

By Day 21, the chick is fully developed, has hatched out, and is living on its own!

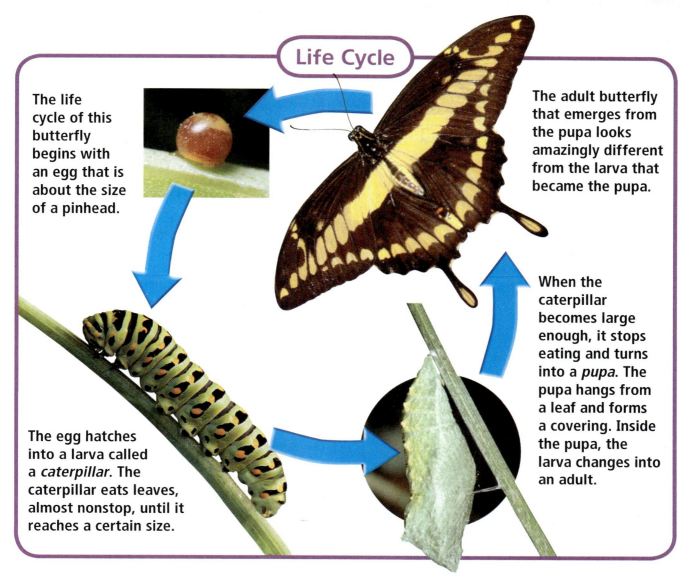

Life Cycle

The life cycle of this butterfly begins with an egg that is about the size of a pinhead.

The adult butterfly that emerges from the pupa looks amazingly different from the larva that became the pupa.

The egg hatches into a larva called a *caterpillar*. The caterpillar eats leaves, almost nonstop, until it reaches a certain size.

When the caterpillar becomes large enough, it stops eating and turns into a *pupa*. The pupa hangs from a leaf and forms a covering. Inside the pupa, the larva changes into an adult.

As living things grow and develop, most pass through several stages. These stages make up an organism's **life cycle**. A life cycle begins with a fertilized egg. Some animals develop inside their mothers' bodies. Then they are born. Others develop inside a protective egg, and then hatch out.

Some organisms, like bacteria and protists, are mature as soon as they are formed. They can reproduce immediately. Others, such as mammals, spend months or years growing and developing before reaching maturity.

Some animals change a great deal as they mature. Animals such as butterflies and frogs actually have one kind of body when they're young and a very different kind of body when they're mature. The changes they undergo as they grow and mature are called *metamorphosis*.

Other animals do not change much during their lives. The young are smaller than the adults, but otherwise look pretty much like the adults. Mammals, birds, reptiles, and most fish have this kind of development.

In summary, a life cycle starts with a fertilized egg. The organism grows and matures. Eventually it reproduces, and a new life cycle starts.

 **MAIN IDEA AND DETAILS** How does cell division help organisms grow?

Cell Division

The process by which most cells divide is called **mitosis** (my•TOH•sis). What makes it happen? Scientists aren't completely sure what triggers it. But they know that the process is directed by the nucleus.

The nucleus contains threadlike structures called **chromosomes**, which are made up of a complex chemical called *DNA*. DNA carries a code in its structure. The DNA code has all the information that directs how a cell functions, including when to divide.

Before mitosis begins, an exact copy of each chromosome is made, producing a pair. During mitosis, the identical chromosomes of each pair separate, resulting in two sets that are identical to the original chromosomes. The sets pull apart. Then the cell membrane pinches in the middle, forming two new cells. Each cell is just like its parent cell.

Have you ever skinned your elbow or knee? Almost immediately, cells in the area started mitosis. New skin cells formed to replace the lost tissue. Soon the scrape disappeared, and your skin was smooth and complete again. This process of replacing tissue is called *regeneration*.

In humans, regeneration is limited to healing wounds. But in some animals, regeneration can replace entire body parts. For example, if a sea star loses an arm, nearby cells undergo rapid mitosis. Soon the sea star has a new arm.

Science Up Close

Mitosis

In mitosis, each new cell gets a copy of the parent cell's chromosomes. This passes along the DNA code. The new cells look and function just like the parent cell.

Before a cell starts mitosis, its chromosomes make copies of themselves. Each original and its copy are joined. The cell now has enough DNA for *two* cells.

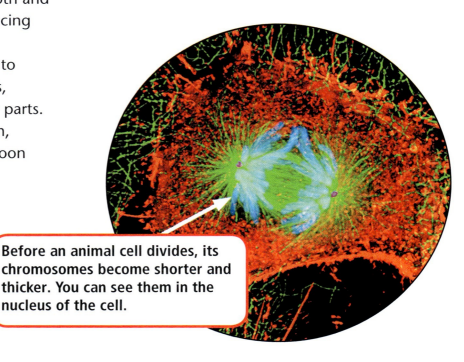

Before an animal cell divides, its chromosomes become shorter and thicker. You can see them in the nucleus of the cell.

As cell division starts, the membrane around the nucleus disappears. The chromosomes become shorter and thicker. Centrioles form at the cell's poles.

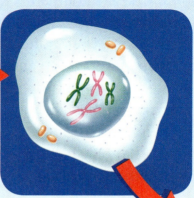

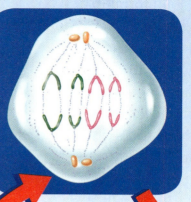

The members of the chromosome pairs separate. One member of each pair moves to one side of the cell, and the other member moves to the opposite side of the cell.

A *spindle* made of thin tubes forms across the cell. The chromosome pairs—with the members of each pair still joined—line up along the center of the spindle.

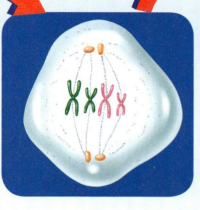

After the chromosomes separate, the spindle breaks down. Each set of chromosomes becomes enclosed by a new nuclear membrane. Finally, the cell membrane pinches in two.

You know that many organisms have only one cell. When the cell divides, the whole organism reproduces. This process is called *asexual reproduction* because there is no joining of cells from different parents. For example, yeast is a single-celled fungus that reproduces when a tiny bud forms on a parent cell. Mitosis takes place in the cell, and a copy of its chromosomes is passed into the growing bud. When the bud is fully grown, it breaks off and begins living on its own.

 MAIN IDEA AND DETAILS Why do members of chromosome pairs separate during mitosis?

Separating Chromosomes

Use two 10-cm pieces of thread to represent chromosomes. Starting at one end, pull apart one of the threads into two threads. Now pull apart the other original thread, but start at the middle. How do you think chromosomes separate during cell division?

Reproduction

Most multicellular organisms reproduce by the joining of cells from two different individuals. This is called *sexual reproduction*. Cells from each parent join, forming a fertilized egg, or *zygote* (ZY•goht). A zygote receives chromosomes from each parent.

It's important for a zygote to contain the right number of chromosomes. The cells of every organism have a specific number of chromosomes. If they have too many or too few, the cells don't work properly.

Organisms that reproduce sexually have two types of cells—body cells and reproductive cells, or *gametes* (GAM•eetz). Gametes contain only half the number of chromosomes of body cells. When two gametes join, the zygote once again has the same number of chromosomes as the rest of the body cells.

Gametes are formed during a process called *meiosis* (my•OH•sis). During meiosis, the number of chromosomes in a cell is divided in half. For example, human body cells have 46 chromosomes. Each human gamete has 23 chromosomes.

Meiosis occurs in two stages. During the first stage, the chromosomes are copied and the cell divides. In the second stage, the two new cells divide again, *without* copying their chromosomes. So, each of the four new cells—the gametes—has only half the number of chromosomes that body cells have.

⭐ **MAIN IDEA AND DETAILS** Why must gametes contain half the number of chromosomes that body cells have?

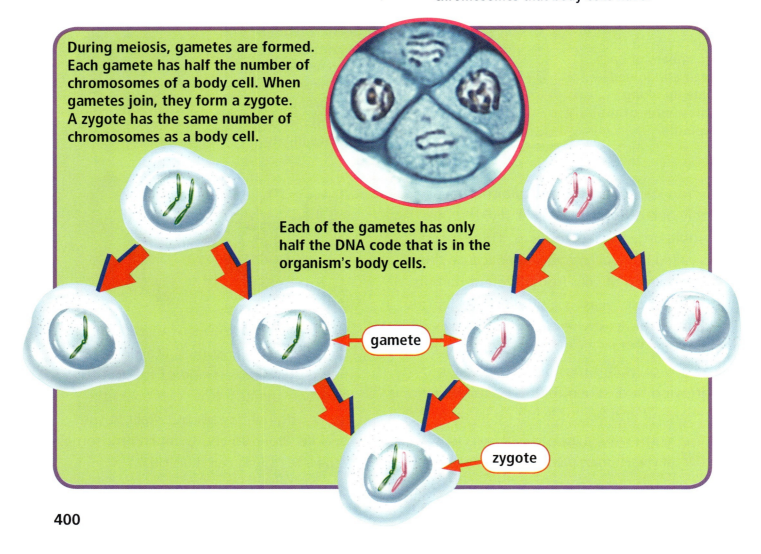

During meiosis, gametes are formed. Each gamete has half the number of chromosomes of a body cell. When gametes join, they form a zygote. A zygote has the same number of chromosomes as a body cell.

Each of the gametes has only half the DNA code that is in the organism's body cells.

gamete

zygote

1. MAIN IDEA AND DETAILS Draw and complete the graphic organizer.

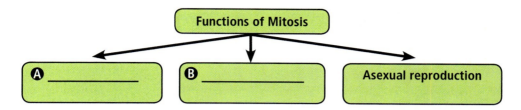

Functions of Mitosis

A _____   **B** _____   **Asexual reproduction**

2. SUMMARIZE Use your graphic organizer to write a sentence that summarizes mitosis.

3. DRAW CONCLUSIONS If an organism has 12 chromosomes in its body cells, how many chromosomes do its gametes and zygotes have?

4. VOCABULARY Without looking back in this lesson, write a definition for each vocabulary term: *life cycle, mitosis, chromosome.*

FCAT Prep

5. Read/Inquire/Explain Why are chromosomes duplicated before mitosis?

6. During mitosis, which part of the cell pinches in to make a new cell?
   A. cell membrane   **C.** cytoplasm
   B. cell wall   **D.** nucleus

Links

Writing
Expository Writing
Suppose you're a science writer for a newspaper. Write a **descriptive article** detailing the process of mitosis.

Math
Display Data
Use library or Internet resources to find out the number of chromosomes in the body cells of five different animals. Make a bar graph to compare the numbers. Which animal has the most? Which has the least?

Health
Mutations
Sometimes, changes occur during the copying of chromosomes. The results are called *genetic mutations*. Use library or Internet resources to identify a genetic mutation. Tell classmates what you learned.

 For more links and activities, go to **www.hspscience.com**

How Are Characteristics Inherited?

Fast Fact

The Code of Life These strands of DNA look oddly twisted. But they contain all the information that cells need to carry out life processes and pass on traits. You'll learn about some inherited traits in the Investigate.

Inherited Characteristics

Materials • mirror

Procedure

1 Make a table like the one shown.

2 Stick out your tongue, and try to roll its edges up, toward the middle. Use the mirror to help you make your observation. Record the result in the table.

3 Use the mirror to observe the shape of your earlobes. Are they attached to your face, or do they hang free? Record the result in the table.

4 Fold your hands in front of you. Observe which of your thumbs falls naturally on top. Record the result in the table.

5 Your teacher will now ask all students to report their results. Tally the results in the table as students report them. Then find the number of students who have each trait. Use numbers to calculate the fraction of the class that has each trait. Then make a graph of the class results.

Characteristic	Result (Circle one.)		Class Totals
Tongue rolling	yes	no	
Earlobes	attached	free	
Folded hands	left	right	

Step 2

Draw Conclusions

1. Which trait in each pair occurred more often in your class?

2. **Inquiry Skill** Scientists often infer an idea after making observations. Infer whether a person could learn to roll his or her tongue. Explain.

Investigate Further

Predict whether the results will be the same for another group. Then gather data to test your prediction.

VOCABULARY

inherited trait p. 404
dominant trait p. 406
recessive trait p. 406
gene p. 408

SCIENCE CONCEPTS

▶ how certain characteristics are passed from parents to their young

▶ how genes influence inherited traits

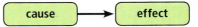

READING FOCUS SKILL

CAUSE AND EFFECT Look for patterns of traits that result from heredity.

cause	→	effect

How Characteristics Are Inherited

You may have a friend who looks a lot like her parents. She may share her mother's eye color and dimples or have the same type of hair or skin color as her father. These and many other traits are inherited. An **inherited trait** is a characteristic passed from parents to their offspring.

In humans, hair color, eye color, and skin color are inherited. Freckles, hair texture, and earlobe shape are inherited, too. So are some behaviors. For example, the tendency to be right-handed or left-handed is inherited.

In animals, eye color is inherited. So are fur color and texture. Each of the puppies

in the picture on this page inherited some traits from its parents, including facial shape and hair texture. All the puppies have faces that are the same shape, and all have similar hair texture. The puppies are not identical, though. One puppy doesn't look much like its parents. But its fur color was inherited.

For thousands of years, farmers have selected animals through breeding. They've bred animals having some desirable traits with animals having other desirable traits so that the offspring would have these traits, too. Farmers knew that traits were passed from parents to their offspring. But they didn't know how.

The way traits are passed from parents to offspring interested Gregor Mendel,

Most of the puppies in this litter look like the parents. But even the one that looks different inherited many of its parents' traits. ▼

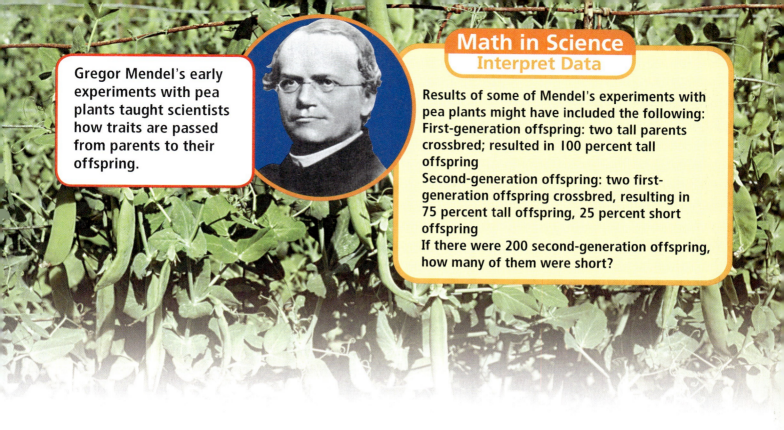

Gregor Mendel's early experiments with pea plants taught scientists how traits are passed from parents to their offspring.

Math in Science
Interpret Data

Results of some of Mendel's experiments with pea plants might have included the following:
First-generation offspring: two tall parents crossbred; resulted in 100 percent tall offspring
Second-generation offspring: two first-generation offspring crossbred, resulting in 75 percent tall offspring, 25 percent short offspring
If there were 200 second-generation offspring, how many of them were short?

a nineteenth-century Austrian monk. Mendel's work in a monastery garden made him want to understand the inheritance of traits. He noticed that some pea plants were tall and others were short. He thought that these traits were inherited, but he didn't know how. In 1857, he began experimenting.

First, he bred tall pea plants with short pea plants. All the offspring—the first generation—were tall. When these tall plants were allowed to breed, three-fourths of the offspring—the second generation—were tall. But one-fourth were short. These results led Mendel to hypothesize that a characteristic is controlled by a pair of *factors.* Each parent passes one of its pair of factors to an offspring. The way the factors combine in the offspring controls which trait appears in each individual.

Mendel learned that traits can skip a generation. As shown above, when he bred tall plants with short plants, the offspring were all tall. But short plants appeared again in the second generation. Inheritance in all organisms, including people, works this way. You can inherit a trait—blue eyes, for example—that neither of your parents shows, as long as people before them in your family had that trait.

 CAUSE AND EFFECT Why are some pea plants short, while others are tall?

Thanks to the work of Gregor Mendel, we know that this child inherited her deep-blue eyes from her parents, even though they both have brown eyes! ▶

Dominant and Recessive Traits

Mendel did hundreds of experiments and kept careful records of his results. Again and again, he found that first-generation offspring of tall plants and short plants were tall, but second-generation offspring included about one-fourth short plants. He hypothesized that the first-generation plants must have a hidden factor for shortness. How else could this trait appear in the second generation?

In pea plants, tallness is a strong trait, or a **dominant trait**. If an organism has one factor for a dominant trait, that trait appears. Shortness in pea plants is a weak trait, or a **recessive trait**. A recessive trait appears only if an organism has two factors for the trait. If both a dominant factor and a recessive factor are present, the dominant trait appears. This explains why three-fourths of Mendel's second-generation pea plants were tall. Plants with one or two factors for tallness were tall. Only plants with two factors for shortness were short.

Look at the example about fur color in mice. Three of the offspring are dark brown, and one is light brown. Both parents have dark brown fur, which is dominant. For light brown fur to appear, both parents must have a factor for light brown fur.

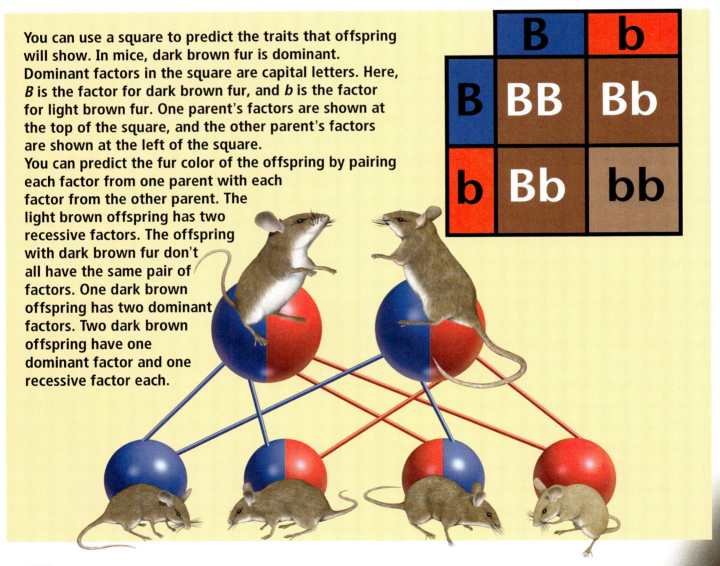

You can use a square to predict the traits that offspring will show. In mice, dark brown fur is dominant. Dominant factors in the square are capital letters. Here, *B* is the factor for dark brown fur, and *b* is the factor for light brown fur. One parent's factors are shown at the top of the square, and the other parent's factors are shown at the left of the square.

You can predict the fur color of the offspring by pairing each factor from one parent with each factor from the other parent. The light brown offspring has two recessive factors. The offspring with dark brown fur don't all have the same pair of factors. One dark brown offspring has two dominant factors. Two dark brown offspring have one dominant factor and one recessive factor each.

In humans, having blue eyes is a recessive trait. Can two brown-eyed parents have a child with blue eyes? Yes, but they must both have a hidden factor for blue eyes.

In the Investigate at the beginning of this lesson, you observed several inherited traits. The ability to roll your tongue is a dominant trait. If you can roll your tongue, you inherited either two dominant factors (one from each parent) or one dominant factor and one recessive factor. If you aren't able to roll your tongue, you inherited two recessive factors (one from each parent).

Unattached earlobes are dominant, and attached earlobes are recessive. If your earlobes are unattached, you inherited at least one dominant factor. If you have attached earlobes, you inherited two recessive factors.

Even though right-handedness is dominant, most people rest the left thumb on top when they fold their hands. Resting the left thumb on top is dominant. If you rest your right thumb on top, what factors did you inherit?

 CAUSE AND EFFECT What are the possible results of breeding a dark brown mouse with a light brown mouse?

◀ **Most dogs have fur, but this dog has hardly any! It inherited a recessive factor for hairlessness from each of its parents.**

Heads or Tails

Toss a pair of coins 32 times, and record how they land. Suppose heads represents a dominant factor and tails represents a recessive factor. Calculate the number of times a dominant trait is expected to appear. Compare this number with your coin tosses.

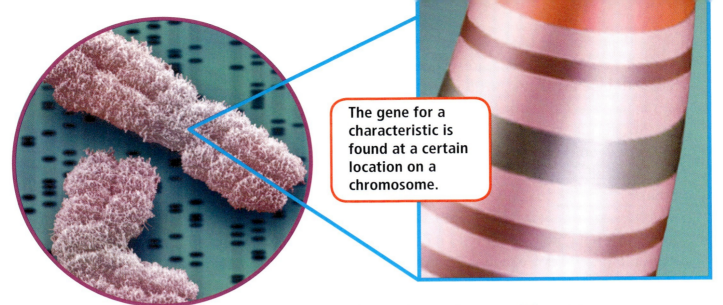

The gene for a characteristic is found at a certain location on a chromosome.

Genes

Today, Mendel's factors are known to be different forms of genes. A **gene** is the part of a chromosome that contains the DNA code for an inherited trait. A gene for a particular trait is found at a specific place on a chromosome. All inherited traits—tongue rolling, thumb position, and thousands more—are controlled by genes.

Like every organism, you are genetically unique. You share some characteristics with most humans, but unless you have an identical twin, there is no one else with exactly the same combination of genes that you have.

What makes you different from everyone else? Remember that during meiosis, each gamete gets only half the chromosomes of a body cell. So each of your parents contributed half of his or her genes to you. You probably inherited many genes for dominant traits. You also inherited some genes for recessive traits. In any case, the particular combination of about 20,000 different genes you inherited is what makes you unique. You may have eyes like your mother's or hair like your father's—but there's no one else exactly like you.

 CAUSE AND EFFECT How does meiosis affect inheritance through genes?

Scientists can now study individual genes to figure out how certain diseases are inherited.

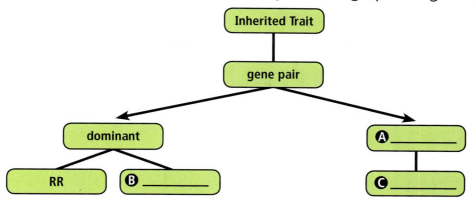

1. CAUSE AND EFFECT Draw and complete this graphic organizer.

Inherited Trait

gene pair

dominant

 RR

B _____

A _____

C _____

2. SUMMARIZE Use your graphic organizer to write a paragraph relating genes and traits.

3. DRAW CONCLUSIONS A dark brown mouse is bred with a light brown mouse. Out of four offspring, how many are likely to be dark brown?

4. VOCABULARY Write clues for the vocabulary terms, and make a word-search puzzle with the terms. Ask a classmate to solve the puzzle.

FCAT Prep

5. Read/Inquire/Explain How can two brown-eyed parents have a blue-eyed child?

6. What are Mendel's "factors"?
- **A.** chromosomes
- **B.** pieces of DNA
- **C.** forms of genes
- **D.** traits

Links

Writing

Expository Writing
Choose one of the traits you've read about. Then write an **explanation** of the inheritance of this trait in your family.

Math
Use Fractions
Suppose a mother has two dominant genes for right-handedness, and a father has two recessive genes. Construct a square to predict the probability of right-handedness in their children.

Health

Genetic Testing
Because some gene combinations cause disease, many states require checking for genetic disorders at birth. Use Internet resources to learn which genetic disorders are checked for in your state.

 For more links and activities, go to **www.hspscience.com**

What Other Factors Affect Characteristics?

Fast Fact

Spiderwebs A spider can spin a complicated web without learning how to do so. It can spin its first web without experience and without even a model of a finished web. The ability to spin a web is inherited. In the Investigate, you'll classify some of your own behaviors as inherited or learned.

410

Learned and Inherited Behaviors

Materials • pen and paper

Procedure

1. Make a table like the one shown.

2. The left-hand column lists common behaviors. Some of these are skills you learned how to do. Others are behaviors you inherited.

3. Think about each behavior. Then record which behaviors you think are learned and which you think are inherited. The first one is classified for you.

4. Think about activities you've done in the last few hours. Then add four behaviors to the table. Record which behaviors you learned and which you inherited.

Behavior	Learned	Inherited
Waking up		l
Brushing teeth		
Eating		
Walking		
Sleeping		
Reading		
Using a computer		

Draw Conclusions

1. Compare the number of learned behaviors to the number of behaviors you inherited.

2. Choose one of the behaviors you learned. Communicate to a classmate how you learned that behavior.

3. Inquiry Skill Scientists often infer the reason for something, based on their observations. Infer whether most human behaviors are learned or inherited. Explain.

Step 3

Investigate Further

Research hunting behavior in lions. Is it inherited, learned, or both? Compare this behavior to some of your behaviors, such as eating and walking.

SC.F.2.2.1.5.1 heredity;
SC.F.2.2.1.5.2 characteristics and environment;
LA.E.2.2.1 cause and effect

VOCABULARY

instinct p. 412
learned behavior p. 414
environment p. 416

SCIENCE CONCEPTS

▶ how instinct and the environment affect characteristics
▶ how learning can affect traits

 **READING FOCUS SKILL**

CAUSE AND EFFECT Look for ways that environment and learning affect traits.

| cause | → | effect |

Instincts

Many of the things you do, such as reading, writing, playing games, and acquiring new skills, are learned. But some, such as eating and sleeping, are *instinctive*. An **instinct** is a behavior that an organism inherits. Since instincts are inherited, they are passed from parents to their offspring.

Have you ever observed a bird making a nest or watched a cat groom itself? If so, you're familiar with some instinctive animal behaviors. These help an animal survive in its surroundings.

Behaviors for building shelters, caring for young, and finding food are usually instinctive. Ospreys, for example, build their nests away from other birds, protect their young, and hunt for fish instinctively.

Canada geese instinctively fly south for the winter and eat grains and water plants.

This osprey chose a particular place for her nest, and she instinctively knows how to build a nest and care for her young. ▶

Some species of ants instinctively "herd" aphids to fresh leaves. There the aphids feed and make a sweet liquid that the ants eat. The ants also defend the aphids against predators.

Squirrels instinctively collect and store nuts and other seeds for the winter.

Cats instinctively eat when they're hungry, sleep when they're tired, and cover their wastes. They also instinctively care for their young, feeding them and protecting them from danger.

Instincts are not just behaviors of individual animals. Instincts are usually shared by all members of a species or by all the males or all the females of a species. Certain species of ants, for example, instinctively take care of aphids, which are insects that provide the ants with food.

In addition to sharing species instincts, different breeds within a species may have slightly different instincts. Beagles, for example, don't have to be taught to track small animals. But they can't herd sheep. Border collies don't have to be taught to round up sheep, but they can't hunt rabbits, as beagles do. These two dog breeds have specific instincts that guide their behavior. However, neither breed needs to be taught fear—both are born knowing to avoid danger.

What instincts were you born with? You were able to eat and sleep when you needed to. And you were able to communicate with your parents when you needed things—your crying was instinctive.

 **CAUSE AND EFFECT** What effect do instincts have on an animal's survival?

Learned Behaviors

Birds instinctively build nests for shelter, but their nests are not all alike. Canada geese, for example, build nests on the ground, using grasses and mosses. Ospreys build nests high above the ground, and they sometimes reuse old nests. Shore birds, such as sea gulls, lay their eggs in shallow depressions in the sand. Swallows use mud, clay, and saliva to cement grass nests to cliffs, buildings, or bridges. Building a nest is instinctive. But using certain kinds of materials is a learned behavior.

A **learned behavior** is a behavior an animal acquires through experience. Cheetahs, for example, are born with the instinct to hunt, kill, and eat other animals. To survive, however, young cheetahs must learn hunting skills from adults. They must have experiences that teach them the best ways to track, hunt, and kill. A young cheetah needs both the instinct to hunt and experiences that develop hunting skills.

You were born with the instinct to cry, but you learned to vary the pitch and loudness of your crying, depending on your needs. As you grew and developed, you learned many other behaviors. You learned how to walk and talk. You learned how to dress yourself, how to bathe, and how to brush your teeth. Though you had the instinct to eat, you learned table manners and how to use spoons, forks, and knives.

Not all learned animal behaviors are used for survival. Animals may learn some less important behaviors from people. A parrot, for example, may mimic simple human speech. Like many people, you may have taught your dog to "shake hands."

These cheetah cubs were born with the instinct to hunt, but their mother teaches them hunting skills. Together, instinct and learned behaviors help the cubs survive. ▼

This service dog has learned behaviors that help its owner.

Have you ever seen dolphins doing tricks or seen a circus act with trained animals? These performances often include behaviors that are similar to instinctive behaviors. But the animals are trained to perform the behaviors at specific times or on command.

Some animals can learn behaviors that are helpful to people. These behaviors aren't necessary for the animals' survival but can be very useful to the animals' human companions.

Service animals are trained to do tasks that help people with disabilities. Guide dogs help owners who can't see, by leading them as the owners walk. Hearing dogs alert their owners to sounds such as ringing phones and doorbells. Mobility-assist dogs help physically disabled people with tasks such as carrying objects or opening doors.

Dogs aren't the only animals that can be trained to help people. Capuchin monkeys, for example, have also been trained to help people do some simple everyday tasks.

CAUSE AND EFFECT How are most animal behaviors learned?

Insta-Lab

Model a Beak
Birds have the instinct to eat certain foods, such as seeds. Place a few beans in a graduate, a narrow cylinder. Try to remove them with a "beak" made up of your thumb and index finger. Then try this with forceps. Why is it important for birds to feed from certain plants?

415

Environmental Influences

Some characteristics or behaviors are the result of *environmental influences.* An organism's ==environment== is everything in its surroundings that affects it, including water, soil, air, weather, landforms, and other living things.

All living things have needs. Animals need food, water, space, and shelter. Plants need nutrients, water, and sunlight. When an environment changes, all the things that live there are affected. Sometimes, animals lose their shelter, or they can't find enough food or water. So they must move to get the things they need.

Sometimes, changes in the environment force animals to change their behavior. In areas where food becomes less plentiful, some animals may learn to eat different foods. Wolves usually eat deer or mountain goats. If there aren't enough of those animals, wolves may learn to eat cattle or sheep.

Sometimes, the environment causes a physical change in a species over time. Pollution kills many plants and animals. But these poisons can also damage the chromosomes of living organisms and can affect their offspring. Look at the frog in the picture. The defects in its body are the result of pollution that changed the frog's DNA. If the DNA change occurs in the frog's gametes, its offspring will inherit the body defects.

 CAUSE AND EFFECT How can the environment affect future generations?

◄ Poisons in an environment harm the populations living there. This frog has defects because pollutants damaged its DNA. How might this damage affect future generations?

Human activities, such as farming, affect the environment. Here, chemicals used in farming have run off from a field, polluting the water.

1. CAUSE AND EFFECT Draw and complete this graphic organizer.

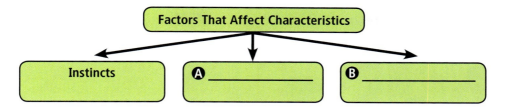

Factors That Affect Characteristics

Instincts

Ⓐ _____

Ⓑ _____

2. SUMMARIZE Use your graphic organizer to write a sentence summarizing the lesson.

3. DRAW CONCLUSIONS How might the number of oak trees in a park affect the number of squirrels that can live there?

4. VOCABULARY Write a definition of the term *instinct*.

FCAT Prep

5. Read/Inquire/Explain What is the difference between an instinct and a learned behavior?

6. Which of the following is **not** a survival instinct for dogs?

A. barking

B. eating

C. shaking hands

D. sleeping

Links

Writing

Persuasive Writing

Choose an animal behavior. Write an essay telling your **opinion** about whether the behavior is instinctive or learned. Give reasons to support your opinion.

Math

Compare Numbers

Use library resources to learn how the number of people in the world has increased since 1650. Make a graph to show the increase. How do you think the increase has affected other living things?

Language Arts

Using Tables

Use your library or the Internet to find out how animals survive cold winter months. Make a cause-and-effect table to summarize your findings. Label causes *instinctive* or *learned*.

For more links and activities, go to **www.hspscience.com**

THE WOLF WITHIN

We love dogs, all types of dogs: small dogs, big dogs, yappy dogs, lap dogs. For their part, dogs love us. They lick our faces, protect our homes, and come when we call them (sometimes).

But where did our favorite four-legged friends come from? How and when did dogs get to be our best friends? Some scientists believe they have found some of the answers.

From Wolf to Woof

Scientists have long known that dogs evolved from wolves. Just when the change from wolf to dog actually took place, however, was a mystery. Some scientists said wolves changed over time to become separate species.

Now, researchers say, those theories are wrong. New studies suggest that tamed dogs first appeared 15,000 years ago in eastern Asia. They also say that every modern dog may be descended from five female Asian wolves.

Old Bones

Scientist Jennifer Leonard and a team of researchers looked into the origins of dogs by collecting the bones of dogs that once lived in North and South America before 1492. Researchers took DNA from

Land Bridge

Scientists suspect dogs first set paw in North America by following settlers across a land bridge that once linked northern Asia and North America. "We can't say in detail how [the dogs got to America]; that's something for the future," said Peter Savolainen, a scientist in Sweden. "But what's certain is that by 9000 years ago, [dogs] were in America and all over Europe and Asia."

the cells in those bones. Genes in the DNA determine a dog's inherited traits, such as eye and fur color. The scientists then compared their samples to the DNA of modern dogs and wolves in Europe, Asia, as well as North and South America.

Scientists found that the genes of the ancient American dogs were similar to the genes of dogs born in Europe and Asia. Scientists also concluded that every breed of dog, from English setters to Labrador retrievers, descended from wolves that lived in Europe and Asia and migrated to North and South America.

Think About It

1. What did scientists look at to study the connection between modern dogs and ancient dogs?
2. What inherited traits do you have from your mother? Your father?

Find out more! Log on to
www.hspscience.com

SC.H.1.2.2.5.1 scientists use different types of investigations;
SC.H.3.2.4.5.1 people can solve problems through science

419

Genes: Building Blocks of Living Things

Gregor Mendel, a monk who lived more than 130 years ago, noticed differences among the pea plants in his garden. Some were tall, while others were short; some had smooth peas and some wrinkled peas. Mendel *cross-pollinated* the plants. He took the pollen from one plant and placed it in the flower of another plant.

Mendel planted the seeds made by the cross-pollinated plant. Based on the traits of the parent plants, he predicted certain traits of the offspring. Mendel had discovered the concept of *genetic heredity,* when the parent of a plant or animal passes along traits through *genes.*

Career   Medical Scientist

Medical scientists research human diseases and their cures. They do most of their work in laboratories. Medical scientists have helped develop vaccines, medicines, and treatments for many diseases.

You Can Do It!

Materials

Quick and Easy Project

How Does DNA Fit?

Materials
- sewing thread
- meterstick
- gelatin capsule

Procedure

1. Measure 1 m of thread. That length of thread represents one chromosome.
2. Make sure your hands are dry. Open the gelatin capsule. The capsule represents the nucleus of a cell.
3. Put all the thread into the capsule in any way you can. Then close the capsule.

Draw Conclusions

How did you get all the thread into the capsule? How do chromosomes fit into the nucleus of a cell? Remember that a nucleus usually contains many chromosomes, not just one.

Design Your Own Investigation

Design a Scale Model

In the activity above, you made a model of how a chromosome fits into the nucleus of a cell. But the model was not to scale. If an actual chromosome were fully stretched out, it would be more than 8000 times the length of a nucleus! Measure the capsule you used. Then calculate how much thread you would need to represent the stretched-out length of a chromosome if the model were to scale.

Vocabulary Review

Use the terms below to complete the sentences. The page numbers tell you where to look in the chapter if you need help.

life cycle p. 397   **dominant trait** p. 406
mitosis p. 398   **gene** p. 408
chromosome p. 398   **environment** p. 416

1. Part of a chromosome that contains the DNA code for a trait is a _____.

2. The stages an organism passes through make up its _____.

3. A strong characteristic that always appears when there is a gene for it is a _____.

4. Body cells divide during _____.

5. A threadlike structure found in the nucleus of the cell is a _____.

6. All the living and nonliving things that affect an organism make up its _____.

Check Understanding

Write the letter of the best choice.

7. In what part of the cell do changes first take place during mitosis?
   A. cell membrane **C.** chloroplasts
   B. cell wall   **D.** nucleus

8. **CAUSE AND EFFECT**
   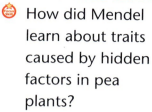 How did Mendel learn about traits caused by hidden factors in pea plants?

   F. They appeared in second-generation offspring.
   G. They appeared in first- and second-generation offspring.
   H. They never appeared in offspring.
   I. They appeared in first-generation offspring.

9. **MAIN IDEA AND DETAILS** During mitosis, what does a new cell get an exact copy of?
   A. cell wall   **C.** dominant traits
   B. chromosomes   **D.** gametes

10. Which is **not** an inherited behavior?
    F. eating   **H.** seeking shelter
    G. reading   **I.** sleeping

11. If an organism has 46 chromosomes in each body cell, how many are in a zygote?
    A. 18   **C.** 46
    B. 23   **D.** 92

12. What are Mendel's *factors* now called?
  F. chromosomes **H.** forms of genes
  G. strands of DNA **I.** nucleus

13. What are inherited behaviors called?
  A. environments **C.** old behaviors
  B. instincts **D.** recessive traits

14. Which sequence describes mitosis?
  F. Chromosomes are copied, chromosomes separate, cell membrane pinches.
  G. Cell membrane pinches, chromosomes are copied, chromosomes separate.
  H. Chromosomes separate, chromosomes are copied, cell membrane pinches.
  I. Cell membrane pinches, chromosomes separate, chromosomes are copied.

15. How is hunting both learned and instinctive in animals?

  A. Animals learn to hunt.
  B. Animals have the instinct to hunt.
  C. Animals have the instinct to hunt but must learn hunting skills.
  D. Animals have the instinct to teach their young how to hunt.

16. Which is an example of a learned behavior?
  F. a snow hare turning white in the winter
  G. a deer standing still in headlight beams
  H. a coyote eating new kinds of prey
  I. a person rolling his tongue

Inquiry Skills

17. Describe the expected results of a cross between two brown-eyed parents. **Predict** the likelihood that their children will have blue eyes.

18. **Compare** meiosis and mitosis. What is the outcome of each?

Read/Inquire/Explain

19. Does a person learn an inherited behavior? Explain.

20. An instinct is a behavior that is passed from parents to their offspring. Instincts are readily observable in animals.
  Part A Explain how instincts can help an animal survive.
  Part B Give an example of learning that improves on an instinct. Explain how the resulting behavior helps an animal.

How Living Things Interact with Their Environments

The chapters in this unit address these Grade Level Expectations from the Florida Sunshine State Standards.

Chapter 12 — **Energy and Ecosystems**

SC.G.1.2.1.5.1	understands the various roles of single-celled organisms in the environment.
SC.G.1.2.1.5.2	knows ways in which protists interact with plants and animals in the environment.
SC.G.1.2.3.5.1	knows that green plants use carbon dioxide, water, and sunlight energy to turn minerals and nutrients into food for growth, maintenance, and reproduction.

Chapter 13 — **Ecosystems and Change**

SC.G.1.2.1.5.1	understands the various roles of single-celled organisms in the environment.
SC.G.1.2.1.5.2	knows ways in which protists interact with plants and animals in the environment.
SC.G.1.2.2.5.1	understands how changes in the environment affect organisms.
SC.G.2.2.1.5.1	knows that adaptations to their environment may increase the survival of a species.

The investigations and experiences in this unit also address many of the Grade Level Expectations in Strand H, The Nature of Science.

Science in Florida

Venice

The Sunshine State

USA

Dear Katherine,

Today I decided that I want to be a marine biologist when I grow up. My class took a field trip to Caspersen Beach in Venice. There were scientists from the Mote Marine Lab in Sarasota doing research on sea turtles. I think it would be so exciting to spend your life studying organisms in the oceans.

See you soon,

Marjorie

Experiment!

Removing Pollution From Water

Living things interact with their environments. Human activity can pollute the physical environment. Living things in the ocean suffer greatly from pollution. How can visible pollution be removed from water? For example, can certain materials be used to filter polluted water? Plan and conduct an experiment to find out.

Chapter

12 Energy and Ecosystems

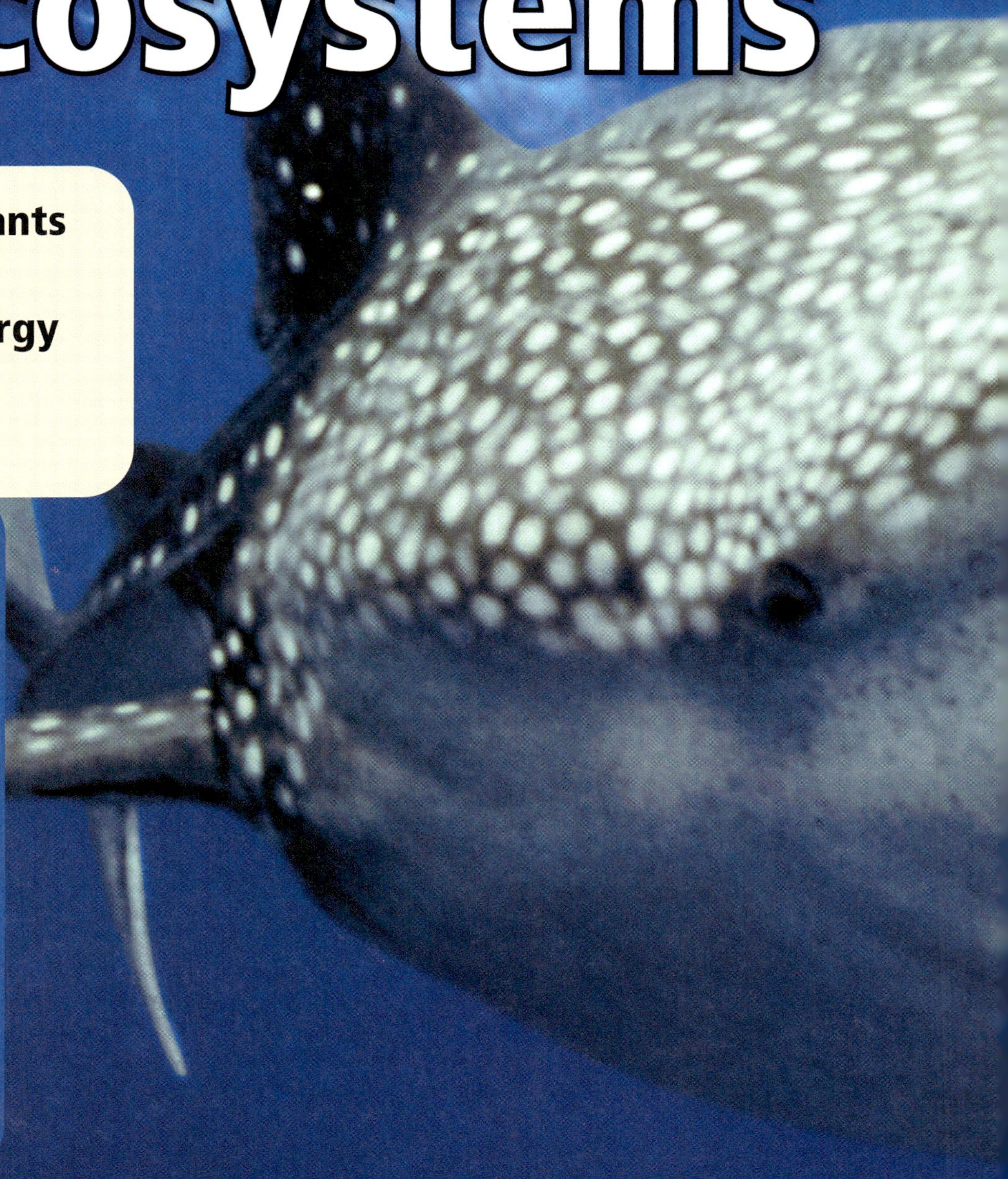

Lesson 1 **How Do Plants Produce Food?**

Lesson 2 **How Is Energy Passed Through an Ecosystem?**

Vocabulary

FCAT-Tested

photosynthesis

producer

consumer

ecosystem

herbivore

carnivore

food chain

decomposer

food web

energy pyramid

Other Terms

transpiration

chlorophyll

What do YOU wonder?

Whale sharks are the largest of all sharks, growing up to 15 m (50 ft) long. They also have the largest mouths, as you can see. What do you think a huge shark like this eats? Where does it get the energy it needs?

How Do Plants Produce Food?

Fast Fact

Working Plants These flowers and trees produce some of the oxygen you breathe. They also take carbon dioxide out of the air. In the Investigate, you will observe that a plant takes in carbon dioxide.

Using Carbon Dioxide

Materials
- safety goggles
- 2 plastic cups
- water
- dropper
- bromothymol blue (BTB)
- 2 test tubes with caps
- *Elodea*
- funnel
- plastic straw

Procedure

1 **CAUTION:** **Wear safety goggles.** Fill one cup about two-thirds full of water. Use the dropper to add BTB until the water is blue.

2 Put the straw into the cup, and blow into it. **CAUTION:** **DO NOT suck on the straw. If the solution gets in your mouth, spit it out and rinse your mouth with water.**

3 Observe and record changes in the water.

4 Put the *Elodea* in one test tube. Use the funnel to fill both test tubes with the BTB solution. Cap both tubes.

5 Turn the tubes upside down, and put them in the empty cup. Place the cup on a sunny windowsill. Predict what changes will occur in the test tubes.

6 After 1 hour, observe both tubes and record your observations.

Draw Conclusions

1. What changes did you observe in the BTB solution during the activity?

2. **Inquiry Skill** Scientists use what they know to predict what will happen. After you blew into the water, how did your observations help you predict what would happen next?

Step 2

Step 5

Investigate Further

Plan and conduct an experiment to test the effect of sunlight on the changes in the BTB solution. Predict what will happen. Then carry out your experiment.

SCIENCE CONCEPTS

▶ how leaves use carbon dioxide and give off oxygen

▶ how the parts of plants make food by means of photosynthesis

 READING FOCUS SKILL

MAIN IDEA AND DETAILS Look for details about how plants make and store food.

Plant Structures

You are probably familiar with the basic parts of plants. These parts include roots, stems, and leaves. Some of those parts produce food for the plant.

Roots Roots have two main jobs. They anchor plants, and they take in water and nutrients. Tubes in the roots carry water to the stems. The roots of some plants, such as carrots, also store food.

Different plants have different types of roots. For example, the roots of desert plants spread out just below the surface to catch any rain that falls. Some plants, like the dandelion, have one main root to reach water deep underground.

Stems Stems support a plant and enable its leaves to reach the sunlight. Stems also contain tubes that carry water and nutrients to the leaves. Other tubes carry food to all parts of the plant. The stems of some plants, such as sugar cane, store food.

Just as plants have different roots, they also have different stems. Small plants tend to have flexible, green stems. Most of these plants live for just one year. Larger plants and

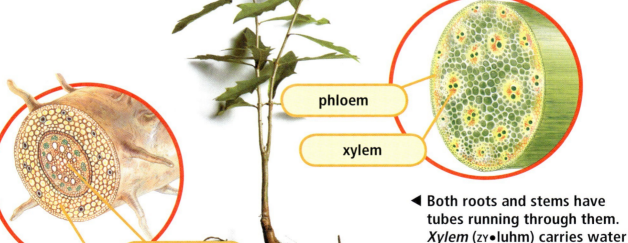

phloem

xylem

xylem

phloem

◀ Both roots and stems have tubes running through them. *Xylem* (ZY•luhm) carries water and nutrients from the soil to the leaves. *Phloem* (FLOH•em) carries food from the leaves to other parts of the plant.

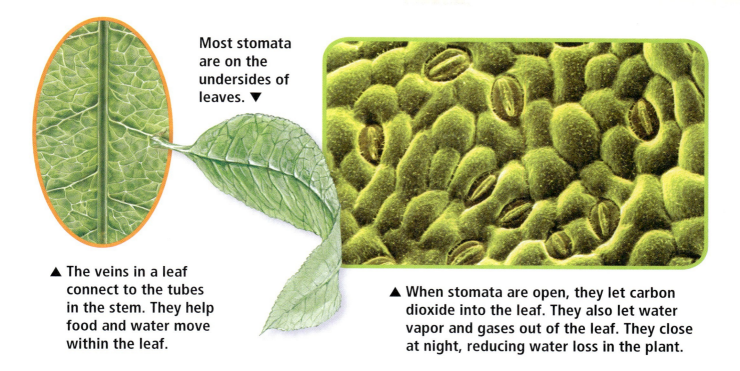

Most stomata are on the undersides of leaves. ▼

▲ The veins in a leaf connect to the tubes in the stem. They help food and water move within the leaf.

▲ When stomata are open, they let carbon dioxide into the leaf. They also let water vapor and gases out of the leaf. They close at night, reducing water loss in the plant.

trees need more support. They usually have stiff, woody stems, and live for many years.

Leaves Leaves have one main job—to make food for the plant. A leaf can be as small as the head of a pin, or it can be wide enough to support a frog on the surface of a pond. Some leaves are very specialized. The leaves of the Venus' flytrap are able to catch food for the plant. They snap shut when an insect lands on them. Then the leaves help digest the insect.

Most leaves are thin and have several layers of cells. The outer layer, called the *epidermis* (ep•uh•DER•mis), keeps the leaf from drying out. The upper epidermis is often covered with a layer of wax. This helps keep water in. The lower epidermis has many small openings called *stomata*.

Stomata usually open during the day so the leaf can take in carbon dioxide to make food. Stomata close at night to keep the plant from drying out. The loss of water through leaves is called <mark>transpiration</mark>.

Just below the upper epidermis is a closely packed layer of cells in which most of the food is made. Just above the lower epidermis is a spongy layer of cells. Air spaces among these cells contain carbon dioxide, oxygen, and water vapor.

Veins, which connect to the tubes in the stems, are found in the center of most leaves. In broad leaves, the veins have many branches. They bring the water needed to make food to cells throughout the leaf.

Focus Skill **MAIN IDEA AND DETAILS** What is the main job of each plant part?

Moving Out
Partially break five toothpicks, leaving the halves connected. Arrange them in a grouping, as shown. Wet the center of the grouping with several drops of water. How does this activity show the way water moves through plants?

Photosynthesis

Plants make food in a process that uses water from the soil, carbon dioxide from the air, and energy from sunlight. This process, called **photosynthesis**, produces food for the plant and releases oxygen into the air.

Recall that plant cells contain organelles called chloroplasts. Cells with chloroplasts are found in the inner layers of leaves on most plants. Only cells with chloroplasts can make food.

Chloroplasts contain a green pigment, or coloring matter, called chlorophyll (KLAWR•uh•fil). **Chlorophyll** enables a plant to absorb light energy so that it can produce food. It also makes plants green. Plants contain small amounts of other pigments as well. In autumn, many plants stop producing chlorophyll, so you can see the other pigments. This is what makes some leaves change color in autumn.

Photosynthesis begins when sunlight hits the chloroplasts. The energy absorbed by the chlorophyll causes water and carbon dioxide to combine to form sugar—the food that plants need to live and grow.

Oxygen is produced as a byproduct of photosynthesis. It is released into the air through the stomata. About 90 percent of the oxygen you breathe is produced during photosynthesis by plants and plantlike protists. Plants also help you by taking carbon dioxide, which your body does not need, out of the air.

 **MAIN IDEA AND DETAILS** What does a plant need for photosynthesis?

Photosynthesis

Sunlight provides energy for plants to make food.

Plants take in carbon dioxide from the air.

After making food, the leaves release oxygen through their stomata.

Chlorophyll absorbs energy from sunlight. The plant needs this energy, along with carbon dioxide and water, to make food.

The food made by the plant is stored in the plant's leaves, stems, seeds, and—in some plants—roots.

Plant roots take in water, which is necessary for photosynthesis.

For more links and activities, go to www.hspscience.com

It All Starts with Plants

All organisms need energy to live and grow. That energy comes from food. Plants are called **producers** because they produce, or make, their own food. Animals can't make their own food, but they need energy from food to survive. When animals eat plants, the animals receive the energy that's stored in those plants. The word *consume* means "to eat," so we call animals that eat plants or other animals **consumers**.

You are a consumer. For example, when you eat a salad, you take in the energy stored in the lettuce leaves and carrot roots. When you eat strawberries, you get the energy that was stored in the fruit and seeds of the strawberry plants.

In fact, you and every animal on Earth depend on plants. Even animals that eat only other animals depend on plants. Without plants, animals such as deer and rabbits, which eat only plants, would starve. Then animals such as wolves, which eat deer and rabbits, would have nothing to eat. They, too, would starve.

The energy from sunlight moves from plants, to animals that eat plants, to animals that eat other animals. Without sunlight, every living thing on Earth would die.

 **MAIN IDEA AND DETAILS** Define the terms *producer* and *consumer*.

These bison get the energy they need by eating grasses. Without plants, the bison couldn't survive.

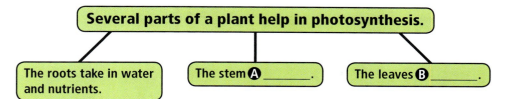

1. MAIN IDEA AND DETAILS Draw and complete the graphic organizer.

> **Several parts of a plant help in photosynthesis.**
>
> - The roots take in water and nutrients.
> - The stem **A** _____.
> - The leaves **B** _____.

2. SUMMARIZE Write two sentences that explain what this lesson is about.

3. DRAW CONCLUSIONS What would happen if all plants had the same kind of roots?

4. VOCABULARY Make a crossword puzzle, including clues, using this lesson's vocabulary terms. Then exchange puzzles with a partner, and solve his or her puzzle.

FCAT Prep

5. Read/Inquire/Explain How would Earth's atmosphere change if plants stopped carrying out photosynthesis?

6. Which gas do plants need for photosynthesis?
 A. carbon dioxide
 B. carbon monoxide
 C. nitrogen
 D. oxygen

Links

Writing

Narrative Writing

Write a **myth** that "explains" a concept in this lesson, such as why plants have roots, why some leaves change color in the fall, or why animals depend on plants. Illustrate your story.

Math

Make a Table

Suppose you want to conduct a two-week experiment to see how different amounts of sunlight affect five sunflower seedlings. Make a table that you could use to record your results.

Language Arts

Word Meanings

Identify the parts of the word *photosynthesis.* Explain how the parts' meanings relate to the fact that plants make their own food. Then list at least three other words that have one of the word parts found in *photosynthesis.*

 For more links and activities, go to **www.hspscience.com**

How Is Energy Passed Through an Ecosystem?

Fast Fact

Bear Chow Bears eat just about anything. A bear weighing 91 kg (200 lb) can eat more than 13 kg (29 lb) of salmon in one day. Or it might eat nearly 32 kg (70 lb) of berries or apples. In the Investigate, you will classify and order organisms that eat one another.

Ordering What Eats What

Materials
- index cards
- markers
- pushpins
- bulletin board
- yarn

Procedure

1. You will be assigned an organism. On an index card, draw it, write its name, or both.

2. Do some research to classify your organism. Is it a producer, a plant-eating consumer, or a meat-eating consumer? Is it a consumer that eats both plants and meat? Or is it an organism that gets its energy from the remains of dead organisms?

3. Work with members of your group to put your cards in an order that shows what eats what.

4. Pin your team's cards in order on the bulletin board. Connect your cards with yarn to show what eats what. Then use yarn to show which of your team's organisms eat organisms from other teams.

Draw Conclusions

1. Classify each organism on your group's cards. In which group does each belong?

2. **Inquiry Skill** When scientists order things, they better understand relationships between them. Could you put your team's cards in another order? Why or why not? Which card must always be first? Which card must always be last?

Step 1

Step 4

Investigate Further

Draw the order of organisms that eat one another in the ocean. Share your drawing with the class.

Reading in Science

 SC.B.1.2.1.5.1 energy flow in a system; **SC.G.1.2.1.5.1** micro-organisms serve many roles; **SC.G.1.2.1.5.2** protists interact with plants and animals; **LA.A.2.2.1** sequence

VOCABULARY

ecosystem p. 438
herbivore p. 438
carnivore p. 438
food chain p. 439
decomposer p. 439
food web p. 440
energy pyramid p. 443

SCIENCE CONCEPTS

▶ how food energy is passed from plant to animal to animal in an ecosystem

▶ how food chains make up food webs

 READING FOCUS SKILL

SEQUENCE Look for the order of events in the transfer of energy.

Energy Transfer

You read that plants make their own food through the process of photosynthesis. So do a few other organisms, such as algae and lichens (LY•kuhnz). Plants are the main producers in most land ecosystems.

An **ecosystem** (EE•koh•sis•tuhm) includes all the organisms in an area and the environment in which they live. This is a tundra ecosystem. All the organisms shown here are part of a tundra ecosystem. An ecosystem includes many kinds of organisms.

Some tundra animals, like caribou, eat plants and other producers. The food energy stored in the reindeer moss is transferred to the caribou. An animal that eats plants or other producers is an **herbivore**. Herbivores are also called first-level consumers.

Other tundra animals, such as wolves, don't eat plants. They get their energy by eating other animals, like caribou. Food energy stored in the caribou is transferred to the wolf. An animal that eats mainly other animals is a **carnivore**. Carnivores are also called second-level consumers.

Reindeer moss, a lichen, makes food by photosynthesis. The food energy is stored in the organism.

The caribou gets its energy by eating reindeer moss.

Some animals, called *omnivores*, eat both plants and other animals. Omnivores can be first-level or second-level consumers. The bear shown on the first page of the lesson is an omnivore. So are most people.

In another ecosystem, a large carnivore, such as a hawk, might eat a smaller carnivore, such as a snake. That makes the hawk a third-level consumer. Each time something eats something else, food energy is transferred from one organism to the next. The transfer of food energy between organisms is called a **food chain**.

When plants and animals die, what happens to the food energy stored in their remains? The remains are broken down and the food energy is used by decomposers. A **decomposer** is a consumer that gets its food energy by breaking down the remains of dead organisms. Decomposers can be animals, such as earthworms. Many decomposers are fungi. Others are single-celled organisms—protists or bacteria.

Decomposers use some of the nutrients as food. The rest become mixed into the soil. Then plant roots can take up these nutrients. In this way, decomposers connect both ends of a food chain.

You know that all the organisms in an ecosystem depend on producers to make food. Then food energy is transferred through the ecosystem from one consumer level to another. All along the way, decomposers get energy from the remains of dead organisms. Any nutrients not used are returned to the soil.

 SEQUENCE What can happen next to food energy taken in by a second-level consumer?

The wolf gets the energy it needs by eating caribou.

When the moss, caribou, and wolf die, decomposers break down their remains. Then the reindeer moss and other producers can take up any remaining nutrients.

Food Webs

You know that most animals eat more than one kind of food. For example, a hawk might eat a mouse that ate seeds. The same hawk might also eat a small snake that ate grasshoppers and other insects. The insects, in turn, might have eaten grass. An organism, such as the hawk, can be a part of several food chains. In this way, food chains overlap. A **food web** shows the relationships among different food chains.

Carnivores eat herbivores, omnivores, and sometimes other carnivores. Carnivores also

Prairie Food Web

The producers in this prairie ecosystem include grasses, clover, and purple coneflowers. First-level consumers, or herbivores, include insects, mice, ground squirrels, and bison. Second-level and third-level consumers—carnivores— include spiders, snakes, and hawks. The decomposers that you can see are mushrooms. What you can't see are the millions of single-celled decomposers. They are in the soil, helping recycle nutrients.

Pond Food Web

In this pond ecosystem, the producers include water plants and algae. Here the first-level consumers, or herbivores, include insects and tadpoles. Second-level and third-level consumers include fish. Some of the birds, such as ducks, are herbivores, while others are carnivores. The turtle is an omnivore, eating insects, tiny fish, and plants. The water is full of decomposers, such as snails, worms, and single-celled protists.

limit the number of animals below them in a food web. For example, without snakes, the number of mice in the prairie ecosystem would keep increasing. In time, the mice would eat all the available food. Then the mice would starve, and so would hawks, which eat mice.

Organisms in an ecosystem depend on one another for survival. A change in the number of one kind of organism can affect the entire ecosystem!

SEQUENCE If all the mosquitoes in a pond died, what might happen next?

Energy Pyramid

Not all the food energy of plants is passed on to the herbivores that eat them. Producers use about 90 percent of the food energy they produce for their own life processes. They store the other 10 percent in their leaves, stems, roots, fruits, and seeds.

Animals that eat the producers get only 10 percent of the energy the producers made. These herbivores then use for their life processes 90 percent of the energy they got from the producers. They store the other 10 percent in their bodies.

Math in Science
Interpret Data

Suppose the grasses at the base of this energy pyramid produce 100,000 kilocalories of energy. How many kilocalories would be passed to each of the other levels?

The owl is a third-level consumer. It takes a lot of grass, locusts, and snakes to provide the owl with the energy it needs.

Owl

The snakes are second-level consumers. They pass on to the owl only 10 percent of the energy they receive from the locusts.

Snakes

The locusts are first-level consumers. They pass on to the snakes only 10 percent of the energy they receive from the grasses.

Locusts

The grasses are producers. They pass on to the locusts only 10 percent of the energy they produce.

Grasses

An **energy pyramid** shows that each level of a food chain passes on less food energy than the level before it. Most of the energy in each level is used at that level. Only a little energy is passed on to the next level.

Because each level passes so little energy to the next, the first-level consumers need many producers to support them. In the same way, the second-level consumers need many first-level consumers to support them. This pattern continues up to the top of the food chain.

That's why the base of an energy pyramid is so wide. That's also why only one or two animals are at the top of the pyramid.

Most food chains have only three or four levels. If there were more, a huge number of producers would be needed at the base of the pyramid! Sometimes, things in the environment may cause the number of organisms at one level of the pyramid to change. Then the whole food chain is affected. Suppose a drought kills most of the grasses in an area. Then some of the first-level consumers will starve. Many second-level and third-level consumers will go hungry, too.

Suppose people cut down a forest to provide space for houses. The second-level and third-level consumers may not be able to find enough small animals to eat, so they may leave that ecosystem. With fewer carnivores to eat them, the number of small animals will increase over time. If there isn't enough food for their larger numbers, many will starve.

When a change in numbers occurs at any level of a food chain, the entire chain will be affected.

 SEQUENCE What can happen to a food chain if the number of second-level consumers increases?

Insta-Lab

A Tale of Two Pyramids

Compare the energy pyramid with this pyramid that was once used to classify foods. How are they alike? How are they different? Who are the consumers at each level of the food pyramid?

Natural Cycles

Most ecosystems depend on the water cycle to provide plants with the water they need for photosynthesis. Other cycles affect ecosystems, too.

For example, nitrogen also has a cycle. Nitrogen compounds are important for all living organisms. Nitrogen is a gas that makes up most of Earth's atmosphere. Before nitrogen gas can be used as a nutrient, it must be changed to a form that plants can take up through their roots.

Some nitrogen is changed, or fixed, by lightning. Lightning burns air, producing nitrogen-rich compounds that dissolve in rain. Plant roots can absorb these compounds. Bacteria found in some plant roots also change nitrogen gas into compounds that plants can use.

When a plant or animal dies and decays, nitrogen returns to the soil. Animal wastes also contain nitrogen. Decomposers change these wastes and remains of organisms into the nitrogen compounds plants need.

Carbon and oxygen also have a cycle. You learned that plants use carbon dioxide to make food and that they release oxygen as a byproduct. Plants and animals use this oxygen and release more carbon dioxide.

Carbon is stored in organisms, too. Burning wood, coal, and natural gas releases carbon dioxide into the air.

 SEQUENCE What part do decomposers play in the nitrogen cycle?

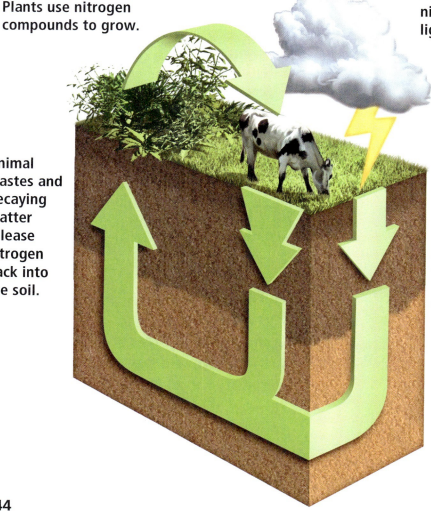

Plants use nitrogen compounds to grow.

A small amount of nitrogen is "fixed" by lightning.

Animal wastes and decaying matter release nitrogen back into the soil.

Animals eat plants that contain nitrogen compounds.

Bacteria in nodules (NAH•joolz), or lumps, on some plant roots change nitrogen into a form plants can use.

1. SEQUENCE Draw and complete this graphic organizer. Put the organisms in an order that forms a food chain, ending with a decomposer.

bear   grass   grasshopper   mushroom   salmon

Ⓐ _____ → Ⓑ _____ → Ⓒ _____ → Ⓓ _____ → Ⓔ _____

2. SUMMARIZE Write a summary of this lesson, beginning with this sentence: *Energy moves through an ecosystem.*

3. DRAW CONCLUSIONS What is your role in a food chain or a food web? Explain your answer.

4. VOCABULARY Write a sentence for each of this lesson's vocabulary terms. Leave a blank space in each sentence for the term. Have a partner fill in the correct terms.

FCAT Prep

5. Read/Inquire/Explain What is your favorite food? What level of consumer are you for that food?

6. Which of these is **not** essential in a food chain?

    A. decomposer
    B. first-level consumer
    C. producer
    D. second-level consumer

Links

Writing

Expository Writing

Imagine that you have discovered an animal that was thought to be extinct. Write a **paragraph** that describes the animal and explains how it fits into a food web in its ecosystem.

Math

Solve a Problem

An eagle ate 2 fish and received 20 kilocalories of energy. The fish had eaten many insects. How many kilocalories were produced by the plants that the insects ate?

Social Studies

Food Choices

In some parts of the world, meat protein is scarce. Find out what kinds of insects some people eat to add protein to their diets. Present a report to share what you learn.

For more links and activities, go to
www.hspscience.com

Trash Man

Chad Pregracke grew up on the banks of the Mississippi River. He spent summers fishing, sailing, water-skiing, and canoeing. When Pregracke was 15, he started working with his brother, a commercial shell diver.

Like a modern-day Tom Sawyer and Huck Finn, the brothers spent their nights camping on river islands and their days combing the pitch-black river bottom for clamshells.

During their travels, Pregracke noticed that the riverbanks were lined with trash. "We're talking refrigerators, barrels, tires. There was this one pile of 50 or 60 barrels that had been there for [more than] 20 years. ... I saw there was a problem, basically in my backyard. And I wanted to do something about it," explained Pregracke.

Taking Action

In addition to collecting clamshells, Pregracke started picking up garbage. He

also wrote letters to local companies requesting donations to launch a river cleanup. When he started in 1997, Pregracke single-handedly cleaned 160 kilometers (100 miles) of the Mississippi River shoreline with community donations and a grant from a local corporation.

Since then, Pregracke's project has grown. He now has a ten-person crew, a fleet of barges and boats, and thousands of volunteers to help keep the Mississippi and other rivers in the United States clean. "There's been a lot of accomplishments, and I've had a lot of help," said Pregracke. "But I feel like I'm just getting started."

Phantom Garbage

Although Pregracke has hauled tons of garbage from the Mississippi, the river is still polluted by a type of waste that can't be picked up with a forklift: runoff.

Rainwater either soaks into the ground or flows over Earth's surface as runoff. Runoff transports ground pollution to rivers, oceans, lakes, and wetlands. Many of the pollutants in runoff come from oil, antifreeze, and gasoline leaked by automobiles; pesticides sprayed on lawns; and fertilizers spread on fields. Other water pollutants include heavy metals, such as iron, copper, zinc, tin, and lead; oil from spills; and sewage.

Water pollution can cause human health problems and harm aquatic ecosystems. An ecosystem is a community of living things and its environment.

Think About It

1. How might runoff pollution affect your drinking water?
2. What can you do to help keep rivers clean?

Did You Know?

- The majority of Americans live within 10 miles of a polluted body of water.

- Water pollution has caused fishing and swimming to be prohibited in 40 percent of the nation's rivers, lakes, and coastal waters.

- Your own daily habits can help reduce water pollution. For more information, visit the U.S. Environmental Protection Agency's water Web site for kids.

Find out more! Log on to
www.hspscience.com

SC.G.1.2.2.5.1 environmental changes affect organisms;
SC.H.3.2.4.5.1 people can solve problems through science

Looking for Trouble

Most people think of marine biologists as swimming in the open ocean, studying whales or sharks. Fu Lin Chu is a marine biologist, but the animals she studies are usually a lot smaller than a whale and can be found in the creeks and shallow areas of the Chesapeake Bay, on the east coast of the United States.

Chu works at the Virginia Institute of Marine Science. She spends most of her time studying shellfish and how they are affected by their environment. This is especially important research in the Chesapeake Bay region, where oysters, a type of shellfish, are in trouble because of pollution and overfishing.

Career Lab Technician

When water samples from field research are sent to the laboratory, they are not just thrown under a microscope and analyzed. Samples have to be catalogued, prepared, and tested. Lab technicians usually are given specific instructions by scientists about how to test or analyze a sample.

SC.F.2.2.1.5.2 some characteristics affected by environment; **SC.G.1.2.2.5.1** environmental changes affect organisms; **SC.H.3.2.4.5.1** people can solve problems through science

SCIENCE Projects
for Home or School

You Can Do It!

Quick and Easy Project

Clover's Secret

Materials
- clover plant
- trowel
- outside faucet or hose

Procedure

1. Find in a field a clover plant at least 15 cm (6 in.) tall. Get permission to dig it up.
2. Use the trowel to dig up the soil around the plant. Then carefully lift the roots out of the soil.
3. Gently shake the loose soil off the roots. Then use water to rinse off the rest of the soil.
4. Look for light-colored lumps on the roots. These lumps are nodules. They contain bacteria that change nitrogen gas from the air into nitrogen compounds that plants can use.

Draw Conclusions

How does nitrogen gas reach the nodules? Are the bacteria in the nodules helpful or harmful? Explain. How do the nodules affect any plants growing around the clover plant?

Design Your Own Investigation

Sweaty Leaves

You read in Lesson 1 that plant leaves can lose water vapor through their stomata. How could you use a green plant and a plastic bag to show that this happens? Design an experiment. Write down the steps you will use to carry it out. Then do your experiment. Be sure to get permission before using someone else's plant. After observing what happens and recording your findings, draw some conclusions about your results.

Review and FCAT Preparation

Vocabulary Review

Use the terms below to complete the sentences. The page numbers tell you where to look in the chapter if you need help.

producers p. 434   **decomposers** p. 439
herbivores p. 438   **food web** p. 440
food chain p. 439   **energy pyramid** p. 443

1. To survive, all consumers rely on

_____.

2. Nutrients are returned to the soil by

_____.

3. Animals that eat producers are _____.

4. Grass-insect-bird-hawk is an example of

a _____.

5. The fact that each level of a food chain passes on less food energy than the level before it is shown in an _____.

6. The relationship among different food chains in an ecosystem is a _____.

Check Understanding

Write the letter of the best choice.

7. Which of the following is the process in which stomata release water from a leaf?
   A. chlorophyll
   B. photosynthesis
   C. respiration
   D. transpiration

8. Which of the following is the substance that enables a leaf to use sunlight to produce food?
   F. chlorophyll
   G. photosynthesis
   H. respiration
   I. transpiration

9. How much energy is passed from each level of an energy pyramid to the next?
   A. 10 percent
   B. 20 percent
   C. 80 percent
   D. 90 percent

10. **SEQUENCE** To which group do herbivores pass their energy?
   F. first-level consumers
   G. plants
   H. producers
   I. second-level consumers

11. **MAIN IDEA AND DETAILS** What is the source of all food energy on Earth?
   A. decomposers
   B. herbivores
   C. producers
   D. carnivores

12. Which process produces most of the oxygen in Earth's atmosphere?
   F. burning
   G. photosynthesis
   H. respiration
   I. transpiration

13. Which of these is **not** a consumer?

A. caribou   C. owl

B. mouse   D. reindeer moss

14. The relationships between organisms in an ecosystem can be shown in many ways. Which way is shown here?

F. energy pyramid

G. food chain

H. food pyramid

I. food web

15. Which gas does photosynthesis produce?

A. ammonia

B. carbon dioxide

C. nitrogen

D. oxygen

16. Which of the following must plants have for photosynthesis?

F. soil   H. warmth

G. stems   I. water

Inquiry Skills

17. Which three of the organisms below should be **classified** in the same group? Explain your answer.

18. Kendra will perform an experiment in which she cuts the stem of a sunflower and then puts the stem into the soil. **Predict** what will happen, and explain why.

 ## Read/Inquire/Explain

19. Not all producers are plants. Some protists are also producers. How can you tell by looking at a protist whether it is a producer?

20. The diagram shows a sequence of four organisms.

grass → grasshopper → snake → hawk

Part A What does the direction of the arrows tell you?

Part B If this were part of a food web, would more arrows point toward the second-level consumer or away from the second-level consumer? Explain.

13 Ecosystems and Change

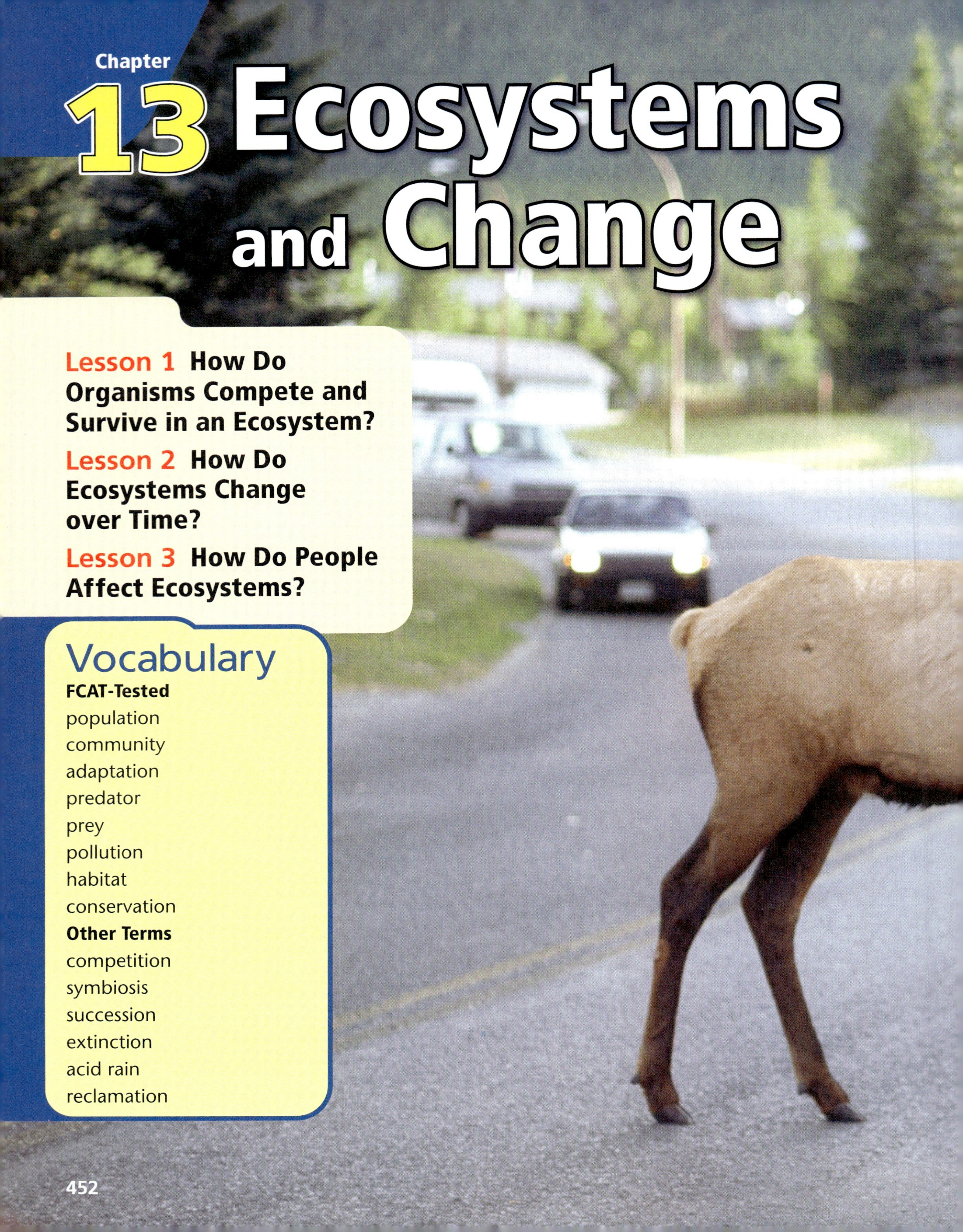

Lesson 1 How Do Organisms Compete and Survive in an Ecosystem?

Lesson 2 How Do Ecosystems Change over Time?

Lesson 3 How Do People Affect Ecosystems?

Vocabulary

FCAT-Tested

population

community

adaptation

predator

prey

pollution

habitat

conservation

Other Terms

competition

symbiosis

succession

extinction

acid rain

reclamation

Many animals share their ecosystems with people. Here an elk is searching for food and water in a neighborhood. How might the neighborhood—a dramatic change in the natural ecosystem of elk— affect the survival of these animals?

How Do Organisms Compete and Survive in an Ecosystem?

Fast Fact

That's Fast! This chameleon's tongue shoots out at about 21.6 km/hr (13.4 mi/hr)! This enables the chameleon to catch fast-moving insects. It can even zap insects more than one and a half body lengths away. In the Investigate, you'll find out how some insects avoid being captured, even by chameleons.

Using Color to Hide

Materials
- hole punch
- red, blue, green, and yellow sheets of acetate
- large green cloth
- clock or watch with a second hand

Procedure

① Make a table like the one shown.

② Using the hole punch, make 50 small "insects" from each color of acetate.

③ Predict which color would be the easiest and which would be the hardest for a bird to find in grass. Record your predictions.

④ Spread the green cloth on the floor, and randomly scatter the insects over it.

⑤ At the edge of the cloth, kneel with your group. In 15 seconds, each of you should pick up as many insects as you can, one at a time.

⑥ Count the number of each color your group collected. Record the data in the table.

⑦ Repeat Steps 5 and 6 three more times. Then total each column.

Draw Conclusions

1. Which color did you predict would be easiest to find? Which color was collected most often? Least often? Why?

2. **Inquiry Skill** Scientists predict what they expect to happen and then observe what happens. Predict what might happen to green insects if the grass turns brown.

Step 2

Number of Insects Found

	Red	Blue	Green	Yellow
Hunt 1				
Hunt 2				
Hunt 3				
Hunt 4				
Total				

Investigate Further

Predict how different body shapes might help insects hide in grass. Then plan an investigation to test your prediction.

SCIENCE CONCEPTS

► how populations depend on and compete with one another

► how adaptations help plants and animals compete

READING FOCUS SKILL

MAIN IDEA AND DETAILS Look for details about how organisms interact.

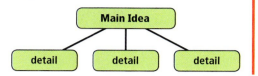

Interactions in Nature

In the last chapter, you learned about different kinds of ecosystems. You also learned that ecosystems include many kinds of plants and animals. All the organisms of one kind in an ecosystem are called a **population**. For example, a pond ecosystem might have populations of frogs, waterlilies, insects, duckweed, and protists.

Populations living and interacting with each other form a **community**. For example, in a pond community, some insects eat plants. Then frogs eat insects.

Another part of an ecosystem is the physical environment, which includes the sun, air, and water. The soil and climate are also part of the environment. Populations interact with the environment. Plants grow in sunlight and take water and nutrients from soil. Fish and frogs live in water that birds and other animals drink.

To survive, each population needs a certain amount of food, water, shelter, and space. The challenge of meeting these

Competition can take many forms. These moray eels compete for shelter in a coral reef.

As this water hole dries up, many organisms compete for water.

Counting the Survivors

This graph shows the average number of young produced and the number that survive the first year. What can you say about survival rates compared to the numbers of young produced?

Survivors

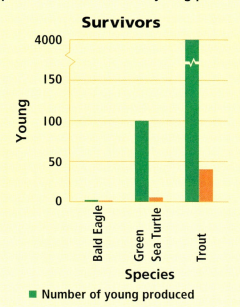

Y-axis: Young — 0, 50, 100, 150, 4000
X-axis: Species — Bald Eagle, Green Sea Turtle, Trout

■ Number of young produced
■ Number of young that survive the first year

After sea horses hatch, they are on their own. Many starve or are eaten by other fish. Sea horses have as many as 1000 young, which helps increase their chances of survival.

Some animals have few young, but take care of them after birth. This care helps the young survive.

needs leads to **competition**, a kind of contest among populations.

Populations often compete for the same sources of food. For example, alligators and snapping turtles both eat fish. When there isn't much food, individuals of the same population compete with each other.

In winter, deer compete with each other for food.

Too little food leads to increased competition. Increased competition limits the number of organisms that can share an ecosystem. For this reason, food is a *limiting factor*. It limits the size of a population.

To survive and compete in an ecosystem, animals have developed many kinds of adaptations. An **adaptation** is a characteristic that helps an organism compete in an ecosystem. A turtle survives the winter by burrowing into the mud. A tiger's coloring enables it to sneak up on prey. Some plants smell so bad that animals won't eat them. All of these characteristics are adaptations.

MAIN IDEA AND DETAILS What do organisms compete for in an ecosystem?

457

Mistletoe sends its roots into the tree on which it grows. It takes nutrients from the tree. The mistletoe benefits, but the tree is harmed.

▲ The barnacles on this humpback whale eat scraps the whale misses. The barnacles benefit, but the whale is not affected.

Symbiosis

Populations don't always compete with each other. Sometimes a relationship between organisms helps each of them meet basic needs. A relationship between different kinds of organisms is called <mark>symbiosis</mark> (sim•by•OH•SIS).

There are three kinds of symbiosis. In the first kind, both organisms benefit. For example, some ants take care of tiny insects called aphids. The ants guide the aphids to leaves. Then the ants protect the aphids while the aphids eat. When an ant rubs an aphid, the aphid gives off a sweet liquid. The ant drinks this liquid. This relationship, called *mutualism*, helps both the ant and the aphid.

In the second kind of symbiosis, only one organism benefits and the other isn't affected. An example is the relationship between sharks and small fish called remora.

A remora attaches itself to the shark by using a sucker on its head. Being near a shark protects the remora. The remora also eats scraps from the shark's meals. The remora benefits, and the shark isn't affected much. This relationship is called *commensalism*.

Some bacteria in your large intestine have this kind of relationship with you. They feed on the food in your intestine without harming you. Other bacteria help supply you with vitamin K. This relationship is an example of mutualism. You provide food, and the bacteria help keep you well. You both benefit.

In the third kind of symbiosis, called *parasitism*, one organism benefits but the other is harmed. The organism that benefits is called a *parasite*. The organism that is harmed is called a *host*. Parasites steal food

▲ The birds on this rhino are eating insects that bother the rhino. The birds get dinner, and the rhino gets relief from the insects. Both benefit.

from hosts or harm them in some other way. Some parasites release chemicals into the host. In time, these chemicals may kill the host.

Viruses and many one-celled organisms—such as bacteria, some protists, and some fungi—are parasites. They cause diseases such as polio, measles, and influenza. During the Middle Ages, a parasite caused an illness called the Black Plague, which killed about one-third of the population of Europe.

Bacteria and viruses spread as long as they can find hosts. Vaccinations can stop the spread of some of these parasites. When the parasites can't find new hosts, they die.

Roundworms and tapeworms are parasites that live in their hosts' intestines. They absorb food from their hosts, harming or killing them.

The sea lamprey is also a parasite. This eel attaches itself to a fish. Unlike the remora, the lamprey drills a hole into the fish and sucks its blood. The wound often becomes infected.

 MAIN IDEA AND DETAILS Give examples of the three kinds of symbiosis.

Human Symbiosis
With a partner, think of human activities that are examples of symbiosis. Then act out your examples. Have classmates classify the types of symbiosis being acted out.

459

Predator-Prey Relationships

To survive, animals must eat. They must also avoid being eaten. An animal that eats other animals is called a **predator**. For example, hawks and wolves are predators. Animals that are eaten, such as mice and rabbits, are called **prey**.

It's easy to see why predators need prey. However, prey need predators, too. Otherwise, prey populations would grow very large. Then the prey would have to compete with each other to meet their basic needs. Many would end up starving.

The number of prey and the number of predators are closely related. Any change in one leads to a change in the other. For example, if a prey animal's food supply increases, it will be easier for more prey to survive long enough to reproduce. More prey means more food for predators, so the number of predators goes up, too.

On the other hand, a drought might kill much of the grass and other plants in an ecosystem. Then the number of prey that eat the plants is likely to drop. Soon the ecosystem will have fewer predators, too.

Predators help keep the number of prey in balance. For example, wolves keep the deer in some ecosystems to a manageable number. If there were too many deer, they might eat all of the available food. Then more deer would die of starvation than from the attacks of wolves.

 MAIN IDEA AND DETAILS What symbiotic relationship is most like a predator-prey relationship?

The cheetah's markings keep it hidden until it gets close to its prey—an antelope. Then the predator's speed enables it to chase down its prey. ▼

1. **MAIN IDEA AND DETAILS** Draw this graphic organizer, and add the missing details.

> **Organisms depend on and compete with one another.**
>
> **Ⓐ Two examples of mutualism:**
> _____
> _____
>
> **Ⓑ Four things that organisms compete for to meet their needs:**
> _____
> _____
> _____
> _____

2. **SUMMARIZE** Write a summary of this lesson by using the vocabulary terms in a paragraph.

3. **DRAW CONCLUSIONS** A certain forest is home to a large number of hawks. What does this tell you about the number of mice and other small animals that live there?

4. **VOCABULARY** Use the lesson vocabulary terms to create a quiz that uses matching.

FCAT Prep

5. **Read/Inquire/Explain** What are three of the populations in an ecosystem near you?

6. Which of these is an adaptation that helps a skunk defend itself against predators?

A. its stripe   **C.** its odor

B. its tail   **D.** its size

Links

Writing

Expository Writing

You have discovered a new kind of organism in a rain forest. Write a brief **description** explaining how this organism meets its needs. Include any symbiotic relationships it has.

Math

Solve a Problem

For a certain fish, only 5 of every 100 eggs hatch and survive to adulthood. If this fish lays 5,000 eggs, how many will become adults?

Health

Parasites

Learn more about the parasites that affect people, such as tapeworms or the viruses that cause smallpox or influenza. Then, in an oral or written report, share what you learned.

 For more links and activities, go to **www.hspscience.com**

How Do Ecosystems Change over Time?

Fast Fact

Missing Marshes Many of the world's ecosystems are changing. Salt marshes like this one are quickly disappearing. By 2025, two-thirds of Africa's farmable land will be too dry for growing crops. In the Investigate, you'll model how an ecosystem can change from a pond into dry land.

Observing Changes

Materials
- ruler
- potting soil
- plastic dishpan
- water
- duckweed
- birdseed

Procedure

1. Make a model of a pond by spreading 5 cm of potting soil in the dishpan. Dig out a low space in the center, leaving 1 cm of soil. Pile up soil around the low space to make sides about 10 cm high.

2. Slowly pour water into the low spot until the water is 4 cm deep. Put duckweed in the "pond."

3. Sprinkle birdseed over the soil. Do not water it. Make a drawing or take a photograph to record how your pond looks.

4. After three or four days, measure and record the depth of the water in the pond. Record how the pond looks now.

5. Sprinkle more birdseed over the soil, and water it lightly.

6. Wait three or four more days, and observe how your pond has changed. Measure and record the depth of the water. Compare your three observations.

Draw Conclusions

1. What caused the changes you observed?

2. **Inquiry Skill** Scientists often make models and observe changes, just as you did. Which of the changes you observed might occur in a real pond? What other changes do you think might occur in a real pond?

Step 1

Step 3

Investigate Further

Make a model of another ecosystem, such as a forest floor. If possible, include some insects. Observe and record the changes that take place over time.

VOCABULARY
succession p. 464
extinction p. 468

SCIENCE CONCEPTS
▶ how changes in ecosystems affect the organisms there
▶ how these changes can cause the extinction of some organisms

 READING FOCUS SKILL

CAUSE AND EFFECT Look for the causes of changes in ecosystems.

cause	→	effect

Primary Succession

Ecosystems change every day, but the changes are usually too slow to notice. Some organisms die out, while others start to thrive. A gradual change in the kinds of organisms living in an ecosystem is called **succession**. Unlike the changes you observed in the Investigate, succession in nature can take thousands of years.

What causes succession? One cause is a change in climate. When a region becomes drier, for example, some of the organisms that live there will no longer be able to meet their needs. If fewer plants survive in the dry climate, herbivores will have to move to find food or they'll die. A loss of herbivores leads to a loss of predators. Meanwhile, plants and animals that can live with less water begin to thrive. They will slowly replace the organisms that cannot live in the drier climate.

Succession can also be caused by the organisms living in an ecosystem. For example, a large herd of deer can kill many trees by eating too many leaves. Then the deer and other animals in the ecosystem

Primary Succession

1 At the edge of a pond, plants trap soil in their roots. As the plants die and decay, the soil gains nutrients.

2 More plants begin to grow in the rich new soil at the edge of the pond. The pond is starting to get smaller.

can no longer find enough food or shelter. To survive, they must move to a new area. With fewer small animals to eat, the predators also leave or die. Because fewer trees shade the forest floor, plants that thrive in the sun begin to grow. Much of the ecosystem has changed.

Adding new plants or animals to an ecosystem is another cause of succession. For example, a vine called *kudzu* has taken over many ecosystems of the southern United States. Kudzu was brought to the United States from Japan in 1876. Farmers were paid to plant it because, they were told, kudzu could control erosion and feed animals.

The climate of the South was perfect for kudzu. It could grow 30 cm (1 ft) a day! Soon this vine was everywhere. It killed whole forests by climbing on trees and preventing sunlight from reaching the trees' leaves. In 1972, kudzu was declared to be a weed. By then, it had affected many ecosystems in the South by changing both the plants and the animals that lived there.

Succession can be primary or secondary. *Primary succession* begins with bare rock. The first plants to grow, such as lichens, are called *pioneer plants*. Lichens can grow without soil, and they can survive harsh conditions. As they grow, lichens produce chemicals that help weather the rock they grow on. In time, a thin layer of soil forms, allowing mosses to grow.

As mosses grow and die, they add nutrients to the thin soil. Soon grass seeds begin to sprout. Then birds and other animals come to eat the grasses and their seeds. The animals' droppings add more nutrients to the soil. When the soil is deep enough and rich enough, larger plants, including trees, begin to grow. In time, the ecosystem becomes stable, and changes stop. The result is known as a *climax community*.

 CAUSE AND EFFECT What are three causes of succession?

The pond ecosystem continues to grow smaller, while the land ecosystem grows larger.

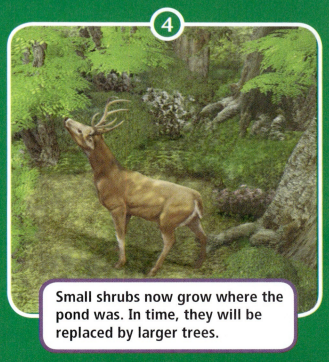

Small shrubs now grow where the pond was. In time, they will be replaced by larger trees.

Secondary Succession

Rebirth of a Forest

1. Fire destroys all the organisms living above ground.

2. Roots that survive underground and seeds blown in by the wind begin to sprout, forming new plants.

Secondary Succession

Secondary succession helps rebuild damaged ecosystems. This kind of succession occurs in places that already have soil. It often happens after a forest fire or a volcanic eruption has destroyed the original ecosystem.

Primary succession is a very slow process. Secondary succession is not. It happens quickly because soil is already there and the soil usually contains many seeds. Animals and wind bring in more seeds. Some roots of original plants survive underground, and they start sending up new shoots. In secondary succession, as with primary succession, the first plants are hardy. But

they don't have to be as hardy as those growing on bare rock. The soil is deep enough for strong roots, and ashes from burned trees add nutrients to the soil.

You might have heard about eruptions of Mount St. Helens in Washington State. This volcano exploded on May 18, 1980, covering the mountain with a thick layer of ash and mud. Yet by the summer of 1981, the mountainside bloomed with pink fireweed flowers. A few years later, shrubs began to grow there. Many insects, birds, and other animals have already returned. Now you can find young fir trees on the mountain's slopes. Even with more eruptions, a mature forest will one day cover Mount St. Helens again.

3. New growth appears among the blackened tree trunks. Many insects and other small animals return to the forest.

For more links and activities, go to
www.hspscience.com

Where secondary succession occurs, there is also some primary succession. Secondary succession cannot occur without primary succession. You can find bare rock after a volcanic eruption. Fire, followed by erosion of the soil, also uncovers bare rock. Lichens would begin growing on the rock. Mosses would grow next, and so on, until the ecosystem of the bare rock would be the same as that restored by secondary succession. But this may take hundreds of years. Remember, primary succession happens very slowly.

 CAUSE AND EFFECT What is the main result of primary succession and of secondary succession?

Insta-Lab

Regrowth
Make a drawing showing regrowth of a climax community in an area that has had a fire, a flood, a volcano, or other natural disaster. Be sure to include several stages of secondary succession in your drawing.

Extinction

Sometimes changes in an ecosystem cause the extinction of an entire species. **Extinction** is the death of all the organisms of a species.

Many organisms can adapt to slow changes in an ecosystem. But some cannot. When an environment changes, some organisms living in it will die. Plants and some animals can't move to other ecosystems to meet their needs.

A species with just a few small populations in different places is more likely to become extinct than a species with many large populations. A population that lives in a small area, such as on a remote island, is in more danger than a population spread out over a large area. Any change in the island environment could wipe out an entire population.

An environmental change can be so great that it affects many populations of different species. You might know that most dinosaurs became extinct about 65 million years ago. But did you know that more than 70 percent of all the other organisms on Earth were also wiped out? This mass extinction was probably due to a drastic change in the worldwide climate.

Some scientists hypothesize that the cause may have been a huge meteor. It may have thrown up a dust cloud so big that it blocked out the sun. Some plants died, followed by many herbivores and most carnivores. Of course, most changes in ecosystems are more gradual.

Many human actions, too, can lead to extinctions. You'll learn more about that in the next lesson.

 CAUSE AND EFFECT How can a change in climate cause extinctions?

Beginning 40,000 years ago, thousands of plants and animals became trapped in tar that rose to Earth's surface. Fossils of nearly 200 kinds of organisms, including saber-toothed cats, have been identified in the La Brea tar pits in California. ▼

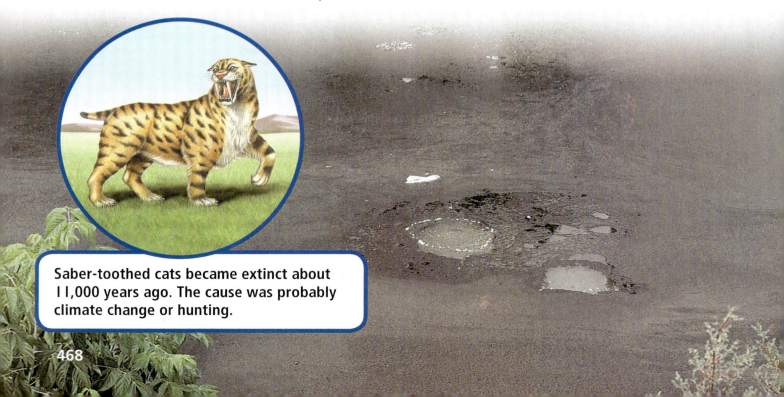

Saber-toothed cats became extinct about 11,000 years ago. The cause was probably climate change or hunting.

1. CAUSE AND EFFECT Draw and complete these graphic organizers. For B–D, describe three causes of the same effect.

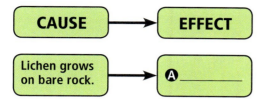

| CAUSE | → | EFFECT |

Lichen grows on bare rock. → Ⓐ _____

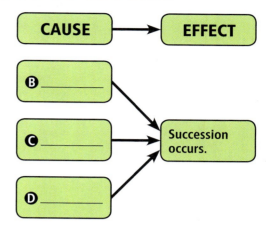

| CAUSE | → | EFFECT |

Ⓑ _____

Ⓒ _____

Ⓓ _____

→ Succession occurs.

2. SUMMARIZE Write two sentences to summarize this lesson.

3. DRAW CONCLUSIONS How are pioneer plants different from plants in a climax community?

4. VOCABULARY Write a paragraph using each vocabulary term twice.

FCAT Prep

5. Read/Inquire/Explain Describe ways that people affect succession.

6. Which of these is the final result of secondary succession?

 A. adaptation
 B. rebuilt ecosystem
 C. competition
 D. final extinction

Links

Writing

Narrative Writing
Choose a wild area or park near you. Write a **description** of its present stage of succession. Describe how human activities have influenced its natural succession.

Math

Make an Estimate
Florida is 65,700 sq mi in area. Texas covers 268,600 sq mi. Florida has 111 species in danger of extinction. Texas has 91. Which state has more endangered species per square mile?

Art

Succession
Use any kind of media to illustrate the stages of primary or secondary succession. Set the succession in a certain climate, and research the plants that should be shown.

 For more links and activities, go to **www.hspscience.com**

How Do People Affect Ecosystems?

Fast Fact

Too Much Paper! More than 40 percent of the trash in this landfill is paper! Despite widespread recycling programs, paper is still the most common item tossed in the trash. Unfortunately, paper buried in a landfill is very slow to decay. Newspapers can still be read 40 years after they were buried. In the Investigate, you'll explore how human actions can affect other parts of our ecosystems.

Observing Effects of Fertilizer

Materials
- marker
- 4 jars with lids
- pond water
- dropper
- liquid fertilizer

Procedure

1. Use the marker to number the jars 1–4.

2. Fill each jar with the same amount of pond water.

3. Use the dropper to put 10 drops of liquid fertilizer in Jar 1, 20 drops in Jar 2, and 40 drops in Jar 3. Do not put any fertilizer in Jar 4.

4. Put the lids on the jars, and place them in a sunny window.

5. Observe the jars every day for two weeks, and record your observations.

Step 1

Draw Conclusions

1. Which jar had the most plant growth? Which had the least? What conclusion can you draw about fertilizer and plant growth?

2. As organisms die and decay in water, they use up the oxygen in the water. Which jar do you infer will eventually contain the least amount of oxygen? Explain your answer.

3. **Inquiry Skill** Scientists identify and control variables in their experiments so they can observe the effect of one variable at a time. Which variables did you control in setting up the four jars? Which variable did you change?

Step 3

Investigate Further

Suppose you want to study the effect of sunlight on fertilizer in pond water. Plan an experiment that will identify and control the variables. Then carry out your experiment.

VOCABULARY
pollution p. 472
acid rain p. 472
habitat p. 473
conservation p. 474
reclamation p. 476

SCIENCE CONCEPTS
▶ how people's actions can change the environment
▶ how the environment can be protected and restored

READING FOCUS SKILL

MAIN IDEA AND DETAILS Look for details about how people damage ecosystems.

Damaging Ecosystems

In the Investigate, you observed how fertilizer affects pond water. You observed that it speeds up plant growth. But isn't plant growth a good thing?

In time, plants in water will die. As they decay, they will use up oxygen in the water. Without oxygen, any fish living there will also die. The decaying fish will use up still more oxygen.

Decaying organic matter can pollute water. **Pollution** is any waste product that damages an ecosystem. Chemicals used on crops and lawns also pollute water. Heavy rain carries them from the fields to streams, rivers, and lakes.

Air can be polluted, too. Burning fossil fuels, such as coal, oil, and gas, is a major cause of air pollution. Certain chemicals in fossil fuels mix with water vapor in the air. The combination produces acids. When these acids fall to Earth with rain, we call it **acid rain**.

Acid rain can damage trees, crops, and other plants. It has made many bodies of clean-looking water acidic. Acidic water affects organisms differently. For example, it might kill all the small fish in a pond but not harm the larger fish. Then that pond's food chain would be affected.

A strip mine can pollute the groundwater as well as the land.▼

This bear now has to share its ecosystem with people.

Trash threatens wildlife in many ways. Animals can get cut by broken glass or snared by plastic drink-can holders. Small animals can even get trapped inside containers.

▲ Every year, snowmobiles add tons of pollutants to the air in places such as Yellowstone National Park.

Ecosystems can also be damaged by changing them. For example, most of our prairie ecosystems have been turned into farms. Prairies once had many communities. Now most of them are used to grow only one crop.

People fence off many ecosystems. This reduces the size of habitats or forces animals to share habitats with people. A **habitat** is an area where an organism can find everything it needs to survive. Fences make it hard for animals to migrate, or move, to different habitats. Fences also cut through hunting grounds of predators such as mountain lions and wolves.

When people cut down forests for timber, they destroy habitats. Habitats are also destroyed when people fill wetlands to make space for houses and shopping malls.

Sometimes people introduce organisms from other regions, such as the kudzu vine you read about. These organisms crowd out native plants and animals, changing and often damaging the ecosystem.

 MAIN IDEA AND DETAILS What are three ways that people damage ecosystems?

Insta-Lab

Melting a Sculpture

Make a "sculpture" from a piece of chalk. Use a paper clip to carve the chalk. Then stand the chalk upright in a clay base. Drip vinegar or lemon juice onto your sculpture. How does the vinegar, an acid, affect your sculpture? How is this like acid rain affecting a statue?

473

▲ Beach walkovers help protect the fragile ecosystem of the dunes.

Protecting Ecosystems

Many laws have been passed to protect ecosystems. For example, most wetlands can no longer be filled in. Regulations control how industries can get rid of possible pollutants. New cars must have devices that reduce air pollution. And before developers can build, they must describe how a project might affect the environment.

But laws alone are not enough. Each person can have a role in protecting ecosystems. One way is through the **conservation**, or saving, of resources.

Conservation of resources includes three actions: reduce, reuse, and recycle.

Reduce means "use fewer resources." For example, if you walk or ride your bike instead of riding in a car, you save gasoline. Opening windows instead of turning on an air conditioner helps reduce the amount of coal burned to produce electricity. Burning gasoline and coal also causes acid rain.

Reuse means "use resources again, instead of throwing them away." For example, you can give outgrown clothes and toys to a charity. That way, someone else can use them. You can also use glasses and dishes that can be washed and used again and again. That saves plastic and paper that would be thrown away.

Some items can be reused for a new purpose. For example, a plastic drink bottle can be reused as a planter, a bird feeder, or a funnel. Reusing items saves resources and space in landfills, too.

Recycle means "collect used items so their raw materials can be used again." For example, glass, paper, aluminum, and some plastics can be ground up or melted and made into new products. And recycling often uses less energy than producing the same items from new resources.

Most glass can be recycled. Recycled glass melts at a lower temperature than the resources used to make new glass. Recycling glass requires 30 percent less energy than making new glass.

Nearly all kinds of paper can be recycled. Making new paper from old paper uses 20 percent less energy than making paper from trees. However, paper coated with wax, foil, or plastic is too costly to recycle.

Recycling aluminum helps a lot. Recycling just two cans saves the energy equal to a cup of gasoline. Making a can from recycled aluminum uses only 4 percent of the energy needed to make a can from new resources.

Plastics make up about 10 percent of our waste. Some kinds of plastic are hard to recycle. However, soft-drink bottles are easy. The recycled bottles can be used to make carpeting, boards, new bottles, and many other products.

Reducing, reusing, and recycling save resources and energy. These actions reduce pollution and help protect ecosystems.

 **MAIN IDEA AND DETAILS** List six ways you can help protect ecosystems.

Juice boxes are hard to recycle because most contain paper, plastic, and aluminum. Pouring juice from a large container into a glass means fewer juice boxes end up in landfills.

Discarded batteries can leak pollutants into the soil. In some states, it is illegal to put batteries in the trash. Instead, use rechargeable batteries.

Old newspapers take up about 13 percent of all the space in landfills. Yet they are easy to recycle into new paper.

Restoring Ecosystems

Damaged ecosystems are not always lost. Some can be cleaned and restored. The process is called <mark>reclamation</mark>. But reclamation is costly and takes time.

Removing pollutants is often part of reclamation. We now know that wetlands can help filter pollutants out of water. Yet the United States has lost most of its wetlands. In the 1970s, builders were filling in 500,000 acres of wetlands a year.

Now the rate of wetland loss has slowed. Many programs are helping to protect remaining wetlands or even to restore them.

For example, many wetlands have been restored along Florida's Gulf Coast. The bays of Fort DeSoto Park, near St. Petersburg, Florida, had become clogged with soil. The water quality was poor. The plants and animals were struggling to survive. Now the water moves freely. This change has also improved water quality in wetlands nearby.

Fragile ecosystems are being restored across the nation. Perhaps there is a reclamation project near you.

 MAIN IDEA AND DETAILS Why are wetlands important in reclamation?

This area used to be a strip mine. The first step in reclaiming a strip mine is removing mining wastes. Then soil must be added to provide a base for trees and plants. Reclamation of a large strip mine can take many years and cost millions of dollars. ▼

1. MAIN IDEA AND DETAILS Draw and complete this graphic organizer by adding two details to support the main idea.

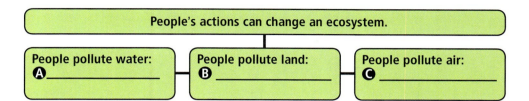

People's actions can change an ecosystem.

People pollute water: **A**_____

People pollute land: **B**_____

People pollute air: **C**_____

2. SUMMARIZE Write one sentence that describes three ways people affect ecosystems.

3. DRAW CONCLUSIONS How is conservation different from reclamation?

4. VOCABULARY Make up quiz-show answers for the vocabulary terms. See if a partner knows the correct questions for the answers, such as "What is pollution?"

FCAT Prep

5. Read/Inquire/Explain What specific things can people do to avoid the cost of restoring an ecosystem?

6. Which of these is a cause of acid rain?
A. burning forests
B. burning fuels
C. runoff from farmers' fields
D. decaying organisms in the water

Links

Writing

Persuasive Writing
Some people think recycling is not worth the effort. Write a **letter** for your school or community newspaper, urging readers to recycle. Try to motivate them to help protect ecosystems.

Math 9÷3

Make a Pictograph
Make a pictograph showing U.S. recycling rates: cardboard, 70%; newspaper, 60%; aluminum cans, 49%; soft-drink bottles, 36%; glass, 22%.

Literature

Life Preservers
Read about the life of a well-known naturalist, such as Rachel Carson, Henry David Thoreau, John Burroughs, or John Muir. In a written or oral report, share what you learned.

 For more links and activities, go to **www.hspscience.com**

Saving the
EVERGLADES

What blood is to the human body, water is to Florida's Everglades. And over the past half-century, the Everglades have been slowly and steadily bleeding to death. In 2001, the federal government passed the Everglades Restoration Act to stop the bleeding and save the Everglades. The restoration will cost more than $8 billion and continue for 30 years.

River of Grass

The Everglades is a slow-moving river that is less than 30 centimeters (1 foot) deep and 80 kilometers (50 miles) wide and covers millions of acres from Lake Okeechobee to Florida Bay. In 1947, the federal government established Everglades National Park. In 1948, Congress ordered the U.S. Army Corps of Engineers to drain large parts of the Everglades outside the park.

The corps began construction on a series of dams and canals that drained hundreds of thousands of acres. That changed the natural flow of water and eventually funneled 6.4 billion liters (1.7 billion gallons) of fresh water into the ocean every day. Builders put up new housing developments, and even whole cities, on drained Everglades.

The canals and other artificial barriers prevented some animal species from migrating. Drainage caused the populations of some wading birds, for instance, to plummet by 90 percent. Chemical and sewage runoff from Florida's growing towns and factories also spilled into natural areas, killing both animals and plants.

Undoing the Damage

The Everglades Restoration Act is aimed at restoring the Everglades to its natural state. One important part of the plan calls for the removal of dams, dikes, and flood-control gates that stop or slow the flow of water. The act also aims to improve water treatment plants. Those plants clean wastewater coming from farms and towns near the Everglades. The improved plants will allow less-polluted water to flow into the Everglades.

Many people, from environmental groups to private citizens, applaud the

The Whole World Is Watching

This is the first time the restoration of an entire ecosystem has been tried.

plan, saying it is a major step in stopping the destruction of a great natural resource.

Think About It

1. Why would the government want to drain wetlands such as the Everglades?
2. Why might it be harmful to change the flow of water in the Everglades?

Find out more! Log on to
www.hspscience.com

Working on the River

Most field trips allow students to see cool sights or visit historical places. However, Portia Johnson recently had a chance to spend a day up to her knees in mud helping to protect an important river in Virginia. Portia and her classmates were part of a project organized by the Friends of the Rappahannock.

During the project, students planted seedlings from the school's nursery along eroded sections of the river. The trees will help to keep the riverbank's soil in place and slow down erosion.

The Rappahannock River runs about 184 miles through Virginia until it empties into the Chesapeake Bay. This river is an important source of water and habitat for many plants and animals.

SC.H.1.2.3.5.1 *scientists communicate*

You Can Do It!

Quick and Easy Project

Plant Power

Materials
- 2 pots filled with soil
- 6 beans
- water
- flour

Procedure

1. Plant 3 beans in each pot, and water both pots in the same way.
2. Mix some flour and water until it forms a thick batter.
3. Pour the batter into one pot, covering the soil with a thick layer.
4. Put both pots at a sunny window.
5. Observe the pots for 10 to 14 days. Water the uncovered pot when it feels dry.

Draw Conclusions

What conclusion can you draw from your observations? What variable did you test? What does this experiment tell you about plants' role in restoring damaged ecosystems?

Design Your Own Investigation

Taking Out the Trash

Which kinds of trash decay quickly in a landfill, and which kinds take up space forever? Form a hypothesis. Then check your hypothesis by designing an investigation and carrying it out. For example, you might make a model of a landfill and bury different kinds of trash in it. Be sure to ask for permission before you start your investigation. Also, wear plastic gloves when you check your results.

Vocabulary Review

Use the terms below to complete the sentences. The page numbers tell you where to look in the chapter if you need help.

competition p. 456
adaptation p. 457
predators p. 460
prey p. 460
succession p. 464
extinction p. 468
conservation p. 474
reclamation p. 476

1. Grasses replace mosses in a process called _____.

2. Recycling is one kind of _____.

3. The number of organisms in a population is limited by _____.

4. A hummingbird's long beak is an _____.

5. Cleaning up polluted water is an example of _____.

6. Earthworms can be _____.

7. The death of all earthworms would be an _____.

8. Big cats are usually _____.

Check Understanding

Write the letter of the best choice.

9. How can we reduce the amount of acid rain that falls?
   A. by driving less
   B. by restoring wetlands
   C. by planting more trees
   D. by cleaning up polluted water

10. What forms a community?
   F. symbiotic relationships
   G. several populations
   H. an ecosystem
   I. succession

11. Which of these is usually in the last stage of succession?
   A. bushes   C. mosses
   B. lichen   D. trees

12. CAUSE AND EFFECT Which of these could possibly lead to an extinction?
   F. adaptation   H. reclamation
   G. pollution   I. symbiosis

13. MAIN IDEA AND DETAILS Which statement is most accurate?
   A. All ecosystems change in a way that is often gradual.
   B. People cause all the changes in ecosystems.
   C. Succession is a cause of change in ecosystems.
   D. Competition is the main cause of change in ecosystems.

14. Which of these is **not** a predator or prey?

    F. corn

    G. alligator

    H. ant

    I. antelope

15. Which of these is **not** a result of human actions?

    A. acid rain

    B. conservation

    C. extinction

    D. symbiosis

16. What is shown in the photo below?

    F. competition

    G. extinction

    H. succession

    I. symbiosis

Inquiry Skills

17. In an experiment, you water one plant with a certain amount of plain water. You water an identical plant with the same amount of a mixture of vinegar and water. You put both plants in a sunny window. Which **variables are you controlling** in this experiment?

18. Suppose the number of organisms in one population in a community suddenly increases. **Predict** what might happen, and explain why.

Read/Inquire/Explain

19. Explain how recycling is like mutualism.

20. Study the photograph below, and answer both questions.

Part A What concept from this chapter does the photograph illustrate?

Part B What organisms probably grew here before this photograph was taken? What kinds of organisms will grow here next?

References

Contents

Your Skin

Your skin is your body's largest organ. It provides your body with a tough protective covering. It produces sweat to help control your body temperature. It protects you from disease. Your skin also provides your sense of touch, which allows you to feel pressure, textures, temperature, and pain.

When you play hard or exercise, your body produces sweat, which cools you as it evaporates. The sweat from your skin also helps your body eliminate excess salts and other wastes.

Epidermis
Many layers of dead skin cells form the top of the epidermis. Cells in the lower part of the epidermis are always making new cells.

The skin is the body's largest organ. ▼

Pore
These tiny holes on the surface of your skin lead to your dermis.

Oil Gland
Oil glands produce oil that keeps your skin soft and smooth.

Dermis
The dermis is much thicker than the epidermis. It is made up of tough, flexible fibers.

Sweat Gland
Sweat glands produce sweat, which contains water, salt, and various wastes.

Hair Follicle
Each hair follicle has a muscle that can contract and make the hair "stand on end."

Fatty Tissue
This tissue layer beneath the dermis stores food, provides warmth, and attaches your skin to underlying bone and muscle.

Caring for Your Skin

- To protect your skin and to keep it healthy, you should wash your body, including your hair and your nails, every day. This helps remove germs, excess oils and sweat, and dead cells from the epidermis, the outer layer of your skin. Because you touch many things during the day, you should wash your hands with soap and water frequently.

- If you get a cut or scratch, you should wash it right away and cover it with a sterile bandage to prevent infection and promote healing.

- Protect your skin from cuts and scrapes by wearing proper safety equipment when you play sports or skate, or when you're riding your bike or scooter.

- Always protect your skin from sunburn by wearing protective clothing and sunscreen when you are outdoors in bright sun.

Your Senses

Eyes

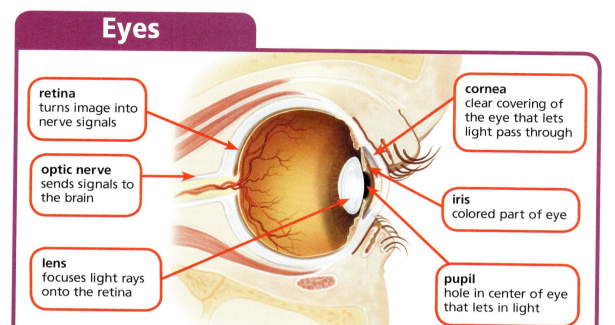

retina
turns image into nerve signals

optic nerve
sends signals to the brain

lens
focuses light rays onto the retina

cornea
clear covering of the eye that lets light pass through

iris
colored part of eye

pupil
hole in center of eye that lets in light

Light rays bounce off objects and enter the eye through the pupil. A lens inside the eye focuses the light rays, and the image of the object is projected onto the retina at the back of the eye. In the retina the image is turned into nerve signals. Your brain analyzes these signals to "tell" you what you're seeing.

Ears

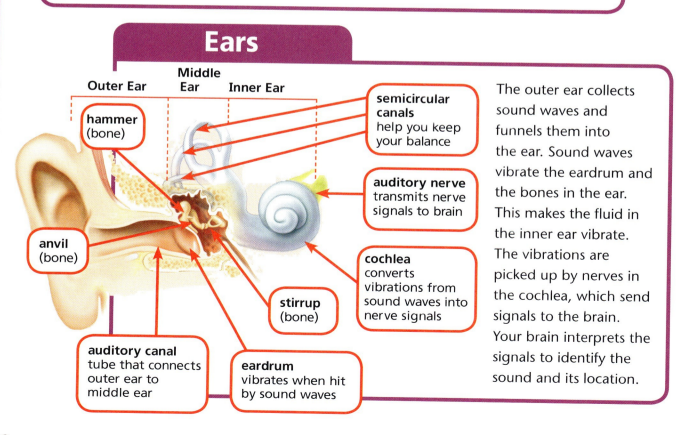

Middle
Ear

Outer Ear   Inner Ear

hammer
(bone)

semicircular canals
help you keep your balance

auditory nerve
transmits nerve signals to brain

anvil
(bone)

cochlea
converts vibrations from sound waves into nerve signals

stirrup
(bone)

auditory canal
tube that connects outer ear to middle ear

eardrum
vibrates when hit by sound waves

The outer ear collects sound waves and funnels them into the ear. Sound waves vibrate the eardrum and the bones in the ear. This makes the fluid in the inner ear vibrate. The vibrations are picked up by nerves in the cochlea, which send signals to the brain. Your brain interprets the signals to identify the sound and its location.

Nose

When you breathe in, air is swept upward to nerve cells in the nasal cavity. The nasal cavity is the upper part of the nose, inside the skull. Different nerve cells respond to different chemicals in the air and send signals to your brain.

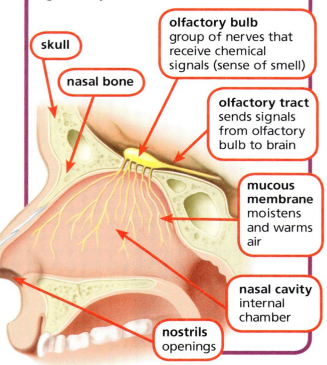

skull

nasal bone

olfactory bulb group of nerves that receive chemical signals (sense of smell)

olfactory tract sends signals from olfactory bulb to brain

mucous membrane moistens and warms air

nasal cavity internal chamber

nostrils openings

Skin

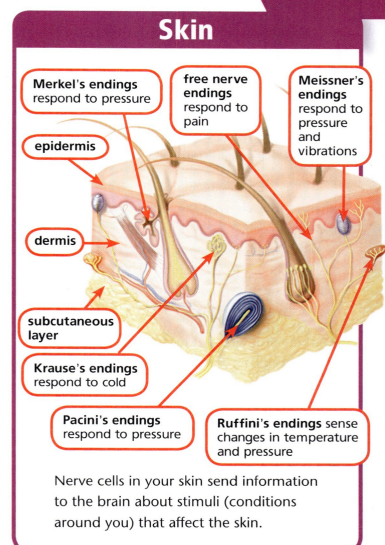

Merkel's endings respond to pressure

free nerve endings respond to pain

Meissner's endings respond to pressure and vibrations

epidermis

dermis

subcutaneous layer

Krause's endings respond to cold

Pacini's endings respond to pressure

Ruffini's endings sense changes in temperature and pressure

Nerve cells in your skin send information to the brain about stimuli (conditions around you) that affect the skin.

Caring for Your Senses

- Injuries to these organs can affect your senses.

- Protect your skin and eyes by wearing sunscreen and sunglasses. Protect your ears from loud sounds. Protect your nose from harsh chemicals and your tongue from hot foods and drinks.

Tongue

The tongue is covered with about 10,000 tiny nerve cells, or taste buds, that detect basic tastes in things you eat and drink. Different taste buds respond to different chemicals and send signals to your brain.

taste buds

Your Digestive System

Your body systems need nutrients from food for energy and for proper cell function. Your digestive system breaks down the food you eat into tiny particles that can be absorbed by your blood and carried throughout your body, so various cells and tissues can use the nutrients.

Digestion begins in your mouth when food is chewed, mixed with saliva, and swallowed. Your tongue pushes the food into your esophagus, which pushes the food down to your stomach with a muscular action, much like the one you use to squeeze toothpaste from a tube.

Your stomach produces gastric juices and mixes them with your food to begin breaking down proteins. Partially digested food leaves your stomach and moves to your small intestine.

Most of the digestive process occurs in your small intestine, where partially digested food is mixed with bile from your liver. This helps break down fats. Your pancreas also produces digestive juices that continue the process of digesting fats and proteins in the small intestine. Your pancreas also produces a special substance called insulin, which helps your body move sugar from your blood into your cells.

As food moves through your small intestine, nutrients are absorbed by the villi and pass into your blood.

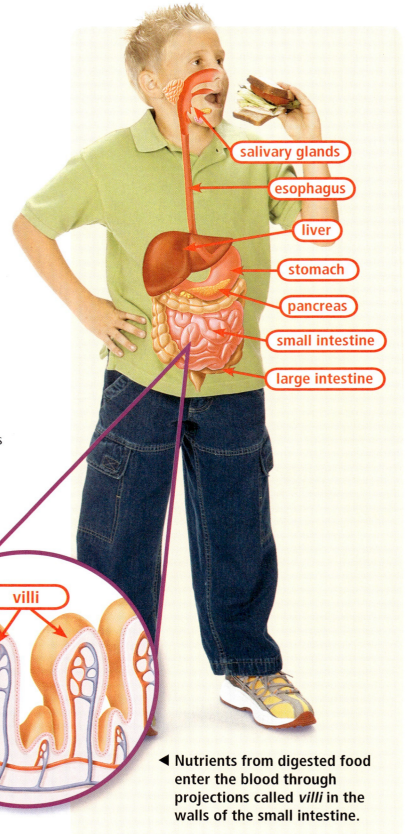

salivary glands

esophagus

liver

stomach

pancreas

small intestine

large intestine

villi

◀ Nutrients from digested food enter the blood through projections called *villi* in the walls of the small intestine.

Specialized Digestive Organs

Your liver produces a fluid called bile that helps break down fats. Bile is stored in your gallbladder. During digestion, the stored bile flows through the bile duct into your small intestine, to help with the digestive process.

Material that is not absorbed by your small intestine passes into your large intestine. This organ absorbs water and vitamins from the undigested materials. The remaining solid wastes are stored by your large intestine until it leaves your body.

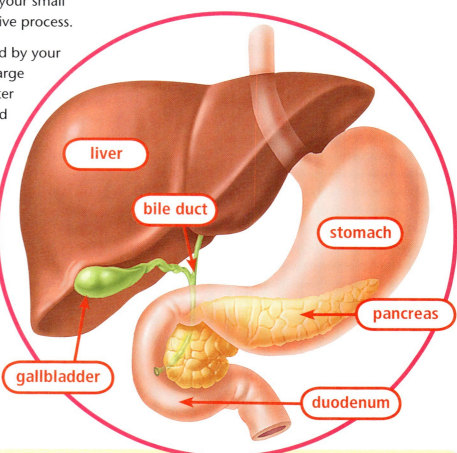

liver

bile duct

stomach

pancreas

gallbladder

duodenum

Caring for Your Digestive System

- Drink plenty of water every day. Water helps move food through your digestive system and helps your body replenish saliva, gastric juices, and bile consumed during digestion.

- Eat a variety of foods, choose a well-balanced diet, and maintain a healthy weight.

- Eat plenty of fruits and vegetables. These foods contain essential nutrients and help your digestive system function effectively.

- Chew your food thoroughly before swallowing.

Your Circulatory System

Your body relies on your circulatory system to deliver essential nutrients and oxygen to your organs, tissues, and cells. These materials are carried by your blood. As it circulates, your blood also removes wastes from your tissues. Your circulatory system includes your heart, arteries that carry oxygen and nutrient-rich blood away from your heart, tiny capillaries that exchange gases and nutrients between your blood and your body's tissues, and veins that carry blood and wastes back to your heart. Your veins have a system of one-way valves that maintains the direction of blood flow within your circulatory system and helps maintain an even distribution of oxygen and nutrients to all parts of your body.

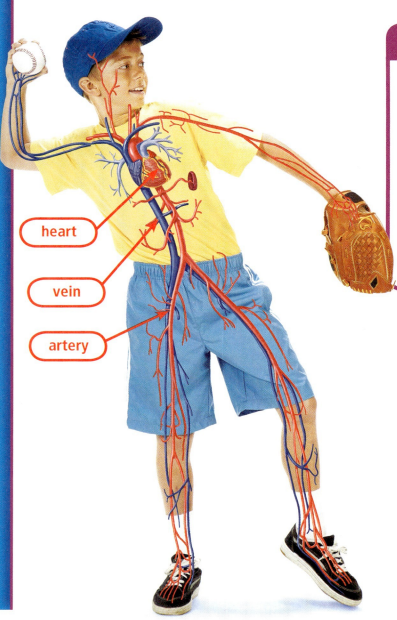

heart

vein

artery

Your Heart

Your heart is a strong, muscular organ that contracts rhythmically to pump blood throughout your circulatory system. When you exercise or work your muscles hard, your heart beats faster to deliver more oxygen and nutrient-rich blood to your muscles. When you rest, your heartbeat slows. Regular exercise helps keep your heart muscle and the rest of your circulatory system strong.

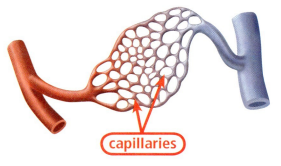

capillaries

▲ Oxygen and nutrients pass from the blood, through capillary walls, and into the cells. Cell wastes pass through capillary walls and into the blood.

Blood Flow and Your Excretory System

Your veins carry blood from your tissues back to your lungs, where carbon dioxide and other waste gases are removed from your red blood cells and expelled when you exhale. Your blood also travels through your kidneys, where small structures called nephrons remove salts and liquid wastes. Urine formed in your kidneys is held in your bladder until it is eliminated. Your liver removes other wastes from your blood, including blood cells. Red blood cells live for only 120 days. Specialized cells in your spleen and liver destroy damaged or dead red blood cells.

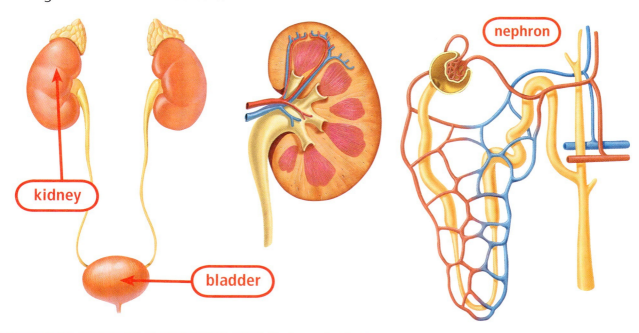

kidney

bladder

nephron

Caring for Your Circulatory System

• Eat foods that are low in fat and high in fiber. Fiber helps take away substances that can lead to fatty buildup in your blood vessels. Eat foods high in iron to help your red blood cells carry oxygen.

• Drink plenty of water to help your body replenish your blood fluid.

• Avoid contact with another person's blood.

• Exercise regularly to keep your heart and blood vessels strong.

• Never smoke or use tobacco. It can strain your heart and damage your blood vessels.

• Don't use illegal drugs or alcohol. They can damage your liver and your heart.

• Follow directions for all medicines carefully. Misuse of medicine can damage your blood's ability to clot after a cut, and can damage your liver and heart.

Your Immune System

A pathogen is an organism or virus that causes illness. An infection is the growth of pathogens in the body. Some pathogens weaken or kill body cells. A disease is an illness that damages or weakens the body, so you are not able to do the things you normally do. You may have a sore throat, or you may feel achy or tired, or you may have an unusually high body temperature, or fever. These are signs that your body is fighting an infection.

Infectious diseases have different symptoms because they are caused by different pathogens. There are four main types of pathogens: viruses, bacteria, fungi, and protozoa.

Diseases Caused by Pathogens

Pathogen	Characteristics	Diseases
Viruses	The smallest pathogens; the ones that cause most infectious diseases	Colds, chicken pox, HIV, infectious hepatitis, influenza (flu), measles, mumps, polio, rabies, rubella (German measles)
Bacteria	One-celled organisms that can—but do not always—cause disease; they make people ill by producing harmful wastes	Strep throat, pertussis (whooping cough), some kinds of pneumonia, Salmonella food poisoning, tetanus, tuberculosis (TB), Lyme disease
Fungi	Small, simple organisms like yeasts and molds; they most often invade the skin or respiratory system	Ringworm, athlete's foot, allergies
Protozoa	One-celled organisms somewhat larger than bacteria; they can cause serious diseases	Ameobic dysentery, giardiasis, malaria

There are pathogens all around you. You don't become ill often because your body has a complex system of defenses that prevents most pathogens from entering your body and destroys the ones that get through.

Sometimes pathogens do manage to overcome your body's defenses. When they do, your body's next line of defense is in your blood. Your blood contains white blood cells that have their own role to play in fighting infection.

Some white blood cells manufacture substances called antibodies. Each antibody is designed to fight a specific kind of pathogen. The antibodies attach themselves to the pathogen and either kill it or mark it to be killed by another kind of white blood cell. When a pathogen enters your body, your immune system produces antibodies to fight it. This process may take several days, during which you may have a fever and feel some other symptoms of the disease. When you have recovered from an illness, your white blood cells "remember" how to make the antibody needed to fight the pathogen that made you ill. The ability to recognize pathogens and "remember" how to make antibodies to fight disease is called *immunity*.

You can also develop immunity to certain diseases by getting vaccinations from your doctor that prevent the disease. A vaccine is usually a killed or weakened form of the pathogen that causes a particular disease.

Your Body's Defenses

1 Tears kill and wash away pathogens that enter your eyes.

2 Earwax traps pathogens that enter your ears.

3 Chemicals in saliva kill pathogens that enter your mouth.

4 Mucus traps pathogens in your nose and keeps them from getting into your respiratory system.

5 Cilia along breathing passages keep pathogens out of your lungs.

6 The skin's outer layers block pathogens. Sweat kills some of them.

7 Stomach acid kills most pathogens in your digestive system.

Caring for Your Immune System

• Exercise regularly and get plenty of rest. This helps your body rebuild damaged tissues and cells.

• Eat a healthful, balanced diet. Good nutrition keeps your immune system strong.

• Avoid substances like illegal drugs, tobacco, and alcohol, that can weaken your immune system.

• Wash your hands frequently and avoid touching your eyes, nose, and mouth.

Your Skeletal System

All of the bones in your body form your skeletal system. Your bones protect many vital organs and support the soft tissues of your body. Your skeletal system includes more than two hundred bones that fit together and attach to muscles at joints.

Types of Bones

Your skeleton includes four basic types of bones: long, short, flat, and irregular. Long bones, like the ones in your arms and legs, are narrow and have large ends. These bones support weight. Short bones, found in your wrists and ankles, are chunky and wide. They allow maximum movement around a joint. Flat bones, like the ones in your skull and ribs, protect your body. Irregular bones, like your vertebrae, have unique shapes and fall outside of the other categories.

Types of Joints

Each of the three types of joints is designed to do a certain job.

Ball-and-socket joints, like your hips and shoulders allow rotation and movement in many directions.

Hinge joints, like your elbow and knees, only move back and forth.

Gliding joints, like those between the vertebrae in your spine or the bones in your wrists and feet, allow side-to-side and back-and-forth movement.

Some joints, like the ones in your skull, do not allow any movement. These flat bones fit tightly together to protect your brain.

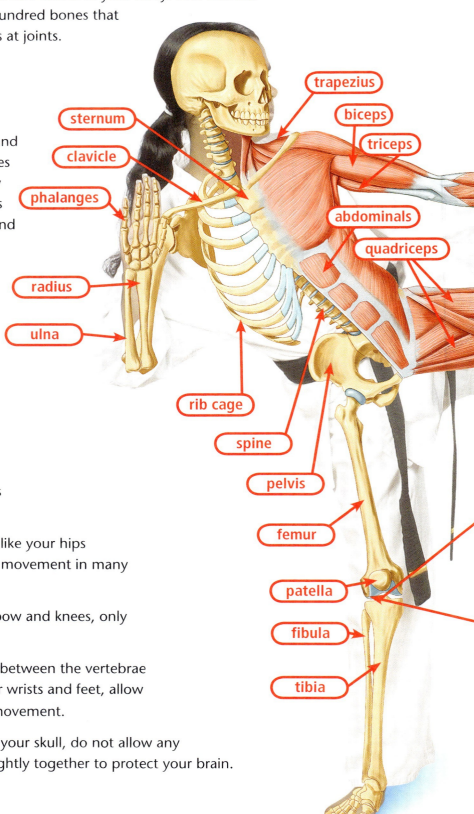

sternum
clavicle
phalanges
radius
ulna
rib cage
spine
pelvis
femur
patella
fibula
tibia
trapezius
biceps
triceps
abdominals
quadriceps

Parts of a Joint

Your bones attach to your muscles and to each other at joints. Your muscles and bones work together to allow your body to move. Joints are made up of ligaments and cartilage. Ligaments are tough, elastic tissues that attach one bone to another. Cartilage is a soft cushioning material at the ends of bones that helps bones move smoothly and absorbs some of the impact when you move. Tendons are dense, cordlike material that joins muscles to bones.

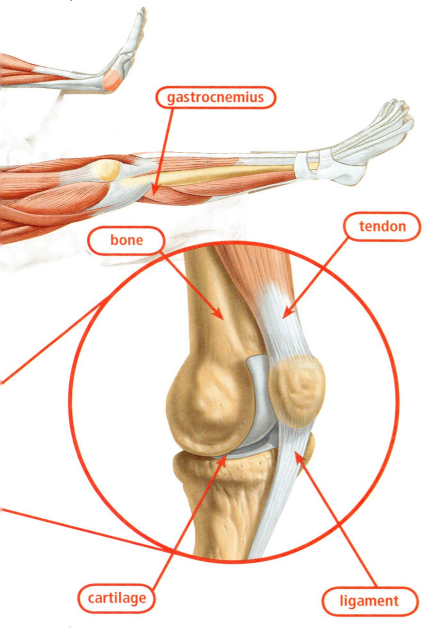

gastrocnemius

bone

tendon

cartilage

ligament

Caring for Your Skeletal System

- Always wear a helmet and proper safety gear when you play sports, skate, or ride a bike or a scooter.
- Your bones are made mostly of calcium and other minerals. To keep your skeletal system strong and to help it grow, you should eat foods that are high in calcium like milk, cheese, and yogurt. Dark green, leafy vegetables like broccoli, spinach, and collard greens are also good sources of calcium.
- Exercise to help your bones stay strong and healthy.
- Always warm up before you exercise.
- Get plenty of rest to help your bones grow.
- Stand and sit with good posture. Sitting slumped over puts strain on your muscles and on your bones.

Your Muscular System

A muscle is a body part that produces movement by contracting and relaxing. All of the muscles in your body make up the muscular system.

Types of Muscle

Your muscular system is made up of three types of muscle. The muscles that make your body move are attached to the bones of your skeletal system. These muscles are called skeletal muscles. A skeletal muscle has a bulging middle and narrow tendons at each end. Tendons are strong flat bands of tissue that attach muscles to bones near your joints. Skeletal muscles are usually under your control, so they are also called voluntary muscles.

Your muscular system includes two other types of muscle. The first of these is called smooth muscle. This specialized muscle lines most of your digestive organs. As these muscles contract and relax, they move food through your digestive system.

Your heart is made of another specialized muscle called cardiac muscle. Your heart's muscle tissue squeezes and relaxes every second of every day to pump blood through your circulatory system. Smooth muscle and cardiac muscle operate automatically. Their contraction is not under your control, so they are also called involuntary muscles.

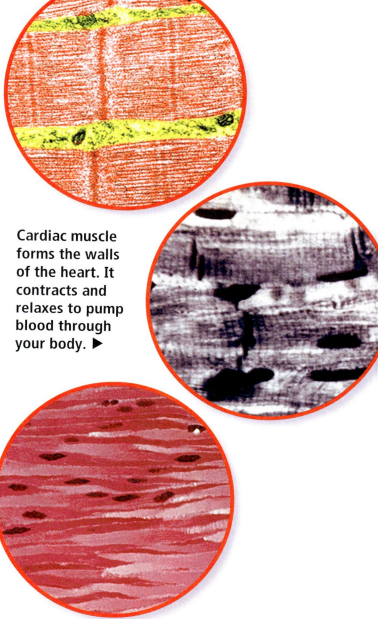

▼ Skeletal muscle appears striped. It is the kind of muscle that moves bones.

Cardiac muscle forms the walls of the heart. It contracts and relaxes to pump blood through your body. ▶

▲ Smooth muscle lines the walls of blood vessels and of organs such as your esophagus and stomach.

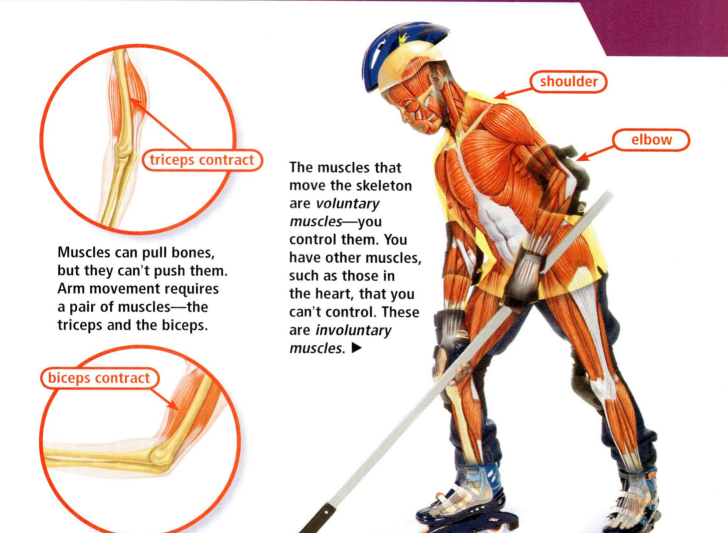

triceps contract

Muscles can pull bones, but they can't push them. Arm movement requires a pair of muscles—the triceps and the biceps.

biceps contract

The muscles that move the skeleton are *voluntary muscles*—you control them. You have other muscles, such as those in the heart, that you can't control. These are *involuntary muscles.* ▶

shoulder

elbow

Caring for Your Muscular System

- Always stretch and warm up your muscles before exercising or playing sports. Do this by jogging slowly or walking for at least ten minutes. This brings fresh blood and oxygen to your muscles, and helps prevent injury or pain.

- Eat a balanced diet of foods to be sure your muscles have the nutrients they need to grow and remain strong.

- Drink plenty of water when you exercise or play sports. This helps your blood remove wastes from your muscles and helps you build endurance.

- Always cool down after you exercise. Walk or jog slowly for five or ten minutes to let your heartbeat slow and your breathing return to normal. This helps you avoid pain and stiffness after your muscles work hard.

- Stop exercising if you feel pain in your muscles.

- Get plenty of rest before and after you work your muscles hard. They need time to repair themselves and to recover from working hard.

Your Nervous System

Your body consists of a number of different systems. Each of your body's systems plays a different role. The different systems of your body work together to keep you alive and healthy.

Just as a leader directs the work of a group, your nervous system controls your body's activities. Some activities, like the beating of your heart and breathing, are controlled automatically by your nervous system.

Your nervous system allows you to move and to see, hear, taste, touch, and smell the world around you. Your brain also allows you to learn, remember, and feel emotions.

Your nervous system is made up of your brain, your spinal cord, and your nerves.

Your spinal cord is a thick bundle of nerves inside the column of bone formed by your vertebrae. Your nerves are bundles of specialized cells branching from your spinal cord. They send messages about your environment to your brain and send signals to your muscles.

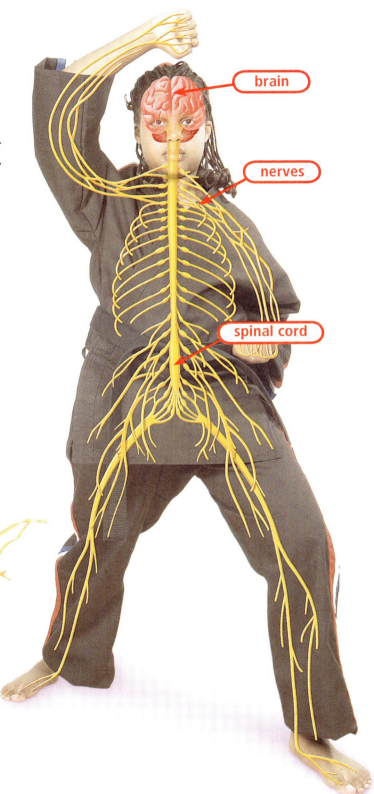

brain

nerves

spinal cord

A nerve cell is called a neuron. Signals travel to and from your brain along branching fibers of one neuron to branching fibers of other neurons.

Your brain contains about 100 billion neurons.
Different areas of your brain control different activities.

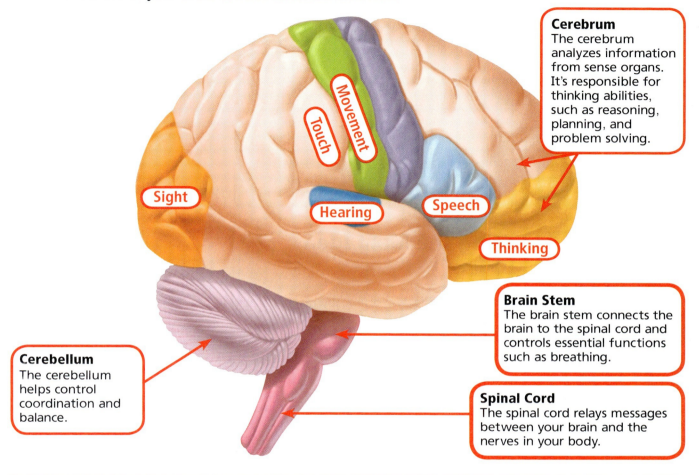

Cerebrum
The cerebrum analyzes information from sense organs. It's responsible for thinking abilities, such as reasoning, planning, and problem solving.

Movement

Touch

Sight

Hearing

Speech

Thinking

Brain Stem
The brain stem connects the brain to the spinal cord and controls essential functions such as breathing.

Cerebellum
The cerebellum helps control coordination and balance.

Spinal Cord
The spinal cord relays messages between your brain and the nerves in your body.

Caring for Your Nervous System

• Don't take illegal drugs, and avoid alcohol. These substances can impair your judgment, which may cause you to react slowly or improperly to danger. They can also damage your nervous system.

• When your doctor prescribes medicines, follow the instructions your doctor gives you. Too much medicine can affect your nervous system. Never take medicine prescribed for someone else.

• Eat a well-balanced diet to be sure your nervous system receives the nutrients it needs.

• Protect your brain and spine from injury by wearing proper safety equipment when you play sports, ride a bike or scooter, or skate.

• Get plenty of rest. Sleep helps keep your mind sharp. Like all of your body's systems, your nervous system requires rest to stay healthy.

Identify the Main Idea and Details

Focus Skill

Many of the lessons in this science book are written so that you can understand main ideas and the details that support them. You can use a graphic organizer like this one to show a main idea and details.

Main Idea: The most important idea of a selection

Detail: Information that tells more about the main idea

Detail: Information that tells more about the main idea

Detail: Information that tells more about the main idea

Tips for Identifying the Main Idea and Details

- To find the main idea, ask—*What is this mostly about?*
- Remember that the main idea is not always stated in the first sentence.
- Be sure to look for details that help you answer questions such as *Who?, What?, Where?, When?, Why?* and *How?*
- Use pictures as clues to help you figure out the main idea.

Here is an example.

Main Idea

All living things are made up of one or more cells. Cells that work together to perform a specific function form tissues. Tissues that work together make up an organ. Each organ in an animal's body is made up of several kinds of tissues. Organs working together form a body system.

Detail

You could record this in the graphic organizer.

Main Idea: All living things are made up of one or more cells.

Detail: Cells that work together form tissues.

Detail: Tissues that work together make up an organ.

Detail: Organs that work together form a body system.

More About Main Idea and Details

Sometimes the main idea of a passage is at the end instead of the beginning. The main idea may not be stated. However, it can be understood from the details. Look at the following graphic organizer. What do you think the main idea is?

Main Idea:

Detail:
Bones make up the skeletal system.

Detail:
The muscular system is made up of voluntary muscles, smooth muscles, and cardiac muscles.

Detail:
Muscles are controlled by the central nervous system.

A passage can contain details of different types. In the following paragraph, identify each detail as a reason, an example, a fact, a step, or a description.

> Digestion begins as you chew food. When you swallow, food passes through the esophagus. Gastric juice breaks down proteins. After several hours in the stomach, partly digested food moves into the small intestine. Digestion of food into nutrients is completed in the small intestine. From the small intestine, undigested food passes into the large intestine. In the large intestine, water and minerals pass into the blood and wastes are removed from the body.

Skill Practice

Read the following paragraph. Use the Tips for Identifying Main Idea and Details to answer the questions.

> The circulatory, respiratory, digestive, and excretory systems work together to keep the body alive. The circulatory system transports oxygen, nutrients, and wastes through the body. In the respiratory system, oxygen diffuses into the blood and carbon dioxide diffuses out of the blood. The digestive system provides the nutrients your cells need to produce energy. The excretory system removes cell wastes from the blood.

1. What is the main idea of the paragraph?

2. What supporting details give more information?

3. What details answer any of the questions *Who?*, *What?*, *Where?*, *When?*, *Why?* and *How?*

Compare and Contrast

Some lessons are written to help you see how things are alike or different. You can use a graphic organizer like this one to compare and contrast.

> **Topic:** Name the topic—the two things you are comparing and contrasting.

> **Alike**
> List ways the things are alike.

> **Different**
> List ways the things are different.

Tips for Comparing and Contrasting

- To compare, ask—*How are people, places, objects, ideas, or events alike?*

- To contrast, ask—*How are people, places, objects, ideas, or events different?*

- When you compare, look for signal words and phrases such as *similar, both, too,* and *also.*

- When you contrast, look for signal words and phrases such as *unlike, however, yet,* and *but.*

Here is an example.

Compare

The two basic kinds of energy are kinetic energy and potential energy. Kinetic energy is the energy of motion. Any matter in motion has kinetic energy. However, potential energy is the energy of position or condition. Transformation of energy is the change between kinetic energy and potential energy. The total amount of energy does not change when energy is transformed.

Contrast

Here is what you could record in the graphic organizer.

> **Topic:** Kinetic and Potential Energy

> **Alike**
> Both are basic kinds of energy.
> The total amount of energy stays the same when it changes forms.

> **Different**
> Kinetic energy is the energy of motion.
> Potential energy is the energy of position or condition.

More About Comparing and Contrasting

Identifying how things are alike and how they're different can help you understand new information. Use a graphic organizer to sort the following information about kinetic energy and potential energy.

| kinetic energy | electric energy | thermal energy | mechanical energy | light energy |

| potential energy | elastic potential energy | gravitational potential energy | chemical energy |

Sometimes a paragraph compares and contrasts more than one topic. In the following paragraph, one topic of comparison is underlined. Find a second topic for comparison or contrast.

> <u>Material that conducts electrons easily is called a conductor.</u> An insulator is a material that does not carry electrons. An electric circuit is any path along which electrons can flow. Some circuits are series circuits. They have only one path for the electrons. Other circuits are parallel circuits, where each device is on a separate path.

Skill Practice

Read the following paragraph. Use the Tips for Comparing and Contrasting to answer the questions.

> Within an atom, electrons have a negative charge and protons have a positive charge. Most objects have equal numbers of protons and electrons. Both protons and electrons attract each other. Sometimes, however, electrons are attracted to the protons of another object and rub off. These objects become negatively charged.

1. What are two ways protons and electrons are alike?

2. Explain a difference between protons and electrons.

3. Name two signal words that helped you identify likenesses or differences in this paragraph.

Cause and Effect

Some of the lessons in this science book are written to help you understand why things happen. You can use a graphic organizer like this one to show cause and effect.

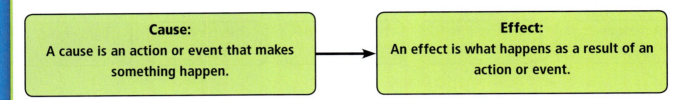

Cause:
A cause is an action or event that makes something happen.

Effect:
An effect is what happens as a result of an action or event.

Tips for Identifying Cause and Effect

- To find an effect, ask—*What happened?*

- To find a cause, ask—*Why did this happen?*

- Remember that events can have more than one cause or effect.

- Look for signal words and phrases, such as *because* and *as a result* to help you identify causes and effects.

Here is an example.

Earth's surface is made up of many plates. Plates are rigid blocks of crust and upper mantle rock. Earth's plates fit together like the pieces of a puzzle. Plate movement is very slow. As plates move around, they cause great changes in Earth's landforms. Where plates collide, energy is released, and new landforms are produced. On land, mountains rise and volcanoes erupt.

Here is what you could record in the graphic organizer.

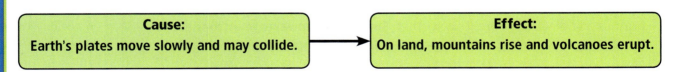

Cause:
Earth's plates move slowly and may collide.

Effect:
On land, mountains rise and volcanoes erupt.

More About Cause and Effect

Events can have more than one cause or effect. For example, suppose a paragraph included a sentence that said "On the ocean floor, deep trenches form." You could then identify two effects of Earth's plates colliding.

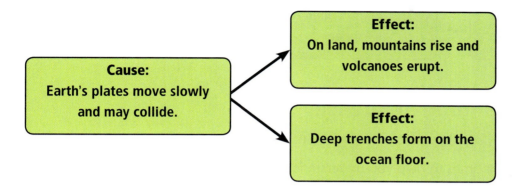

Cause:
Earth's plates move slowly and may collide.

Effect:
On land, mountains rise and volcanoes erupt.

Effect:
Deep trenches form on the ocean floor.

Some paragraphs contain more than one cause and effect. In the paragraph below, one cause and its effect are underlined. Find the second cause and its effect.

As Earth's plates pull apart on land, valleys with volcanoes develop. Africa's Great Rift Valley was formed by the African and Arabian plates pulling apart. When plates pull apart under the sea, ridges and volcanoes form. New sea floor is formed at the ridges.

Skill Practice

Read the following paragraph. Use the Tips for Identifying Cause and Effect to help you answer the questions.

When energy is suddenly released in Earth's crust, the ground shakes and an earthquake occurs. The earthquake is a result of plates crushing together, scraping past each other, or bending along jagged boundaries. Because Earth shakes in an earthquake, great damage can occur, such as streets splitting open and bridges collapsing.

1. What causes an earthquake to occur?

2. What are some effects of an earthquake?

3. What two signal words or phrases helped you identify the causes and effects in this paragraph?

Sequence

Some lessons in this science book are written to help you understand the order in which things happen. You can use a graphic organizer like this one to show sequence.

1. The first thing that happened	→	2. The next thing that happened	→	3. The last thing that happened

Tips for Understanding Sequence

- Pay attention to the order in which events happen.

- Remember dates and times to help you understand the sequence.

- Look for signal words such as *first, next, then, last,* and *finally.*

- Sometimes it's helpful to add your own time-order words to help you understand the sequence.

Here is an example.

Time-order words

> A substance is buoyant, or will float in a liquid, if its density is less than that of the liquid. Here is a procedure that will show you what it takes for an egg to float in water. First, place an egg in a cup of water. Observe whether or not it floats. Next, remove the egg and stir several spoonfuls of salt into the water. Finally, replace the egg in the water and observe whether or not it floats. By changing the density of the water, you allow its density to become greater than the density of the egg.

You could record this in the graphic organizer.

1. First, place an egg in a cup of water and observe.	→	2. Next, remove the egg and stir salt into the water.	→	3. Finally, replace the egg in the water and observe.

More About Sequence

Sometimes information is sequenced by dates. For example, models of the atom have changed since the late 1800s. Use the graphic organizer to sequence the order of how the model of an atom has changed over time.

1. Near the end of the 1800s, Thomson's model of an atom was the first to include subatomic particles.	→	2. In the early 1900s, Rutherford's model suggested that the atom was made up mostly of empty space. Bohr's model showed different orbits for electrons.	→	3. Today, the modern model of an atom includes a cloud of electrons around the central positive nucleus.

When time-order words are not given, add your own words to help you understand the sequence. In the paragraph below, one time-order word has been included and underlined. What other time-order words can you add to help understand the paragraph's sequence?

> A person riding a bicycle changes the chemical energy in their cells to mechanical energy in order to push the pedals. The energy is transferred from the pedals through the chain to the rear wheel. Finally, the kinetic energy of the turning of the wheel is transferred to the whole bicycle.

Skill Practice

Read the following paragraph. Use the Tips for Understanding Sequence to answer the questions.

> First, a flashlight is switched on. Then the chemical energy stored in the battery is changed into electric energy. Next, the circuit is closed. Finally, the electric energy is changed to light energy in the flashlight bulb.

1. What is the first thing that happened in this sequence?

2. About how long did the process take?

3. What signal words helped you identify the sequence in this paragraph?

Draw Conclusions

At the end of each lesson in this science book, you will be asked to draw conclusions. To draw conclusions, use information from the text you are reading and what you already know. Drawing conclusions can help you understand what you read. You can use a graphic organizer like this.

What I Read		What I Know		Conclusion:
List facts from the text.	**+**	List related ideas from your own experience.	**=**	Combine facts from the text with your own experience.

Tips for Drawing Conclusions

- Ask—*What text information do I need to think about?*

- Ask—*What do I know from my own experience that could help me draw a conclusion?*

- Pay close attention to the information in the text and to your experience to be sure the conclusion is valid, or makes sense.

Here is an example.

> The shore is the area where the ocean and land meet and interact. Waves grind pebbles and rocks against the shore which can cause erosion. The water pressure from a wave can loosen pebbles and small rocks, which outgoing waves carry into the ocean. Long shore currents move sand, pebbles, and shells along the shore.

Here is what you could record in the graphic organizer.

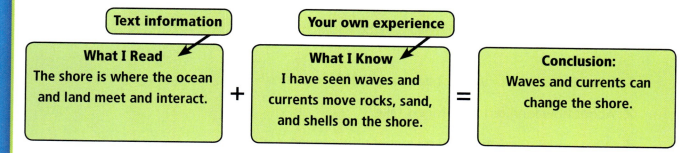

Text information

Your own experience

What I Read		What I Know		Conclusion:
The shore is where the ocean and land meet and interact.	**+**	I have seen waves and currents move rocks, sand, and shells on the shore.	**=**	Waves and currents can change the shore.

More About Drawing Conclusions

Sensible conclusions based on your experience and the facts you read are valid. For example, suppose a paragraph had ended with the sentence "Human activities can also change the shore." You might have come to a different conclusion about what changes the shore.

What I Read		What I Know		Conclusion:
The shore is where the ocean and land meet and interact.	**+**	Waves loosen rocks and pebbles. Currents move sand, pebbles, and shells. Structures can be built to prevent erosion.	**=**	Waves, currents, and human activities can change the shore.

Sometimes a paragraph might not contain enough information for drawing a valid conclusion. Read the paragraph below. Think of one valid conclusion you could draw. Then think of one invalid conclusion someone might draw from the given information.

> A jetty is a wall-like structure made of rocks that sticks out into the ocean. Jetties are usually built on either side of an opening to a harbor. Jetties catch sand and pebbles that normally flow down the coast with the current. Jetties can change the shore by building up the beach.

Skill Practice

Read the following paragraph. Use the Tips for Drawing Conclusions to answer the questions.

> Most of the movement of water on the ocean's surface is due to waves. A wave is the up-and-down movement of surface water. On a calm day, ocean waves may only be 1.5 meters high or less. However, during a storm, waves can reach heights of 30 meters.

1. What conclusion did you draw about the height of a wave?

2. What information from your personal experience did you use to draw the conclusion?

3. What text information did you use?

Summarize

Focus Skill

At the end of every lesson in this science book, you will be asked to summarize. When you summarize, you use your own words to tell what something is about. In the lesson, you will be given ideas for writing your summary. You can also use a graphic organizer like this one to summarize.

Main Idea: Tell about the most important information you have read.	+	Details: Add details that answer important questions Who?, What?, Where?, When?, Why?, and How?	=	Summary: Retell what you have just read, include only the most important details.

Tips for Summarizing

- To write a summary, ask—*What is the most important idea of the paragraph?*
- To include details with your summary, ask—*Who?, What?, When?, Where?, Why? and How?*
- Remember to use fewer words than the original has.
- Don't forget to use your own words when you summarize.

Here is an example.

Main Idea

Sound waves are carried by vibrating matter. Most sound waves travel through air, but they may also travel through liquids and even some solids. As the sound waves travel, the energy of the wave decreases. The frequency at which the sound wave moves determines the pitch of the sound. The greater the frequency, the higher the pitch. The strength of a sound wave can also be measured. The more energy a sound has, the louder it is.

Details

Here's what you could record in your graphic organizer.

Main Idea: Sound waves are carried by vibrating matter.	+	Details: Pitch is determined by the frequency at which the sound wave moves. The more energy a sound has, the louder it is.	=	Summary: Sound waves are carried by vibrating matter. Pitch is determined by the frequency at which the sound wave moves. The loudness of a sound is determined by how much energy it has.

R26

More About Summarizing

Sometimes a paragraph includes information that should not be included in a summary. For example, suppose a paragraph included a sentence that said "High musical notes have high pitch and high frequency, and low musical notes have low pitch and low frequency." The graphic organizer would remain the same, because that detail is not important to understanding the paragraph's main idea.

Sometimes the main idea of a paragraph is not in the first sentence. In the following paragraph, two important details are underlined. What is the main idea?

> Air, water, clear glass, and clear plastic are substances which objects can clearly be seen through. Substances that light can travel through are transparent. Substances that are transparent are used to make things like windows and eyeglasses. Some substances are transparent only to certain colors of light. They are described as clear since you can see objects through them, but they have a color.

Skill Practice

Read the following paragraph. Use the Tips for Summarizing to answer the questions.

> Light can be absorbed, reflected, or refracted. Sometimes light waves are absorbed when they strike an object. Most objects absorb some colors of light. Other colors of light bounce off objects, or are reflected. These are the colors we see. The change in speed of light causes it to bend. This bending of light waves is called refraction.

1. If a friend asked you what this paragraph was about, what information would you include? What would you leave out?

2. What is the main idea of the paragraph?

3. What two details would you include in a summary?

Using Tables, Charts, and Graphs

As you do investigations in science, you collect, organize, display, and interpret data. Tables, charts, and graphs are good ways to organize and display data so that others can understand and interpret your data.

The tables, charts, and graphs in this Handbook will help you read and understand data. You can also use the information to choose the best ways to display data so that you can use it to draw conclusions and make predictions.

Reading a Table

A bird-watching group is studying the wingspans of different birds. They want to find out the birds with the greatest wingspans. The table shows the data the group has collected.

Largest Wingspans

Type of Bird	Wingspan (in feet)
Albatross	12
Trumpeter Swan	11
California Condor	10
Marabou Stork	10

Title
Headings
Data

How to Read a Table

1. **Read the title** to find out what the table is about.

2. **Read the headings** to find out what information is given.

3. **Study the data.** Look for patterns.

4. **Draw conclusions.** If you display the data in a graph, you might be able to see patterns easily.

By studying the table, you can see the birds with the greatest wingspans. However, suppose the group wants to look for patterns in the data. They might choose to display the data in a different way, such as in a bar graph.

Reading a Bar Graph

The data in this bar graph is the same as in the table. A bar graph can be used to compare the data about different events or groups.

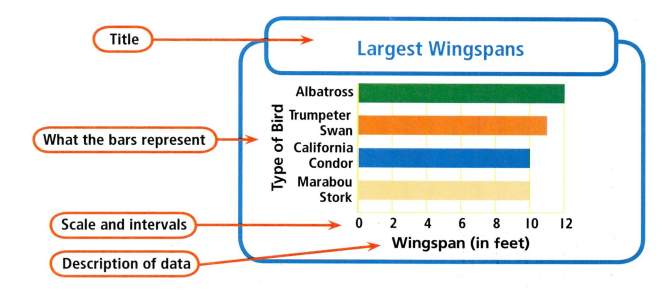

Title → **Largest Wingspans**

What the bars represent →

Scale and intervals →

Description of data →

How to Read a Bar Graph

1. **Look** at the graph to determine what kind of graph it is.

2. **Read** the graph. Use the labels to guide you.

3. **Analyze** the data. Study the bars to compare the measurements. Look for patterns.

4. **Draw conclusions.** Ask yourself questions, like the ones in the Skills Practice.

Skills Practice

1. Which two birds have the same wingspan?

2. How much greater is the wingspan of an albatross than the wingspan of a California condor?

3. A red-tailed hawk has a wingspan of 4 feet. Which type of bird has a wingspan that is three times that of the hawk?

4. **Predict** A fifth-grade student saw a bird that had a wingspan that was about the same as her height. Could the bird have been an albatross?

5. Was the bar graph a good choice for displaying this data? Explain your answer.

Reading a Line Graph

A scientist collected this data about how the amount of ice in the Nordic Sea area of the Arctic Ocean has changed over the years.

Nordic Sea Area Ice

Year	Number of Square Kilometers (in millions)
1860	2.8
1880	2.7
1900	2.2
1920	2.4
1940	2.0
1960	1.8
1980	1.5
2000	1.6

Here is the same data displayed in a line graph. A line graph is used to show changes over time.

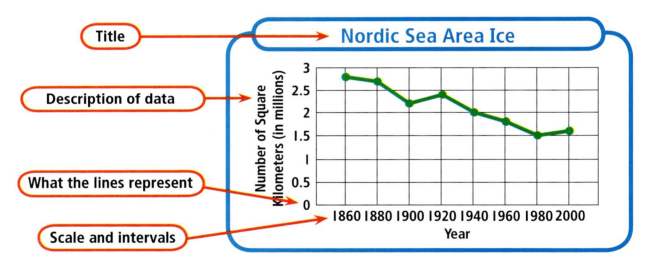

Title

Description of data

What the lines represent

Scale and intervals

How to Read a Line Graph

1. **Look** at the graph to determine what kind of graph it is.

2. **Read** the graph. Use the labels to guide you.

3. **Analyze** the data. Study the points along the lines. Look for patterns.

4. **Draw conclusions.** Ask yourself questions, like the ones in the Skills Practice to help you draw conclusions.

Skills Practice

1. By how much did the ice in the Nordic Sea area change from 1940 to 1980?

2. **Predict** Will there be more or less than 2.5 million square kilometers of ice in the Nordic Sea area in 2020?

3. Was the line graph a good choice for displaying this data? Explain why.

Reading a Circle Graph

A fifth-grade class is studying U.S. energy sources. They want to know which energy sources are used in the U.S. They classified the different sources by making a table. Here is the data they gathered.

U.S. Energy Sources

Source of Energy	Amount Used
Petroleum	0.38
Natural Gas	0.24
Coal	0.22
Hydroelectric and Nuclear Power	0.12
Other	0.04

The circle graph shows the same data as the table. A circle graph can be used to show data as a whole made up of different parts.

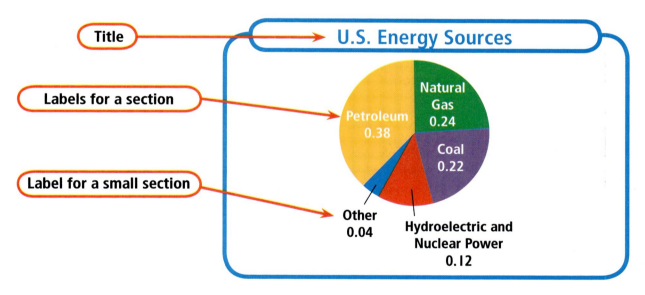

Title

Labels for a section

Label for a small section

U.S. Energy Sources

Natural Gas 0.24

Petroleum 0.38

Coal 0.22

Other 0.04

Hydroelectric and Nuclear Power 0.12

How to Read a Circle Graph

1. **Look** at the title of the graph to learn what kind of information is shown.

2. **Read** the graph. Look at the label of each section to find out what information is shown.

3. **Analyze** the data. Compare the sizes of the sections to determine how they are related.

4. **Draw conclusions.** Ask yourself questions, like the ones in the Skills Practice.

Skills Practice

1. Which source of energy is used most often?

2. **Predict** If wind, geothermal, and solar make up some of the other energy sources, will they be a greater or lesser part of U.S. energy sources in the future?

3. Was the circle graph a good choice for displaying this data? Explain why.

Using Metric Measurements

A measurement is a number that represents a comparison of something being measured to a unit of measurement. Scientists use many different tools to measure objects and substances as they work. Scientists almost always use the metric system for their measurements.

Measuring Length and Capacity

When you measure length, you find the distance between two points. The distance may be in a straight line, along a curved path, or around a circle. The table shows the metric units of **length** and how they are related.

Equivalent Measures
1 centimeter (cm) = 10 millimeters (mm)
1 decimeter (dm) = 10 centimeters (cm)
1 meter (m) = 1,000 millimeters
1 meter = 10 decimeters
1 kilometer (km) = 1,000 meters

You can use these comparisons to help you understand the size of each metric unit of length.

A **millimeter (mm)** is about the thickness of a dime.	A **centimeter (cm)** is about the width of your index finger.	A **decimeter (dm)** is about the width of an adult's hand.	A **meter (m)** is about the width of a door.

Sometimes you may need to change units of length. The following diagram shows how to multiply and divide to change to larger and smaller units.

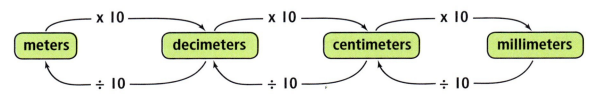

The photos below show the metric units of **capacity** and common comparisons. The metric units of volume are the milliliter (mL) and the liter (L). You can use multiplication to change liters to milliliters. You can use division to change milliliters to liters.

A **milliliter (mL)** is the amount of liquid that can fill part of a medicine dropper.

 1 mL

A **liter (L)** is the amount of liquid that can fill a plastic bottle.

 **1 L**
1 L = 1,000 mL

To change *larger* units to *smaller* units, you need more of the *smaller units*. So, **multiply** by 10, 100, or 1,000. To change *smaller* units to *larger* units, you need *fewer of the larger units*. So, **divide** by 10, 100, or 1,000.

500 dm = ___ cm

Think: There are 10 cm in 1 dm.

500 dm = 500 × 10 = 5,000

So, 500 dm = 5,000 cm.

4,000 mL = ____ L

Think: There are 1,000 mL in 1 L.

4,000 ÷ 1,000 = 4

So, 4,000 mL = 4 L.

Skills Practice

Complete. Tell whether you multiply or divide by 10, 100, or 1,000.

1. 7 m = _____ cm

2. 4 m = _____ dm

3. 800 _____ = 8 m

4. 9,000 mm = _____ m

5. 9 L = _____ mL

6. 6,000 mL = _____ L

7. 3,000 mL = _____ L

8. 8 _____ = 8,000 mL

Measuring Mass

Matter is what all objects are made of. Mass is the amount of matter that is in an object. The metric units of mass are the gram (g) and the kilogram (kg).

You can use these comparisons to help you understand the masses of some everyday objects.

A paper clip is about **1 gram** (g).

A slice of wheat bread is about **20 grams**.

A box of 12 crayons is about **100 grams**.

A large wedge of cheese is **1 kilogram** (kg).

You can use multiplication to change kilograms to grams.

You can use division to change grams to kilograms.

2 kg = ___ g

Think: There are 1,000 g in 1 kg.

2 kg = 2 x 1,000 = 2,000 g

So, 2 kg = 2,000 g.

4,000 g = ____ kg

Think: There are 1,000 g in 1 kg.

4,000 ÷ 1,000 = 4

So, 4,000 g = 4 kg.

Skills Practice

Complete. Tell whether you multiply or divide by 1,000.

1. 4,000 g = _____ kg

2. 3,000 g = _____ kg

3. 7 kg = _____ g

4. 8 _____ = 8,000 g

Measurement Systems

SI Measures (Metric)

Temperature

Ice melts at 0 degrees Celsius (°C)

Water freezes at 0°C

Water boils at 100°C

Length and Distance

1000 meters (m) = 1 kilometer (km)

100 centimeters (cm) = 1 m

10 millimeters (mm) = 1 cm

Force

1 newton (N) = 1 kilogram x

  1 meter/second/second (kg-m/s^2)

Volume

1 cubic meter (m^3) = 1 m x 1 m x 1 m

1 cubic centimeter (cm^3) =

  1 cm x 1 cm x 1 cm

1 liter (L) = 1000 millimeters (mL)

1 cm^3 = 1 mL

Area

1 square kilometer (km^2) =

  1 km x 1 km

1 hectare = 10 000 m^2

Mass

1000 grams (g) = 1 kilogram (kg)

1000 milligrams (mg) = 1 g

Rates (Metric and Customary)

km/hr = kilometers per hour

m/s = meters per second

mi/hr = miles per hour

Customary Measures

Volume of Fluids

2 c = 1 pint (pt)

2 pt = 1 quart (qt)

4 qt = 1 gallon (gal)

Temperature

Ice melts at 32 degrees

  Fahrenheit (°F)

Water freezes at 32°F

Water boils at 212°F

Length and Distance

12 inches (in.) = 1 foot (ft)

3 ft = 1 yard (yd)

5,280 ft = 1 mile (mi)

Weight

16 ounces (oz) = 1 pound (lb)

2,000 pounds = 1 ton (T)

Safety in Science

Doing investigations in science can be fun, but you need to be sure you do them safely. Here are some rules to follow.

1. **Think ahead.** Study the steps of the investigation so you know what to expect. If you have any questions, ask your teacher. Be sure you understand any caution statements or safety reminders.

2. **Be neat.** Keep your work area clean. If you have long hair, pull it back so it doesn't get in the way. Roll or push up long sleeves to keep them away from your activity.

3. **Oops!** If you should spill or break something, or get cut, tell your teacher right away.

4. **Watch your eyes.** Wear safety goggles anytime you are directed to do so. If you get anything in your eyes, tell your teacher right away.

5. **Yuck!** Never eat or drink anything during a science activity.

6. **Don't get shocked.** Be especially careful if an electric appliance is used. Be sure that electric cords are in a safe place where you can't trip over them. Don't ever pull a plug out of an outlet by pulling on the cord.

7. **Keep it clean.** Always clean up when you have finished. Put everything away and wipe your work area. Wash your hands.

Visit the Multimedia Science Glossary to see illustrations of these words and to hear them pronounced.
www.hspscience.com

Glossary

As you read your science book, you will notice that new or unfamiliar terms have been respelled to help you pronounce them while you are reading. Those respellings are called *phonetic respellings.* In this Glossary you will see the same kind of respellings.

In phonetic respellings, syllables are separated by a bullet (•). Small, uppercase letters show stressed syllables.

The boldfaced letters in the examples in the Pronunciation Key below show how certain letters and combinations of letters are pronounced in the respellings.

The page number (in parens) at the end of a definition tells you where to find the term, defined in context, in your book. Depending on the context in which it is used, a term may have more than one definition.

Pronunciation Key

Sound	As in	Phonetic Respelling	Sound	As in	Phonetic Respelling
a	b**a**t	(BAT)	oh	**o**ver	(OH•ver)
ah	l**o**ck	(LAHK)	oo	p**oo**l	(POOL)
air	r**a**re	(RAIR)	ow	**ou**t	(OWT)
ar	**ar**gue	(AR•gyoo)	oy	f**oi**l	(FOYL)
aw	l**aw**	(LAW)	s	**c**ell	(SEL)
ay	f**a**ce	(FAYS)		**s**it	(SIT)
ch	**ch**apel	(CHAP•uhl)	sh	**sh**eep	(SHEEP)
e	t**e**st	(TEST)	th	**th**at	(THAT)
	m**e**tric	(MEH•trik)		**th**in	(THIN)
ee	**ea**t	(EET)	u	p**u**ll	(PUL)
	f**ee**t	(FEET)	uh	med**a**l	(MED•uhl)
	sk**i**	(SKEE)		tal**e**nt	(TAL•uhnt)
er	pap**er**	(PAY•per)		penc**i**l	(PEN•suhl)
	f**er**n	(FERN)		**o**nion	(UHN•yuhn)
eye	**i**dea	(eye•DE•uh)		play**fu**l	(PLAY•fuhl)
i	b**i**t	(BIT)		d**u**ll	(DUHL)
ing	go**ing**	(GOH•ing)	y	**y**es	(YES)
k	**c**ard	(KARD)		r**i**pe	(RYP)
	kite	(KYT)	z	bag**s**	(BAGZ)
ngk	ba**nk**	(BANGK)	zh	trea**s**ure	(TREZH•er)

A

acceleration [ak•sel•er•AY•shuhn] The rate at which velocity changes **(180)**

acid rain [AS•id RAYN] A mixture that falls to Earth of rain and acids from air pollution **(472)**

adaptation [ad•uhp•TAY•shuhn] A trait or characteristic that helps an organism survive **(457)**

air mass [AIR MASS] A large body of air that has the same temperature and humidity throughout **(304)**

air pressure [AIR PRESH•er] The weight of the atmosphere pressing down on Earth **(287)**

atmosphere [AT•muhs•feer] The blanket of air surrounding Earth **(286)**

atom [AT•uhm] The smallest unit of an element that has all the properties of that element **(66)**

axis [AK•sis] An imaginary line that passes through Earth's center and its North and South Poles **(322)**

B

balance [BAL•uhns] A tool that measures the amount of matter in an object (the object's mass) **(7)**

balanced forces [BAL•uhnst FAWRS•iz] Forces that act on an object but cancel each other out **(152)**

buoyant force [BOY•uhnt FAWRS] The upward force exerted on an object by water **(156)**

C

carnivore [KAHR•nuh•vawr] An animal that eats other animals; also called a second-level consumer **(438)**

cell [SEL] The basic unit of structure and function of all living things **(360)**

cell membrane [SEL MEM•brayn] The thin covering that surrounds every cell **(362)**

change of state [CHAYNJ uhv STAYT] A physical change that occurs when matter changes from one state to another, such as from a liquid to a gas **(74)**

chemical change [KEM•ih•kuhl CHAYNJ] A reaction or change in a substance, produced by chemical means, that results in a different substance **(84)**

chemical energy [KEM•ih•kuhl EN•er•jee] Energy that can be released by a chemical reaction **(110)**

chemical property [KEM•ih•kuhl PRAHP•er•tee] A property that involves how a substance interacts with other substances **(83)**

chemical reaction [KEM•ih•kuhl ree•AK•shuhn] A chemical change **(84)**

chlorophyll [KLAWR•uh•fihl] A green pigment that allows a plant to absorb the sun's light energy **(432)**

chromosome [KROH•muh•sohm] A threadlike structure in the nucleus, made up of DNA **(398)**

circulatory system [SER•kyoo•luh•tawr•ee sis•tuhm] The organ system—made up of the heart, blood vessels, and blood—that transports materials throughout the body **(376)**

climate [KLY•muht] The pattern of weather an area experiences over a long period of time **(306)**

community [kuh•MYOO•nuh•tee] A group of populations that live together **(456)**

competition [kahm•puh•TISH•uhn] A kind of contest among populations that need to get a certain amount of food, water, and shelter to survive **(457)**

compound [KAHM•pownd] A substance made of two or more different elements **(84)**

condensation [kahn•duhn•SAY•shuhn] The process of a gas changing into a liquid **(295)**

conduction [kuhn•DUK•shuhn] The transfer of heat from one object directly to another **(120)**

conservation [kahn•ser•VAY•shuhn] The use of less of something to make the supply last longer **(127)**

conservation [kahn•ser•VAY•shuhn] The practice of saving resources **(474)**

constellation [kahn•stuh•LAY•shuhn] A pattern of stars, named after a mythological or religious figure, an object, or an animal **(339)**

consumer [kuhn•SOOM•er] An animal that eats plants, other animals, or both **(434)**

convection [kuhn•VEK•shuhn] The transfer of heat through the movement of a gas or a liquid **(120)**

crater [KRAYT•er] A bowl-shaped, low area on the surface of a planet or moon **(330)**

cytoplasm [SYT•oh•plaz•uhm] The jellylike material inside a cell between the cell membrane and the nucleus **(362)**

decomposer [dee•kuhm•POHZ•er] A consumer that obtains food energy by breaking down the remains of dead plants and animals **(439)**

delta [DEL•tuh] An area of new land at the mouth of a river, formed from sediments carried by the river **(261)**

density [DEN•suh•tee] The measure of how closely packed matter is in an object **(34)**

deposition [dep•uh•ZISH•uhn] The process in which sediment settles out of water or is dropped by wind **(224)**

digestive system [dih•JES•tiv SIS•tuhm] The organ system that turns food into nutrients that body cells need for energy, growth, and repair **(370)**

dominant trait [DAHM•uh•nuhnt TRAYT] A trait that appears even if an organism has only one factor for the trait **(406)**

earthquake [ERTH•kwayk] A movement of the ground, caused by a sudden release of energy in Earth's crust **(270)**

eclipse [ih•KLIPS] An event that occurs when one object in space passes through the shadow of another object in space **(334)**

ecosystem [EE•koh•sis•tuhm] A community of organisms and the environment in which they live **(438)**

electric energy [ee•LEK•trik EN•er•jee] Energy that comes from an electric current **(112)**

element [EL•uh•muhnt] A substance made up of only one kind of atom **(68)**

energy [EN•er•jee] The ability to cause changes in matter **(100)**

energy pyramid [EN•er•jee PIR•uh•mid] A diagram that shows how much food energy is passed from each level in a food chain to the next **(443)**

energy transfer [EN•er•jee TRANS•fer] Movement of energy from one place or object to another **(104)**

environment [en•VY•ruhn•muhnt] All the living and nonliving things that surround and affect an organism **(416)**

epicenter [EP•ih•sent•er] The point on Earth's surface directly above the focus of an earthquake **(270)**

equator [ee•KWAYT•er] An imaginary line around Earth equally distant from the North and South Poles **(324)**

erosion [uh•ROH•zhuhn] The process of wearing away and moving sediment by wind, moving water, or ice **(235)**

evaporation [ee•vap•uh•RAY•shuhn] The process of a liquid changing into a gas **(295)**

excretory system [EKS•kruh•tawr•ee SIS•tuhm] The organ system, including the kidneys and bladder, that removes waste materials from the blood **(384)**

experiment [ek•SPEHR•uh•muhnt] A procedure carried out under controlled conditions to test a hypothesis **(15)**

extinction [ek•STINGK•shuhn] The death of all the organisms of a species **(468)**

fault [FAWLT] A break in Earth's crust **(270)**

food chain [FOOD CHAYN] The transfer of food energy between organisms in an ecosystem **(439)**

food web [FOOD WEB] A diagram that shows the relationships between different food chains in an ecosystem **(440)**

force [FAWRS] A push or pull that causes an object to move, stop, or change direction **(144)**

fossil [FAHS•uhl] The remains or traces of past life, found in sedimentary rock **(126)**

frequency [FREE•kwuhn•see] The number of vibrations per second **(198)**

friction [FRIK•shuhn] A force that opposes motion **(145)**

front [FRUHNT] The border where two air masses meet **(305)**

fulcrum [FUHL•kruhm] The balance point on a lever that supports the arm but does not move **(162)**

galaxy [GAL•uhk•see] A grouping of gas, dust, and many stars, plus any objects that orbit those stars **(344)**

gas [GAS] The state of matter that does not have a definite shape or volume **(41)**

gene [JEEN] The part of a chromosome that contains the DNA code for an inherited trait **(408)**

glacier [GLAY•sher] A large, thick sheet of ice **(252)**

gravitational force [grav•ih•TAY•shuhn•uhl FAWRS] The pull of all objects in the universe on one another **(146)**

gravity [GRAV•ih•tee] The force of attraction between objects **(146)**

habitat [HAB•i•tat] An area where an organism can find everything it needs to survive **(473)**

hardness [HARD•nis] A mineral's ability to resist being scratched **(218)**

heat [HEET] The transfer of thermal energy between objects with different temperatures **(118)**

herbivore [HER•buh•vawr] An animal that eats only producers **(438)**

humidity [hyoo•MID•uh•tee] A measurement of the amount of water vapor in the air **(296)**

igneous rocks [IG•nee•uhs RAHKZ] Rocks that form when melted rock cools and hardens **(224)**

inclined plane [in•KLYND PLAYN] A ramp or another sloping surface **(163)**

inertia [in•ER•shuh] The property of matter that keeps it at rest or moving in a straight line **(187)**

inherited trait [in•HAIR•it•ed TRAYT] A characteristic passed from parents to their offspring **(404)**

inquiry [IN•kwer•ee] An organized way to gather information and answer questions **(12)**

instinct [IN•stinkt] A behavior that an organism inherits **(412)**

investigation [in•ves•tuh•GAY•shuhn] A procedure carried out to gather data about an object or event **(12)**

kinetic energy [kih•NET•ik EN•er•jee] The energy of motion **(102)**

landform [LAND•fawrm] A natural land shape or feature **(250)**

lava [LAH•vuh] Molten (melted) rock that reaches Earth's surface **(272)**

learned behavior [LERND bee•HAYV•yer] A behavior that an animal acquires through experience **(414)**

lever [LEV•er] A bar that makes it easier to move things **(162)**

life cycle [LYF CY•kuhl] The stages that a living thing passes through as it grows and changes **(397)**

light [LYT] Radiation that we can see **(108)**

liquid [LIK•wid] The state of matter that has a definite volume but no definite shape **(41)**

local wind [LOH•kuhl WINDZ] Movements of air that result from local changes in temperature **(289)**

luster [LUS•ter] The way a mineral's surface reflects light **(217)**

magma [MAG•muh] Molten (melted) rock beneath Earth's surface **(272)**

magnetism [MAG•nuh•tiz•uhm] The force produced by a magnet **(148)**

mass [MAS] The amount of matter in an object **(33)**

matter [MAT•er] Anything that has mass and takes up space **(32)**

mechanical energy [muh•KAN•ih•kuhl EN•er•jee] The combination of all the kinetic and potential energy that something has **(110)**

metamorphic rocks [met•uh•MAWR•fik RAHKZ] Rocks formed when high heat and great pressure change existing rocks into a new form **(228)**

microscope [MY•kruh•skohp] A tool that makes small objects appear larger **(4)**

microscopic [my•kruh•SKAHP•ik] Too small to be seen without using a microscope **(360)**

mineral [MIN•er•uhl] A naturally occurring, nonliving solid that has a specific chemical makeup and a repeating structure **(216)**

mitosis [my•TOH•sis] The process by which most cells divide **(398)**

mixture [MIKS•chuhr] A blending of two types of matter that are not chemically combined **(48)**

moon [MOON] Any natural body that revolves around a planet **(330)**

moon phase [MOON FAYZ] One of the shapes the moon seems to have as it orbits Earth **(333)**

muscular system [MUHS•kyoo•ler SIS•tuhm] The organ system that includes the muscles and allows the body to move **(380)**

nervous system [NER•vuhs SIS•tuhm] The organ system—including the brain, spinal cord, and nerves—that senses your surroundings and controls other organs **(382)**

net force [NET FAWRS] The combination of all the forces acting on an object **(154)**

nonrenewable resource [nahn•rih•NOO•uh•buhl REE•sawrs] A resource that, once used, cannot be replaced in a reasonable amount of time **(127)**

nucleus [NOO•klee•uhs] The part of a cell that directs all of the cell's activities **(362)**

orbit [AWR•bit] The path one body takes in space as it revolves around another body **(324)**

organ [AWR•guhn] A group of tissues that work together to perform a certain function **(369)**

organ system [AWR•guhn SIS•tuhm] A group of organs that work together to do a job for the body **(370)**

photosynthesis [foht•oh•SIHN•thuh•sis] The process in which plants make food by using water from the soil, carbon dioxide from the air, and energy from sunlight **(432)**

physical change [FIZ•ih•kuhl CHAYNJ] A change in matter from one form to another that doesn't result in a different substance **(76)**

physical property [FIZ•ih•kuhl PRAHP•er•tee] A property that involves a substance by itself **(83)**

pitch [PICH] A measurement of how high or low a sound is **(198)**

planet [PLAN•it] A body that revolves around a star **(341)**

plate [PLAYT] A section of Earth's crust and mantle that fits together with other sections like puzzle pieces **(269)**

pollution [puh•LOO•shuhn] Anything that dirties or harms the environment **(130, 472)**

population [pahp•yuh•LAY•shuhn] A group of organisms of one kind that live in one location **(456)**

position [puh•ZISH•uhn] The location of an object in space **(176)**

potential energy [poh•TEN•shuhl EN•er•jee] The energy an object has because of its condition or position **(102)**

precipitation [pree•sip•uh•TAY•shuhn] Water that falls from the air to Earth **(296)**

predator [PRED•uh•ter] An animal that kills and eats other animals **(460)**

prevailing winds [pree•VAYL•ing WINDZ] Global winds that blow constantly from the same direction **(290)**

prey [PRAY] An animal that is eaten by a predator **(460)**

producer [pruh•DOOS•er] A living thing, such as a plant, that makes its own food **(434)**

protist [PROHT•ist] A single-celled organism with a nucleus and organelles **(364)**

pulley [PUHL•ee] A wheel with a rope that lets you change the direction in which you move an object **(163)**

radiation [ray•dee•AY•shuhn] The transfer of energy by means of waves that move through matter and space **(121)**

recessive trait [rih•SES•iv TRAYT] A trait that appears only if an organism has two factors for the trait **(406)**

reclamation [rek•luh•MAY•shuhn] The process of cleaning and restoring a damaged ecosystem **(476)**

reflection [rih•FLEK•shuhn] The bouncing of heat or light off an object **(121)**

refraction [rih•FRAK•shuhn] The bending of light **(334)**

renewable resource [rih•NOO•uh•buhl REE•sawrs] A resource that can be replaced within a reasonable amount of time **(128)**

respiratory system [RES•per•uh•tawr•ee sis•tuhm] The organ system, including the lungs, that exchanges oxygen and carbon dioxide between the body and the environment **(379)**

revolve [rih•VAHLV] To travel in a closed path **(324)**

rock [RAHK] A natural substance made of one or more minerals **(224)**

rock cycle [RAHK CY•kuhl] The continuous process in which one type of rock changes into another type **(236)**

rotate [ROH•tayt] To spin on an axis **(322)**

sand dune [SAND DOON] A hill of sand, made and shaped by wind **(253)**

scientific method [sy•uhn•TIF•ik METH•uhd] A series of steps that scientists use when performing an experiment **(20)**

sedimentary rocks [sed•uh•MEN•tuh•ree RAHKZ] Rocks formed when sediments are cemented together **(224)**

simple machine [SIM•puhl muh•SHEEN] A device that makes a task easier by changing the size or direction of a force or the distance over which the force acts **(162)**

sinkhole [SINGK•hohl] A large hole formed when the roof of a cave collapses **(262)**

skeletal system [SKEL•uh•tuhl SIS•tuhm] The organ system, including the bones, that protects the body and gives it structure **(380)**

solar energy [SOH•ler EN•er•jee] Energy that comes from the sun **(108)**

solar system [SOH•ler SIS•tuhm] A star and all the planets and other objects that revolve around it **(338)**

solid [SAHL•id] The state of matter that has a definite shape and a definite volume **(40)**

solubility [sahl•yoo•BIL•uh•tee] The measure of how much of a material will dissolve in another material **(51)**

solution [suh•LOO•shuhn] A uniform mixture of two or more substances in a single state of matter **(50)**

speed [SPEED] The distance an object travels in a certain amount of time **(178)**

star [STAR] A huge ball of very hot gases in space **(338)**

state of matter [STAYT uhv MAT•er] One of the three forms (solid, liquid, and gas) that matter can exist in **(40)**

streak [STREEK] The color of the powder left behind when you rub a mineral against a rough white tile or a streak plate **(217)**

succession [suhk•SESH•uhn] A gradual change in the kinds of organisms living in an ecosystem **(464)**

sun [SUHN] The star at the center of our solar system **(322)**

suspension [suh•SPEN•shuhn] A kind of mixture in which particles of one ingredient are floating in another ingredient **(52)**

symbiosis [sim•by•OH•sis] A relationship between different kinds of organisms **(458)**

system [SIS•tuhm] A group of separate elements that work together to accomplish something **(119)**

tissue [TISH•oo] A group of cells that work together to perform a certain function **(368)**

topography [tuh•PAHG•ruh•fee] All the kinds of landforms in a certain place **(250)**

transpiration [tran•spuh•RAY•shuhn] The loss of water from a leaf through the stomata **(431)**

troposphere [TROH•puh•sfeer] The layer of air closest to Earth's surface **(286)**

unbalanced forces [uhn•BAL•uhnst FAWRS•iz] Forces that act on an object and don't cancel each other out; unbalanced forces cause a change in motion **(152)**

universe [YOO•nuh•vers] Everything that exists, including such things as stars, planets, gas, dust, and energy **(344)**

velocity [vuh•LAHS•uh•tee] A measure of an object's speed in a particular direction **(178)**

vibration [vy•BRAY•shuhn] A back-and-forth movement of matter **(196)**

volcano [vahl•KAY•noh] A mountain made of lava, ash, or other materials from eruptions that occur at an opening in Earth's crust **(272)**

volume [VAHL•yoom] The amount of space an object takes up **(34)** A measurement of how soft or loud a sound is **(197)**

water cycle [WAW•ter SY•kuhl] The process in which water continuously moves from Earth's surface into the atmosphere and back again **(294)**

weathering [WETH•er•ing] The process of wearing away rocks by natural processes **(234)**

wheel-and-axle [weel•and•AK•suhl] A wheel with a rod, or axle, in the center **(162)**

work [WERK] The use of a force to move an object through a distance **(160)**

Index

Index

Wind(s)
  erosion by, 235
  landform changes from, 258
  local, 289
  prevailing, 290
  as renewable energy source, 128–129
  sand landforms and, 253
  weather patterns and, 306
Windsocks, 303
Wind vanes, 303
Winter, 324
  at North and South Poles, 326
Winter Park, Florida, 262
Winter solstice, 325
Wolves, 418–419
Work, 160–161
  definition of, 160
  done by machines, 162
World Ice Art Championships (Alaska), 38
Wright, Orville and Wilbur, 10

X-rays, 108–109
Xylem, 430

Years (on planets), 340–343
Yellowstone National Park, 473

Zapata, Yesenia, 312
Zygote, 400

VISION Jaguars see better at night than during the day.

MOVEMENT If possible, jaguars live near water. from most cats—they LIKE to swim!

They are different

CAMOUFLAGE Most jaguars have brownish-yellow fur.

YOUNG Jaguar cubs weigh about two pounds, less than most human babies, when they are born. Their eyes are shut to protect them from sunlight.

Some jaguars have black rosettes and black fur.

COLOR